A REGISTER OF DECEASED PERSONS
*at Sea and on Grosse Île
in 1847*

A REGISTER OF DECEASED PERSONS
at Sea and on Grosse Île in 1847

ANDRÉ CHARBONNEAU
DORIS DROLET-DUBÉ
with the collaboration of
ROBERT GRACE *and* SYLVIE TREMBLAY

Canadian Heritage / Patrimoine canadien

Parks Canada / Parcs Canada

1997

Writing : ANDRÉ CHARBONNEAU
and DORIS DROLET-DUBÉ

Research Supervision : ANDRÉ CHARBONNEAU

Project Supervision : MICHEL P. DE COURVAL

Art Direction and Printing Supervision : PIERRE DEMERS

Drawings : DANIEL RAINVILLE

Cartography : CHRISTIANE HÉBERT

Standardization of Names : ROBERT GRACE

Data Capture : RENÉ GÉLINAS and SYLVIE TREMBLAY

Word Processing : NOËLLA GAUTHIER

Translation : CAROLINE ARAI and SUSAN PATRICK

Graphics Design : NORMAN DUPUIS inc.

Printing : IMPRIMERIE LA RENAISSANCE

Cover : *THE CELTIC CROSS*
(Parks Canada / M. Boucher)

Canadian cataloguing in Publication Data

Charbonneau, André, 1950-

A Register of Deceased Persons at Sea and on Grosse Île in 1847

Issued also in French under title : Répertoire des décès de 1847 à la Grosse-Île et en mer.

Includes bibliographical references.

ISBN 0-660-16877-4

N° de cat. R64-198/1-1997E

1. Registers of birth etc. — Quebec (Province) — Grosse Île, (Montmagny). 2. Irish — Quebec (Province) — Grosse Île, (Montmagny) — Mortality. 3. Grosse Île, (Montmagny, Quebec) — History — 19th Century. 4. Quarantine — Quebec (Province) — Grosse Île, (Montmagny). I. Drolet-Dubé, Doris, 1947- . II. Grace, Robert J. (Robert John), 1960-   . III. Tremblay, Sylvie. IV. Parks Canada. V.Title.

FC2908.IC42 1997   971.4'735   C97-980114-1   F1035-16C42 1997

© Minister of Public Works and Government Services Canada, 1997.

All rights reserved. No part of this book may be reproduced or utilized in any form or by any means, electronic or mechanical, or by any information storage and retrieval system, without permission in writing from Parks Canada.

Legal deposit (Québec and Ottawa)
2nd trimester 1997

Published under the authority of the Minister of Canadian Heritage, Ottawa, 1997.

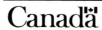

Table of contents

Acknowledgements — ix

Calendar — x

Introduction — 1

1. Lists of people who died and were buried on Grosse Île, in 1847
   a. The emigrants who died and were buried on Grosse Île — 12
   b. The employees who died and were buried on Grosse Île — 61
   c. The sailors who died and were buried on Grosse Île — 62

2. List of people who died on ships at sea or in quarantine at Grosse Île, in 1847 — 63

Appendices

1. List of married women who died and were buried on Grosse Île, in 1847 — 100

2. List of ships that arrived at Grosse Île and Québec City, in 1847 — 101

Sources — 108

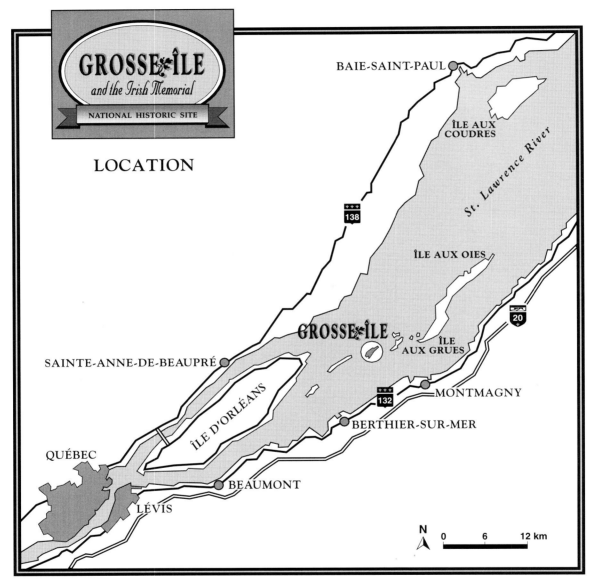

(Parks Canada/Christiane Hébert, 1997.)

Acknowledgements

First of all, a very special thank you to Antony Lorraine who put us on the trail of the lists found in the *Quebec Morning Chronicle*. We would also like to express our thanks to Michel de Courval and Pierre Demers who, throughout the publication process, always listened to our needs.

Our gratitude is also directed toward all the Parks Canada personnel who helped us. We would particularly like to mention the involvement of those people who, at one time or another, were part of the Grosse Île project research team. Our colleagues Christine Chartré, Rémi Chénier, Yvon Desloges, René Gélinas, Robert Grace, Johanne Lachance, André Sévigny and Sylvie Tremblay all contributed in their diverse ways to the completion of this listing. Noëlla Gauthier also shared in our work when it came time to do the editing and word processing. We offer all of these people our most heartfelt thanks.

André CHARBONNEAU and Doris DROLET-DUBÉ

Calendar 1847

JANUARY
S	M	T	W	T	F	S
					1	2
3	4	5	6	7	8	9
10	11	12	13	14	15	16
17	18	19	20	21	22	23
24	25	26	27	28	29	30
31						

FEBRUARY
S	M	T	W	T	F	S
	1	2	3	4	5	6
7	8	9	10	11	12	13
14	15	16	17	18	19	20
21	22	23	24	25	26	27
28						

MARCH
S	M	T	W	T	F	S
	1	2	3	4	5	6
7	8	9	10	11	12	13
14	15	16	17	18	19	20
21	22	23	24	25	26	27
28	29	30	31			

APRIL
S	M	T	W	T	F	S
				1	2	3
4	5	6	7	8	9	10
11	12	13	14	15	16	17
18	19	20	21	22	23	24
25	26	27	28	29	30	

MAY
S	M	T	W	T	F	S
						1
2	3	4	5	6	7	8
9	10	11	12	13	14	15
16	17	18	19	20	21	22
23	24	25	26	27	28	29
30	31					

JUNE
S	M	T	W	T	F	S
		1	2	3	4	5
6	7	8	9	10	11	12
13	14	15	16	17	18	19
20	21	22	23	24	25	26
27	28	29	30			

JULY
S	M	T	W	T	F	S
				1	2	3
4	5	6	7	8	9	10
11	12	13	14	15	16	17
18	19	20	21	22	23	24
25	26	27	28	29	30	31

AUGUST
S	M	T	W	T	F	S
1	2	3	4	5	6	7
8	9	10	11	12	13	14
15	16	17	18	19	20	21
22	23	24	25	26	27	28
29	30	31				

SEPTEMBER
S	M	T	W	T	F	S
			1	2	3	4
5	6	7	8	9	10	11
12	13	14	15	16	17	18
19	20	21	22	23	24	25
26	27	28	29	30		

OCTOBER
S	M	T	W	T	F	S
					1	2
3	4	5	6	7	8	9
10	11	12	13	14	15	16
17	18	19	20	21	22	23
24	25	26	27	28	29	30
31						

NOVEMBER
S	M	T	W	T	F	S
	1	2	3	4	5	6
7	8	9	10	11	12	13
14	15	16	17	18	19	20
21	22	23	24	25	26	27
28	29	30				

DECEMBER
S	M	T	W	T	F	S
			1	2	3	4
5	6	7	8	9	10	11
12	13	14	15	16	17	18
19	20	21	22	23	24	25
26	27	28	29	30	31	

Introduction

THE PRESENT REGISTER HAS BEEN DRAWN UP ESSENTIALLY TO MAKE AVAILABLE to the general public some of the information on family histories that was collected during the research stages of developing Grosse Île and the Irish Memorial National Historic Site. Given that most passenger lists dating back to the first half of the 19th century have been lost, this publication takes on a special significance for it somewhat personalizes the vast migratory movement which characterized that period of Canadian history.

This register contains two lists of names of those who died and groups together emigrants, quarantine station employees, and sailors. The first list identifies mainly those who died and were buried at the Grosse Île quarantine station during the 24-week shipping season in 1847. The second lists a number of emigrants who died on the ships, at sea and in quarantine, during the same season. Most of the names on these lists come from the deaths listed in the *Quebec Morning Chronicle* during the summer and autumn of 1847, at the request of the authorities.

By lifting the cloak of anonymity that shrouded these deaths at sea and on Grosse Île, we wish above all to pay homage, some 150 years later, to the thousands of unfortunate people, most of whom were of Irish origin, who invested so much effort in the hope of improving their lot in life, only to have that hope so unfortunately dissipated along the way.

A sombre record

The 1847 wave of emigration was unquestionably a significant event of the 19th century. At the port of Québec City, the rate of newly arriving emigrants, a total of 90 150 people, was triple the average of the preceeding years. This emigration was first and foremost Irish since Ireland was going through the worst year of the Great Famine. Already weakened by malnutrition and deprivation, the Irish emigrants were crowded aboard filthy sailing ships unfit for human transportation. They arrived in deplorable condition and a number of them were sick with typhus which quickly spread to epidemic proportions. In 1847, the number of hospitalizations that occured between the emigrants' departure in Europe and their arrival somewhere in Canada was very high and affected approximately one half of the emigrants who landed in Québec City in 1847. The mortality rate also reached record levels, affecting eighteen percent of the emigrants heading for Québec City (Table 1). This sombre record remained unchallenged throughout the 19th century.

PREPARATIONS FOR EMBARKATION ON THE WHARFS OF LIVERPOOL.
(McGill University, McLellan Library, Illustrated London News, July 6, 1850.)

A quick analysis of the mortality rate on board ship and in quarantine clearly identifies the ports of departure with the worst reports: Liverpool (England) and Cork (Ireland) (Table 2). Vessels leaving Liverpool had a mean of 58.8 deaths per average 375.5 passengers, a mortality rate of almost 16%. Ships out of Cork reflected a similar toll to that of Liverpool: a mean of 58.3 deaths out of an average of 312.8 passengers, for a death rate of about 19%. This poses an enormous contrast to the ships coming from the German ports of Bremen and Hamburg, where the death rate varied between 0.01% and 0.02% of the average number of travellers. In fact, some contaminated ships came close to total tragedy. Over 56% of the passengers on the *Naomi* and the *Virginius* coming from Liverpool died at sea or in quarantine. Some 44% of the emigrants aboard the *Avon* and the *Bee*, which set out from Cork, had already died when their ship arrived in Québec City! Of the 442 vessels that arrived at the port of Québec City in 1847, over 35 ships from Liverpool and Cork had a death toll of over 15%.

This situation tends to confirm what Dr. Douglas and emigration agent Buchanan had to say at the end of the 1847 season: in addition to the overcrowded ships, the poor hygienic conditions and the lack of food on board, the high toll of the 1847 season can be attributed to the condition of the emigrants before they embarked on the journey as well as the latent presence of the germ of the disease amongst them. The ships coming from Liverpool and Cork transported mainly Irish emigrants who were already very much affected and weakened by the Famine.

INTRODUCTION

The total number of deaths on the ships and at the quarantine station, estimated at 8745, accounts for 50% of all the deaths amongst the emigrants of 1847 who passed in transit through Québec City. The total number of deaths on board ship is an astonishing 5293, a little more than 5% of all the emigrants who set sail. This figure includes deaths at sea, those on the ships at the moment of the quarantine and, according to Buchanan, the deaths of 11 women in child-birth. The average age of those who died on the boats is 20. Human losses at the quarantine station number 3452, of which 3238 were registered in the hospital and 214 others were amongst the so-called "healthy emigrants". Spread over the 24 weeks the quarantine station was operating in 1847, this works out to an average of 144 deaths per week (Table 3). The average age at the time of death was 24.4 years.

It is more difficult to provide the precise number of people who were buried on Grosse Île than it is to determine the number of deaths at sea. Nevertheless, the number 5424, which is inscribed on the Medical Officers' Monument, would seem to be the maximum possible (Table 4). The calculation becomes rather difficult because the number of deaths which occurred on board the ships while in quarantine at Grosse Île is not accurate; it is not known how many bodies were removed from the ships to be buried at the cemetery on Grosse Île. The data furnished by superintendent Douglas between December 1847 and February 1848 accounts for 4292 burials on Grosse Île in 1847, of which 3452 were deaths on the island, and 842 deaths on board the quarantined ships. However, according to the data taken from the register of ships inspected at Grosse Île and the register of arrivals in Québec City, the total number of deaths is calculated at 3501 in the hospital on Grosse Île plus 1190 on the quarantined ships, for a total of

ONE OF THE CAUSES OF DEATH ABOARD SAILBOATS TRANSPORTING EMIGRANTS: OVERCROWDING.
(McGill University, McLellan Library, Illustrated London News, July 6, 1850.)

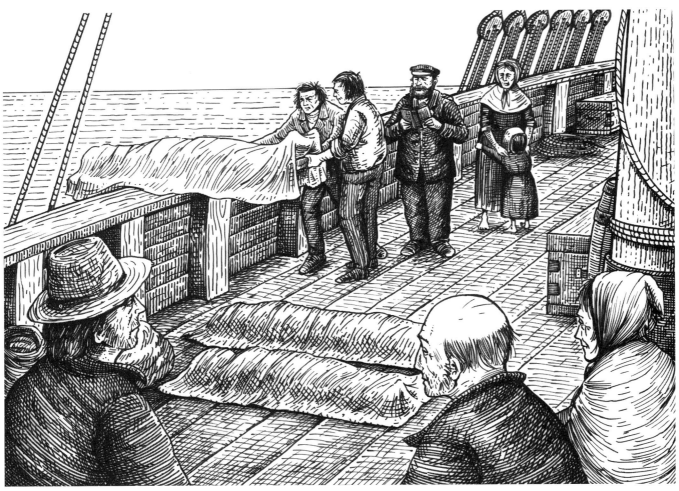

BURIAL AT SEA.
(Parks Canada/Daniel Rainville, 1997.)

4691 burials. In an 1848 report, Bishop Mountain states that approximatively 5400 bodies were buried on Grosse Île during the 1847 season. And finally, in another report of statistics compiled some time later and annexed to the hospitalization records of Grosse Île for the year 1897, it is recorded that there were 3226 deaths in hospital and 2198 deaths on the quarantined ships or during the landing of sicks emigrants before they could be hospitalized. Despite the divergences in these reports, the various figures given provide an idea of the dimension of the tragedy and tend to confirm the maximum number of 5424 burials in the cemeteries of the Grosse Île quarantine station in 1847.

The cemeteries on Grosse Île

Two of the three cemeteries on Grosse Île are linked to the deaths of 1847. The largest, which is situated on the south-west peninsula of the island, is likely the resting place of the remains of most of the people who died in hospital or on the ships in quarantine during the 1847 season. Because of the high rate of daily mortality, the bodies were buried in mass graves lined up in rectangular rows along the north-south axis of the island. According to certain accounts, the remains were all laid in wooden coffins then placed one on top another in three rows. Thus, despite the urgency of the situation in 1847, the mortal remains seem to have been interred in a most respectful manner.

INTRODUCTION

This cemetery, which was set up during the first quarantine season in 1832, is known today as the "Irish cemetery" after the main victims of the 1847 typhus epidemic. For this reason, it remains one of the most important witnesses to the 1847 tragedy. The surface of the cemetery today is still marked by the alternating mounds and furrows created by the rows of coffins which have settled into the earth over the years. A second cemetery located at the east end of the island probably contains the remains of those who died in the "healthy division" which was set up in this eastern sector of the island during the summer of 1847.

The cemeteries are amongst the most important cultural and symbolic assets of the national historic site that Grosse Île has become. Mrs. Jeannette Vekeman-Masson, who was born and lived on Grosse Île at the beginning of the century, puts it so well, *"the immigrants rest there in peace. Most of them were fleeing poverty and seeking a promised land. They found it on Quarantine Island. Now they sleep in a enchanting and peaceful place, and we should not disturb their dreams. "* [translation] (*Grand-maman raconte la Grosse Île,* Corporation pour la mise en valeur de Grosse-Ile inc., Sainte-Foy, Éditions La Liberté, 1981, p. 147).

BURIAL ON GROSSE ÎLE.
(Parks Canada/Daniel Rainville, 1997.)

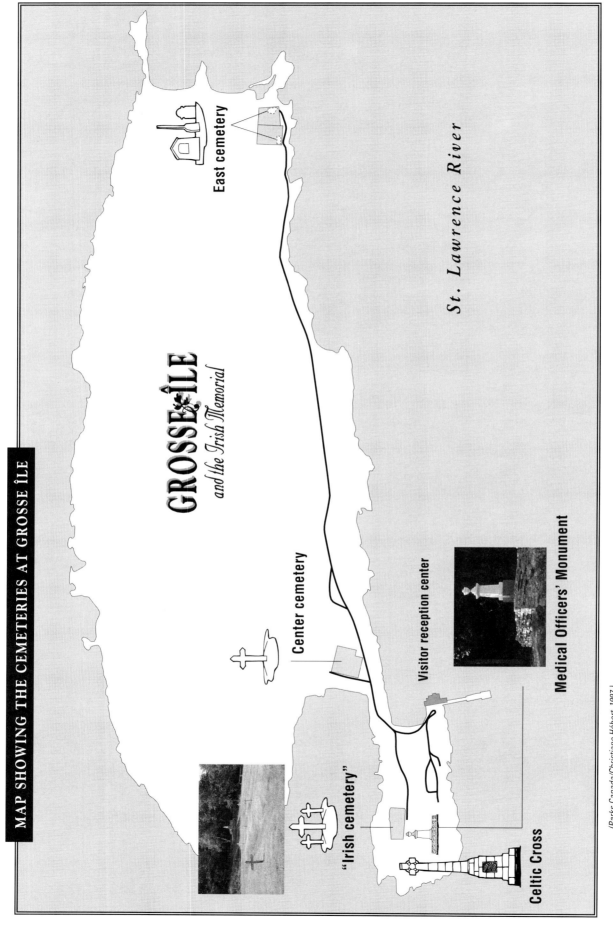

(Parks Canada/Christiane Hébert, 1997.)

Introduction

THE WESTERN CEMETERY: IN THE BACKGROUND, THE MONUMENT DEDICATED TO THE DOCTORS INCLUDING THOSE WHO DIED DURING THE TYPHUS EPIDEMIC OF 1847. IN FRONT, DEPRESSIONS IN THE GROUND SUGGEST THE PLACEMENT OF GRAVES.
(Parks Canada/Bonacorsi, 1996.)

The lists

The two lists presented in this index include a total of 8308 entries. The first contains the names of 3879 people buried on Grosse Île in 1847. These are mainly the people who died in hospital or in the quarantine station's "healthy division"; added to these are names of emigrants who died on the quarantined ships and whose deaths were recorded in the register of burials at the Anglican and Catholic chapels.

The first list is divided into three parts: emigrants (3826), sailors (38) and employees (15) who died and were interred on Grosse Île. In each of these groups, the names appear in alphabetical order and each entry includes the family name, given name, age (if available), name of the ship and its port of departure, the country in which the emigrant boarded ship, and the date of death, in that order. In most cases, the date mentioned is an indication of the week in which the death occurred, including the first and last days of that week. If the date mentioned is followed by an asterisk (*), it indicates the date of burial.

The second list, taken mainly from the *Quebec Morning Chronicle,* contains the names of 4429 people who died on the ships, at sea or in quarantine. Even if we know that the emigrants who died on the ships during the quarantine period were buried on Grosse Île, we unfortunately cannot distinguish them from those who died during the voyage. Once again, the names appear in alphabetical order and each entry includes the family name, given name, age, name of the ship, its port of departure, and the country the emigrant left from. Since we do not have a precise date of death, we have chosen to indicate the interval during which the death occurred by presenting, for each individual, the date of departure from Europe and the date of the ship's arrival in Québec City. The difference in figures between 5293, the total number of deaths on the ships at sea and in quarantine, and 4429, the number of names presented in this index, could probably be explained by the fact that the names of infants under one year of age who died during the voyage were not recorded.

WEEKLY RETURN OF SICK IN THE QUARANTINE HOSPITAL GROSSE ISLE FROM 16 TO 22 MAY 1847. ONE OF ONLY TWO HANDWRITTEN HOSPITALIZATION REPORTS BY MEDICAL SUPERINTENDENT GEORGE MELLIS DOUGLAS THAT ARE AVALAIBLE FOR 1847.
(NAC, PRO, CO42/542, fol. 171, microfilm reel-407.)

The names appearing in this index were gathered from a variety of often handwritten sources by a number of researchers who respected the variant spellings encountered in the various reference documents. Preparing these lists for publication thus required painstaking attention to detail in order to avoid confusion amongst the variant forms. For this reason, the spelling of family names has been standardized. However, we leave it up to the reader to draw the obvious links between names such as Barron and Barrow, or Reilly and O'Reilly...

Sometimes the same name appears on both lists, since the Anglican registers indicate on which ship in quarantine an emigrant died. It should be mentioned here that the Catholic and Anglican chapel registers as well as the *Quebec Morning Chronicle* identify deaths of emigrants coming from boats that were not registered on the ships inspection lists at Grosse Île or in Québec City. Could these ships have been local vessels plying the St. Lawrence and carrying passengers who landed downstream? At this point, we don't know.

We also came across some married women's maiden names which are listed in appendix 1 of this register. These names are entered as follow: Barry, Margaret, 32 years, Avon, Cork, Ireland, see Reilly, Margaret. We felt that the list of ships which stopped at the quarantine station before arriving at the port of Québec City in 1847 would also be an indispensable tool for those researching family history. This appendix contains 478 entries including the sailing country, the number of ships from same origine, the average number of passengers, the mean of deaths on the voyage and in quarantine at Grosse Île.

Table 1
TOTAL NUMBER OF DEATHS AMONGST EMIGRANTS HEADING FOR QUÉBEC CITY IN 1847

Deaths in quarantine on Grosse Île	3452
Deaths on the ships during the voyage and in quarantine	5293 *
Deaths at the Marine and Emigrants Hospital of Québec	1041
Deaths at Montréal at the Pointe-Saint-Charles Hospital (as of January 1, 1848)	3579
Deaths in Saint-Jean (Quebec)	71
Deaths in Lachine	130
Deaths at the Emigrants Hospital of Toronto (as of February 2, 1848)	863
Deaths in other towns in Upper Canada	3048
Total	17477

December 1847 and March 1848

* This figure includes the 842 people who died on the quarantined ships and were buried at the cemetery on Grosse Île.

Table 2
AVERAGE MORTALITY RATE PER SHIP DURING THE VOYAGE AND AT THE QUARANTINE STATION

Port	Country	Number of ships	Average number of passengers	Average number of deaths during the voyage	Average number of deaths on board ship in quarantine	Average number of deaths at the quarantine station	Total average number of deaths	Mortality rate (%)
Aberdeen	Scotland	4	93	0	0	0	0	0
Aberystwyth	Wales	1	243	1	0	0	1	0.41
Ballyshannon	Ireland	1	66	0	0	0	0	0
Belfast	Ireland	21	329.19	6.67	1.71	6.05	14.43	4.38
Benicarlo	Spain	1	3	0	0	0	0	0
Bideford	England	2	9.5	0	0	0	0	0
Bremen	Germany	24	226.38	2.21	0.13	0	2.33	1.03
Bremerhaven	Germany	2	265.5	3	0	0	3	1.13
Bridgwater	England	1	55	0	0	0	0	0
Bristol	England	5	31.4	0	0	0.2	0.2	0.64
Cardiff	Wales	2	4.5	0	0	0	0	0
Chepstow	England	1	1	0	0	0	0	0
Cork	Ireland	33	312.79	26.91	7.58	23.85	58.33	18.64
Donegal	Ireland	5	167.2	3	0	1.20	4.2	2.51
Dublin	Ireland	27	243.26	8.93	0.81	9.89	19.63	8.07
Dundee	Scotland	2	36	0	0	0	0	0
Falmouth	England	2	159.5	0	0	0	0	0
Galway	Ireland	4	187.25	3.5	1.75	4.75	10	5.34
Glasgow	Scotland	30	67.3	2.03	0.37	0.9	3.3	4.9
Greenock	Scotland	5	228.4	1.8	0	1.2	3	1.31
Hamburg	Germany	10	164.6	3.3	0.1	0.2	3.6	2.19
Hull	England	4	87.5	0.25	0	0	0.25	2.29
Killala	Ireland	5	277.5	6.6	2.8	11.6	21	7.57
Kilrush	Ireland	1	119	0	0	0	0	0
Limerick	Ireland	50	183.48	4.22	0.6	1.28	6.1	3.32
Liverpool	England	72	375.54	25.76	9.32	23.69	58.78	15.65
Loch Saxford	Scotland	1	279	0	0	0	0	0
Londonderry	Ireland	11	320.55	5.64	2.73	7.36	15.73	4.91
London	England	19	104.47	1.68	0	0.16	1.84	1.76
Maryport	England	2	15.5	0	0	0	0	0
Milford	England	1	32	0	0	0	0	0
New Ross	Ireland	15	293	7.8	1.73	6.13	15.67	5.35
Newport	England	1	364	5	0	7	12	3.30
Newry	Ireland	5	300.4	4.2	0.2	2.4	6.8	2.26
Padstow	England	3	228	0.67	0	0	0.67	0.29
Penzance	England	1	66	0	0	0	0	0
Plymouth	England	7	146.43	0.43	0	0	0.43	0.29
Poole	England	2	5	0	0	0	0	0
Saint-Hélier	Jersey	1	19	0	0	0	0	0
Sligo	Ireland	26	220.46	14.23	3.35	7.31	24.88	11.29
Southampton	England	2	126	0	0	0	0	0
St.Ives	England	2	33	0	0	0	0	0
Stockton	England	2	3.5	0	0	0	0	0
Sunderland	England	2	3.5	0	0	0	0	0
Torquay	England	2	6.5	0	0	0	0	0
Waterford	Ireland	14	217.86	2.64	0.07	0.71	3.43	1.57
Westport	Ireland	2	37	0.5	0	0	0.5	1.35
Weymouth	England	1	4	0	0	0	0	0
Whitehaven	England	1	2	0	0	0	0	0
Youghal	Ireland	3	106	0.67	0	0.33	1	0.94

Table 3
BREAKDOWN OF DEATHS PER WEEK ON GROSSE ÎLE DURING THE 1847 SEASON

Week	Number of deaths	Week	Number of deaths
From May 8 to 15	1	From August 1 to 7	220
From May 16 to 22	16	From August 8 to 14	322
From May 23 to 29	71	From August 15 to 21	288
From May 30 to June 5	119	From August 22 to 28	256
From June 6 to 12	154	From August 29 to September 4	191
From June 13 to 19	202	From September 5 to 11	143
From June 20 to 26	156	From September 12 to 18	133
From June 27 to July 3	144	From September 19 to 25	121
From July 4 to 10	165	From September 26 to October 2	86
From July 11 to 17	171	From October 3 to 9	61
From July 18 to 24	197	From October 10 to 16	33
From July 25 to 31	188	From October 17 to 23	14
		TOTAL	3452*
		October 1847	

* This figure includes the 3228 deaths registered in the hospital and the 214 others that occurred at the "healthy division" set up on the east side of the island.

Table 4
REPORT OF BURIALS ON GROSSE ÎLE IN 1847

Sources	Deaths on Grosse Île	Deaths on board quarantined ships	Total
Statistics published in the *Quebec Morning Chronicle* of October 28, 1847	3452	1282	4734
Statistical data provided by Douglas (December 1847 to February 1848)	3452	842	4294
Report annexed to the 1897 hospitalization register	3226 *	2198 **	5424
Commemorative monument at the cemetery on the west end of the island			5424
Calculation of the data collected for each ship	3501	1190	4691

* This figure only concerns the deaths in hospital.
** This figure takes into account the deaths which occurred on the quarantined ships or during the landing of emigrants before they were registered in the hospital records.

1

Lists of people who died and were buried on Grosse Île, in 1847

a. The emigrants
b. The employees
c. The sailors

OVERALL VIEW OF THE "IRISH" CEMETERY.
(Parks Canada/L. McNicoll, 1984.)

LISTS OF PEOPLE WHO DIED AND WERE BURIED ON GROSSE ÎLE, IN 1847

a. The emigrants

Name	Age	Vessel	Port	Country	Date of death
Acton, John	26	Erin's Queen	Liverpool	England	between August 1 and 7, 1847
Acton, Mary	23	Erin's Queen	Liverpool	England	between July 25 and 31, 1847
Adams, Edward	2 months				1847/08/09*
Adams, Mary	40	Sir Henry Pottinger	Belfast	Ireland	1847/08/29
Addy, Francis	1	Champion	Liverpool	England	between August 29 and September 4, 1847
Agnew, Margaret	30	Caithness-shire	Belfast	Ireland	between June 20 and 26, 1847
Ahern, Bridget	40	Erin's Queen	Liverpool	England	between July 25 and 31, 1847
Ahern, Bridget	21	Emily	Cork	Ireland	between August 1 and 7, 1847
Ahern, John	30	Naomi	Liverpool	England	between August 8 and 14, 1847
Aldgate, William	18	Saguenay	Cork	Ireland	between August 29 and September 4, 1847
Alexander, Francis	5	Sobraon	Liverpool	England	between July 11 and 17, 1847
Alexander, James	11	Sobraon	Liverpool	England	between August 15 and 21, 1847
Alexander, John	18	Broom	Liverpool	England	between August 1 and 7, 1847
Alexander, Joseph	13	Sobraon	Liverpool	England	between August 1 and 7, 1847
Allen, David	57	Triton	Liverpool	England	1847/09/16
Allen, David	47	Triton	Liverpool	England	between September 12 and 18, 1847
Allen, John	20	John Munn	Liverpool	England	between August 15 and 21, 1847
Allen, Margaret	54	Colonist	New Ross	Ireland	between August 29 and September 4, 1847
Allen, Mary	28	Bridgetown	Liverpool	England	between August 22 and 28, 1847
Allen, Sarah	24	Lord Seaton	Belfast	Ireland	between June 13 and 19, 1847
Allen, Sarah Ann	24	Christiana	Londonderry	Ireland	1847/06/19
Allen, Thomas					
Alton, Ann	3	Bridgetown	Liverpool	England	1847/08/29
Anderson, Alice	40	Lively	Cork	Ireland	between July 11 and 17, 1847
Anderson, Ann	6 months	Bridgetown	Liverpool	England	between August 22 and 28, 1847
Anderson, B.					
Anderson, Frances	20	Maria Somes	Cork	Ireland	1847/09/01
Anderson, James	3	George	Liverpool	England	between June 13 and 19, 1847
Anderson, James	5 years & 9 months				1847/06/16
Anderson, John	4 months	Maria Somes	Cork	Ireland	1847/09/06
Anderson, John	23	George	Liverpool	England	between June 27 and July 3, 1847
Anderson, John	28	George	Liverpool	England	between June 20 and 26, 1847
Anderson, Margaret	53	Thistle	Liverpool	England	between July 18 and 24, 1847
Anderson, Mary	5 months	Maria Somes	Cork	Ireland	between September 5 and 11, 1847
Anderson, Robert	40	John Bolton	Liverpool	England	between June 20 and 26, 1847

Name	Age	Vessel	Port	Country	Date of death
Anderson, William	1	Lively	Cork	Ireland	between July 18 and 24, 1847
Andrews, Francis	36	Maria Somes	Cork	Ireland	between August 29 and September 4, 1847
Andrews, James	36	Gilmour	Cork	Ireland	between June 6 and 12, 1847
Andrews, Mary Ann	37				1847/06/27
Andrews, William	18	Abbotsford	Dublin	Ireland	between June 6 and 12, 1847
Ansley, Ann	76	Lotus	Liverpool	England	1847/06/07*
Armour, Robert	46	Progress	New Ross	Ireland	1847/07/08
Armstrong, Ann	4	Christiana	Londonderry	Ireland	1847/05/29
Armstrong, Catherine	1 year & 6 months	Royalist	Liverpool	England	between May 23 and 29, 1847
Armstrong, John	1				1847/05/23
Armstrong, John	23	Free Trader	Liverpool	England	between August 29 and September 4, 1847
Arthur, Matthew	59	Aberdeen	Liverpool	England	between May 29 and June 5, 1847
Ashe, Thomas	40	Jessie	Cork	Ireland	between July 18 and 24, 1847
Atkinson, Mary	23	Naomi	Liverpool	England	between August 8 and 14, 1847
Austin, Hamilton		Constitution	Belfast	Ireland	1847/05/27
B___, C___					
B___, C___					
B___, D___					
B___, R___					
B___, Rose		Argo	Liverpool	England	between June 6 and 12, 1847
Bagnel, Ann	6	Marinus	Dublin	Ireland	between September 5 and 11, 1847
Bagnel, Bridget	28	Marinus	Dublin	Ireland	between September 12 and 18, 1847
Bagnel, Michael	2 years & 6 months	Marinus	Dublin	Ireland	between August 22 and 28, 1847
Bailey, Eliza	3	Christiana	Londonderry	Ireland	1847/06/06
Bailey, George		Goliah	Liverpool	England	
Baker, Isabella	1 year & 9 months	Emigrant	Liverpool	England	between September 26 and October 2, 1847
Baker, John	25	Sir Henry Pottinger	Belfast	Ireland	1847/10/01
Baker, Mary					1847/07/01
Baldwin, Mary	25	Wm S. Hamilton	New Ross	Ireland	between July 25 and 31, 1847
Baldwin, William	2 months	Wm S. Hamilton	New Ross	Ireland	between July 18 and 24, 1847
Bale, Henry	66	Nelson's Village	Belfast	Ireland	between July 4 and 10, 1847
Banks, Alexander	25	Avon	Cork	Ireland	between August 8 and 14, 1847
Bannon, Honora	25	Larch	Sligo	Ireland	between August 15 and 21, 1847
Barnes, Jane Maxwell	30				1847/06/12
Barnes, Jean	30	Eliza Caroline	Liverpool	England	between June 6 and 12, 1847
Barnes, Judy	30	Wellington	Liverpool	England	between October 17 and 23, 1847
Barnes, Robert	7	Eliza Caroline	Liverpool	England	between June 13 and 19, 1847

The emigrants

Name	Age	Vessel	Port	Country	Date of death
Barnes, Sally	24	Lady Milton	Liverpool	England	between July 4 and 10, 1847
Barnes, Samuel	30	Marinus	Dublin	Ireland	between August 15 and 21, 1847
Barnes, William	40	Progress	New Ross	Ireland	between July 4 and 10, 1847
Barrett, B.	9 months	John Francis	Cork	Ireland	between June 6 and 12, 1847
Barrett, Bridget	18	Constitution	Belfast	Ireland	between August 15 and 21, 1847
Barrett, Catherine	19	John Munn	Liverpool	England	between August 8 and 14, 1847
Barrett, Mary	50	John Francis	Cork	Ireland	between June 13 and 19, 1847
Barrett, Mary	18	Broom	Liverpool	England	between August 8 and 14, 1847
Barrett, Michael	3	Larch	Sligo	Ireland	between August 22 and 28, 1847
Barrett, Sydney	18	Yorkshire Lass	Killala	Ireland	between August 8 and 14, 1847
Barrett, Thadeus	16	Lady Flora Hastings	Cork	Ireland	between July 18 and 24, 1847
Barron, Ann Maxwell		Eliza Caroline	Liverpool	England	1847/06/10
Barron, John	5	Eliza Caroline	Liverpool	England	1847/06/06
Barron, Richard	9	Eliza Caroline	Liverpool	England	between June 20 and 26, 1847
Barron, Robert	7	Eliza Caroline	Liverpool	England	1847/06/14
Barrow, Joseph	22	Gilmour	Cork	Ireland	between July 25 and 31, 1847
Barry, Ann	21	Caithness-shire	Belfast	Ireland	between June 6 and 12, 1847
Barry, Ellen	3	Sir Henry Pottinger	Belfast	Ireland	between August 22 and 28, 1847
Barry, Ellen	30	Sir Henry Pottinger	Belfast	Ireland	between August 29 and September 4, 1847
Barry, Ellen	1	Avon	Cork	Ireland	between August 22 and 28, 1847
Barry, John	26	Britain			between July 11 and 17, 1847
Barry, John	40	Lady Flora Hastings	Cork	Ireland	between June 20 and 26, 1847
Barry, John	40	Wandsworth	Dublin	Ireland	between June 6 and 12, 1847
Barry, John	35	Avon	Cork	Ireland	between August 1 and 7, 1847
Barry, John	40	Wandsworth	Dublin	Ireland	between June 6 and 12, 1847
Barry, John		Free Briton	Cork	Ireland	
Barry, Margaret	30	Agnes	Cork	Ireland	between June 13 and 19, 1847
Barry, Mary	21	Agnes	Cork	Ireland	between July 11 and 17, 1847
Barry, Mary	20	Aberdeen	Liverpool	England	between June 13 and 19, 1847
Barry, Thadeus	37	Greenock	Liverpool	England	between July 25 and 31, 1847
Barry, Timothy	24	Sir Henry Pottinger	Belfast	Ireland	between September 12 and 18, 1847
Barry, William	40	Sarah	Liverpool	England	between August 8 and 14, 1847
Barry, William	42	Colonist	New Ross	Ireland	between August 22 and 28, 1847
Barton, Johanna	26	Bee	Cork	Ireland	between July 24 and 31, 1847
Bassett, George	40	John Francis	Cork	Ireland	1847/06/19
Bateman, Hugh	36	Triton	Liverpool	England	1847/07/20
Bateman, Joseph	8	Triton	Liverpool	England	between July 25 and 31, 1847
Bath, Margaret	3	Julius Caesar	Liverpool	England	between September 19 and 25, 1847
Bath, Priscilla	7	Julius Caesar	Liverpool	England	between September 19 and 25, 1847
Battle, Bridget	29	Sarah	Liverpool	England	between August 29 and September 4, 1847
Battle, John	4	Avon	Cork	Ireland	between August 8 and 14, 1847
Beatty, Eliza	14	Wellington	Liverpool	England	between October 3 and 9, 1847
Behan, Ann	22	Emigrant	Liverpool	England	between October 3 and 9, 1847
Behan, John	17	Scotland	Cork	Ireland	between May 23 and 29, 1847
Behan, Mary	27	Covenanter	Cork	Ireland	between September 5 and 11, 1847
Bell, Ann	28	Junior	Liverpool	England	between July 11 and 17, 1847
Bell, Henry					1847/07/05
Bell, James	30	Sobraon	Liverpool	England	between July 4 and 10, 1847
Bennett, Anthony	24	Erin's Queen	Liverpool	England	between July 25 and 31, 1847
Bennett, B.	9 months	John Francis	Cork	Ireland	between May 29 and June 5, 1847
Bennett, John	7	Jessie	Limerick	Ireland	between August 22 and 28, 1847
Bennett, Thomas	4	Wandsworth	Dublin	Ireland	1847/05/21
Benson, Dr John	45	Wandsworth	Dublin	Ireland	1847/05/26
Benson, Mary	34	Sir Henry Pottinger	Belfast	Ireland	between August 22 and 28, 1847
Best, James	23	Rose	Liverpool	England	between July 18 and 24, 1847
Best, Mary Ann					
Bird, Mary	19	Sarah Maria	Sligo	Ireland	1847/07/23
Birney, Thomas		Progress	New Ross	Ireland	
Bishop, Alexander	7	John Munn	Liverpool	England	between August 15 and 21, 1847
Bishop, Alice	7	Free Trader	Liverpool	England	between August 22 and 28, 1847
Bishop, Amelia	14	Free Trader	Liverpool	England	1847/09/13
Bishop, Daniel	3	Naomi	Liverpool	England	between August 15 and 21, 1847
Bishop, Ferdinand	12	Free Trader	Liverpool	England	1847/09/08
Bishop, Martha	9	Free Trader	Liverpool	England	1847/08/30
Bishop, Martha	9 years & 6 months	Broom	Liverpool	England	between August 29 and September 4, 1847
Bishop, Mary	37	Free Trader	Liverpool	England	between August 8 and 14, 1847
Bishop, Mary	11	Free Trader	Liverpool	England	between August 8 and 14, 1847
Bishop, Olive	27	Free Trader	Liverpool	England	1847/08/18
Bishop, Stephen		Free Trader	Liverpool	England	
Bishop, William	55	Maria Somes	Cork	Ireland	between August 29 and September 4, 1847
Black, James	21	Zealous	London	England	1847/08/16
Black, William	24	Pursuit	Liverpool	England	between June 27 and July 3, 1847
Blake, Andrew	21	Standard	New Ross	Ireland	between June 20 and 26, 1847
Blake, James		Zealous	London	England	
Blake, John	2	Marinus	Dublin	Ireland	between September 5 and 11, 1847
Blake, Joseph		Zealous	London	England	
Blake, Nicholas	25	Lively	Cork	Ireland	between July 11 and 17, 1847
Blake, Sally	60	Marchioness of Bute	Belfast	Ireland	between August 8 and 14, 1847
Blakely, John	14	Christiana	Londonderry	Ireland	1847/06/22
Blakely, William	1 year & 3 months	Christiana	Londonderry	Ireland	1847/06/05
Blanch, William	24				1847/06/28
Bloomer, David	16	Rose	Liverpool	England	between July 25 and 31, 1847

13

Lists of people who died and were buried on Grosse Île, in 1847

Name	Age	Vessel	Port	Country	Date of death
Bogue, John	56	Unicorn	Londonderry	Ireland	1847/07/26
Bogue, Thomas	12	Unicorn	Londonderry	Ireland	between August 1 and 7, 1847
Boland, Ann	40	Erin's Queen	Liverpool	England	between July 11 and 17, 1847
Boland, Helen	19	Free Trader	Liverpool	England	between August 21 and 28, 1847
Boland, Mary	3	Wm S. Hamilton	New Ross	Ireland	between August 1 and 7, 1847
Bolger, Bridget	60	Broom	Liverpool	England	between August 8 and 14, 1847
Bolger, Michael	60	Cape Breton	Dublin	Ireland	between June 13 and 19, 1847
Bolger, Michael	13	Cape Breton	Dublin	Ireland	between August 1 and 7, 1847
Bolton, Bridget	30	Ajax	Liverpool	England	between July 18 and 24, 1847
Bolton, John	28	John Bolton	Liverpool	England	between May 29 and June 5, 1847
Bonner, Thomas	3	Lady Milton	Liverpool	England	between June 27 and July 3, 1847
Borden, John	10	Sobraon	Liverpool	England	between June 27 and July 3, 1847
Borden, Michael	50	Sobraon	Liverpool	England	between June 27 and July 3, 1847
Bourke, Richard	54	John and Robert	Liverpool	England	between August 15 and 21, 1847
Bowen, Susan	20	Saguenay	Cork	Ireland	between August 22 and 28, 1847
Bowers, Francis	23	Free Trader	Liverpool	England	between August 15 and 21, 1847
Bowes, John		Unicorn	Londonderry	Ireland	
Bowes, William	2 months	Lotus	Liverpool	England	1847/07/14
Boyd, Joseph	3	Euclid	Glasgow	Scotland	between July 25 and 31, 1847
Boyle, Bridget	10	Triton	Liverpool	England	between July 11 and 17, 1847
Boyle, Catherine	10	Triton	Liverpool	England	between August 8 and 14, 1847
Boyle, Ellen	38	John Munn	Liverpool	England	between September 5 and 11, 1847
Boyle, Honora	50	John Munn	Liverpool	England	between August 15 and 21, 1847
Boyle, Mary	2	Goliah	Liverpool	England	between July 11 and 17, 1847
Boyle, Mary	12	Triton	Liverpool	England	between August 1 and 7, 1847
Boyle, Mary Ann	6 months	Eliza Morrison	Belfast	Ireland	1847/07/14
Bracken, Patrick	50	Naomi	Liverpool	England	between August 15 and 21, 1847
Bradley, Charles	45	John Francis	Cork	Ireland	between June 6 and 12, 1847
Bradley, Charles	40	Agnes	Cork	Ireland	between June 20 and 26, 1847
Bradley, Christopher	30	Pursuit	Liverpool	England	between June 27 and July 3, 1847
Bradshaw, Agnes	60	Caithness-shire	Belfast	Ireland	between July 4 and 10, 1847
Bradshaw, Margaret	25				1847/06/13
Bradshaw, Mary	25	Caithness-shire	Belfast	Ireland	between June 6 and 12, 1847
Bradshaw, William	25	Sir Henry Pottinger	Belfast	Ireland	between August 15 and 21, 1847
Brady, Atty	40	Erin's Queen	Liverpool	England	between July 25 and 31, 1847
Brady, Catherine	16	Free Trader	Liverpool	England	between August 15 and 21, 1847
Brady, Catherine	40	Superior	Londonderry	Ireland	between September 26 and October 2, 1847
Brady, Eliza	26	John Jardine	Liverpool	England	between August 22 and 28, 1847
Brady, Elizabeth	24	Eliza Morrison	Belfast	Ireland	between August 22 and 28, 1847
Brady, Hugh	22	James Moran	Liverpool	England	between August 8 and 14, 1847
Brady, Joseph	40	Erin's Queen	Liverpool	England	1847/08/23
Brady, Michael	30	Greenock	Liverpool	England	between August 15 and 21, 1847
Branagan, Joseph		Cape Breton	Dublin	Ireland	
Branagan, Joshua	28	Cape Breton	Dublin	Ireland	between June 20 and 26, 1847
Brannan, Patrick	3	John Munn	Liverpool	England	between August 15 and 21, 1847
Brannan, Thomas	40	Covenanter	Cork	Ireland	between August 8 and 14, 1847
Brawley, George		Goliah	Liverpool	England	
Bray, Nelly	30	George	Liverpool	England	between June 20 and 26, 1847
Breen, Bridget	23	Scotland	Cork	Ireland	between June 13 and 19, 1847
Breen, Robert	30	Sesostris	Londonderry	Ireland	between June 20 and 26, 1847
Brennan, Ann	34	Naomi	Liverpool	England	between September 12 and 18, 1847
Brennan, Bernard	22	Virginius	Liverpool	England	between August 1 and 7, 1847
Brennan, Bridget	36	Harry Lorrequer			between August 1 and 7, 1847
Brennan, Bridget	11	Marinus	Dublin	Ireland	between August 15 and 21, 1847
Brennan, Catherine	36	Perseverance	Dublin	Ireland	between June 6 and 12, 1847
Brennan, Catherine	35	Covenanter	Cork	Ireland	between August 15 and 21, 1847
Brennan, Charles	60	Free Trader	Liverpool	England	between August 15 and 21, 1847
Brennan, Daniel	36	Covenanter	Cork	Ireland	between August 15 and 21, 1847
Brennan, Daniel	35	Scotland	Cork	Ireland	between August 8 and 14, 1847
Brennan, David	60	Forester			between June 20 and 26, 1847
Brennan, James	36	Emigrant	Liverpool	England	between October 10 and 16, 1847
Brennan, James		John Munn	Liverpool	England	
Brennan, John	6	Perseverance	Dublin	Ireland	between September 19 and 25, 1847
Brennan, Joseph	18	Coromandel	Dublin	Ireland	between July 4 and 10, 1847
Brennan, Margaret	5	Emigrant	Liverpool	England	between October 3 and 9, 1847
Brennan, Martin	50	Virginius	Liverpool	England	between August 8 and 14, 1847
Brennan, Mary	65	Virginius	Liverpool	England	between August 8 and 14, 1847
Brennan, Mary	10	Pursuit	Liverpool	England	between June 20 and 26, 1847
Brennan, Mary	25	Aberdeen	Liverpool	England	between July 4 and 10, 1847
Brennan, Mary	14	Emigrant	Liverpool	England	between September 26 and October 2, 1847
Brennan, Michael	35	Sir Henry Pottinger	Belfast	Ireland	between August 29 and September 4, 1847
Brennan, Michael	3	Emigrant	Liverpool	England	between October 3 and 9, 1847
Brennan, Owen	30	Saguenay	Cork	Ireland	between August 22 and 28, 1847
Brennan, Patrick	10	Covenanter	Cork	Ireland	between August 8 and 14, 1847
Brennan, Sarah	40	Odessa	Dublin	Ireland	between August 1 and 7, 1847
Brennan, Thomas	40	Gilmour	Cork	Ireland	between June 6 and 12, 1847
Brennan, Timothy		John Munn	Liverpool	England	
Brennan, William	8	Virginius	Liverpool	England	between August 15 and 21, 1847

The emigrants

Name	Age	Vessel	Port	Country	Date of death
Brewer, Michael	30	Avon	Cork	Ireland	between July 18 and 24, 1847
Brick, John	26	Broom	Liverpool	England	between August 15 and 21, 1847
Brickley, Michael	22	Manchester	Liverpool	England	between July 25 and 31, 1847
Brien, Catherine	17	John Jardine	Liverpool	England	between July 11 and 17, 1847
Brien, Catherine	12	Mail	Cork	Ireland	between July 11 and 17, 1847
Brien, Edward	19	Syria	Liverpool	England	between August 8 and 14, 1847
Brien, James	22	Pursuit	Liverpool	England	between July 4 and 10, 1847
Brien, John		Avon	Cork	Ireland	
Brien, Mary	5	John Munn	Liverpool	England	between August 22 and 28, 1847
Brien, Thomas	50	Naomi	Liverpool	England	between August 22 and 28, 1847
Briody, Edward	45				1847/07/05
Broder, Mary	30	Naomi	Liverpool	England	between August 15 and 21, 1847
Broderick, Edward	32	Champion	Liverpool	England	between August 22 and 28, 1847
Broderick, William	15	Naparina	Dublin	Ireland	between August 29 and September 4, 1847
Brogan, James	29	Superior	Londonderry	Ireland	between September 19 and 25, 1847
Brookes, Eliza	9	Saguenay	Cork	Ireland	1847/08/24
Brown, Agnes	30				1847/07/12
Brown, Alexander		Wilhelmina	Belfast	Ireland	
Brown, Allan	19	Gilmour	Cork	Ireland	between June 20 and 26, 1847
Brown, Ann Pharson	30				1847/05/31
Brown, Eleanor Sloame	1 year & 4 months				1847/06/01
Brown, Ellen	1 year & 6 months	Constitution	Belfast	Ireland	between May 29 and June 5, 1847
Brown, James	36	Pandora	New Ross	Ireland	between August 1 and 7, 1847
Brown, Jane	11	Agamemnon	Liverpool	England	1847/07/28
Brown, Johanna	1	Scotland	Cork	Ireland	between June 20 and 26, 1847
Brown, John	6	Gilmour	Cork	Ireland	between June 6 and 12, 1847
Brown, Margaret	50	Sovereign			1847/06/25
Brown, Mary	2	Free Trader	Liverpool	England	between August 15 and 21, 1847
Brown, Mary	9	Lord Seaton	Belfast	Ireland	between August 15 and 21, 1847
Brown, Mary	9	Euclid	Glasgow	Scotland	1847/08/18
Brown, Mary	4	Gilmour	Cork	Ireland	between July 4 and 10, 1847
Brown, Michael	24	Goliah	Liverpool	England	between August 1 and 7, 1847
Brown, Patrick	11	Covenanter	Cork	Ireland	between September 19 and 25, 1847
Brown, Peter	12	Odessa	Dublin	Ireland	between August 8 and 14, 1847
Brown, Rose	17				between August 22 and 28, 1847
Brown, Thomas	27	Scotland	Cork	Ireland	between May 29 and June 5, 1847
Brown, Thomas	1	Lord Seaton	Belfast	Ireland	between May 23 and 29, 1847
Bruce, Robert	21	Sarah Maria	Sligo	Ireland	between August 8 and 14, 1847
Bryan, Bridget	23	Scotland	Cork	Ireland	between June 13 and 19, 1847
Bryan, Daniel	26	Sisters	Liverpool	England	between June 13 and 19, 1847
Bryan, Henry	4	Mail	Cork	Ireland	between June 27 and July 3, 1847
Bryan, James	1	Bee	Cork	Ireland	between July 4 and 10, 1847
Bryan, John	4 months	Lord Sandon	Cork	Ireland	between June 20 and 26, 1847
Bryan, John		Junior	Liverpool	England	
Bryan, Judith	6				1847/05/14
Bryan, Morgan	30	Numa	Sligo	Ireland	between August 15 and 21, 1847
Bryan, William		Junior	Liverpool	England	
Bryans, James	28	Sir Robert Peel	Liverpool	England	between October 10 and 16, 1847
Buck, John		Unicorn	Londonderry	Ireland	
Buckley, D.					
Buckley, Joseph	24	Elizabeth	Limerick	Ireland	between July 4 and 10, 1847
Buckley, Timothy	28	Agnes	Cork	Ireland	between May 29 and June 5, 1847
Buggy, Thomas	7	Wandsworth	Dublin	Ireland	between June 27 and July 3, 1847
Burgess, Mary	40	Clarendon	Liverpool	England	between June 27 and July 3, 1847
Burgess, Thomas	3	Clarendon	Liverpool	England	between June 13 and 19, 1847
Burke, Alexander		Erin's Queen	Liverpool	England	
Burke, Ann	9	Goliah	Liverpool	England	between August 8 and 14, 1847
Burke, Anthony	55	Erin's Queen	Liverpool	England	between August 22 and 28, 1847
Burke, Arthur	46	Odessa	Dublin	Ireland	between August 15 and 21, 1847
Burke, Bridget	19	Champion	Liverpool	England	between October 3 and 9, 1847
Burke, Catherine	10	Asia	Cork	Ireland	between September 5 and 11, 1847
Burke, Helen	35	Avon	Cork	Ireland	between July 25 and 31, 1847
Burke, James	8	Champion	Liverpool	England	between September 5 and 11, 1847
Burke, John	3	Odessa	Dublin	Ireland	between August 15 and 21, 1847
Burke, Kate	55	Naomi	Liverpool	England	between August 15 and 21, 1847
Burke, Margaret	14	Champion	Liverpool	England	between September 19 and 25, 1847
Burke, Margaret	22	Jessie	Cork	Ireland	between July 25 and 31, 1847
Burke, Margaret	20	John Munn	Liverpool	England	between August 29 and September 4, 1847
Burke, Mary	2	Asia	Cork	Ireland	between August 1 and 7, 1847
Burke, Mary	22	Roseanna	Cork	Ireland	between August 1 and 7, 1847
Burke, Mary	23	Minerva	Galway	Ireland	between August 8 and 14, 1847
Burke, Mary	22	Asia	Cork	Ireland	between September 5 and 11, 1847
Burke, Michael	32	Pursuit	Liverpool	England	between June 27 and July 3, 1847
Burke, Michael	50	Triton	Liverpool	England	between July 18 and 24, 1847
Burke, Michael	23	Lady Flora Hastings	Cork	Ireland	between July 4 and 10, 1847
Burke, Michael	6	Champion	Liverpool	England	between September 5 and 11, 1847
Burke, Nelly	8	Champion	Liverpool	England	between September 26 and October 2, 1847
Burke, Noreen	17	Pursuit	Liverpool	England	between July 11 and 17, 1847
Burke, Patrick	30	Achilles	Liverpool	England	between June 6 and 12, 1847

Lists of people who died and were buried on Grosse Île, in 1847

Name	Age	Vessel	Port	Country	Date of death
Burke, Patrick	24	Abbotsford	Dublin	Ireland	between June 13 and 19, 1847
Burke, Patrick	10	Sir Henry Pottinger	Belfast	Ireland	between August 1 and 7, 1847
Burke, Thomas	23	Agnes	Cork	Ireland	between May 23 and 29, 1847
Burke, Winifred	6	Free Trader	Liverpool	England	between August 15 and 21, 1847
Burns, Ann	60	Ajax	Liverpool	England	between June 20 and 26, 1847
Burns, Bridget	6	Rankin	Liverpool	England	between June 20 and 26, 1847
Burns, Bridget	8	John Munn	Liverpool	England	between September 26 and October 2, 1847
Burns, Catherine	29	Syria	Liverpool	England	between June 6 and 12, 1847
Burns, Catherine	20	Avon	Cork	Ireland	between August 1 and 7, 1847
Burns, Denis		John Munn	Liverpool	England	
Burns, Denis	30	Covenanter	Cork	Ireland	between August 22 and 28, 1847
Burns, Ellen	3 months	Scotland	Cork	Ireland	between June 13 and 19, 1847
Burns, Helen	65	Colonist	New Ross	Ireland	between August 29 and September 4, 1847
Burns, James	6	Avon	Cork	Ireland	between August 8 and 14, 1847
Burns, Jane	3	John Munn	Liverpool	England	between August 29 and September 4, 1847
Burns, Jane	41	Columbia	Sligo	Ireland	between September 19 and 25, 1847
Burns, John	17	Triton	Liverpool	England	between August 15 and 21, 1847
Burns, John	40	John Munn	Liverpool	England	between August 15 and 21, 1847
Burns, Judith	30	Champion	Liverpool	England	between September 5 and 11, 1847
Burns, M.	4	Scotland	Cork	Ireland	between June 20 and 26, 1847
Burns, Margaret	1	Lady Bagot	Dublin	Ireland	between September 5 and 11, 1847
Burns, Martha	12	Herald	Dublin	Ireland	between June 27 and July 3, 1847
Burns, Mary	65	Colonist	New Ross	Ireland	between September 12 and 18, 1847
Burns, Mary	14	Sobraon	Liverpool	England	between July 25 and 31, 1847
Burns, Michael	41	Caledonia	Glasgow	Scotland	between September 19 and 25, 1847
Burns, Noreen	30	Erin's Queen	Liverpool	England	between August 8 and 14, 1847
Burns, Patrick	21	Pandora	New Ross	Ireland	between July 25 and 31, 1847
Burns, Patrick	9 months	Wellington	Liverpool	England	between September 19 and 25, 1847
Burns, Peter	10	Triton	Liverpool	England	between August 1 and 7, 1847
Burns, Thomas	56	Scotland	Cork	Ireland	between June 6 and 12, 1847
Burns, Thomas	18	Scotland	Cork	Ireland	between June 20 and 26, 1847
Burns, Thomas	50	Avon	Cork	Ireland	between July 25 and 31, 1847
Burton, Thomas	18	Marchioness of Abercorn	Londonderry	Ireland	between August 8 and 14, 1847
Butler, John	28	Covenanter	Cork	Ireland	between August 1 and 7, 1847
Butler, Judith	16	John Munn	Liverpool	England	between August 15 and 21, 1847
Butler, Richard	23	John Munn	Liverpool	England	between August 22 and 28, 1847
Butler, William	34	Elizabeth	Liverpool	England	between July 18 and 24, 1847
Butler, William	35	Progress	New Ross	Ireland	between July 4 and 10, 1847
Butt, James	10	Sir Henry Pottinger	Cork	Ireland	between August 1 and 7, 1847
Butterby, Edward	30	James Moran	Liverpool	England	between August 1 and 7, 1847
Byrne					
Byrne, Ann	11	Champion	Liverpool	England	between September 5 and 11, 1847
Byrne, Ann	20	Numa	Sligo	Ireland	between August 1 and 7, 1847
Byrne, Bartholomew	20	Naomi	Liverpool	England	between September 12 and 18, 1847
Byrne, Edmund	16	Avon	Cork	Ireland	between August 22 and 28, 1847
Byrne, Edward	10	John Munn	Liverpool	England	between August 15 and 21, 1847
Byrne, Eliza	4 months	Erin's Queen	Liverpool	England	between July 18 and 24, 1847
Byrne, Elizabeth	32	Wellington	Liverpool	England	between September 19 and 25, 1847
Byrne, Henry	20	John Munn	Liverpool	England	between September 12 and 18, 1847
Byrne, John	40	John Munn	Liverpool	England	between August 29 and September 4, 1847
Byrne, John	10	John Munn	Liverpool	England	between August 29 and September 4, 1847
Byrne, John		John Munn	Liverpool	England	
Byrne, John	40				between August 1 and 7, 1847
Byrne, Luke	23	James Moran	Liverpool	England	between July 24 and 31, 1847
Byrne, Margaret	8	John Munn	Liverpool	England	between August 8 and 14, 1847
Byrne, Mary	5	Erin's Queen	Liverpool	England	between July 18 and 24, 1847
Byrne, Mary	20	Virginius	Liverpool	England	between August 22 and 28, 1847
Byrne, Mary	36	John Munn	Liverpool	England	between September 26 and October 2, 1847
Byrne, Michael	20	Scotland	Cork	Ireland	between June 27 and July 3, 1847
Byrne, Sally	15	Virginius	Liverpool	England	between August 22 and 28, 1847
Byrne, Thomas	26	Phoenix	Liverpool	England	1847/05/26
Byrne, William		Progress	New Ross	Ireland	
Byrne, William	17	Sarah	Liverpool	England	between August 8 and 14, 1847
Byrne, William	21	Asia	Cork	Ireland	between August 8 and 14, 1847
Byron, John	25	Lotus	Liverpool	England	between June 27 and July 3, 1847
C___, Bridget	45	Ann	Liverpool	England	between June 27 and July 3, 1847
C___, D.M.					
C___, F___					
C___, J___					
C___, W___					
Cadden, Bridget	60	Triton	Liverpool	England	between August 29 and September 4, 1847
Cadden, John	5	Wolfville	Sligo	Ireland	between May 29 and June 5, 1847
Caffrey, Ellen	40	Sir Henry Pottinger	Cork	Ireland	between August 8 and 14, 1847
Cahalane, Judith	30	Bee	Cork	Ireland	between June 13 and 19, 1847
Cahill, Bernard	36	Virgilia	Liverpool	England	between September 26 and October 2, 1847
Cahill, John	40	Achilles	Liverpool	England	between June 13 and 19, 1847

The emigrants

Name	Age	Vessel	Port	Country	Date of death
Cahill, Mary	20	Agnes	Cork	Ireland	between June 13 and 19, 1847
Cahill, Matthew	1	John Jardine	Liverpool	England	between July 11 and 17, 1847
Cahill, William	53	Sisters	Liverpool	England	between June 20 and 26, 1847
Cain, Ann	14	Scotland	Cork	Ireland	between June 6 and 12, 1847
Cain, Bridget	10	Wolfville	Sligo	Ireland	between May 29 and June 5, 1847
Cain, Bridget		Marinus	Dublin	Ireland	
Cain, Bud		Marinus	Dublin	Ireland	
Cairns, Patrick	24	Broom	Liverpool	England	between September 12 and 18, 1847
Callaghan, Daniel	22	Triton	Liverpool	England	between August 15 and 21, 1847
Callaghan, Edward	18	Erin's Queen	Liverpool	England	between July 11 and 17, 1847
Callaghan, Eliza	30	Wakefield	Cork	Ireland	between July 25 and 31, 1847
Callaghan, Francis	59	Avon	Cork	Ireland	between July 25 and 31, 1847
Callaghan, Honora	29	Sir Henry Pottinger	Belfast	Ireland	between September 5 and 11, 1847
Callaghan, Johanna	50	Colonist	New Ross	Ireland	between August 22 and 28, 1847
Callaghan, John	22	Sir Henry Pottinger	Cork	Ireland	between August 1 and 7, 1847
Callaghan, John	66	Wakefield	Cork	Ireland	between July 4 and 10, 1847
Callaghan, John	26	Wakefield	Cork	Ireland	between August 8 and 14, 1847
Callaghan, Mary	30	Sir Henry Pottinger	Cork	Ireland	between August 1 and 7, 1847
Callaghan, Owen	60	Lotus	Liverpool	England	between July 18 and 24, 1847
Callaghan, Owen	22	Erin's Queen	Liverpool	England	between July 18 and 24, 1847
Callaghan, William	28	Champion	Liverpool	England	between August 22 and 28, 1847
Callaghan, William	30	Sir Henry Pottinger	Belfast	Ireland	between August 29 and September 4, 1847
Calvey, Mary	25	Isabella	Killala	Ireland	between October 3 and 9, 1847
Calvin, ___		Emigrant	Liverpool	England	
Calvin, Mary	6	Mail	Cork	Ireland	between June 27 and July 3, 1847
Cameron, Alexander	4	Euclid	Glasgow	Scotland	between July 25 and 31, 1847
Cameron, Donald	5				1847/08/09*
Cameron, Eliza	4	Euclid	Glasgow	Scotland	between July 25 and 31, 1847
Cameron, Hannah	6	Ann	Liverpool	England	between July 25 and 31, 1847
Cameron, Hugh	49	Wellington	Liverpool	England	1847/10/08
Cameron, Hugh	2	Euclid	Glasgow	Scotland	between July 25 and 31, 1847
Cameron, Margaret	1	Euclid	Glasgow	Scotland	between July 25 and 31, 1847
Campbell, Arthur	16	Elliotts	Dublin	Ireland	between July 11 and 17, 1847
Campbell, Catherine	24	Maria Somes	Cork	Ireland	between September 26 and October 2, 1847
Campbell, Daniel	32	Ganges	Liverpool	England	between September 26 and October 2, 1847
Campbell, Dougall	35				1847/09/30
Campbell, James	1 year & 6 months	Broom	Liverpool	England	between August 15 and 21, 1847
Campbell, James	3	Christiana	Londonderry	Ireland	1847/06/05
Campbell, Jane	25	Roseanna	Cork	Ireland	between August 1 and 7, 1847
Campbell, John	29	Champion	Liverpool	England	1847/08/30
Campbell, Margaret		Tamarac	Liverpool	England	1847/07/05
Campbell, Timothy	20	Ellen Simpson	Limerick	Ireland	between August 29 and September 4, 1847
Campbell, William	1	Ganges	Liverpool	England	between August 22 and 28, 1847
Capless, David	50	Urania	Cork	Ireland	between June 20 and 26, 1847
Cardwell, Alfred	1 year & 6 months	Eliza Morrison	Belfast	Ireland	1847/07/09
Cardwell, Alice	44	Eliza Morrison	Belfast	Ireland	1847/07/13
Cardwell, Ann	9	Eliza Morrison	Belfast	Ireland	1847/07/12
Cardwell, David	3	Eliza Morrison	Belfast	Ireland	1847/07/09
Carey, Bridget	60	Ganges	Liverpool	England	between August 22 and 28, 1847
Carey, Catherine	50	Argo	Liverpool	England	between June 27 and July 3, 1847
Carey, Catherine	43	Argo	Liverpool	England	between June 27 and July 3, 1847
Carey, Michael	40	Argo	Liverpool	England	between July 11 and 17, 1847
Carmody, Catherine	7	Lord Sandon	Cork	Ireland	between June 20 and 26, 1847
Carmody, Edward	24	Free Trader	Liverpool	England	between August 29 and September 4, 1847
Carmody, Mary	7	Lord Sandon	Cork	Ireland	between June 20 and 26, 1847
Carney, Diana	22	Larch	Sligo	Ireland	between August 8 and 14, 1847
Carney, Frances	47	Sir Henry Pottinger	Cork	Ireland	between August 15 and 21, 1847
Carney, Hugh	49	Wellington	Liverpool	England	between October 3 and 9, 1847
Carney, James	19	Jane Black	Limerick	Ireland	between May 29 and June 5, 1847
Carney, John	22	Sir Henry Pottinger	Cork	Ireland	between August 1 and 7, 1847
Carney, Judith	24	Gilmour	Cork	Ireland	between June 27 and July 3, 1847
Carney, Mary	13	Jessie	Cork	Ireland	between August 1 and 7, 1847
Carney, Nancy	40	Progress	New Ross	Ireland	between July 25 and 31, 1847
Carney, Patrick	40	Avon	Cork	Ireland	between July 18 and 24, 1847
Carney, Patrick	40	Emigrant	Liverpool	England	between October 17 and 23, 1847
Carr, C___	40	Eliza Caroline	Liverpool	England	between June 20 and 26, 1847
Carr, James	25	Bridgetown	Liverpool	England	1847/09/29
Carr, Mary	30	Larch	Sligo	Ireland	between August 15 and 21, 1847
Carr, Patrick	22	Eliza Caroline	Liverpool	England	between August 15 and 21, 1847
Carr, Peter	45	Eliza Caroline	Liverpool	England	between June 13 and 19, 1847
Carrick, Thomas	4 years & 6 months	Champion	Liverpool	England	between August 29 and September 4, 1847
Carrier, Margaret	6 months	Champion	Liverpool	England	between September 5 and 11, 1847
Carrigan, Brian	46	Ann	Liverpool	England	between July 4 and 10, 1847
Carrigan, Owen	5	Rankin	Liverpool	England	between June 13 and 19, 1847
Carroll, Ann	50	Jane Avery	Dublin	Ireland	between June 27 and July 3, 1847
Carroll, Bridget	18	Sarah	Liverpool	England	between August 22 and 28, 1847
Carroll, Catherine	35	Free Trader	Liverpool	England	between September 5 and 11, 1847
Carroll, Daniel	23	Wandsworth	Dublin	Ireland	between June 27 and July 3, 1847

Lists of people who died and were buried on Grosse Île, in 1847

Name	Age	Vessel	Port	Country	Date of death
Carroll, Elizabeth	9	Naparina	Dublin	Ireland	between August 22 and 28, 1847
Carroll, John	9 months	John Munn	Liverpool	England	between August 8 and 14, 1847
Carroll, Margaret	28	John Munn	Liverpool	England	between September 5 and 11, 1847
Carroll, Patrick		Wandsworth	Dublin	Ireland	
Carroll, Susan	9	Champion	Liverpool	England	between September 19 and 25, 1847
Carroll, Thomas	26	Brothers	Dublin	Ireland	between August 15 and 21, 1847
Carroll, William	18	Wandsworth	Dublin	Ireland	between July 4 and 10, 1847
Carter, Mary	25	Superior	Londonderry	Ireland	between September 19 and 25, 1847
Carty, Bryan	25	Numa	Sligo	Ireland	between August 8 and 14, 1847
Carty, Ellen	6	Agnes	Cork	Ireland	between June 6 and 12, 1847
Casey, Catherine		Covenanter	Cork	Ireland	
Casey, Eliza	4 years & 6 months	Argo	Liverpool	England	between June 13 and 19, 1847
Casey, John		Sobraon	Liverpool	England	
Casey, John	19	Covenanter	Cork	Ireland	between August 22 and 28, 1847
Casey, Julia	6	Coromandel	Dublin	Ireland	between August 8 and 14, 1847
Casey, Martin	18	Covenanter	Cork	Ireland	between August 8 and 14, 1847
Casey, Mary	1	Free Trader	Liverpool	England	between August 22 and 28, 1847
Casey, Mary	23	Saguenay	Cork	Ireland	between August 8 and 14, 1847
Casey, Mary	20	Larch	Sligo	Ireland	between August 22 and 28, 1847
Casey, Patrick	9 months	Argo	Liverpool	England	between June 13 and 19, 1847
Casey, Timothy	48	Scotland	Cork	Ireland	between June 6 and 12, 1847
Casey, William	1	Sir Robert Peel	Liverpool	England	between September 19 and 25, 1847
Casey, William	25	Covenanter	Cork	Ireland	between August 1 and 7, 1847
Casey, William	28	Lively	Cork	Ireland	between August 29 and September 4, 1847
Cash, Patrick	22	Syria	Liverpool	England	between July 11 and 17, 1847
Cassells, Eliza	43	Argo	Liverpool	England	between June 27 and July 3, 1847
Cassidy, Ann	30	Tamarac	Liverpool	England	between July 11 and 17, 1847
Cassidy, Catherine	26	Clarendon	Liverpool	England	between June 13 and 19, 1847
Cassidy, Ellen	40	Lady Campbell	Dublin	Ireland	between August 29 and September 4, 1847
Cassidy, Jerry M.		Bee	Cork	Ireland	
Cassidy, Mary	12	Lady Campbell	Dublin	Ireland	between August 22 and 28, 1847
Cassin, John		Sobraon	Liverpool	England	
Caulfield, A.	50	Wandsworth	Dublin	Ireland	between June 13 and 19, 1847
Cavanagh, Ann	10	Pursuit	Liverpool	England	between June 13 and 19, 1847
Cavanagh, George	12	Pursuit	Liverpool	England	between July 18 and 24, 1847
Cavanagh, Mary	10	Greenock	Liverpool	England	between August 8 and 14, 1847
Cavanagh, Michael	30	Lively	Cork	Ireland	between July 18 and 24, 1847
Cavanagh, Robert	18	Greenock	Liverpool	England	between July 25 and 31, 1847
Chadwick, Alice	31	Champion	Liverpool	England	1847/09/15
Chambers, Catherine	50	Ganges	Liverpool	England	between September 5 and 11, 1847
Chambers, John					
Chambers, Thomas	55	John and Robert	Liverpool	England	1847/08/10
Cherick, Ann	47				1847/07/12
Chesty, Ann	40	Sobraon	Liverpool	England	between July 11 and 17, 1847
Chittick, James	5	Yorkshire Lass	Killala	Ireland	between August 1 and 7, 1847
Chou, Jude	60	Johana			between July 11 and 17, 1847
Clancy, Catherine	7	Dykes	Sligo	Ireland	between July 25 and 31, 1847
Clancy, Mary		Westmoreland	Sligo	Ireland	
Clancy, Michael	26	Agnes	Cork	Ireland	between June 6 and 12, 1847
Clark, Bernard	33	Lady Milton	Liverpool	England	between July 18 and 24, 1847
Clark, Catherine	20	Ann	Liverpool	England	between June 27 and July 3, 1847
Clark, James	35	Champion	Liverpool	England	1847/09/02
Clark, James	56	Superior	Londonderry	Ireland	between September 12 and 18, 1847
Clark, Judith	30	John Munn	Liverpool	England	between August 22 and 28, 1847
Clark, Judith	3	Syria	Liverpool	England	between June 27 and July 3, 1847
Clark, Mary	22	Champion	Liverpool	England	1847/09/24
Clark, Mary	23	Lotus	Liverpool	England	between June 20 and 26, 1847
Clark, Mary	4	Goliah	Liverpool	England	between July 25 and 31, 1847
Clark, Michael	23	John Munn	Liverpool	England	between August 1 and 7, 1847
Clark, Michael	29	Clarendon	Liverpool	England	between June 13 and 19, 1847
Clark, Patrick	20	Aberdeen	Liverpool	England	between July 4 and 10, 1847
Clark, Patrick	45	Champion	Liverpool	England	between September 5 and 11, 1847
Clark, Patrick C.	18	Wolfville	Sligo	Ireland	between June 20 and 26, 1847
Clark, Peter	3	Goliah	Liverpool	England	between August 1 and 7, 1847
Clark, Sally	4	Sobraon	Liverpool	England	between August 1 and 7, 1847
Clark, Thomas	49	Superior	Londonderry	Ireland	between September 12 and 18, 1847
Clark, Thomas	7	Rankin	Liverpool	England	between June 20 and 26, 1847
Cleary, John	30	Margaret	New Ross	Ireland	between July 4 and 10, 1847
Cleary, Margaret	1	John Francis	Cork	Ireland	between May 29 and June 5, 1847
Cleary, W.	30	George	Liverpool	England	between May 29 and June 5, 1847
Clegg, Eliza	65	Emigrant	Liverpool	England	1847/10/07
Clifford, Daniel	52	Avon	Cork	Ireland	between July 18 and 24, 1847
Clinton, Ann	15	Huron	Belfast	Ireland	between August 29 and September 4, 1847
Clinton, Thomas	26	Broom	Liverpool	England	between August 22 and 28, 1847
Cloherty, Catherine	10	Avon	Cork	Ireland	between August 8 and 14, 1847
Cloherty, Michael	37	John Munn	Liverpool	England	between August 8 and 14, 1847
Clohessy, Henry	20	Avon	Cork	Ireland	between July 25 and 31, 1847
Clough, John	24	Lotus	Liverpool	England	between July 4 and 10, 1847
Clune, James	9	George	Liverpool	England	between July 11 and 17, 1847

The emigrants

Name	Age	Vessel	Port	Country	Date of death
Clune, Ned	16	George	Liverpool	England	between June 13 and 19, 1847
Clune, Thomas	21	Naomi	Liverpool	England	between August 29 and September 4, 1847
Clune, William	10	Rankin	Liverpool	England	between June 20 and 26, 1847
Cluvane, Hugh	5	Odessa	Dublin	Ireland	between August 8 and 14, 1847
Clyne, Daniel		Naomi	Liverpool	England	
Clyne, John	2	Odessa	Dublin	Ireland	between August 8 and 14, 1847
Clyne, Mary	55	George	Liverpool	England	between July 25 and 31, 1847
Clyne, Onny	15	Yeoman			between August 22 and 28, 1847
Clyne, Owen	61	Naomi	Liverpool	England	between August 22 and 28, 1847
Clyne, Patrick	32				between August 22 and 28, 1847
Clyne, William	22	George	Liverpool	England	between June 6 and 12, 1847
Coakley, Honora	60	Agnes	Cork	Ireland	between July 25 and 31, 1847
Coakley, Maria	22	Bee	Cork	Ireland	between June 20 and 26, 1847
Coates, Ellen	6	Odessa	Dublin	Ireland	between August 29 and September 4, 1847
Cochrane, ___		Junior	Liverpool	England	
Cochrane, Eliza	26	Virginius	Liverpool	England	between August 8 and 14, 1847
Cody, Mary	30	Rose	Liverpool	England	between July 11 and 17, 1847
Coen, Catherine	34	John Bolton	Liverpool	England	between June 27 and July 3, 1847
Coen, Mary	6	George	Liverpool	England	between June 6 and 12, 1847
Coen, Michael	35	Larch	Sligo	Ireland	between September 12 and 18, 1847
Coen, Thomas	50	George	Liverpool	England	between June 6 and 12, 1847
Coffey, Mary	5	Julius Caesar	Liverpool	England	between September 12 and 18, 1847
Coffey, Mary		Larch	Sligo	Ireland	
Coffey, William	34	Ganges	Liverpool	England	between August 15 and 21, 1847
Cogan, Elizabeth	30	Avon	Cork	Ireland	between August 22 and 28, 1847
Coke, Philip	20	Zealous	London	England	between August 22 and 28, 1847
Colbert, Ellen	35	Agnes	Cork	Ireland	between June 13 and 19, 1847
Colbert, Johanna	50	John Francis	Cork	Ireland	between June 6 and 12, 1847
Coleman, Dennis	23	Scotland	Cork	Ireland	between May 23 and 29, 1847
Coleman, Dennis	27	Scotland	Cork	Ireland	between June 20 and 26, 1847
Coleman, John	29	Scotland	Cork	Ireland	between July 25 and 31, 1847
Coleman, Mary	18	Urania	Cork	Ireland	between May 23 and 29, 1847
Coleman, Michael	25	Gilmour	Cork	Ireland	between June 20 and 26, 1847
Colgan, Honora	19	Industry	Dublin	Ireland	between October 17 and 23, 1847
Colgan, Judith	17	John Munn	Liverpool	England	between September 5 and 11, 1847
Colgan, Mary	16	Marinus	Dublin	Ireland	between August 15 and 21, 1847
Collins, Barbara	35	Urania	Cork	Ireland	between May 23 and 29, 1847
Collins, Catherine	40	Lady Flora Hastings	Cork	Ireland	between June 20 and 26, 1847
Collins, Daniel	45	Wolfville	Sligo	Ireland	between June 6 and 12, 1847
Collins, David	45	Urania	Cork	Ireland	between May 29 and June 5, 1847
Collins, Dennis	33	Avon	Cork	Ireland	between August 1 and 7, 1847
Collins, Dennis	12	Avon	Cork	Ireland	between August 29 and September 4, 1847
Collins, Francis	22	Caithness-shire	Belfast	Ireland	between July 25 and 31, 1847
Collins, John	6	Urania	Cork	Ireland	between May 23 and 29, 1847
Collins, Margaret	20	Scotland	Cork	Ireland	between June 6 and 12, 1847
Collins, Mary	8	Urania	Cork	Ireland	between May 23 and 29, 1847
Collins, Mary	33	Aberdeen	Liverpool	England	between July 4 and 10, 1847
Collins, Michael	4	Avon	Cork	Ireland	between July 25 and 31, 1847
Collins, Patrick	32	Bee	Cork	Ireland	between June 27 and July 3, 1847
Colvin, John	84	Perseverance	Dublin	Ireland	between May 16 and 22, 1847
Comber, Thomas	40	Syria	Liverpool	England	1847/05/21
Compton, David	20	Avon	Cork	Ireland	between August 29 and September 4, 1847
Conaghan, Catherine	2	Emigrant	Liverpool	England	between October 17 and 23, 1847
Condon, Edward	28	Eliza Caroline	Liverpool	England	between June 27 and July 3, 1847
Condon, James	30	Triton	Liverpool	England	between July 25 and 31, 1847
Condon, John	30	Saguenay	Cork	Ireland	between August 22 and 28, 1847
Condron, John	1	Eliza Caroline	Liverpool	England	between June 6 and 12, 1847
Condy, John	45	Scotland	Cork	Ireland	between June 27 and July 3, 1847
Conefry, Maria	40	Wandsworth	Dublin	Ireland	between June 13 and 19, 1847
Conlan, Catherine	4	John Francis	Cork	Ireland	between June 20 and 26, 1847
Conlan, Ellen	8	John Francis	Cork	Ireland	between June 20 and 26, 1847
Conlan, James	40	Sarah	Liverpool	England	between August 15 and 21, 1847
Conlan, James	26	Lotus	Liverpool	England	between June 20 and 26, 1847
Conlan, Joseph	30	Yorkshire Lass	Killala	Ireland	between July 4 and 10, 1847
Conlan, Lawrence					
Conlan, Luke	19	Charles Richard	Sligo	Ireland	between August 22 and 28, 1847
Conlan, Mary Ann	9	Achilles	Liverpool	England	between June 27 and July 3, 1847
Conlan, Mary Blair	36				1847/06/16
Conlan, Thomas	9	James Moran	Liverpool	England	between August 22 and 28, 1847
Connaughton, ___		Wm S. Hamilton	New Ross	Ireland	
Connaughton, Catherine	40	Triton	Liverpool	England	between August 22 and 28, 1847
Connaughton, James	7	Erin's Queen	Liverpool	England	between July 18 and 24, 1847
Connaughton, William	30	Triton	Liverpool	England	between August 15 and 21, 1847
Connell, Ann	16	Ann	Liverpool	England	between July 11 and 17, 1847
Connell, Ann	2	Champion	Liverpool	England	between August 29 and September 4, 1847
Connell, Ann	4	Larch	Sligo	Ireland	between August 22 and 28, 1847

LISTS OF PEOPLE WHO DIED AND WERE BURIED ON GROSSE ÎLE, IN 1847

Name	Age	Vessel	Port	Country	Date of death
Connell, Catherine	13	Bee	Cork	Ireland	between June 6 and 12, 1847
Connell, Daniel	32	Wolfville	Sligo	Ireland	between May 29 and June 5, 1847
Connell, Denis	22	Wellington	Liverpool	England	between September 26 and October 2, 1847
Connell, E.		Urania	Cork	Ireland	
Connell, Elizabeth	30	Julius Caesar	Liverpool	England	between September 26 and October 2, 1847
Connell, Francis	36	Urania	Cork	Ireland	between May 23 and 29, 1847
Connell, Honora	50	Wellington	Liverpool	England	between September 12 and 18, 1847
Connell, James	10 months	Pursuit	Liverpool	England	between June 20 and 26, 1847
Connell, Johanna	25	Scotland	Cork	Ireland	between June 20 and 26, 1847
Connell, Johanna	1	Julius Caesar	Liverpool	England	between September 26 and October 2, 1847
Connell, John	27	Scotland	Cork	Ireland	between May 23 and 29, 1847
Connell, John	15	Mary	Sligo	Ireland	between July 25 and 31, 1847
Connell, Mary	4 months	John Bolton	Liverpool	England	between June 6 and 12, 1847
Connell, Mary	60	John Francis	Cork	Ireland	between May 29 and June 5, 1847
Connell, Mary	14	Bee	Cork	Ireland	between July 4 and 10, 1847
Connell, Michael	30	Bee	Cork	Ireland	between May 29 and June 5, 1847
Connell, Patrick	12	Ann	Liverpool	England	between August 1 and 7, 1847
Connell, Peter	40	Urania	Cork	Ireland	between May 23 and 29, 1847
Connell, Philip	3	Pursuit	Liverpool	England	between July 4 and 10, 1847
Connell, Thomas	5	Bee	Cork	Ireland	between July 4 and 10, 1847
Connell, William	47	Bee	Cork	Ireland	between June 6 and 12, 1847
Connell, William	50	Triton	Liverpool	England	between August 15 and 21, 1847
Connell, William	13	Ann	Liverpool	England	between June 27 and July 3, 1847
Connery, Nelly	16	Roseanna	Cork	Ireland	between August 22 and 28, 1847
Connery, Thomas	17	Triton	Liverpool	England	between July 11 and 17, 1847
Connolly, Ann	16	Larch	Sligo	Ireland	between August 15 and 21, 1847
Connolly, Ann	50	John Munn	Liverpool	England	between August 15 and 21, 1847
Connolly, Bridget	28	Scotland	Cork	Ireland	between May 23 and 29, 1847
Connolly, Bridget	28	James Moran	Liverpool	England	between July 4 and 10, 1847
Connolly, Bridget	24	Virginius	Liverpool	England	between August 22 and 28, 1847
Connolly, Catherine		Sir Henry Pottinger	Cork	Ireland	1847/08/05
Connolly, Catherine	46	Naomi	Liverpool	England	between August 15 and 21, 1847
Connolly, Christopher	10	Erin's Queen	Liverpool	England	between July 18 and 24, 1847
Connolly, Daniel	6	Yorkshire	Liverpool	England	between September 5 and 11, 1847
Connolly, Edward	45	Lotus	Liverpool	England	between July 4 and 10, 1847
Connolly, Ellen	21	Clarendon	Liverpool	England	between May 23 and 29, 1847
Connolly, Ferry	56	John & Robert	Liverpool	England	between August 22 and 28, 1847
Connolly, M.					
Connolly, Margaret	26	Lotus	Liverpool	England	between July 4 and 10, 1847
Connolly, Mary	28	Agnes	Cork	Ireland	between May 23 and 29, 1847
Connolly, Mary	6 months	Lotus	Liverpool	England	between June 20 and 26, 1847
Connolly, Patrick	14	Free Trader	Liverpool	England	between August 22 and 28, 1847
Connor, Ann	26	Greenock	Liverpool	England	between August 29 and September 4, 1847
Connor, Bridget	2	Wolfville	Sligo	Ireland	between May 29 and June 5, 1847
Connor, Bridget	44	Ganges	Liverpool	England	between August 8 and 14, 1847
Connor, Dominic	20	Triton	Liverpool	England	between July 25 and 31, 1847
Connor, Eliza	40	Naomi	Liverpool	England	between August 8 and 14, 1847
Connor, Ellen	24	Lady Flora Hastings	Cork	Ireland	between July 25 and 31, 1847
Connor, James	21	Julius Caesar	Liverpool	England	between September 19 and 25, 1847
Connor, John	25	Wm S. Hamilton	New Ross	Ireland	between August 8 and 14, 1847
Connor, John	40	Jessie	Cork	Ireland	between July 18 and 24, 1847
Connor, John	27	Triton	Liverpool	England	between July 25 and 31, 1847
Connor, John	28	Jessie	Cork	Ireland	between August 8 and 14, 1847
Connor, John	16	Marchioness of ___			between September 5 and 11, 1847
Connor, Mary	3	Champion	Liverpool	England	between August 29 and September 4, 1847
Connor, Michael	20	Larch	Sligo	Ireland	between August 15 and 21, 1847
Connor, Michael	6	Marchioness of ___			between August 29 and September 4, 1847
Connor, Morris	23	Scotland	Cork	Ireland	between June 20 and 26, 1847
Connor, Nancy	12	Marchioness of ___			between August 29 and September 4, 1847
Connor, Patrick	1 year & 6 months	Scotland	Cork	Ireland	between May 23 and 29, 1847
Connor, Patrick	37	Marchioness of ___			between September 5 and 11, 1847
Connor, Sally	40	Champion	Liverpool	England	between August 29 and September 4, 1847
Connor, Tiernan					
Connor, Winifred	3	Champion	Liverpool	England	between August 29 and September 4, 1847
Connors, Bridget	31	Lotus	Liverpool	England	between July 25 and 31, 1847
Connors, Catherine	21	Sarah Milledge	Galway	Ireland	between October 10 and 16, 1847
Connors, Ellen	27	Margaret	New Ross	Ireland	between July 4 and 10, 1847
Connors, James	21	Marchioness of Bute	Belfast	Ireland	between August 1 and 7, 1847
Connors, James	28	Sir Henry Pottinger	Cork	Ireland	between August 1 and 7, 1847
Connors, James	16	Marinus	Dublin	Ireland	between August 15 and 21, 1847
Connors, Jeremiah	44	Henrietta Mary	Cork	Ireland	between October 3 and 9, 1847
Connors, John	2	Covenanter	Cork	Ireland	between August 8 and 14, 1847
Connors, Nancy	26	Avon	Cork	Ireland	between August 8 and 14, 1847

The emigrants

Name	Age	Vessel	Port	Country	Date of death
Connors, Patrick	35	Sarah Milledge	Galway	Ireland	between October 17 and 23, 1847
Conroy, Catherine	18	George	Liverpool	England	between June 13 and 19, 1847
Conroy, Dennis	5	Ann Kenny	Waterford	Ireland	between August 29 and September 4, 1847
Conroy, Margaret	28	George	Liverpool	England	between June 6 and 12, 1847
Conroy, Patrick	19	George	Liverpool	England	between August 8 and 14, 1847
Considine, Thomas	22	Sir Henry Pottinger	Cork	Ireland	between August 1 and 7, 1847
Convey, John	18	Jane Avery	Dublin	Ireland	between July 11 and 17, 1847
Convey, Sarah	50	Triton	Liverpool	England	between July 11 and 17, 1847
Conway, ___					
Conway, Ann	34	Jessie	Cork	Ireland	between June 27 and July 3, 1847
Conway, Darby	21	Syria	Liverpool	England	between July 18 and 24, 1847
Conway, Dennis		Sisters	Liverpool	England	
Conway, Elizabeth	40	George	Liverpool	England	between June 27 and July 3, 1847
Conway, Elizabeth	13	George	Liverpool	England	between June 27 and July 3, 1847
Conway, Mary	16	Erin's Queen	Liverpool	England	between July 18 and 24, 1847
Conway, Michael	4	Triton	Liverpool	England	between July 25 and 31, 1847
Conway, Michael	26	Syria	Liverpool	England	between September 5 and 11, 1847
Cook, Bridget	22	John Bolton	Liverpool	England	between July 11 and 17, 1847
Cook, Mary	19	Gilmour	Cork	Ireland	between August 8 and 14, 1847
Cook, Morris	17	Jessie	Limerick	Ireland	between September 12 and 18, 1847
Cook, Thomas	28	Virginius	Liverpool	England	between August 1 and 7, 1847
Cooney, Catherine	22	Goliah	Liverpool	England	between August 22 and 28, 1847
Cooney, Margaret	25	Triton	Liverpool	England	between July 25 and 31, 1847
Cooney, Mary	6 months	Clarendon	Liverpool	England	between June 6 and 12, 1847
Cooney, Mary	45	Wm S. Hamilton	New Ross	Ireland	between July 25 and 31, 1847
Cooney, Mary	32	Triton	Liverpool	England	between July 25 and 31, 1847
Cooney, Philip	30	Triton	Liverpool	England	between August 1 and 7, 1847
Coote, Charles	3	Ganges	Liverpool	England	between August 15 and 21, 1847
Coote, Ellen	6	Odessa	Dublin	Ireland	1847/09/04
Coote, Margaret	33	Odessa	Dublin	Ireland	1847/08/24
Coote, Martha	1	Virginius	Liverpool	England	between August 8 and 14, 1847
Coote, Samuel	40	Odessa	Dublin	Ireland	1847/08/19
Coote, Samuel	40	Naomi	Liverpool	England	between August 15 and 21, 1847
Copes, Henry	61	Naomi	Liverpool	England	between September 26 and October 2, 1847
Corbett, James	30	Yorkshire Lass	Killala	Ireland	between August 8 and 14, 1847
Corbett, James	25	Goliah	Liverpool	England	1847/08/11
Corbett, James	20	Cape Breton	Dublin	Ireland	between August 8 and 14, 1847
Corbett, James	10	Agent	New Ross	Ireland	between July 4 and 10, 1847
Corbett, Johanna	25	Asia	Cork	Ireland	between August 8 and 14, 1847
Corbett, Julia	27	Agent	New Ross	Ireland	between July 18 and 24, 1847
Corbett, Lucinda	18	Goliah	Liverpool	England	1847/09/22
Corbett, Lucy	18	Goliah	Liverpool	England	between September 19 and 25, 1847
Corbett, Samuel	30	Superior	Londonderry	Ireland	between October 3 and 9, 1847
Corbett, Thomas	12	James Moran	Liverpool	England	between September 5 and 11, 1847
Corcoran, Barry	37				between August 1 and 7, 1847
Corcoran, Bridget		Washington		England	
Corcoran, Catherine	25	Virginius	Liverpool	England	between August 15 and 21, 1847
Corcoran, James	5	John Munn	Liverpool	England	between August 8 and 14, 1847
Corcoran, Martin	22	Free Trader	Liverpool	England	between August 15 and 21, 1847
Corcoran, Mary	23	Avon	Cork	Ireland	between July 25 and 31, 1847
Corcoran, Michael	4	Virginius	Liverpool	England	between August 8 and 14, 1847
Corish, Elizabeth	40	Sarah	Liverpool	England	1847/08/14
Corkery, Bridget	2	John Munn	Liverpool	England	between August 1 and 7, 1847
Corkery, Denis	10	Agnes	Cork	Ireland	between July 11 and 17, 1847
Corkin, Samuel		Superior	Londonderry	Ireland	1847/10/03
Corless, Margaret	23	Larch	Sligo	Ireland	between August 22 and 28, 1847
Corley, Margaret	23	Sarah	Liverpool	England	between August 8 and 14, 1847
Cormack, Bridget	30	Lady Campbell	Dublin	Ireland	between September 19 and 25, 1847
Cormack, Michael	4	Lady Campbell	Dublin	Ireland	between September 19 and 25, 1847
Cormack, Michael	30	Junior	Liverpool	England	between July 11 and 17, 1847
Corrigan, Ann	22	John Munn	Liverpool	England	between August 22 and 28, 1847
Corrigan, Irvine	5 years & 6 months				1847/06/18
Corrigan, James	22	Rankin	Liverpool	England	1847/06/08
Cosgrove, Daniel	45	Erin's Queen	Liverpool	England	between July 25 and 31, 1847
Cosgrove, Margaret	18	Lotus	Liverpool	England	between June 20 and 26, 1847
Cosgrove, Mary	60	Erin's Queen	Liverpool	England	between July 25 and 31, 1847
Costello, Edward	25	Avon	Cork	Ireland	between August 1 and 7, 1847
Costello, Ellen	7	Sisters	Liverpool	England	between June 20 and 26, 1847
Costello, Honora	12	Sisters	Liverpool	England	between July 4 and 10, 1847
Costello, Mary	17	Sisters	Liverpool	England	between June 20 and 26, 1847
Costello, Michael	20	Covenanter	Cork	Ireland	between August 29 and September 4, 1847
Costely, Michael	20	Covenanter	Cork	Ireland	between August 29 and September 4, 1847
Cotter, Thomas	25	Avon	Cork	Ireland	between August 1 and 7, 1847
Cotton, Thomas	14	James Moran	Liverpool	England	between August 8 and 14, 1847
Coughlan, Bartholomew	2 years & 6 months	Wakefield	Cork	Ireland	between August 15 and 21, 1847
Coughlan, Catherine	20	Sir Henry Pottinger	Cork	Ireland	between August 1 and 7, 1847
Coughlan, Catherine		Achilles	Liverpool	England	
Coughlan, Jeremiah	25	James Moran	Liverpool	England	between August 15 and 21, 1847

Lists of people who died and were buried on Grosse Île, in 1847

Name	Age	Vessel	Port	Country	Date of death
Coughlan, John	23	Agnes	Cork	Ireland	between May 29 and June 5, 1847
Coughlan, Mary	20	Covenanter	Cork	Ireland	between August 15 and 21, 1847
Coughlan, Thadeus	1	Mail	Cork	Ireland	between July 18 and 24, 1847
Courtney, Denis	40	Agnes	Cork	Ireland	between June 13 and 19, 1847
Courtney, Nanny	30	Wakefield	Cork	Ireland	between July 4 and 10, 1847
Cousens, Catherine	30	Colonist	New Ross	Ireland	between September 5 and 11, 1847
Cousens, Margaret	57	Virginius	Liverpool	England	between September 12 and 18, 1847
Coveny, Eliza	15	Ayrshire	Newry	Ireland	between September 12 and 18, 1847
Coveny, John		Triton	Liverpool	England	
Coveny, Martin	50	Yorkshire Lass	Killala	Ireland	between August 8 and 14, 1847
Coveny, William		Triton	Liverpool	England	
Cowley, Noreen	5	Bee	Cork	Ireland	between May 29 and June 5, 1847
Cox, Denis	2	Saguenay	Cork	Ireland	between August 15 and 21, 1847
Cox, George		Virginius	Liverpool	England	
Cox, John	3	Larch	Sligo	Ireland	between September 5 and 11, 1847
Cox, John	9	Odessa	Dublin	Ireland	between August 22 and 28, 1847
Cox, John	33	Wellington	Liverpool	England	between October 17 and 23, 1847
Cox, Mary	40	Covenanter	Cork	Ireland	between August 15 and 21, 1847
Cox, Mary		Virginius	Liverpool	England	
Cox, Michael	30	Virginius	Liverpool	England	between August 15 and 21, 1847
Coyle, Ann	60	Virginius	Liverpool	England	between August 22 and 28, 1847
Coyle, Catherine	14	Sir Henry Pottinger	Cork	Ireland	between August 8 and 14, 1847
Coyle, George	3 years & 6 months	Christiana	Londonderry	Ireland	1847/06/01
Coyle, Jane	2	Larch	Sligo	Ireland	between August 15 and 21, 1847
Coyle, Peter	8	Emigrant	Liverpool	England	between October 3 and 10, 1847
Coyle, Philip	24	Alexander Stewart	Limerick	Ireland	between August 15 and 21, 1847
Coyle, Robert	12	Christiana	Londonderry	Ireland	1847/05/27
Coyle, William	14	Christiana	Londonderry	Ireland	between June 20 and 26, 1847
Craig, Hugh		Huron	Belfast	Ireland	
Craig, John	28	Isabella	Killala	Ireland	between September 19 and 25, 1847
Craig, Martha Arlwekle	40	Rankin	Liverpool	England	1847/06/12
Crane, Denis	22	John Munn	Liverpool	England	between August 8 and 14, 1847
Cranny, Ann	30	Lady Campbell	Dublin	Ireland	between August 22 and 28, 1847
Cranny, Mary		Lady Campbell	Dublin	Ireland	
Cranny, Patrick	3	Lady Campbell	Dublin	Ireland	between August 22 and 28, 1847
Crawford, Edward	29	Sarah	Liverpool	England	1847/07/20
Crawford, Jane	19	Ajax	Liverpool	England	between August 1 and 7, 1847
Crawford, Susanna	40	George	Liverpool	England	1847/07/13
Crawley, Catherine	30	Emily	Cork	Ireland	between July 4 and 10, 1847
Crawley, John	40	Goliah	Liverpool	England	between August 8 and 14, 1847
Creagh, Cecily	25	Minerva	Galway	Ireland	between August 22 and 28, 1847
Creed, Ellen	8	Bridgetown	Liverpool	England	between August 29 and September 4, 1847
Creed, John	11	Elliotts	Dublin	Ireland	between July 4 and 10, 1847
Creed, Stephen	22	Elliotts	Dublin	Ireland	between July 11 and 17, 1847
Creen, David	9	Scotland	Cork	Ireland	between July 4 and 10, 1847
Creen, Mary	1 week	Scotland	Cork	Ireland	between June 13 and 19, 1847
Cremin, Michael	20	Wandsworth	Dublin	Ireland	between May 29 and June 5, 1847
Cromie, Barclay	30	Ann Kenny	Waterford	Ireland	between August 15 and 21, 1847
Cromie, Mary	14	Royalist	Liverpool	England	between June 27 and July 3, 1847
Cromie, William	1 year & 6 months	Orlando	Newry	Ireland	1847/06/05
Cronin, John	50	Triton	Liverpool	England	between August 1 and 7, 1847
Cronin, Patrick	40	Triton	Liverpool	England	between August 15 and 21, 1847
Cronin, Thomas	23	Agnes	Cork	Ireland	between June 20 and 26, 1847
Cross, Hugh	18	Huron	Belfast	Ireland	between July 18 and 24, 1847
Crowe, Mary	21	Avon	Cork	Ireland	between July 11 and 17, 1847
Crowley, David	35	John and Robert	Liverpool	England	between August 8 and 14, 1847
Crowley, John	40	Emigrant	Liverpool	England	between September 26 and October 2, 1847
Crowley, John	50	Goliah	Liverpool	England	between August 8 and 14, 1847
Crowley, Patrick		Bee	Cork	Ireland	
Crowley, Timothy	5	Emily	Cork	Ireland	between July 11 and 17, 1847
Cuddy, Mary	19	Superior	Londonderry	Ireland	between September 26 and October 2, 1847
Cuffe, Ann	16	Larch	Sligo	Ireland	between September 12 and 18, 1847
Cuffe, Mary	19	Westmoreland	Sligo	Ireland	between August 15 and 21, 1847
Culhane, Michael	25	James Moran	Liverpool	England	between July 11 and 17, 1847
Cullen, James	1	Champion	Liverpool	England	between September 5 and 11, 1847
Cullen, Margaret	23	Lady Flora Hastings	Cork	Ireland	between July 4 and 10, 1847
Cullen, Martha	50	Odessa	Dublin	Ireland	1847/08/10
Cullen, Mary	40	Superior	Londonderry	Ireland	between October 10 and 16, 1847
Cullen, Patrick	6	Champion	Liverpool	England	between October 10 and 16, 1847
Culligan, Ann	20	Naomi	Liverpool	England	between August 8 and 14, 1847
Cully, Luke	4	Eliza Caroline	Liverpool	England	between June 20 and 26, 1847
Cummings, Bartholomew	6 months	Naparina	Dublin	Ireland	between August 15 and 21, 1847
Cummins, Bridget	8	Sarah	Liverpool	England	between August 1 and 7, 1847
Cummins, Catherine	7 months				between August 8 and 14, 1847
Cummins, Jane	1	Sarah	Liverpool	England	between July 18 and 24, 1847
Cummins, John	25				between August 22 and 28, 1847
Cummins, Lawrence	32	Covenanter	Cork	Ireland	between August 8 and 14, 1847
Cummins, Martin	50	Goliah	Liverpool	England	between July 11 and 17, 1847

The Emigrants

Name	Age	Vessel	Port	Country	Date of death
Cummins, Martin	60	Sarah	Liverpool	England	between July 11 and 17, 1847
Cummins, Patrick	3	Sarah	Liverpool	England	between July 11 and 17, 1847
Cunningham, James	26	Agnes	Cork	Ireland	between May 29 and June 5, 1847
Cunningham, Jeremiah	2	John Francis	Cork	Ireland	between June 6 and 12, 1847
Cunningham, John	30	Champion	Liverpool	England	between September 12 and 18, 1847
Cunningham, Patrick	35	John Francis	Cork	Ireland	between June 20 and 26, 1847
Cunningham, Patrick	25	Argo	Liverpool	England	between June 13 and 19, 1847
Cunningham, Patrick	36	Agnes	Cork	Ireland	between July 4 and 10, 1847
Cunningham, T.	1 year & 2 months	John Francis	Cork	Ireland	between May 29 and June 5, 1847
Curran, Catherine	60	Marchioness of Breadalbane	Sligo	Ireland	between August 8 and 14, 1847
Curran, John	10	Scotland	Cork	Ireland	between May 29 and June 5, 1847
Curran, Julia	20	Lady Campbell	Dublin	Ireland	between August 1 and 7, 1847
Curry, Mary	30	Marinus	Dublin	Ireland	between August 15 and 21, 1847
Curtin, David	30	Avon	Cork	Ireland	between September 12 and 18, 1847
Curtin, Edward		Saguenay	Cork	Ireland	
Curtin, Ellen		Saguenay	Cork	Ireland	
Curtin, James	17	Jessie	Limerick	Ireland	between August 29 and September 4, 1847
Curtin, John	27	Avon	Cork	Ireland	between September 5 and 11, 1847
Curtin, Thomas	23	Avon	Cork	Ireland	between July 25 and 31, 1847
Curtis, William	27	Broom	Liverpool	England	between September 12 and 18, 1847
Cushely, Rose	50	Ganges	Liverpool	England	between August 15 and 21, 1847
Cushman, Johan	27	Bee	Cork	Ireland	between June 20 and 26, 1847
Cussane, John	30	Sobraon	Liverpool	England	between August 22 and 28, 1847
D___, D___					
Dalton, Patrick	26	Ajax	Liverpool	England	between August 1 and 7, 1847
Daly, Ann	21	Naomi	Liverpool	England	between September 12 and 18, 1847
Daly, Bridget	1	Jessie	Cork	Ireland	between August 1 and 7, 1847
Daly, Carol	22	John Munn	Liverpool	England	between September 19 and 25, 1847
Daly, Denis	35	Wakefield	Cork	Ireland	between July 11 and 17, 1847
Daly, Honora	4	Scotland	Cork	Ireland	between July 4 and 10, 1847
Daly, James	6 months	Bee	Cork	Ireland	between May 29 and June 5, 1847
Daly, James	34	Jessie	Cork	Ireland	between July 18 and 24, 1847
Daly, John	2	Covenanter	Cork	Ireland	between August 29 and September 4, 1847
Daly, Margaret	46	John Munn	Liverpool	England	between October 10 and 16, 1847
Daly, Margaret	23	Scotland	Cork	Ireland	between July 4 and 10, 1847
Daly, Mary	45	Clarendon	Liverpool	England	between June 6 and 12, 1847
Daly, Mary	13	Clarendon	Liverpool	England	between June 13 and 19, 1847
Daly, Michael	12	John Munn	Liverpool	England	between September 5 and 11, 1847
Daly, Michael	10	Wakefield	Cork	Ireland	between July 18 and 24, 1847
Daly, Patrick	7	Albion	Cork	Ireland	between October 3 and 9, 1847
Daly, Patrick	15	John Munn	Liverpool	England	between August 22 and 28, 1847
Daly, Timothy	30	John Munn	Liverpool	England	between September 12 and 18, 1847
Dalzell, Alexander	23	Lady Gordon	Belfast	Ireland	1847/06/14
Damery, John	24	Agnes	Cork	Ireland	between May 29 and June 5, 1847
Dansy, James	28	Elizabeth	Liverpool	England	between July 11 and 17, 1847
Darcy, Johanna	40	Scotland	Cork	Ireland	between July 4 and 10, 1847
Darcy, Judith	50				1847/06/16*
Darcy, Thomas	20	Virginius	Liverpool	England	between August 1 and 7, 1847
Darcy, William	38	John Jardine	Liverpool	England	between July 18 and 24, 1847
Dargan, James	1	Lady Campbell	Dublin	Ireland	between August 29 and September 4, 1847
Davis, James	28	Elizabeth	Liverpool	England	between July 18 and 24, 1847
Davis, Michael	40	James Moran	Liverpool	England	between August 22 and 28, 1847
Davis, William	2	Argo	Liverpool	England	1847/06/06
Davitt, Martha	30	Larch	Sligo	Ireland	between August 15 and 21, 1847
Davitt, Patrick	8	Odessa	Dublin	Ireland	between August 22 and 28, 1847
Dawley, Thomas	14	Superior	Londonderry	Ireland	between September 26 and October 2, 1847
Dawson, Abraham	13	Erin's Queen	Liverpool	England	1847/08/16
Dawson, Eliza	40	Britannia	Greenock	Scotland	1847/08/18
Dawson, Mary	6	Erin's Queen	Liverpool	England	between July 18 and 24, 1847
Day, W.O.	2	Wandsworth	Dublin	Ireland	between May 23 and 29, 1847
Dea, John	40	Bee	Cork	Ireland	between May 29 and June 5, 1847
Dea, Mary	62	Elizabeth	Liverpool	England	between June 27 and July 3, 1847
Dean, Edward	20	Syria	Liverpool	England	between June 6 and 12, 1847
Dean, Mary		Syria	Liverpool	England	
Dean, Peter	26	Syria	Liverpool	England	between May 23 and 29, 1847
Deasey, Cornelius	4	Scotland	Cork	Ireland	between June 20 and 26, 1847
Deasey, David	23	Lady Gordon	Belfast	Ireland	between June 20 and 26, 1847
Deasey, Ellen	21	Gilmour	Cork	Ireland	between July 11 and 17, 1847
Deasey, H.	4	Jane Avery	Dublin	Ireland	between June 27 and July 3, 1847
Deasey, Margaret	40	Jane Avery	Dublin	Ireland	between June 27 and July 3, 1847
Deasey, Margaret	7	Jane Avery	Dublin	Ireland	between June 27 and July 3, 1847
Deasey, Mary	12	Scotland	Cork	Ireland	between May 23 and 29, 1847
Deasey, Mary	8	Scotland	Cork	Ireland	between June 6 and 12, 1847
Deasey, Mary	13	Scotland	Cork	Ireland	between June 6 and 12, 1847
Deasey, Mary	17	Gilmour	Cork	Ireland	between August 8 and 14, 1847
Deasey, Michael	12	Scotland	Cork	Ireland	between May 23 and 29, 1847
Deely, Daniel	25	Alexander Stewart	Limerick	Ireland	between September 5 and 11, 1847

Lists of people who died and were buried on Grosse Île, in 1847

Name	Age	Vessel	Port	Country	Date of death
Deery, James	40	Syria	Liverpool	England	between May 23 and 29, 1847
Deery, John	43	Scotland	Cork	Ireland	between May 23 and 29, 1847
Deevy, Mary	6	Elizabeth			between June 27 and July 3, 1847
Delacour, Eliza	5	Covenanter	Cork	Ireland	between September 12 and 18, 1847
Delaney, Henry	15	Lillias	Dublin	Ireland	1847/09/05
Delaney, Margaret	21	Free Trader	Liverpool	England	between August 29 and September 4, 1847
Delmage, Martha	18	Sir Henry Pottinger	Belfast	Ireland	1847/09/17
Dempsey, Honora	14	Naparina	Dublin	Ireland	between September 19 and 25, 1847
Dempsey, John	16	Free Trader	Liverpool	England	between August 22 and 28, 1847
Dempsey, Margaret	14	Free Trader	Liverpool	England	between August 29 and September 4, 1847
Dempsey, Mary	37	Lady Campbell	Dublin	Ireland	between August 1 and 7, 1847
Dempsey, Mary	7	Free Trader	Liverpool	England	between August 15 and 21, 1847
Dempsey, Mary	50	John Francis	Cork	Ireland	between June 27 and July 3, 1847
Dempsey, Michael	15	Ann Kenny	Waterford	Ireland	between August 1 and 7, 1847
Dempsey, Michael	22	Gilmour	Cork	Ireland	between July 4 and 10, 1847
Dempsey, Miles	33	Achilles	Liverpool	England	between August 22 and 28, 1847
Dempsey, Stephan	2	Naparina	Dublin	Ireland	between September 12 and 18, 1847
Dempsey, Thomas	9	Naparina	Dublin	Ireland	between September 19 and 25, 1847
Dempsey, William	40	Naparina	Dublin	Ireland	between September 5 and 11, 1847
Dempster, H.	24	Royalist	Liverpool	England	between June 6 and 12, 1847
Dennehy, Eliza	33	Agnes	Cork	Ireland	between June 20 and 26, 1847
Dennehy, Francis	12	Agnes	Cork	Ireland	between June 6 and 12, 1847
Dennehy, Michael	4	Agnes	Cork	Ireland	between June 6 and 12, 1847
Dennis, John	5	John Francis	Cork	Ireland	between June 20 and 26, 1847
Dennison, Bartholomew	45	Columbia	Sligo	Ireland	between June 13 and 19, 1847
Dennison, Bartholomew jr	15	Columbia	Sligo	Ireland	between June 13 and 19, 1847
Dennison, James		Columbia	Sligo	Ireland	
Dennison, John	6	Columbia	Sligo	Ireland	between June 13 and 19, 1847
Dennison, John	2	Columbia	Sligo	Ireland	between June 13 and 19, 1847
Dennison, Mary	30	Columbia	Sligo	Ireland	between June 6 and 12, 1847
Dennison, Mary	30	Clarendon	Liverpool	England	between June 13 and 19, 1847
Dennison, Michael		Columbia	Sligo	Ireland	
Dennison, William	16	Marinus	Dublin	Ireland	between September 5 and 11, 1847
Derby, Ann	60	John Bolton	Liverpool	England	between July 4 and 10, 1847
Derbyshire, George	21	Sir Robert Peel	Liverpool	England	1847/09/14
Derrig, Michael	36	Larch	Sligo	Ireland	between August 15 and 21, 1847
Devaney, Ann	33	Columbia	Sligo	Ireland	between June 20 and 26, 1847
Devery, Michael	6	Columbia	Sligo	Ireland	between June 6 and 12, 1847
Devine, Andrew	46	Yorkshire Lass	Killala	Ireland	between August 1 and 7, 1847
Devine, Ann	15	John Bolton	Liverpool	England	between July 18 and 24, 1847
Devine, Ann	25	Larch	Sligo	Ireland	between August 29 and September 4, 1847
Devine, Anthony	24	Yorkshire Lass	Killala	Ireland	between August 1 and 7, 1847
Devine, Bridget	20	Yorkshire Lass	Killala	Ireland	between September 5 and 11, 1847
Devine, Catherine	24	Yorkshire Lass	Killala	Ireland	between July 11 and 17, 1847
Devine, John	1	Yorkshire Lass	Killala	Ireland	between July 4 and 10, 1847
Devine, Thomas	33	Sesostris	Londonderry	Ireland	between August 8 and 14, 1847
Devlin, Margaret	30	Lord Seaton	Belfast	Ireland	1847/06/19
Devlin, Mary	30	Lord Seaton	Belfast	Ireland	between June 13 and 19, 1847
Devoy, Ellen	30	Ganges	Liverpool	England	between September 12 and 18, 1847
Dickinson, George	2	Primrose	Limerick	Ireland	between July 4 and 10, 1847
Dickinson, Margaret	26	Cape Breton	Dublin	Ireland	between June 20 and 26, 1847
Dickson, Thomas	10	Free Trader	Liverpool	England	between August 15 and 21, 1847
Dignan, Thomas	60	Progress	New Ross	Ireland	between June 27 and July 3, 1847
Dillon, Maurice	8	Covenanter	Cork	Ireland	between August 15 and 21, 1847
Dillon, Michael	45	Covenanter	Cork	Ireland	between September 19 and 25, 1847
Dillon, Patrick	35	George	Liverpool	England	between June 6 and 12, 1847
Dinan, Timothy	2	Agnes	Cork	Ireland	between June 13 and 19, 1847
Dinneen, Mary	10	Covenanter	Cork	Ireland	between August 22 and 28, 1847
Dinning, Daniel	6	Agnes	Cork	Ireland	between June 20 and 26, 1847
Dinning, Eliza	22	Agnes	Cork	Ireland	between July 4 and 10, 1847
Dinsmore, Thomas	32				between August 8 and 14, 1847
Dixon, Matilda	37	Superior	Londonderry	Ireland	between October 10 and 16, 1847
Dobbin, Bridget	30	Bee	Cork	Ireland	between June 6 and 12, 1847
Dobbin, John		Bee	Cork	Ireland	
Dobbin, William	36	Bee	Cork	Ireland	between June 13 and 19, 1847
Dobson, Jane	12	Ajax	Liverpool	England	between July 18 and 24, 1847
Dobson, William	19				1847/07/05
Dodds, Thomas	16	Ayrshire	Newry	Ireland	between September 26 and October 2, 1847
Doheny, Jane	7	Naparina	Dublin	Ireland	between August 15 and 21, 1847
Doherty, Alexander	43	Maria Somes	Cork	Ireland	between September 5 and 11, 1847
Doherty, Charles	24	Lively	Cork	Ireland	between August 15 and 21, 1847
Doherty, John	35	Yorkshire Lass	Killala	Ireland	between July 4 and 10, 1847
Doherty, M.	24				between July 18 and 24, 1847
Doherty, Patrick	60	Yorkshire Lass	Killala	Ireland	between July 18 and 24, 1847
Doherty, Rose	19	Wolfville	Sligo	Ireland	between July 25 and 31, 1847
Doherty, Thomas	28	Yorkshire Lass	Killala	Ireland	between August 1 and 7, 1847
Dolly, Margaret					
Dolly, Theresa					

The Emigrants

Name	Age	Vessel	Port	Country	Date of death
Donaghue, Ann	22	Covenanter	Cork	Ireland	between September 19 and 25, 1847
Donaghue, Darby	35	Bee	Cork	Ireland	between May 29 and June 5, 1847
Donaghue, John	13	John Francis	Cork	Ireland	between May 4 and 10, 1847
Donaghue, Mary	44	Larch	Sligo	Ireland	between August 29 and September 4, 1847
Donaghue, Patrick	60	Colonist	New Ross	Ireland	between August 29 and September 4, 1847
Donahoe, Bridget	40	Numa	Sligo	Ireland	between August 8 and 14, 1847
Donahoe, Catherine	23	Wellington	Liverpool	England	between October 3 and 9, 1847
Donahoe, Jeremiah	28	Odessa	Dublin	Ireland	between August 15 and 21, 1847
Donahoe, John	27	Saguenay	Cork	Ireland	between October 10 and 16, 1847
Donahoe, Margaret	20	Covenanter	Cork	Ireland	between August 1 and 7, 1847
Donahoe, Mary	40	Pursuit	Liverpool	England	between July 4 and 10, 1847
Donahoe, Mary	15	Odessa	Dublin	Ireland	between August 15 and 21, 1847
Donahoe, Michael	30	Triton	Liverpool	England	between July 25 and 31, 1847
Donahoe, Michael	60	Pandora	New Ross	Ireland	between August 1 and 7, 1847
Donahoe, Patrick	2	Triton	Liverpool	England	between July 25 and 31, 1847
Donahoe, Thomas	15	John Munn	Liverpool	England	between August 8 and 14, 1847
Donahoe, Timothy	30	Pacha	Cork	Ireland	between July 11 and 17, 1847
Donaldson, Mary	2	Free Trader	Liverpool	England	between August 22 and 28, 1847
Donaldson, Massay	2 years & 6 months	Free Trader	Liverpool	England	1847/08/28
Donnell, John	5 weeks	Rankin	Liverpool	England	between June 6 and 12, 1847
Donnell, John	45	Eliza Caroline	Liverpool	England	between June 13 and 19, 1847
Donnell, Judith	40	Eliza Caroline	Liverpool	England	between June 6 and 12, 1847
Donnell, Margaret	8	Eliza Caroline	Liverpool	England	between June 13 and 19, 1847
Donnell, William	9	Eliza Caroline	Liverpool	England	between June 20 and 26, 1847
Donnellan, Catherine	7	Naomi	Liverpool	England	between August 8 and 14, 1847
Donnellan, Luke	30	Naomi	Liverpool	England	between August 8 and 14, 1847
Donnellan, Peter	22	Sarah	Liverpool	England	between July 11 and 17, 1847
Donnelly, Bridget	7	Free Trader	Liverpool	England	between August 15 and 21, 1847
Donnelly, Jeremiah	2	Agnes	Cork	Ireland	between June 13 and 19, 1847
Donnelly, John	10	Naparina	Dublin	Ireland	between August 29 and September 4, 1847
Donnelly, Mary	25	Junior	Liverpool	England	between July 4 and 10, 1847
Donnelly, Mary	56	Progress	New Ross	Ireland	between July 4 and 10, 1847
Donnelly, Patrick	34	Urania	Cork	Ireland	between June 6 and 12, 1847
Donnelly, Patrick	76	Rankin	Liverpool	England	between June 13 and 19, 1847
Donovan, Andrew	4	Bee	Cork	Ireland	between June 6 and 12, 1847
Donovan, Catherine	8	Agnes	Cork	Ireland	between June 13 and 19, 1847
Donovan, Catherine	26	Bee	Cork	Ireland	between June 6 and 12, 1847
Donovan, Catherine	5 months	Sir Henry Pottinger	Cork	Ireland	between August 8 and 14, 1847
Donovan, Cornel	20	Agnes	Cork	Ireland	between May 23 and 29, 1847
Donovan, Curly	45	Agnes	Cork	Ireland	between July 18 and 24, 1847
Donovan, Daniel	25	Scotland	Cork	Ireland	between August 8 and 14, 1847
Donovan, Dennis	30	Scotland	Cork	Ireland	between May 23 and 29, 1847
Donovan, Donald	28	Wolfville	Sligo	Ireland	between June 20 and 26, 1847
Donovan, Ellen	3	Scotland	Cork	Ireland	between May 23 and 29, 1847
Donovan, Ellen	20	Bee	Cork	Ireland	between June 6 and 12, 1847
Donovan, H.	3	Bee	Cork	Ireland	between June 13 and 19, 1847
Donovan, Joanna	8	Bee	Cork	Ireland	between June 20 and 26, 1847
Donovan, John	14	Bee	Cork	Ireland	between May 29 and June 5, 1847
Donovan, John	22	Gilmour	Cork	Ireland	between June 20 and 26, 1847
Donovan, Mary	20	Scotland	Cork	Ireland	between June 13 and 19, 1847
Donovan, Mary	18	Agnes	Cork	Ireland	between June 27 and July 3, 1847
Donovan, Mary	55	Scotland	Cork	Ireland	between July 4 and 10, 1847
Donovan, Michael	37	Agnes	Cork	Ireland	between June 6 and 12, 1847
Donovan, Nancy	20	Goliah	Liverpool	England	between September 19 and 25, 1847
Donovan, Noreen	1 year & 6 months	Bee	Cork	Ireland	between May 29 and June 5, 1847
Donovan, Noreen	28	Avon	Cork	Ireland	between July 25 and 31, 1847
Donovan, Thomas	20	Agnes	Cork	Ireland	between June 13 and 19, 1847
Donovan, Thomas	8	Agnes	Cork	Ireland	between June 13 and 19, 1847
Donovan, Timothy	30	Agnes	Cork	Ireland	between June 20 and 26, 1847
Donovan, Timothy	20	Bee	Cork	Ireland	between August 15 and 21, 1847
Doohan, James	40	Rose	Liverpool	England	between August 8 and 14, 1847
Doohan, Mary	23	Free Trader	Liverpool	England	between August 29 and September 4, 1847
Doolan, Bridget	68	Naparina	Dublin	Ireland	between August 22 and 28, 1847
Doolan, Ellen	12	Westmoreland	Sligo	Ireland	between August 8 and 14, 1847
Doolan, James	30	Marinus	Dublin	Ireland	between August 15 and 21, 1847
Doolan, Michael	60	Avon	Cork	Ireland	between September 5 and 11, 1847
Dooley, Ann	22	Washington	Liverpool	England	between October 10 and 16, 1847
Dooley, James	26	Larch	Sligo	Ireland	between August 29 and September 4, 1847
Dooley, James		Washington	Liverpool	England	
Dooley, Jeremiah	28	John Munn	Liverpool	England	between August 22 and 28, 1847
Dooley, John	50	Washington	Liverpool	England	between September 12 and 18, 1847
Dooley, Michael	22	Naomi	Liverpool	England	between September 12 and 18, 1847
Doolin, Bridget	30	Ann Kenny	Waterford	Ireland	between October 3 and 9, 1847

Lists of people who died and were buried on Grosse Île, in 1847

Name	Age	Vessel	Port	Country	Date of death
Doonan, Daniel	1	Free Trader	Liverpool	England	between August 8 and 14, 1847
Doonan, Thomas	32	George	Liverpool	England	between May 29 and June 5, 1847
Doorly, James	24	Washington	Liverpool	England	between October 10 and 16, 1847
Doran, Edward	73	Sarah	Liverpool	England	between July 18 and 24, 1847
Doran, Mary Ann	6 months	Urania	Cork	Ireland	between June 27 and July 3, 1847
Doran, Phillip	22	John and Robert	Liverpool	England	between September 26 and October 2, 1847
Dormer, Patrick	67	Perseverance	Dublin	Ireland	between May 29 and June 5, 1847
Douglas, Ellen	12	Pursuit	Liverpool	England	between June 20 and 26, 1847
Douglas, Thomas	7	Pursuit	Liverpool	England	1847/06/07
Dowd, James	26	Oregon	Killala	Ireland	between August 1 and 7, 1847
Dowd, John	26	Avon	Cork	Ireland	between August 1 and 7, 1847
Dowd, Mary	26	Bee	Cork	Ireland	between May 29 and June 5, 1847
Dowdall, Robert	60	Erin's Queen	Liverpool	England	between July 18 and 24, 1847
Dowling, James	22	Bee	Cork	Ireland	between May 29 and June 5, 1847
Downes, Michael					
Downes, Owen	24	Julius Caesar	Liverpool	England	between September 12 and 18, 1847
Downes, Patrick	25	Triton	Liverpool	England	between July 18 and 24, 1847
Downes, Patrick	24	Jessie	Limerick	Ireland	between August 1 and 7, 1847
Downey, Nancy	35	Urania	Cork	Ireland	between June 6 and 12, 1847
Doyle, Ann	1	Sarah	Liverpool	England	between July 25 and 31, 1847
Doyle, Francis	1	Bridgetown	Liverpool	England	between August 29 and September 4, 1847
Doyle, Honora	63	Progress	New Ross	Ireland	between July 4 and 10, 1847
Doyle, Honora	20	Sir Henry Pottinger	Cork	Ireland	between August 1 and 7, 1847
Doyle, John	23	Perseverance	Dublin	Ireland	between May 23 and 29, 1847
Doyle, John		Syria	Liverpool	England	
Doyle, Margaret	30	Rankin	Liverpool	England	between June 13 and 19, 1847
Doyle, Mary	18	Virginius	Liverpool	England	between August 8 and 14, 1847
Doyle, Patrick	18	Margaret	New Ross	Ireland	between June 27 and July 3, 1847
Doyle, Patrick	56	Colonist	New Ross	Ireland	between August 22 and 28, 1847
Drennan, Ann	36	Wandsworth	Dublin	Ireland	between May 23 and 29, 1847
Drennan, Ann	2 months	Syria	Liverpool	England	between June 13 and 19, 1847
Drennan, Dennis	6	Agnes	Cork	Ireland	between May 23 and 29, 1847
Drennan, Jane	65	Wandsworth	Dublin	Ireland	between June 20 and 26, 1847
Drew, John	60	Superior	Londonderry	Ireland	between September 12 and 18, 1847
Driscoll, Catherine	24	Free Trader	Liverpool	England	between August 8 and 14, 1847
Driscoll, Mary	3	Agnes	Cork	Ireland	between June 13 and 19, 1847
Driscoll, Mary	6	Covenanter	Cork	Ireland	between September 5 and 11, 1847
Driscoll, William	21	John Munn	Liverpool	England	between August 15 and 21, 1847
Drum, John James	6	Rose	Liverpool	England	1847/06/16
Duffy, Catherine	26	Sarah	Liverpool	England	between July 25 and 31, 1847
Duffy, Ellen	8	Wolfville	Sligo	Ireland	between July 4 and 10, 1847
Duffy, Honora	24	Wellington	Liverpool	England	between September 19 and 25, 1847
Duffy, Isabella	2 months	Manchester	Liverpool	England	between July 11 and 17, 1847
Duffy, James	40	Wm S. Hamilton	New Ross	Ireland	between August 15 and 21, 1847
Duffy, James	23	Virginius	Liverpool	England	between August 8 and 14, 1847
Duffy, John	3	Naomi	Liverpool	England	between August 15 and 21, 1847
Duffy, Letitia	40	Manchester	Liverpool	England	between July 18 and 24, 1847
Duffy, Margaret	17	Ganges	Liverpool	England	between August 22 and 28, 1847
Duffy, Michael	40	Ann	Liverpool	England	1847/06/23*
Duffy, Patrick	35	Manchester	Liverpool	England	between July 18 and 24, 1847
Duffy, Patrick	3	Manchester	Liverpool	England	between August 1 and 7, 1847
Duffy, Peter	50	Sarah	Liverpool	England	between July 25 and 31, 1847
Duffy, Thomas	10	Aberdeen	Liverpool	England	between June 20 and 26, 1847
Duggan, Bridget	14	Naomi	Liverpool	England	between August 8 and 14, 1847
Duggan, Catherine	40	Virginius	Liverpool	England	between August 15 and 21, 1847
Duggan, Catherine	22	Naomi	Liverpool	England	between August 15 and 21, 1847
Duggan, Charles	3	Covenanter	Cork	Ireland	between August 15 and 21, 1847
Duggan, Daniel	21	Jessie	Cork	Ireland	between July 11 and 17, 1847
Duggan, James	20	Wakefield	Cork	Ireland	between August 15 and 21, 1847
Duggan, Margaret	7	Covenanter	Cork	Ireland	between August 8 and 14, 1847
Duggan, Mary	7	Pandora	New Ross	Ireland	between July 25 and 31, 1847
Duggan, Thomas	22	John Bolton	Liverpool	England	between July 4 and 10, 1847
Duhig, Thomas	7	Erin's Queen	Liverpool	England	between July 18 and 24, 1847
Duke, Thomas					
Dundas, Hebe	3 years & 6 months	Tay	Sligo	Ireland	1847/06/01
Dundas, Sarah	5	Rankin	Liverpool	England	between June 13 and 19, 1847
Dunn, Catherine	40	Ganges	Liverpool	England	between August 15 and 21, 1847
Dunworth, Stephen	31	Emily	Cork	Ireland	between July 4 and 10, 1847
Durham, Bridget	7	John Munn	Liverpool	England	between September 19 and 25, 1847
Durkin, Mary	30	John Munn	Liverpool	England	between September 5 and 11, 1847
Durkin, Peter	20	Sarah	Liverpool	England	between August 1 and 7, 1847
Durnan, Mary	21	Thistle	Liverpool	England	between July 11 and 17, 1847
Dutch, Charles	20	Triton	Liverpool	England	between July 18 and 24, 1847
Dwane, Patrick	30	George	Liverpool	England	between June 6 and 12, 1847
Dwyer, Catherine	17	Larch	Sligo	Ireland	between August 15 and 21, 1847
Dwyer, James		Wakefield	Cork	Ireland	
Dwyer, John	1	Yorkshire Lass	Killala	Ireland	between July 4 and 10, 1847

The emigrants

Name	Age	Vessel	Port	Country	Date of death
Dwyer, Margaret	26	Saguenay	Cork	Ireland	between September 12 and 18, 1847
Dwyer, Richard	40	Washington	Liverpool	England	between August 22 and 28, 1847
Dwyer, Timothy	25	Wakefield	Cork	Ireland	between July 11 and 17, 1847
Dyer, John	40	Scotland	Cork	Ireland	between June 27 and July 3, 1847
E___, P___					
Earl, Edward	30	Wm S. Hamilton	New Ross	Ireland	1847/09/15
Earl, Eliza	22	Wm S. Hamilton	New Ross	Ireland	1847/08/27
Earls, Daniel	30	Abbotsford	Dublin	Ireland	between May 29 and June 5, 1847
Edwards, George	32				1847/06/29
Edwards, Henry	24	Charles Richard	Sligo	Ireland	between July 18 and 24, 1847
Edwards, Michael	25	Lotus	Liverpool	England	between July 11 and 17, 1847
Egan, Bridget	16	Erin's Queen	Liverpool	England	between September 5 and 11, 1847
Egan, John	40	Naomi	Liverpool	England	between August 15 and 21, 1847
Egan, John	7	Naomi	Liverpool	England	between August 8 and 14, 1847
Egan, Mary					
Egan, Mary	21	Yorkshire	Liverpool	England	between September 12 and 18, 1847
Egan, Mary	25	Larch	Sligo	Ireland	between September 5 and 11, 1847
Egan, O.	4				between August 15 and 21, 1847
Egan, Thomas	32	Virginius	Liverpool	England	between August 22 and 28, 1847
Egan, Thomas	35	Triton	Liverpool	England	between August 21 and 28, 1847
Egerton, Richard	40	Champion	Liverpool	England	between August 22 and 28, 1847
Elliott, Andrew	50	Pursuit	Liverpool	England	1847/06/06
Elliott, James	50	Ganges	Liverpool	England	between September 5 and 11, 1847
English, Edward	40	Wm S. Hamilton	New Ross	Ireland	between August 1 and 7, 1847
English, Edward		Pandora	New Ross	Ireland	
Ennis, Catherine	17	John Jardine	Liverpool	England	between July 11 and 17, 1847
Enright, Thomas	45	Nerio	Limerick	Ireland	between September 26 and October 2, 1847
Erwin, Andrew	24	Elizabeth	Liverpool	England	between July 18 and 24, 1847
Erwin, Eliza	33	Jessie	Limerick	Ireland	between August 8 and 14, 1847
Erwin, Mary	50	Sobraon	Liverpool	England	between July 25 and 31, 1847
Evans, James	37	Sir Henry Pottinger	Belfast	Ireland	1847/08/28
Evans, John	3	Triton	Liverpool	England	between July 18 and 24, 1847
Evans, Thomas	21	Erin's Queen	Liverpool	England	between July 18 and 24, 1847
Everell, William	50	Ann	Liverpool	England	between August 8 and 14, 1847
Fagan, Owen	30	Lotus	Liverpool	England	between July 25 and 31, 1847
Fagan, Patrick	13	Wandsworth	Dublin	Ireland	1847/05/22
Fahey, Bridget		Princess Royal	Liverpool	England	
Fahey, Michael	5	Princess Royal	Liverpool	England	between June 20 and 26, 1847
Fahey, Michael	24	Lady Milton	Liverpool	England	between September 5 and 11, 1847
Fahey, Patrick	36	Sarah Maria	Sligo	Ireland	between July 18 and 24, 1847
Fair, John	29	Triton	Liverpool	England	between September 19 and 25, 1847
Fallon, Bridget	36	Saguenay	Cork	Ireland	between August 15 and 21, 1847
Fallon, Catherine	45	Erin's Queen	Liverpool	England	between August 8 and 14, 1847
Fallon, Eliza	3	Free Trader	Liverpool	England	between August 15 and 21, 1847
Fallon, John	10	Naomi	Liverpool	England	between August 22 and 28, 1847
Fallon, John	7	Virginius	Liverpool	England	between August 1 and 7, 1847
Fallon, Patrick	50	Naomi	Liverpool	England	between September 12 and 18, 1847
Fallon, Susan	3	Naomi	Liverpool	England	between August 15 and 21, 1847
Fallon, Thadeus	14	Virginius	Liverpool	England	between August 29 and September 4, 1847
Falvey, John	21	Dominica	Cork	Ireland	between July 11 and 17, 1847
Fannin, Ann	7	Wakefield	Cork	Ireland	between July 18 and 24, 1847
Fannin, Margaret	11 months				1847/05/20
Farley, Francis	8 months	Ajax	Liverpool	England	1847/06/02
Farley, Margaret	66	Covenanter	Cork	Ireland	between August 15 and 21, 1847
Farley, Mary	30	Pursuit	Liverpool	England	between July 4 and 10, 1847
Farley, William	17	Ajax	Liverpool	England	between July 18 and 24, 1847
Farrell, Ann	21	John Munn	Liverpool	England	between August 8 and 14, 1847
Farrell, Edward	12	Lady Campbell	Dublin	Ireland	between August 15 and 21, 1847
Farrell, James	1	Wandsworth	Dublin	Ireland	between May 23 and 29, 1847
Farrell, Jane	15	Naomi	Liverpool	England	between September 12 and 18, 1847
Farrell, John	6	Marchioness of Breadalbane	Sligo	Ireland	between August 8 and 14, 1847
Farrell, John	17	Erin's Queen	Liverpool	England	between August 29 and September 4, 1847
Farrell, John	14	Naomi	Liverpool	England	between August 15 and 21, 1847
Farrell, Margaret	40	Wandsworth	Dublin	Ireland	between June 6 and 12, 1847
Farrell, Margaret	50	Covenanter	Cork	Ireland	between August 29 and September 4, 1847
Farrell, Mary	58				between July 11 and 17, 1847
Farrell, Michael	35	Naomi	Liverpool	England	between August 8 and 14, 1847
Farrell, Michael	12	Covenanter	Cork	Ireland	between August 29 and September 4, 1847
Farrell, Patrick	1 year & 6 months	Royal Adelaide	Killala	Ireland	between August 22 and 28, 1847
Farrell, Peter	26	Royal Adelaide	Killala	Ireland	between September 5 and 11, 1847
Farren, Eliza	19	Royalist	Liverpool	England	1847/05/22
Farrow, John	22	Gilmour	Cork	Ireland	between July 25 and 31, 1847
Fastedy, Catherine	50	Lady Flora Hastings	Cork	Ireland	between June 20 and 26, 1847
Fearon, Ann	33	Champion	Liverpool	England	between August 29 and September 4, 1847
Fearon, Patrick	3	Erin's Queen	Liverpool	England	between September 5 and 11, 1847
Fee, Ann	30	Charles Richard	Sligo	Ireland	between August 22 and 28, 1847
Feehan, Mary	24	Agnes	Cork	Ireland	between July 4 and 10, 1847
Feely, James	40	Scotland	Cork	Ireland	between August 8 and 14, 1847

Lists of people who died and were buried on Grosse Île, in 1847

Name	Age	Vessel	Port	Country	Date of death
Feely, Margaret	50	Numa	Sligo	Ireland	between July 25 and 31, 1847
Feeney, Mary	27	John Munn	Liverpool	England	between August 1 and 7, 1847
Feeney, Michael	26	Sobraon	Liverpool	England	between July 25 and 31, 1847
Feerick, James	13	Greenock	Liverpool	England	between August 1 and 7, 1847
Fegan, Ann		Triton	Liverpool	England	
Fegan, Ann	30	Roseanna	Cork	Ireland	between July 25 and 31, 1847
Fegan, Bridget	50	Rose	Liverpool	England	between July 11 and 17, 1847
Fenlon, Mary	38	Progress	New Ross	Ireland	between July 4 and 10, 1847
Fennell, Thomas	4	Saguenay	Cork	Ireland	between August 15 and 21, 1847
Fergus, Bridget	1	Naomi	Liverpool	England	between August 15 and 21, 1847
Fergus, Catherine	21	Naomi	Liverpool	England	between August 8 and 14, 1847
Ferguson, James	50	Agamemnon	Liverpool	England	between September 12 and 18, 1847
Ferris, Patrick	5 months	Virginius	Liverpool	England	between August 8 and 14, 1847
Ferris, Thomas	4	Covenanter	Cork	Ireland	between August 1 and 7, 1847
Ferriter, H.	4	Gilmour	Cork	Ireland	between June 20 and 26, 1847
Ferriter, Thomas	9	Gilmour	Cork	Ireland	between June 20 and 26, 1847
Ferry, Mary		Lady Flora Hastings	Cork	Ireland	
Ferry, Mary	11	Virginius	Liverpool	England	between August 22 and 28, 1847
Fihilly, Ellen	2	Ann	Liverpool	England	between July 11 and 17, 1847
Fihilly, Honora	16	Numa	Sligo	Ireland	between August 15 and 21, 1847
Finerty, Donald	30	Yorkshire Lass	Killala	Ireland	between August 8 and 14, 1847
Finlay, John	19	Champion	Liverpool	England	between October 3 and 9, 1847
Finlay, Margaret	18	Eliza Morrison	Belfast	Ireland	1847/08/23
Finlay, Margaret	18	Saguenay	Cork	Ireland	between August 22 and 28, 1847
Finn, Bridget	5	Odessa	Dublin	Ireland	between August 29 and September 4, 1847
Finn, Catherine	8	Lord Sandon	Cork	Ireland	between June 20 and 26, 1847
Finn, Henry	34	Larch	Sligo	Ireland	between August 15 and 21, 1847
Finn, Julia	40	Odessa	Dublin	Ireland	between August 1 and 7, 1847
Finn, Mary	1 year & 6 months	Virginius	Liverpool	England	between August 8 and 14, 1847
Finn, Mary	46	Urania	Cork	Ireland	between June 27 and July 3, 1847
Finn, Michael		Pursuit	Liverpool	England	
Finn, Michael	10	Odessa	Dublin	Ireland	between August 22 and 28, 1847
Finn, Thomas	2	Champion	Liverpool	England	between August 29 and September 4, 1847
Finn, Thomas	30	John Bolton	Liverpool	England	between August 8 and 14, 1847
Finn, Timothy	22	Agnes	Cork	Ireland	between June 6 and 12, 1847
Finnegan, Patrick	19	Champion	Liverpool	England	between September 19 and 25, 1847
Finucane, Michael	3	Free Trader	Liverpool	England	between August 29 and September 4, 1847
Fisher, Ellen	5	Gilmour	Cork	Ireland	between June 6 and 12, 1847
Fitzgerald, Ann	2	Rose	Liverpool	England	between June 27 and July 3, 1847
Fitzgerald, David	27	Gilmour	Cork	Ireland	between June 6 and 12, 1847
Fitzgerald, Garrett	20	Sir Henry Pottinger	Belfast	Ireland	between August 29 and September 4, 1847
Fitzgerald, John	40	Try Again	Cork	Ireland	between May 29 and June 5, 1847 or between June 27 and July 3, 1847
Fitzgerald, Margaret	34	Rose	Liverpool	England	between June 20 and 26, 1847
Fitzgerald, Mary	1	Wakefield	Cork	Ireland	between July 25 and 31, 1847
Fitzgerald, Thomas	7	Bridgetown	Liverpool	England	between September 12 and 18, 1847
Fitzgibbon, Michael	40	Manchester	Liverpool	England	between August 8 and 14, 1847
Fitzpatrick, Bridget	30	Washington	Liverpool	England	between August 22 and 28, 1847
Fitzpatrick, Bridget	20	Wolfville	Sligo	Ireland	between June 13 and 19, 1847
Fitzpatrick, John	20	Minerva	Galway	Ireland	between August 22 and 28, 1847
Fitzpatrick, Margaret	30	Erin's Queen	Liverpool	England	between July 25 and 31, 1847
Fitzpatrick, Mary	20	Progress	New Ross	Ireland	between July 11 and 17, 1847
Fitzpatrick, Patrick	40	George	Liverpool	England	between June 27 and July 3, 1847
Fitzpatrick, Thomas	45	Progress	New Ross	Ireland	between June 27 and July 3, 1847
Fitzpatrick, William	30	George	Liverpool	England	between June 20 and 26, 1847
Fitzsimmons, Hugh	32	Free Trader	Liverpool	England	between August 29 and September 4, 1847
Flaherty, Bridget	60	Argo	Liverpool	England	between June 13 and 19, 1847
Flanagan, Edward	35	Ann	Liverpool	England	between August 1 and 7, 1847
Flanagan, Honora	20	George	Liverpool	England	between July 11 and 17, 1847
Flanagan, Honora	16	Wolfville	Sligo	Ireland	between July 4 and 10, 1847
Flanagan, Mary	13	Ganges	Liverpool	England	between August 22 and 28, 1847
Flanagan, Mary	6	Rose	Liverpool	England	between July 25 and 31, 1847
Flanagan, Rose	30	Rose	Liverpool	England	between August 22 and 28, 1847
Flannery, David	28	John Francis	Cork	Ireland	between June 27 and July 3, 1847
Fleming, Diana	7	Agnes	Cork	Ireland	between June 6 and 12, 1847
Fleming, James	15	Mail	Cork	Ireland	between June 27 and July 3, 1847
Fleming, Luke	45	Clarendon	Liverpool	England	between June 13 and 19, 1847
Fleming, Mary	25	Gilmour	Cork	Ireland	between June 6 and 12, 1847
Fleming, Mary	3 years & 6 months	Yorkshire Lass	Killala	Ireland	between July 25 and 31, 1847
Fleming, Matthew	12	Clarendon	Liverpool	England	between June 13 and 19, 1847
Fleming, Patrick	30	John and Robert	Liverpool	England	between August 8 and 14, 1847
Fleming, Patrick	30	Gilmour	Cork	Ireland	between June 6 and 12, 1847
Fletcher, Richard	24	Agnes	Cork	Ireland	between June 6 and 12, 1847
Flood, Andrew	7	Perseverance	Dublin	Ireland	between August 1 and 7, 1847
Flood, Mary	18	Abbotsford	Dublin	Ireland	between June 20 and 26, 1847

The emigrants

Name	Age	Vessel	Port	Country	Date of death
Flynn, Andrew	40	Sisters	Liverpool	England	between June 20 and 26, 1847
Flynn, Daniel	30	Saguenay	Cork	Ireland	between August 22 and 28, 1847
Flynn, Darby	40	Argo	Liverpool	England	between June 27 and July 3, 1847
Flynn, Frances	20	Pacha	Cork	Ireland	between June 13 and 19, 1847
Flynn, Frances	26	Rose	Liverpool	England	between June 20 and 26, 1847
Flynn, Mary	36	Junior	Liverpool	England	between June 27 and July 3, 1847
Flynn, Mary	33	Scotland	Cork	Ireland	between June 6 and 12, 1847
Flynn, Mary	3	Junior	Liverpool	England	between July 4 and 10, 1847
Flynn, Michael	60	Sisters	Liverpool	England	between July 25 and 31, 1847
Flynn, Michael	22	Yorkshire	Liverpool	England	between August 15 and 21, 1847
Flynn, Timothy	20	Pacha	Cork	Ireland	between June 13 and 19, 1847
Flynn, Timothy	10	Eliza Caroline	Liverpool	England	between July 4 and 10, 1847
Fogarty, Andrew	55	Julius Caesar	Liverpool	England	between September 12 and 18, 1847
Fogarty, Patrick	21	Greenock	Liverpool	England	1847/08/16
Foley, James	23	Covenanter	Cork	Ireland	between August 1 and 7, 1847
Foley, Jeremiah	25	Agnes	Cork	Ireland	between June 20 and 26, 1847
Foley, Margaret		Ellen Simpson	Limerick	Ireland	
Foley, Patrick	1	Scotland	Cork	Ireland	between May 29 and June 5, 1847
Foley, Thadeus	30	Agnes	Cork	Ireland	between July 11 and 17, 1847
Foran, Catherine	2	Araminta	Liverpool	England	between July 4 and 10, 1847
Ford, Denis	25	Agnes	Cork	Ireland	between August 22 and 28, 1847
Ford, James	40	Henrietta Mary	Cork	Ireland	between September 26 and October 2, 1847
Ford, Mary	30	Bee	Cork	Ireland	between July 11 and 17, 1847
Ford, Michael	45	Ann	Liverpool	England	between June 27 and July 3, 1847
Ford, Temor					1847/09/30
Fowler, Daniel	40	Sir Robert Peel	Liverpool	England	between September 19 and 25, 1847
Fox, Andrew	46	Lotus	Liverpool	England	between July 4 and 10, 1847
Fox, Ann	33	Lady Campbell	Dublin	Ireland	between August 8 and 14, 1847
Fox, Bridget	27	Free Trader	Liverpool	England	between August 22 and 28, 1847
Fox, Bridget	10	Lotus	Liverpool	England	between July 4 and 10, 1847
Fox, Catherine	15	John and Robert	Liverpool	England	between August 8 and 14, 1847
Fox, John	19	Wolfville	Sligo	Ireland	between July 4 and 10, 1847
Fox, Margaret	40	Lotus	Liverpool	England	between July 11 and 17, 1847
Fox, Mary	13	Bridgetown	Liverpool	England	between August 29 and September 4, 1847
Foy, Bernard	50	Free Trader	Liverpool	England	between August 8 and 14, 1847
Foy, Judith	16	John Munn	Liverpool	England	between August 8 and 14, 1847
Foy, Margaret	22	Pandora	New Ross	Ireland	between August 8 and 14, 1847
Fraher, Mary	50	Virginius	Liverpool	England	between September 12 and 18, 1847
Francis, Margaret	3	Champion	Liverpool	England	between August 29 and September 4, 1847
Fraser, Alexander	50	Avon	Cork	Ireland	between August 8 and 14, 1847
Fraser, Catherine	28	George	Liverpool	England	between August 15 and 21, 1847
Fraser, Catherine	28	Broom	Liverpool	England	1847/08/20
Fraser, Eliza	3	Rankin	Liverpool	England	between June 13 and 19, 1847
Fraser, Hugh	57	Broom	Liverpool	England	between August 1 and 7, 1847
Fraser, Isabella	35	Broom	Liverpool	England	1847/08/18
French, Bridget	30	Royalist	Liverpool	England	between June 20 and 26, 1847
French, Christopher	28	Wandsworth	Dublin	Ireland	between June 20 and 26, 1847
French, P.	2 months	Royalist	Liverpool	England	between May 23 and 29, 1847
Frizell, Mary	25	Argo	Liverpool	England	between June 6 and 12, 1847
Frost, Judith		Odessa	Dublin	Ireland	
Furlong, Thomas	50	Progress	New Ross	Ireland	between July 4 and 10, 1847
Fury, Mary	50	Numa	Sligo	Ireland	between August 8 and 14, 1847
G___, M___					
Gaffney, ___	56	Pandora	New Ross	Ireland	between August 1 and 7, 1847
Gaffney, Ann	45	Pandora	New Ross	Ireland	between August 8 and 14, 1847
Gaffney, Bridget	1	Charles Richard	Sligo	Ireland	between July 25 and 31, 1847
Gaffney, Michael	9	Jessie	Sligo	Ireland	between May 23 and 29, 1847
Gahan, John	6	Free Trader	Liverpool	England	between September 5 and 11, 1847
Gaimbro, Martha		Tamarac	Liverpool	England	1847/07/06
Gainer, John	25	Industry	Sligo	Ireland	between August 29 and September 4, 1847
Galbot, Catherine Williams		Saguenay	Cork	Ireland	1847/08/06
Galbot, Eliza Blair					1847/08/06
Gallagher, Ann	27	Clansman	Greenock	Scotland	between July 25 and 31, 1847
Gallagher, Honora		Sir Henry Pottinger	Cork	Ireland	between September 5 and 11, 1847
Gallagher, James	18	Marchioness of Breadalbane	Sligo	Ireland	between August 8 and 14, 1847
Gallagher, James	25	Brothers	Dublin	Ireland	between August 8 and 14, 1847
Gallagher, Mary	26	Bee	Cork	Ireland	between May 29 and June 5, 1847
Gallagher, Thomas	23	Erin's Queen	Liverpool	England	between August 15 and 21, 1847
Gallagher, William	27	John Francis	Cork	Ireland	between June 27 and July 3, 1847
Gallagher, William	27	Wakefield	Cork	Ireland	between July 25 and 31, 1847
Galligan, Michael	8	Virgilia	Liverpool	England	between September 12 and 18, 1847
Gallivan, Denis	14	Virgilia	Liverpool	England	between September 19 and 25, 1847
Gallivan, Donald	1	Bee	Cork	Ireland	between June 20 and 26, 1847
Galloway, Margaret	1 year & 11 months	Rankin	Liverpool	England	1847/06/01
Galvin, Daniel	21	Emigrant	Liverpool	England	between October 10 and 16, 1847
Galway, John	23	Marinus	Dublin	Ireland	between August 29 and September 4, 1847
Gannon, Catherine	4	Larch	Sligo	Ireland	between August 22 and 28, 1847

Lists of people who died and were buried on Grosse Île, in 1847

Name	Age	Vessel	Port	Country	Date of death
Gargan, James	44	Bridgetown	Liverpool	England	between September 5 and 11, 1847
Gargan, Margaret	10	Bridgetown	Liverpool	England	between August 29 and September 4, 1847
Garry, Francis	3	Maria Somes	Cork	Ireland	between September 19 and 25, 1847
Garry, Patrick	6 months	Maria Somes	Cork	Ireland	between September 19 and 25, 1847
Gately, Margaret	25	Sobraon	Liverpool	England	between July 11 and 17, 1847
Gaughan, Catherine	35	Yorkshire Lass	Killala	Ireland	between August 8 and 14, 1847
Gaughan, Margaret	30	Pandora	New Ross	Ireland	between August 29 and September 4, 1847
Gaughan, Patrick	30	Yorkshire	Liverpool	England	between August 8 and 14, 1847
Gaughan, Patrick	30	Covenanter	Cork	Ireland	between August 8 and 14, 1847
Gaul, John	8	Columbia	Sligo	Ireland	between June 13 and 19, 1847
Gault, Margaret	11	Ajax	Liverpool	England	1847/06/02
Gaynor, Margaret	50	Marinus	Dublin	Ireland	between August 22 and 28, 1847
Geary, Ann	50	Henry	Donegal	Ireland	between June 13 and 19, 1847
Geraghty, Ann	25	Yorkshire Lass	Killala	Ireland	between July 11 and 17, 1847
Geraghty, Ann	20	Yorkshire Lass	Killala	Ireland	between August 15 and 21, 1847
Geraghty, James	60	Araminta	Liverpool	England	between June 13 and 19, 1847
Geraghty, James	42	Araminta	Liverpool	England	between June 20 and 26, 1847
Geraghty, John	36	Dykes	Sligo	Ireland	between June 13 and 19, 1847
Getting, Frances	22	Avon	Cork	Ireland	between July 11 and 17, 1847
Getting, Frances	11	Avon	Cork	Ireland	between August 15 and 21, 1847
Getting, Thomas	40	Avon	Cork	Ireland	between August 8 and 14, 1847
Gibbons, Clement					1847/09/04
Gibbons, John	35	James Moran	Liverpool	England	between July 11 and 17, 1847
Gibbs, Frances	1	Virgilia	Liverpool	England	1847/09/25
Gibson, Daniel	23	Naomi	Liverpool	England	between August 15 and 21, 1847
Gibson, Elzear	32	James Moran	Liverpool	England	between August 4 and 10, 1847
Gibson, George	19	John and Robert	Liverpool	England	1847/08/31
Gibson, James	10	James Moran	Liverpool	England	between July 4 and 10, 1847
Gibson, Mary	19	Marinus	Dublin	Ireland	between September 5 and 11, 1847
Gibson, Sally	8	Aberdeen	Liverpool	England	between June 27 and July 3, 1847
Gilgan, Patrick	35	Aberdeen	Liverpool	England	between July 18 and 24, 1847
Gilhooly, Mary	37	Wonder	Sligo	Ireland	between August 1 and 7, 1847
Gill, John	55	Ann	Liverpool	England	between July 25 and 31, 1847
Gillan, Eliza	3 months	Agent	New Ross	Ireland	between June 27 and July 3, 1847
Gillan, James	36	Agent	New Ross	Ireland	1847/07/09
Gillespie, Archibald	1	Euclid	Glasgow	Scotland	between July 25 and 31, 1847
Gillis, Robert	26	Blonde	Liverpool	England	between October 10 and 16, 1847
Gilman, James	26				1847/07/09
Gilmartin, Patrick	40	Numa	Sligo	Ireland	between August 29 and September 4, 1847
Gilmore, John	34				1847/08/20
Gilmore, Lawrence	50	X.L.	Galway	Ireland	between August 8 and 14, 1847
Gilroy, Edward	50	Argyle	Liverpool	England	between October 10 and 16, 1847
Glass, Jane	46	Maria Somes	Cork	Ireland	1847/09/23
Glass, John	18	Maria Somes	Cork	Ireland	1847/09/20
Gleeson, Eliza	4 months	Syria	Liverpool	England	between June 27 and July 3, 1847
Gleeson, Joanna	10	Urania	Cork	Ireland	between June 20 and 26, 1847
Gleeson, Richard	40	Urania	Cork	Ireland	between July 11 and 17, 1847
Glenn, Patrick	40	Larch	Sligo	Ireland	between August 15 and 21, 1847
Glenny, Mary Jane	8 months	Eliza Caroline	Liverpool	England	1847/06/06
Glynn, Bridget	13	George	Liverpool	England	between July 18 and 24, 1847
Going, Elizabeth	25	John Francis	Cork	Ireland	between June 6 and 12, 1847
Golding, Jeremiah	3	Mail	Cork	Ireland	between July 11 and 17, 1847
Golding, Nancy	40	Charles Walton	Killala	Ireland	between August 1 and 7, 1847
Golding, William	60	Jessie	Sligo	Ireland	between May 23 and 29, 1847
Good, Hannah	20	Lady Gordon	Belfast	Ireland	between June 13 and 19, 1847
Gord, L.	25	Sisters	Liverpool	England	between June 13 and 19, 1847
Gordon, Mary	12	Syria	Liverpool	England	between June 6 and 12, 1847
Gorman, Jeremiah	25	Bee	Cork	Ireland	between May 29 and June 5, 1847
Gorman, Jeremiah	25	Bee	Cork	Ireland	between July 25 and 31, 1847
Gorman, Lawrence	24	Avon	Cork	Ireland	between July 11 and 17, 1847
Gorman, Martha	20	Jessie	Cork	Ireland	between June 27 and July 3, 1847
Gorman, Mary	36	George	Liverpool	England	between June 13 and 19, 1847
Gorman, Thomas	25	Bridgetown	Liverpool	England	between August 22 and 28, 1847
Gorman, William	17				between August 29 and September 4, 1847
Gormley, Francis	45	Superior	Londonderry	Ireland	between September 12 and 18, 1847
Gormley, Martha	5	Sir Henry Pottinger	Belfast	Ireland	between August 22 and 28, 1847
Gough, Bridget	9	Covenanter	Cork	Ireland	between August 15 and 21, 1847
Goulding, Mary	26	Jane Blane	Sligo	Ireland	between July 18 and 24, 1847
Gourley, Denis	22	Roseanna	Cork	Ireland	between August 1 and 7, 1847
Gourley, Hannah	37	Sir Henry Pottinger	Belfast	Ireland	1847/09/20
Gourley, Murtagh	5	Sir Henry Pottinger	Belfast	Ireland	1847/08/27
Gourley, Sarah	48	Sir Henry Pottinger	Belfast	Ireland	between September 19 and 25, 1847
Gowan, Jacob	50	Achilles	Liverpool	England	between June 13 and 19, 1847
Gowan, Mary	2	Syria	Liverpool	England	between June 6 and 12, 1847
Grady, James	4 years & 6 months	Sir Robert Peel	Liverpool	England	1847/09/14
Grady, Mary	11	Elizabeth	Liverpool	England	between July 4 and 10, 1847
Grady, William	22	John Munn	Liverpool	England	between August 22 and 28, 1847
Graham, Catherine	60	Panope	Dublin	Ireland	between July 11 and 17, 1847

The Emigrants

Name	Age	Vessel	Port	Country	Date of death
Graham, Catherine	4 months	Broom	Liverpool	England	1847/08/23
Graham, George	2	Lord Seaton	Belfast	Ireland	1847/06/13
Graham, Helen	13	Lady Campbell	Dublin	Ireland	between October 3 and 9, 1847
Graham, Henry	2 years & 7 months	Broom	Liverpool	England	1847/09/10
Graham, John	28	Argyle	Newport	England	between October 17 and 23, 1847
Graham, Joseph	3 years & 9 months	Lord Seaton	Belfast	Ireland	1847/06/02
Graham, Martha	4	Lady Campbell	Dublin	Ireland	between October 3 and 9, 1847
Graham, Sarah	37	Broom	Liverpool	England	1847/09/27
Graham, Sarah	7	Broom	Liverpool	England	between September 5 and 11, 1847
Graham, Sarah Eliza	2 years & 6 months				1847/05/21
Graham, William	45	Superior	Londonderry	Ireland	1847/09/12
Grant, Daniel	2	Lord Seaton	Belfast	Ireland	between June 6 and 12, 1847
Grant, Malachy	31	Avon	Cork	Ireland	between August 29 and September 4, 1847
Grant, Peter	17	Agamemnon	Liverpool	England	between August 8 and 14, 1847
Gray, Margaret	40	John Munn	Liverpool	England	between August 15 and 21, 1847
Gray, Mary	1	Naomi	Liverpool	England	between August 15 and 21, 1847
Green, Brian	40	Lady Milton	Liverpool	England	between June 20 and 26, 1847
Green, Catherine	25	John Munn	Liverpool	England	between August 8 and 14, 1847
Green, Christopher Thomas	1	Albion	Galway	Ireland	1847/05/27
Green, George	4	Naomi	Liverpool	England	between August 15 and 21, 1847
Green, John	7	Bridgetown	Liverpool	England	between September 19 and 25, 1847
Green, John	60	Tamarac	Liverpool	England	between July 11 and 17, 1847
Green, Mary	14	Progress	New Ross	Ireland	between June 27 and July 3, 1847
Green, Mary Jane	3 years & 2 months	Ellen Thompson	Londonderry	Ireland	1847/05/24
Green, Susan	16	Erin's Queen	Liverpool	England	between August 15 and 21, 1847
Greenan, Catherine	4	Virginius	Liverpool	England	between August 15 and 21, 1847
Greenan, James	35	Lady Campbell	Dublin	Ireland	between August 29 and September 4, 1847
Greenan, Mary	50	Free Trader	Liverpool	England	between August 22 and 28, 1847
Greenaway, John	11 months	Constitution	Belfast	Ireland	1847/06/01
Greenaway, Mary	17	Constitution	Belfast	Ireland	between June 27 and July 3, 1847
Greenaway, Mary	7	Constitution	Belfast	Ireland	1847/06/29
Greenock, Michael		Jessie		Ireland	
Griffin, John	23	Minerva	Galway	Ireland	between August 22 and 28, 1847
Griffin, John	24	Sir Henry Pottinger	Belfast	Ireland	between September 12 and 18, 1847
Griffin, Mary	58	Nerio	Limerick	Ireland	between May 29 and June 5, 1847
Griffin, Michael	50	Clarendon	Liverpool	England	between June 13 and 19, 1847
Griffin, William	21	Rose	Liverpool	England	between July 4 and 10, 1847
Grimes, Thomas	40	Lady Campbell	Dublin	Ireland	between September 19 and 25, 1847
Grogan, James	14				1847/08/03
Grogan, John	28	Bee	Cork	Ireland	between June 13 and 19, 1847
Grogan, Michael	23	Bee	Cork	Ireland	between June 13 and 19, 1847
Grory, Johanna	56	John Francis	Cork	Ireland	between July 18 and 24, 1847
Grory, Patrick	40	John Francis	Cork	Ireland	between June 13 and 19, 1847
Grory, Philip	8	John Francis	Cork	Ireland	between June 27 and July 3, 1847
Gunn, Edward	30	Syria	Liverpool	England	between June 20 and 26, 1847
Gunn, Ellen	25	George	Liverpool	England	between June 27 and July 3, 1847
H__, E___					
H___, I___					
H___, R___		Bee	Cork	Ireland	
H___, W___					
Hadwyn, Jannet	40	Broom	Liverpool	England	1847/09/21
Hagan, John	32	Aberdeen	Liverpool	England	1847/05/26
Haley, Barbara	7	Princess Royal	Liverpool	England	between June 13 and 19, 1847
Haley, Ellen	19	Asia	Cork	Ireland	between September 19 and 25, 1847
Haley, John	24	Bee	Cork	Ireland	between July 4 and 10, 1847
Haley, Thomas	16	Triton	Liverpool	England	between July 11 and 17, 1847
Halfpenny, Bridget	26	Agnes	Cork	Ireland	between June 27 and July 3, 1847
Hall, Ann	22	Covenanter	Cork	Ireland	between August 22 and 28, 1847
Hall, Jane	13	Ganges	Liverpool	England	between September 19 and 25, 1847
Hallissy, Ellen	3	Covenanter	Cork	Ireland	between August 8 and 14, 1847
Hallissy, Mary	8	Washington	Liverpool	England	between August 29 and September 4, 1847
Hamilton, James	45	Greenock	Liverpool	England	between July 25 and 31, 1847
Hamilton, Mary Jane	4	Argo	Liverpool	England	1847/06/05
Hamilton, Susan	55	Eliza Caroline	Liverpool	England	1847/06/02
Hamm, John	10	Bridgetown	Liverpool	England	between August 29 and September 4, 1847
Hammond, Martha	35	Elizabeth	Liverpool	England	between June 27 and July 3, 1847
Hammond, Martin	22	Free Trader	Liverpool	England	between August 15 and 21, 1847
Hanafin, John	30	Wakefield	Cork	Ireland	between August 1 and 7, 1847
Hanafin, Margaret	22	Sisters	Liverpool	England	between July 25 and 31, 1847
Hanafin, William	6 months	Wakefield	Cork	Ireland	between July 18 and 24, 1847
Hanley, Ann	33	Saguenay	Cork	Ireland	between September 12 and 18, 1847
Hanley, Catherine	3	Caithness-shire	Belfast	Ireland	between June 13 and 19, 1847
Hanley, Daniel	11	Virginius	Liverpool	England	between September 5 and 11, 1847
Hanley, Daniel	8	Ganges	Liverpool	England	between October 3 and 9, 1847
Hanley, John	10	Julius Caesar	Liverpool	England	between September 19 and 25, 1847
Hanley, Margaret	4	Virgilia	Liverpool	England	between September 19 and 25, 1847
Hanley, Mary	15	Virginius	Liverpool	England	between August 15 and 21, 1847
Hanley, Mary	19	Sir Robert Peel	Liverpool	England	between September 19 and 25, 1847
Hanley, Mary	30	Virginius	Liverpool	England	between August 1 and 7, 1847

Lists of people who died and were buried on Grosse Île, in 1847

Name	Age	Vessel	Port	Country	Date of death
Hanley, Michael	6	Wolfville	Sligo	Ireland	between June 13 and 19, 1847
Hanley, Patrick	3	Free Trader	Liverpool	England	between August 15 and 21, 1847
Hanley, Rod	45	Washington	Liverpool	England	between September 5 and 11, 1847
Hanley, Rose	34	Naomi	Liverpool	England	between August 29 and September 4, 1847
Hanley, William	3	Ganges	Liverpool	England	between August 22 and 28, 1847
Hanlon, Ann	7	John Munn	Liverpool	England	between August 1 and 7, 1847
Hanlon, Ann	20	Coromandel	Dublin	Ireland	between August 1 and 7, 1847
Hanlon, Catherine	40	Rankin	Liverpool	England	between June 13 and 19, 1847
Hanlon, William	1	Ganges	Liverpool	England	between September 12 and 18, 1847
Hanlon, William	25	Marchioness of Breadalbane	Sligo	Ireland	between August 1 and 7, 1847
Hanna, Margaret	40	Lord Glenelg	Limerick	Ireland	between June 27 and July 3, 1847
Hanna, Margaret	20	John Bolton	Liverpool	England	between June 27 and July 3, 1847
Hanna, Mary	6	Aberdeen	Liverpool	England	between June 13 and 19, 1847
Hanna, Samuel	20	John Bolton	Liverpool	England	between June 13 and 19, 1847
Hannon, Daniel	47	Sir Henry Pottinger	Belfast	Ireland	1847/09/22
Hannon, Elizabeth	20	Wolfville	Sligo	Ireland	between August 29 and September 4, 1847
Hannon, John		Unicorn	Londonderry	Ireland	1847/09/06
Hannon, John	26	Marchioness of ___			between September 5 and 11, 1847
Hannon, Lawrence	24	Avon	Cork	Ireland	between July 18 and 24, 1847
Hare, Bridget	23	Champion	Liverpool	England	between October 3 and 9, 1847
Hare, Elizabeth	15	Broom	Liverpool	England	1847/08/22
Hare, Honora	30	Champion	Liverpool	England	between September 5 and 11, 1847
Hare, John	2	Champion	Liverpool	England	between September 5 and 11, 1847
Hare, John	30	Champion	Liverpool	England	between September 5 and 11, 1847
Hare, Mary		Larch	Sligo	Ireland	
Hare, Matthew	28	Champion	Liverpool	England	between September 12 and 18, 1847
Hare, Michael	4 years & 6 months	Champion	Liverpool	England	between August 29 and September 4, 1847
Hare, P.					
Harkin, James	13	Lotus	Liverpool	England	between June 27 and July 3, 1847
Harkin, Mary	60	Congress	Sligo	Ireland	between June 13 and 19, 1847
Harkin, Michael	26	Wolfville	Sligo	Ireland	between June 13 and 19, 1847
Harkin, Patrick	45	Congress	Sligo	Ireland	between June 13 and 19, 1847
Harmouge, Michael	20	Argyle	Newport	England	between September 26 and October 2, 1847
Harnett, Garret	56	Agnes	Cork	Ireland	between June 6 and 12, 1847
Harney, Ellen	28	Eliza Caroline	Liverpool	England	between June 27 and July 3, 1847
Harney, Patrick	6	Naomi	Liverpool	England	between August 8 and 14, 1847
Harney, Patrick	37	Huron	Belfast	Ireland	between August 8 and 14, 1847
Harold, Catherine	50	Henrietta Mary	Cork	Ireland	between October 10 and 16, 1847
Harold, Christopher	26	Saguenay	Cork	Ireland	between September 19 and 25, 1847
Harold, W.					
Harrington, Cornelius	28	Scotland	Cork	Ireland	between June 6 and 12, 1847
Harrington, Ellen	40	Covenanter	Cork	Ireland	between August 15 and 21, 1847
Harrington, James	19	Urania	Cork	Ireland	between May 23 and 29, 1847
Harrington, James	40	Covenanter	Cork	Ireland	between September 19 and 25, 1847
Harris, James	34	Sarah	Liverpool	England	between July 18 and 24, 1847
Harris, Sarah	35	Erin's Queen	Liverpool	England	between July 18 and 24, 1847
Harris, Thomas	3	Sarah	Liverpool	England	between July 25 and 31, 1847
Harrison, Rebecca	20	Bridgetown	Liverpool	England	1847/08/31
Harrity, Michael	6	Constitution	Belfast	Ireland	between June 6 and 12, 1847
Harrold, John	17	Henrietta Mary	Cork	Ireland	1847/10/03
Hart, John	70	Covenanter	Cork	Ireland	between August 8 and 14, 1847
Hart, Michael	30	Agnes	Cork	Ireland	between May 29 and June 5, 1847
Hart, Patrick	22	Triton	Liverpool	England	between August 15 and 21, 1847
Hartin, Noreen	20	Mary Brack	Limerick	Ireland	between June 13 and 19, 1847
Hartley, John	40	Abbotsford	Dublin	Ireland	between June 13 and 19, 1847
Harvey, Bryan	54	Syria	Liverpool	England	between May 29 and June 5, 1847
Harvey, Thomas	45				between July 11 and 17, 1847
Haslett, Eliza	19	Sarah Maria	Sligo	Ireland	between July 25 and 31, 1847
Haslett, Rebecca	13	Sarah Maria	Sligo	Ireland	between June 27 and July 3, 1847
Hattery, Patrick	5 months				1847/06/16*
Hawe, James	45				1847/06/25
Hawkins, Mary	40	John Bolton	Liverpool	England	between June 20 and 26, 1847
Hawthorn, Hutchison	1 year & 6 months	Achilles	Liverpool	England	1847/06/04
Hawthorn, John	54	Achilles	Liverpool	England	1847/06/02
Hay, Catherine	14	Broom	Liverpool	England	between August 1 and 7, 1847
Hay, Daniel	12	Broom	Liverpool	England	between September 5 and 11, 1847
Hay, Donald	20	Broom	Liverpool	England	1847/09/01
Hay, Duncan	12	Broom	Liverpool	England	1847/09/06
Hay, Ellen	64	Virgilia	Liverpool	England	1847/09/22
Hay, George	10	Araminta	Liverpool	England	between June 20 and 26, 1847
Hay, James		Broom	Liverpool	England	
Hay, John	20	Broom	Liverpool	England	1847/09/27
Hay, Peter	17	Broom	Liverpool	England	1847/09/30
Hayes, Ann	22	John Munn	Liverpool	England	between August 8 and 14, 1847
Hayes, Charles	82	Jessie	Limerick	Ireland	between September 12 and 18, 1847
Hayes, Charlotte	48				1847/09/15
Hayes, Daniel	35	Jessie	Limerick	Ireland	between August 8 and 14, 1847
Hayes, John	23	John Munn	Liverpool	England	between September 5 and 11, 1847
Hayes, John	14	Jessie	Limerick	Ireland	between August 8 and 14, 1847
Hayes, John	23	Triton	Liverpool	England	between August 8 and 14, 1847
Hayes, Joseph	15	Bridgetown	Liverpool	England	between September 5 and 11, 1847

The emigrants

Name	Age	Vessel	Port	Country	Date of death
Hayes, Margaret	23	Scotland	Cork	Ireland	between May 23 and 29, 1847
Hayes, Mary	18	Avon	Cork	Ireland	between August 8 and 14, 1847
Hayes, Mary	12	Jessie	Limerick	Ireland	1847/08/14
Hayes, Nancy	50	John Munn	Liverpool	England	between September 5 and 11, 1847
Hayes, Patrick	22	Agnes	Cork	Ireland	between June 6 and 12, 1847
Hayes, Patrick	14	Agnes	Cork	Ireland	between June 6 and 12, 1847
Hayes, Peter	65	John Munn	Liverpool	England	between August 8 and 14, 1847
Hayes, Sarah		Jessie	Limerick	Ireland	
Hayes, William	41	Jessie	Limerick	Ireland	1847/08/30
Hazelton, Dora	19	Ganges	Liverpool	England	between September 26 and October 2, 1847
Hazelton, Margaret	20	Ganges	Liverpool	England	1847/09/28
Hazelton, Margaret	45	Ganges	Liverpool	England	between August 22 and 28, 1847
Hazelton, Robert	9 months	Rankin	Liverpool	England	between June 13 and 19, 1847
Healy, Catherine	60	Asia	Cork	Ireland	between August 1 and 7, 1847
Healy, Edward	30	Jessie	Cork	Ireland	between July 18 and 24, 1847
Healy, Margaret	19	Agnes King	Limerick	Ireland	between July 11 and 17, 1847
Healy, Mary	16	Erin's Queen	Liverpool	England	between July 25 and 31, 1847
Healy, Michael	22	Durham	Liverpool	England	between September 26 and October 2, 1847
Healy, William	42	Larch	Sligo	Ireland	between August 15 and 21, 1847
Heaney, Michael	40	Odessa	Dublin	Ireland	between August 8 and 14, 1847
Hearn, David	25	Avon	Cork	Ireland	between September 12 and 18, 1847
Heavey, William	18	Ceylon	New York	USA	between July 11 and 17, 1847
Heffernan, Eliza	5	Lady Campbell	Dublin	Ireland	between September 5 and 11, 1847
Heffernan, Mary	38	Lady Campbell	Dublin	Ireland	between August 22 and 28, 1847
Heffernan, Robert	5	Lady Campbell	Dublin	Ireland	between September 5 and 11, 1847
Heffernan, Thomas	38	Lady Campbell	Dublin	Ireland	between August 29 and September 4, 1847
Heffernan, Thomas	6	John Munn	Liverpool	England	between August 15 and 21, 1847
Heffron, Mary	27	Rose	Liverpool	England	between July 4 and 10, 1847
Hegarty, Jeremiah	28	Dominica	Cork	Ireland	between June 13 and 19, 1847
Hegarty, Margaret	45	Ganges	Liverpool	England	1847/08/27
Hegarty, Stephen		Ann	Liverpool	England	
Henaghan, Daniel	2	Sir Henry Pottinger	Cork	Ireland	between August 1 and 7, 1847
Hendrick, Mary	20	Bee	Cork	Ireland	between May 29 and June 5, 1847
Hennelly, Mary	40	Araminta	Liverpool	England	between June 20 and 26, 1847
Hennessy, Isaac	58	Naparina	Dublin	Ireland	between August 22 and 28, 1847
Hennessy, Judith	22	Naparina	Dublin	Ireland	between September 5 and 11, 1847
Hennessy, Michael	35	Covenanter	Cork	Ireland	between August 22 and 28, 1847
Hennessy, Richard	14	Tottenham	Youghal	Ireland	between May 23 and 29, 1847
Hennessy, Sarah	13	Progress	New Ross	Ireland	between July 11 and 17, 1847
Henry, Ann	18	Bridgetown	Liverpool	England	1847/08/27
Henry, Anny Holmes		Rosalinda	Belfast	Ireland	1847/08/04
Henry, Catherine	20	Greenock	Liverpool	England	between August 8 and 14, 1847
Henry, Edward	30	George	Liverpool	England	between June 6 and 12, 1847
Henry, James	2	Ajax	Liverpool	England	1847/05/29
Henry, Nancy	18	Bridgetown	Liverpool	England	between August 22 and 28, 1847
Henry, Thomas	16	Marchioness of Breadalbane	Sligo	Ireland	between August 15 and 21, 1847
Herlihy, John	26	Triton	Liverpool	England	between August 1 and 7, 1847
Heron, Mary	18	Aberdeen	Liverpool	England	between June 13 and 19, 1847
Heron, Patrick	14	George	Liverpool	England	between June 20 and 26, 1847
Heron, Thomas	26	John Francis	Cork	Ireland	between June 20 and 26, 1847
Hess, Henreick	40	Sceptre	Hamburg	Germany	1847/06/14
Hester, Bridget	32	Lord Sandon	Cork	Ireland	between July 4 and 10, 1847
Hester, Thomas	4	Lady Milton	Liverpool	England	between June 27 and July 3, 1847
Hetherington, Ann	8 months	John Francis	Cork	Ireland	between June 13 and 19, 1847
Hetherington, Hugh	40	Dykes	Sligo	Ireland	1847/10/07
Hetherington, James	49	Wandsworth	Dublin	Ireland	between May 29 and June 5, 1847
Hetherington, Jane	30	Dykes	Sligo	Ireland	1847/06/16
Hetherington, John	28	Argo	Liverpool	England	between June 13 and 19, 1847
Hetherington, William	14	Wandsworth	Dublin	Ireland	between May 23 and 29, 1847
Hewson, John	27	Odessa	Dublin	Ireland	1847/08/22
Hickey, Bridget	40	Julius Caesar	Liverpool	England	between September 19 and 25, 1847
Hickey, David	48	Maria Somes	Cork	Ireland	between September 12 and 18, 1847
Hickey, Elizabeth	5	Maria Somes	Cork	Ireland	between October 3 and 9, 1847
Hickey, James	50	Julius Caesar	Liverpool	England	between September 19 and 25, 1847
Hickey, James	9 months	Maria Somes	Cork	Ireland	between September 12 and 18, 1847
Hickey, Jeremiah	14	Julius Caesar	Liverpool	England	between September 12 and 18, 1847
Hickey, John	9	Julius Caesar	Liverpool	England	between September 19 and 25, 1847
Hickey, Margaret	3	Maria Somes	Cork	Ireland	between September 26 and October 2, 1847
Hickey, Mary	3	Maria Somes	Cork	Ireland	between September 5 and 11, 1847
Hickey, Mary	20	Scotland	Cork	Ireland	between June 20 and 26, 1847
Hickey, Michael	26	Jessie	Limerick	Ireland	between July 25 and 31, 1847
Higgins, Henry	25	Greenock	Liverpool	England	between August 8 and 14, 1847
Higgins, Martha	63	Progress	New Ross	Ireland	between July 11 and 17, 1847
Higgins, Matthew	30	Yorkshire Lass	Killala	Ireland	between July 25 and 31, 1847
Higgins, Patrick	29	George	Liverpool	England	between July 25 and 31, 1847
Higgins, Peter	28	Ann	Liverpool	England	between July 11 and 17, 1847
Higgins, Thomas	12	Naomi	Liverpool	England	between August 15 and 21, 1847
Higginson, Martha	24	Yorkshire	Liverpool	England	between September 12 and 18, 1847
Hill, Francis	20	John Munn	Liverpool	England	1847/09/02

Lists of people who died and were buried on Grosse Île, in 1847

Name	Age	Vessel	Port	Country	Date of death
Hilliard, Johanna	30				between August 22 and 28, 1847
Hinchy, ___		Lotus	Liverpool	England	1847/06/14
Hinds, Ann	2	Emigrant	Liverpool	England	between September 26 and October 2, 1847
Hinunane, Ellen	22	Sobraon	Liverpool	England	between July 4 and 10, 1847
Hoban, Catherine	2	Argo	Liverpool	England	between August 15 and 21, 1847
Hoban, Mary	25	Covenanter	Cork	Ireland	between August 8 and 14, 1847
Hoban, Mary	30	Naparina	Dublin	Ireland	between August 15 and 21, 1847
Hobbs, Patrick	5	Rose	Liverpool	England	between June 20 and 26, 1847
Hodgins, Mary	40	Odessa	Dublin	Ireland	between August 1 and 7, 1847
Hodgins, Sarah	17	Odessa	Dublin	Ireland	1847/09/04
Hogan, Bridget	5	Rose	Liverpool	England	between July 4 and 10, 1847
Hogan, Catherine	22	Jessie	Limerick	Ireland	between August 15 and 21, 1847
Hogan, Charles	50	Bridgetown	Liverpool	England	between August 22 and 28, 1847
Hogan, Edmund	9	Jessie	Cork	Ireland	between July 25 and 31, 1847
Hogan, Ellen	40	Blenheim	Cork	Ireland	between August 1 and 7, 1847
Hogan, Mary	7	Rose	Liverpool	England	between July 11 and 17, 1847
Hogan, Mary	21	Virginius	Liverpool	England	between October 17 and 23, 1847
Hogan, Patrick	14	Lillias	Dublin	Ireland	between August 8 and 14, 1847
Hogan, Patrick	24	Dykes	Sligo	Ireland	between June 20 and 26, 1847
Holden, Catherine	44	Royal Adelaide	Killala	Ireland	between August 15 and 21, 1847
Holden, Eliza	10	Coromandel	Dublin	Ireland	between September 19 and 25, 1847
Holden, Samuel	38	Coromandel	Dublin	Ireland	between September 5 and 11, 1847
Holland, Mary	40	Agnes	Cork	Ireland	between July 4 and 10, 1847
Holland, Patrick	30	John Munn	Liverpool	England	between August 15 and 21, 1847
Holleran, James	25	Junior	Liverpool	England	between August 1 and 7, 1847
Holleran, Mary	10	Lively	Cork	Ireland	between August 8 and 14, 1847
Hollinger, Thomas	30	Lord Seaton	Belfast	Ireland	1847/05/22
Hollingsworth, Henry	18	Wm S. Hamilton	New Ross	Ireland	between August 1 and 7, 1847
Hollingsworth, John	14	Wm S. Hamilton	New Ross	Ireland	between July 18 and 24, 1847
Hollingsworth, Thomas	9	Wm S. Hamilton	New Ross	Ireland	between August 1 and 7, 1847
Holly, Margaret		Ellen Simpson	Limerick	Ireland	
Holmes, Cetty	33	Odessa	Dublin	Ireland	between August 8 and 14, 1847
Holmes, Joseph	5	Virginius	Liverpool	England	between August 1 and 7, 1847
Holmes, Mary	50	John Munn	Liverpool	England	between August 29 and September 4, 1847
Hood, Thomas	21	Herald	Dublin	Ireland	between July 11 and 17, 1847
Hooney, Mary	10	George	Liverpool	England	between June 13 and 19, 1847
Hooper, Ann	10	Wandsworth	Dublin	Ireland	1847/05/21
Hooper, Theresa	5	Wandsworth	Dublin	Ireland	1847/05/21
Hooper, William	45	Scotland	Cork	Ireland	between May 23 and 29, 1847
Hopkins, Ann	15	Free Trader	Liverpool	England	between August 15 and 21, 1847
Hopkins, Anthony	30	Sisters	Liverpool	England	between June 27 and July 3, 1847
Hopkins, Brien	20	Virginius	Liverpool	England	between August 8 and 14, 1847
Hopkins, Mary	24	Wandsworth	Dublin	Ireland	between May 23 and 29, 1847
Hopkins, Patrick	45	Argo	Liverpool	England	between June 13 and 19, 1847
Hopkins, Thomas	15	Congress	Sligo	Ireland	between June 13 and 19, 1847
Hopper, Bridget	40	Wanderer			between June 13 and 19, 1847
Horan, Bridget	7	James Moran	Liverpool	England	between August 22 and 28, 1847
Horan, Mary	18	Aberdeen	Liverpool	England	between June 13 and 19, 1847
Horan, Mary	20	Huron	Belfast	Ireland	between July 25 and 31, 1847
Horan, Mary	22	Yorkshire	Liverpool	England	between August 29 and September 4, 1847
Horan, Murphy	25	Roseanna	Cork	Ireland	between July 11 and 17, 1847
Horan, Thomas	53	Jessie	Cork	Ireland	between July 18 and 24, 1847
Horne, Ann	13	George	Liverpool	England	between June 27 and July 3, 1847
Horne, Bridget	45	George	Liverpool	England	between June 6 and 12, 1847
Horner, Samuel	19	John Bolton	Liverpool	England	between June 13 and 19, 1847
Horner, William	45	Rose	Liverpool	England	between June 20 and 26, 1847
Horrigan, Bridget	20	Agnes	Cork	Ireland	between June 13 and 19, 1847
Horrigan, Ellen	60	John Francis	Cork	Ireland	between May 23 and 29, 1847
Horrigan, Esther	34	Lord Seaton	Belfast	Ireland	between May 29 and June 5, 1847
Horrigan, James	30	Avon	Cork	Ireland	between August 8 and 14, 1847
Horrigan, Jeremiah	60	John Francis	Cork	Ireland	between May 23 and 29, 1847
Horrigan, John	3	Gilmour	Cork	Ireland	between June 13 and 19, 1847
Horrigan, John	4	Lord Seaton	Belfast	Ireland	between May 23 and 29, 1847
Horrigan, Mary	3	Free Briton	Cork	Ireland	between July 4 and 10, 1847
Houlihan, Bridget	2	Manchester	Liverpool	England	between August 22 and 28, 1847
Houlihan, John	1	Manchester	Liverpool	England	between July 25 and 31, 1847
Hourihane, Kerne	18	Sir Henry Pottinger	Cork	Ireland	between August 8 and 14, 1847
Howard, Catherine	40	William Pirie	Belfast	Ireland	between June 20 and 26, 1847
Howard, Thomas	55	Julius Caesar	Liverpool	England	1847/09/12
Howell, Thomas	15	Larch	Sligo	Ireland	between September 12 and 18, 1847
Howley, Catherine		Virginius	Liverpool	England	
Howley, Edward	20	Leander	Londonderry	Ireland	between August 15 and 21, 1847
Howley, John	40	John Munn	Liverpool	England	between September 12 and 18, 1847
Howley, Martin	45	Marinus	Dublin	Ireland	between August 15 and 21, 1847
Howley, Mary	14	John Munn	Liverpool	England	between August 8 and 14, 1847
Howlin, James	40	Royal Adelaide	Killala	Ireland	between August 15 and 21, 1847
Hoy, Daniel	25	Naomi	Liverpool	England	between August 8 and 14, 1847

The Emigrants

Name	Age	Vessel	Port	Country	Date of death
Hoy, Margaret	5	Progress	New Ross	Ireland	between July 4 and 10, 1847
Hoy, Phoeby	2	Numa	Sligo	Ireland	between August 1 and 7, 1847
Hoy, William	38	Araminta	Liverpool	England	between July 11 and 17, 1847
Hoyne, Ellen	36	Alert	Waterford	Ireland	between July 25 and 31, 1847
Hoyne, Ellen	29	Virginius	Liverpool	England	between August 8 and 14, 1847
Hoyne, James	12	Rankin	Liverpool	England	between July 25 and 31, 1847
Hughes, Bridget	6	Royal Adelaide	Killala	Ireland	between September 5 and 11, 1847
Hughes, Bridget	3	Colonist	New Ross	Ireland	between August 29 and September 4, 1847
Hughes, Catherine	1	Free Trader	Liverpool	England	between August 15 and 21, 1847
Hughes, Elizabeth	2	Rankin	Liverpool	England	between June 27 and July 3, 1847
Hughes, James	5	Clarendon	Liverpool	England	between June 6 and 12, 1847
Hughes, John	12	Champion	Liverpool	England	between August 29 and September 4, 1847
Hughes, Margaret	3	Bridgetown	Liverpool	England	between September 12 and 18, 1847
Hughes, Maria	25	Colonist	New Ross	Ireland	between September 19 and 25, 1847
Hughes, Martin	1 year & 6 months	Marinus	Dublin	Ireland	between August 15 and 21, 1847
Hughes, Mary	38	Champion	Liverpool	England	between September 5 and 11, 1847
Hughes, Mary	13	Sarah	Liverpool	England	between July 18 and 24, 1847
Hughes, Thomas	50	Champion	Liverpool	England	between August 29 and September 4, 1847
Hughes, Thomas	20	Clarendon	Liverpool	England	between June 6 and 12, 1847
Hughey, Ellen	18	Bee	Cork	Ireland	between June 13 and 19, 1847
Hughey, Jeremiah		Bee	Cork	Ireland	
Humphreys, Eliza	24	Lord Seaton	Belfast	Ireland	1847/06/29
Humphreys, Mary Ann	1 year & 3 months	Lord Seaton	Belfast	Ireland	1847/06/19
Hungerford, Frances Jane	1 year & 1 month				1847/05/20
Hunter, Ann	28	Julius Caesar	Liverpool	England	1847/09/13
Hunter, Clara	44	William Pirie	Belfast	Ireland	1847/07/10
Hunter, Martha J.					
Hurley, Catherine	28	Agnes	Cork	Ireland	between June 13 and 19, 1847
Hurley, Daniel	30	Larch	Sligo	Ireland	between August 15 and 21, 1847
Hurley, Ellen	35	Sisters	Liverpool	England	between June 20 and 26, 1847
Hurley, James	5 years & 6 months	Erin's Queen	Liverpool	England	between July 18 and 24, 1847
Hurley, John	13	Agnes	Cork	Ireland	between June 6 and 12, 1847
Hurley, Mary	7	Try Again	Cork	Ireland	between June 6 and 12, 1847
Hurley, Michael	3	John Francis	Cork	Ireland	between May 29 and June 5, 1847
Hurley, Michael	20	Triton	Liverpool	England	between July 25 and 31, 1847
Hurley, Patrick	1	John Francis	Cork	Ireland	between May 29 and June 5, 1847
Hurley, Timothy	26	Scotland	Cork	Ireland	between June 6 and 12, 1847
Hyland, Margaret	36	Emigrant	Liverpool	England	between October 3 and 9, 1847
Hyland, Martin		Emigrant	Liverpool	England	
Hynes, ___					
Hynes, Bridget	8	Rankin	Liverpool	England	between July 11 and 17, 1847
Hynes, Catherine	3	Covenanter	Cork	Ireland	between August 8 and 14, 1847
Hynes, Denis	30	Huron	Belfast	Ireland	between August 8 and 14, 1847
Hynes, Mary	40	Triton	Liverpool	England	between July 25 and 31, 1847
Igoe, Daniel	19	Naomi	Liverpool	England	between August 22 and 28, 1847
Igoe, John	15	Naomi	Liverpool	England	between August 15 and 21, 1847
Ireland, Mary Rain	46	Odessa	Dublin	Ireland	1847/08/15
Irvine, Elizabeth Reid					1847/08/09
Irvine, John	53	John and Robert	Liverpool	England	between August 15 and 21, 1847
Irvine, John	43	John and Robert	Liverpool	England	1847/08/16
Irwin, Thomas	24	Scotland	Cork	Ireland	between July 25 and 31, 1847
Irwin, William	23	John and Robert	Liverpool	England	1847/08/23
Ivory, John	40	John Francis	Cork	Ireland	between June 6 and 12, 1847
Ivory, Lawrence	3	John Francis	Cork	Ireland	between June 20 and 26, 1847
Jackson, Ann					
Jackson, Edward	43	Triton	Liverpool	England	1847/07/21
Jackson, Elizabeth	40	Junior	Liverpool	England	between July 4 and 10, 1847
Jackson, John	24	Constitution	Belfast	Ireland	between June 6 and 12, 1847
Jackson, Thomas Edward	1 year & 2 months	Constitution	Belfast	Ireland	1847/05/28
Jacobs, W.	26	Wandsworth	Dublin	Ireland	between May 23 and 29, 1847
James, Charles	28	Marchioness of Abercorn	Londonderry	Ireland	between August 1 and 7, 1847
Jameson, Eliza Ann	12	Lord Seaton	Belfast	Ireland	1847/06/30
Jay, Joseph	2 months				1847/05/22
Jeffries, Cornelius		Free Trader	Liverpool	England	
Jenkins, David		Greenock	Liverpool	England	
Jenkins, Edward	20	Jessie	Cork	Ireland	between August 1 and 7, 1847
Jennings, Austin	45	George	Liverpool	England	between June 6 and 12, 1847
Jennings, Margaret	40	Jane Avery	Dublin	Ireland	between June 27 and July 3, 1847
Jennings, Mary	12	George	Liverpool	England	between June 6 and 12, 1847
Jennings, Matthew	3 years & 6 months	Agnes	Cork	Ireland	between June 13 and 19, 1847
Jewel, Sarah	40	Argo	Liverpool	England	1847/06/18
Johnson, James	6	Sir Henry Pottinger	Belfast	Ireland	1847/10/01
Johnson, James	40	Lady Gordon	Belfast	Ireland	1847/06/28
Johnson, Joseph	2	Superior	Londonderry	Ireland	between September 12 and 18, 1847
Johnson, Margaret	20	Yorkshire	Liverpool	England	1847/09/24
Johnston, ___	30	Goliah	Liverpool	England	between July 18 and 24, 1847
Johnston, Alexander	5	Superior	Londonderry	Ireland	1847/09/26
Johnston, Eliza	27	Leander	Londonderry	Ireland	between October 10 and 16, 1847
Johnston, Isabella	1	Superior	Londonderry	Ireland	1847/09/16
Johnston, J.					
Johnston, James					
Johnston, James					
Johnston, James	6	Superior	Londonderry	Ireland	between September 26 and October 2, 1847
Johnston, Lilas	19	Superior	Londonderry	Ireland	1847/09/17
Johnston, Margaret	40	Superior	Londonderry	Ireland	between September 19 and 25, 1847

Lists of people who died and were buried on Grosse Île, in 1847

Name	Age	Vessel	Port	Country	Date of death
Johnston, Mary	40	Superior	Londonderry	Ireland	1847/09/26
Johnston, Mary	50	Superior	Londonderry	Ireland	between September 26 and October 2, 1847
Johnston, Thomas	22	Wolfville	Sligo	Ireland	between August 1 and 7, 1847
Johnston, William	25	John Munn	Liverpool	England	between August 29 and September 4, 1847
Jones, Arthur	1	Bridgetown	Liverpool	England	between August 22 and 28, 1847
Jones, David	3	Bridgetown	Liverpool	England	1847/09/13
Jones, Elizabeth	1	Argo	Liverpool	England	1847/05/27
Jones, Evan	6	Bridgetown	Liverpool	England	1847/08/31
Jones, Grace	30	Goliah	Liverpool	England	1847/07/14
Jones, John	40	Goliah	Liverpool	England	between July 25 and 31, 1847
Jones, Mary A.	1	Colonist	New Ross	Ireland	between August 22 and 28, 1847
Jones, William	18	Sir Henry Pottinger	Belfast	Ireland	1847/09/12
Jordan, Bridget	6	Wandsworth	Dublin	Ireland	between May 23 and 29, 1847
Jordan, James	4	Wandsworth	Dublin	Ireland	between May 23 and 29, 1847
Jordan, John	16	Wandsworth	Dublin	Ireland	between May 23 and 29, 1847
Jordan, John	12	Ellen	Sligo	Ireland	between July 11 and 17, 1847
Jordan, Maria	11	Wandsworth	Dublin	Ireland	between May 23 and 29, 1847
Jordan, Patrick	8	Wandsworth	Dublin	Ireland	1847/05/21
Joyce, J.					
Judge, Bridget	30	Yorkshire Lass	Killala	Ireland	between July 11 and 17, 1847
Judge, Margaret	2	Rankin	Liverpool	England	between August 8 and 14, 1847
Judge, Morris	50	Clarendon	Liverpool	England	between July 4 and 10, 1847
K___, B___					
K___, D___					
K___, J___					
K___, W___					
Kane, ___					
Kane, Catherine	7	Marinus	Dublin	Ireland	between October 10 and 16, 1847
Kane, Ellen	4				1847/05/15
Kane, Mary	18	Sarah	Liverpool	England	between July 25 and 31, 1847
Kastle, John	4	Argo	Liverpool	England	1847/06/01
Kay, George	36	John Jardine	Liverpool	England	between July 25 and 31, 1847
Keady, Elizabeth	22	Agnes	Cork	Ireland	between June 6 and 12, 1847
Keally, Johanna	60	Asia	Cork	Ireland	between August 1 and 7, 1847
Keally, Michael	24	Avon	Cork	Ireland	between July 25 and 31, 1847
Kean, Alexander	35	Triton	Liverpool	England	between July 11 and 17, 1847
Kean, Denis	35	Erin's Queen	Liverpool	England	between August 15 and 21, 1847
Keane, Ann	8	Marinus	Dublin	Ireland	between September 26 and October 2, 1847
Keane, Bridget	40	Sarah	Liverpool	England	between August 8 and 14, 1847
Keane, Bridget	40	Marinus	Dublin	Ireland	between August 22 and 28, 1847
Keane, Christopher	4	Marinus	Dublin	Ireland	between August 29 and September 4, 1847
Keane, Edward	1	Blonde	Liverpool	England	between June 27 and July 3, 1847
Keane, Ellen	4	Syria	Liverpool	England	between May 8 and 15, 1847
Keane, Ellen	29	Blonde	Liverpool	England	between June 27 and July 3, 1847
Keane, John	24	Bee	Cork	Ireland	between June 20 and 26, 1847
Keane, John	55	Agnes	Cork	Ireland	between June 13 and 19, 1847
Keane, Margaret	2	Marinus	Dublin	Ireland	between August 29 and September 4, 1847
Keane, Mary	18	Avon	Cork	Ireland	between August 8 and 14, 1847
Keane, Patrick	16	Larch	Sligo	Ireland	between August 15 and 21, 1847
Keane, Patrick	22	John and Robert	Liverpool	England	between August 29 and September 4, 1847
Kearney, Alexander	2	Eliza Caroline	Liverpool	England	between June 13 and 19, 1847
Kearney, Edward	2	Jessie	Cork	Ireland	between July 18 and 24, 1847
Kearney, James	4	Covenanter	Cork	Ireland	between August 15 and 21, 1847
Kearney, Thomas	25	Gilmour	Cork	Ireland	between July 11 and 17, 1847
Kearney, William	26	Triton	Liverpool	England	between July 25 and 31, 1847
Kearns, Catherine	9	Greenock	Liverpool	England	between August 1 and 7, 1847
Kearns, Francis	5	Argo	Liverpool	England	between August 8 and 14, 1847
Kearns, James	24	Larch	Sligo	Ireland	between August 15 and 21, 1847
Keating, Thomas	1	John Munn	Liverpool	England	between August 29 and September 4, 1847
Keefe, Catherine	25	Despatch	Waterford	Ireland	between June 20 and 26, 1847
Keefe, David	25	Wakefield	Cork	Ireland	between July 11 and 17, 1847
Keefe, David	30	Rodeng	Cork	Ireland	between July 4 and 10, 1847
Keegan, A.	40	Pacha	Cork	Ireland	between June 13 and 19, 1847
Keegan, Ann	40	Bridgetown	Liverpool	England	between September 5 and 11, 1847
Keegan, Ann	2	Bridgetown	Liverpool	England	between September 5 and 11, 1847
Keegan, Catherine	12	Bridgetown	Liverpool	England	between August 22 and 28, 1847
Keegan, Catherine	45	Bridgetown	Liverpool	England	between September 5 and 11, 1847
Keegan, Catherine	13	Bridgetown	Liverpool	England	between August 29 and September 4, 1847
Keegan, Edward	22	Emigrant	Liverpool	England	between September 26 and October 2, 1847
Keegan, Jeremiah	17	Bridgetown	Liverpool	England	between September 5 and 11, 1847
Keegan, Patrick	7	Bridgetown	Liverpool	England	between September 12 and 18, 1847
Keegan, Richard	14	Bridgetown	Liverpool	England	between October 3 and 9, 1847
Keenan, Bridget	7	Saguenay	Cork	Ireland	between August 29 and September 4, 1847
Keenan, Catherine	6	Larch	Sligo	Ireland	between August 15 and 21, 1847
Keenan, James	50	John Munn	Liverpool	England	between August 15 and 21, 1847
Keenan, Margaret	20	Marinus	Dublin	Ireland	between August 29 and September 4, 1847

THE EMIGRANTS

Name	Age	Vessel	Port	Country	Date of death
Keenan, Mary	18	Ayrshire	Newry	Ireland	between August 29 and September 4, 1847
Keenan, Peter	12	Superior	Londonderry	Ireland	between October 3 and 9, 1847
Kelleher, Bridget	40	Superior	Londonderry	Ireland	between September 19 and 25, 1847
Kelleher, Ellen	30	Saguenay	Cork	Ireland	between September 19 and 25, 1847
Kelleher, James	40	Sir Henry Pottinger	Belfast	Ireland	between August 29 and September 4, 1847
Kelleher, Jeremiah	40	Argo	Liverpool	England	between August 15 and 21, 1847
Kelleher, Mary	18	Saguenay	Cork	Ireland	between October 3 and 9, 1847
Kelly, Andrew	22	John Bolton	Liverpool	England	between August 1 and 7, 1847
Kelly, Ann	20	Aberdeen	Liverpool	England	between June 20 and 26, 1847
Kelly, Ann	6	Wolfville	Sligo	Ireland	between May 29 and June 5, 1847
Kelly, Bridget	70	Dunbrody	New Ross	Ireland	between July 18 and 24, 1847
Kelly, Edward	30	Erin's Queen	Liverpool	England	between July 18 and 24, 1847
Kelly, Edward	33	Free Trader	Liverpool	England	between August 15 and 21, 1847
Kelly, Eliza	3	John Munn	Liverpool	England	between August 22 and 28, 1847
Kelly, Eliza	9	Triton	Liverpool	England	between August 15 and 21, 1847
Kelly, James	30	Triton	Liverpool	England	between August 8 and 14, 1847
Kelly, John	50	Free Trader	Liverpool	England	between August 22 and 28, 1847
Kelly, John	35	George	Liverpool	England	between June 13 and 19, 1847
Kelly, John	20	Margaret	New Ross	Ireland	between June 27 and July 3, 1847
Kelly, John	23	Wakefield	Cork	Ireland	between August 22 and 28, 1847
Kelly, John	36	Wolfville	Sligo	Ireland	between May 29 and June 5, 1847
Kelly, Margaret	20	Rosalinda	Belfast	Ireland	between August 22 and 28, 1847
Kelly, Margaret	7	Free Trader	Liverpool	England	between August 22 and 28, 1847
Kelly, Margaret	20	Sarah	Liverpool	England	between July 25 and 31, 1847
Kelly, Mary	20	Covenanter	Cork	Ireland	between August 8 and 14, 1847
Kelly, Mary	50	Triton	Liverpool	England	between July 18 and 24, 1847
Kelly, Mary	33				between August 15 and 21, 1847
Kelly, Mary	2	Greenock	Liverpool	England	between August 1 and 7, 1847
Kelly, Mary	13	Sir Henry Pottinger	Cork	Ireland	between August 15 and 21, 1847
Kelly, Mary	18	Virginius	Liverpool	England	between August 8 and 14, 1847
Kelly, Mary	28	Primrose	Limerick	Ireland	between June 20 and 26, 1847
Kelly, Mary	30	Emily	Cork	Ireland	between July 4 and 10, 1847
Kelly, Mary	30	Rankin	Liverpool	England	between July 4 and 10, 1847
Kelly, Mary	40	Naomi	Liverpool	England	between August 8 and 14, 1847
Kelly, Patrick	21	Numa	Sligo	Ireland	between August 15 and 21, 1847
Kelly, Patrick	25	John Munn	Liverpool	England	between August 8 and 14, 1847
Kelly, Patrick	20	Virginius	Liverpool	England	between August 8 and 14, 1847
Kelly, Patrick	37	Triton	Liverpool	England	between August 22 and 28, 1847
Kelly, Richard	20	Ganges	Liverpool	England	between September 5 and 11, 1847
Kelly, Sarah A.	24	Gilmour	Cork	Ireland	between June 6 and 12, 1847
Kelly, Sylvia	24	Gilmour	Cork	Ireland	between June 6 and 12, 1847
Kelly, Thomas	28	Eliza Caroline	Liverpool	England	between July 25 and 31, 1847
Kelly, Thomas	50	Rosalinda	Belfast	Ireland	between September 26 and October 2, 1847
Kelly, Thomas	22	Odessa	Dublin	Ireland	between August 8 and 14, 1847
Kelly, William	63	Numa	Sligo	Ireland	between August 1 and 7, 1847
Kelly, William	18	Rose	Liverpool	England	between June 20 and 26, 1847
Kenna, Mary	25	Jessie	Cork	Ireland	between July 18 and 24, 1847
Kenna, Michael	26	Jessie	Cork	Ireland	between July 11 and 17, 1847
Kennedy, ___		Sisters	Liverpool	England	
Kennedy, Catherine	25	Unicorn	Londonderry	Ireland	between August 29 and September 4, 1847
Kennedy, Denis	30	John Munn	Liverpool	England	between August 8 and 14, 1847
Kennedy, Ellen	20	Corea	Liverpool	England	between August 29 and September 4, 1847
Kennedy, Honora	23	Wakefield	Cork	Ireland	between August 15 and 21, 1847
Kennedy, Hugh	60	Bridgetown	Liverpool	England	between September 26 and October 2, 1847
Kennedy, Jane	37	Bridgetown	Liverpool	England	between September 12 and 18, 1847
Kennedy, Johanna	27	Bridgetown	Liverpool	England	between September 5 and 11, 1847
Kennedy, John	40	Sir Robert Peel	Liverpool	England	between September 26 and October 2, 1847
Kennedy, John	22	Bridgetown	Liverpool	England	between September 12 and 18, 1847
Kennedy, Margaret	3	Lord Seaton	Belfast	Ireland	1847/05/28
Kennedy, Margaret	1	Nerio	Limerick	Ireland	between September 26 and October 2, 1847
Kennedy, Margaret	38	Sir Robert Peel	Liverpool	England	between September 19 and 25, 1847
Kennedy, Mary	45	Solway	New Ross	Ireland	between July 18 and 24, 1847
Kennedy, Mary	40	Aberdeen	Liverpool	England	between June 13 and 19, 1847
Kennedy, Mary	35	Ganges	Liverpool	England	between August 29 and September 4, 1847
Kennedy, Nelly	12	Bridgetown	Liverpool	England	between September 5 and 11, 1847
Kennedy, Patrick	11	Allan Kerr	Sligo	Ireland	between August 1 and 7, 1847
Kennedy, Sarah	40	Aberdeen	Liverpool	England	between June 13 and 19, 1847
Kennedy, Thomas	22	Wallace	Liverpool	England	between June 6 and 12, 1847
Kennelly, Noreen	7 months	Scotland	Cork	Ireland	between May 29 and June 5, 1847
Kennelly, William	3	Yorkshire Lass	Killala	Ireland	between August 1 and 7, 1847
Kenny, Ann	26	Trade	Waterford	Ireland	between August 22 and 28, 1847
Kenny, Edward	20	Avon	Cork	Ireland	between July 25 and 31, 1847

Lists of people who died and were buried on Grosse Île, in 1847

Name	Age	Vessel	Port	Country	Date of death
Kenny, James	60	Araminta	Liverpool	England	between June 13 and 19, 1847
Kenny, John	26	Larch	Sligo	Ireland	between September 5 and 11, 1847
Kenny, Margaret	2	Trade	Waterford	Ireland	between August 1 and 7, 1847
Kenny, Mary	38	Araminta	Liverpool	England	between June 13 and 19, 1847
Kenny, Mary	20	Free Trader	Liverpool	England	between August 22 and 28, 1847
Kenny, Mary	12	Bridgetown	Liverpool	England	between September 5 and 11, 1847
Kent, John	15	Triton	Liverpool	England	between July 25 and 31, 1847
Kent, Noreen	32	Blenheim	Cork	Ireland	between August 1 and 7, 1847
Kent, Noreen	32	Syria	Liverpool	England	between August 8 and 14, 1847
Kent, Patrick	27	Triton	Liverpool	England	between July 25 and 31, 1847
Kent, Peter	37	Frankfield	Liverpool	England	between September 5 and 11, 1847
Kent, William	14	Triton	Liverpool	England	between August 1 and 7, 1847
Kenyon, Michael	12	Avon	Cork	Ireland	between July 25 and 31, 1847
Keogh, Catherine	3	Virginius	Liverpool	England	between October 10 and 16, 1847
Keogh, Patrick	30	Avon	Cork	Ireland	between August 22 and 28, 1847
Kernan, James		Erin's Queen	Liverpool	England	
Kerr, Marianne	42	Sarah	Liverpool	England	1847/08/20
Kerr, Mary A.	42	Yorkshire	Liverpool	England	between August 15 and 21, 1847
Kerr, Robert		Sisters	Liverpool	England	1847/06/07
Kerr, Samuel	50	Sisters	Liverpool	England	1847/06/04
Kettle, Thomas	20	Free Trader	Liverpool	England	1847/08/20
Kettly, Thomas	20	Saguenay	Cork	Ireland	between August 15 and 21, 1847
Keville, Bridget	17	Larch	Sligo	Ireland	between September 5 and 11, 1847
Keville, Michael	14	Larch	Sligo	Ireland	between August 15 and 21, 1847
Kiernan, Catherine	4	Greenock	Liverpool	England	between August 1 and 7, 1847
Kiernan, Ellen	10	Ann Kenny	Waterford	Ireland	between August 15 and 21, 1847
Kiernan, James	38	Erin's Queen	Liverpool	England	between August 1 and 7, 1847
Kiernan, James	30	Greenock	Liverpool	England	between August 15 and 21, 1847
Kiernan, Margaret	1	Greenock	Liverpool	England	between August 8 and 14, 1847
Kiernan, Mary A.	23	Syria	Liverpool	England	between August 8 and 14, 1847
Kiernan, Rose	32	Erin's Queen	Liverpool	England	between July 18 and 24, 1847
Kiernan, Thomas	7 months	Erin's Queen	Liverpool	England	between July 25 and 31, 1847
Killeen, Timothy	25	Elizabeth	Liverpool	England	between July 4 and 10, 1847
Killeen, Timothy	25	Ajax	Liverpool	England	between July 18 and 24, 1847
Killoran, Bridget	28	Larch	Sligo	Ireland	between August 22 and 28, 1847
Killoran, Robert M.	23	Ganges	Liverpool	England	1847/08/30
Kilmartin, Margaret	21	John Munn	Liverpool	England	between August 8 and 14, 1847
Kilmartin, Mary	19	Numa	Sligo	Ireland	between August 1 and 7, 1847
Kilmartin, Michael	8	Numa	Sligo	Ireland	between August 1 and 7, 1847
Kilmartin, Patrick	16	Numa	Sligo	Ireland	between August 1 and 7, 1847
Kilroy, Denis	29	Covenanter	Cork	Ireland	between September 12 and 18, 1847
King, Daniel	50	Eliza Caroline	Liverpool	England	between June 20 and 26, 1847
King, James	20	Linden	Limerick	Ireland	between July 4 and 10, 1847
King, James	35	Margaret	New Ross	Ireland	between July 4 and 10, 1847
King, John	8	Eliza Caroline	Liverpool	England	between June 6 and 12, 1847
King, Mary	50	Eliza Caroline	Liverpool	England	between July 4 and 10, 1847
Kinsella, William	22	Coromandel	Dublin	Ireland	between July 25 and 31, 1847
Kirby, Elizabeth	48	Erin's Queen	Liverpool	England	1847/09/17
Kirby, James	47	Erin's Queen	Liverpool	England	1847/07/21
Kirby, Jane	7	Erin's Queen	Liverpool	England	1847/08/28
Kirby, Johanna	12	Gilmour	Cork	Ireland	between August 1 and 7, 1847
Kirby, John	4	Covenanter	Cork	Ireland	between August 8 and 14, 1847
Kirby, John	8	Gilmour	Cork	Ireland	between June 20 and 26, 1847
Kirby, Patrick	45	Yorkshire Lass	Killala	Ireland	between August 8 and 14, 1847
Kirby, William	3	Covenanter	Cork	Ireland	between August 8 and 14, 1847
Kirkland, James	1	Erin's Queen	Liverpool	England	between July 25 and 31, 1847
Kirkland, James	33	Larch	Sligo	Ireland	between August 8 and 14, 1847
Kistle, Elizabeth	43	Argo	Liverpool	England	1847/07/01
Knight, Frederick	29	Zealous	London	England	between September 5 and 11, 1847
Kyle, Mary	17	Free Trader	Liverpool	England	between August 8 and 14, 1847
Kyle, William	15	Christiana	Londonderry	Ireland	1847/06/18
L___, W___					
L___, W___					
Lafferty, Mary	40	Herald	Dublin	Ireland	between June 27 and July 3, 1847
Laighin, William	1 month	Caithness-shire	Belfast	Ireland	between May 29 and June 5, 1847
Laird, John	40	Avon	Cork	Ireland	between August 1 and 7, 1847
Lally, Ann	10	John Munn	Liverpool	England	between August 15 and 21, 1847
Lambert, Alice	21	Lady Flora Hastings	Cork	Ireland	between July 4 and 10, 1847
Lambert, Mary	18	Lady Flora Hastings	Cork	Ireland	between July 4 and 10, 1847
Lancaster, John	28	Ajax	Liverpool	England	between July 4 and 10, 1847
Lane, Julia	13	Free Briton	Cork	Ireland	between August 8 and 14, 1847
Lang, Margaret	27	James Moran	Liverpool	England	between August 1 and 7, 1847
Lang, Margaret	40	Free Trader	Liverpool	England	between August 8 and 14, 1847
Lang, Mary Ann	22	John Munn	Liverpool	England	1847/08/31
Lannigan, Patrick	19	Triton	Liverpool	England	between July 18 and 24, 1847
Lannon, Edward	23	Progress	New Ross	Ireland	between July 11 and 17, 1847
Lannon, Thomas	30	Ninian	Limerick	Ireland	between June 13 and 19, 1847
Lanskey, Sally	25	Aberdeen	Liverpool	England	between May 29 and June 5, 1847
Larkin, Ellen					1847/06/28
Larkin, James	50	Greenock	Liverpool	England	between August 1 and 7, 1847
Larkin, Julia	11	Triton	Liverpool	England	between July 25 and 31, 1847

The emigrants

Name	Age	Vessel	Port	Country	Date of death
Laturney, Ellen	34	Goliah	Liverpool	England	between July 18 and 24, 1847
Laughlin, Johanna		Covenanter	Cork	Ireland	
Laughlin, John		Ninian	Limerick	Ireland	
Laughlin, Mary	24	Caithness-shire	Belfast	Ireland	between June 20 and 26, 1847
Lavan, Ann	4	Araminta	Liverpool	England	between June 13 and 19, 1847
Lavan, Ellen	27	Courier			between June 27 and July 3, 1847
Lavan, Ellen	4	Araminta	Liverpool	England	between June 20 and 26, 1847
Lavan, John	40	Araminta	Liverpool	England	between June 13 and 19, 1847
Lavan, Mary	8	Araminta	Liverpool	England	between July 4 and 10, 1847
Lavan, Mary	30	Emigrant	Liverpool	England	between October 3 and 10, 1847
Lavelle, Mary	30	Larch	Sligo	Ireland	between September 19 and 25, 1847
Lavery, George	20	Gilmour	Cork	Ireland	between June 13 and 19, 1847
Lawler, Ellen	16	Lady Campbell	Dublin	Ireland	between August 22 and 28, 1847
Lawless, Ann	18	Pursuit	Liverpool	England	between August 1 and 7, 1847
Lawless, Bridget	45	Superior	Londonderry	Ireland	between September 12 and 18, 1847
Lawless, Rebecca	30	Coromandel	Dublin	Ireland	between July 4 and 10, 1847
Lawlor, James	23	Naparina	Dublin	Ireland	between September 5 and 11, 1847
Lawson, Catherine	60	Agnes	Cork	Ireland	between June 20 and 26, 1847
Lawson, John	19	Agnes	Cork	Ireland	between June 6 and 12, 1847
Leahy, Catherine	3	Wakefield	Cork	Ireland	between July 11 and 17, 1847
Leahy, Michael	30	Wakefield	Cork	Ireland	between July 11 and 17, 1847
Leary, Ann	3	James Moran	Liverpool	England	between July 25 and 31, 1847
Leary, Denis	52	Agnes	Cork	Ireland	between June 13 and 19, 1847
Leary, Dennis	7	Scotland	Cork	Ireland	between July 4 and 10, 1847
Leary, Ellen	3	Scotland	Cork	Ireland	between June 13 and 19, 1847
Leary, Jeremiah	9	Covenanter	Cork	Ireland	between September 12 and 18, 1847
Leary, John	24	John Bolton	Liverpool	England	between May 29 and June 5, 1847
Leary, John	35	Bee	Cork	Ireland	between September 12 and 18, 1847
Leary, John	10	Marinus	Dublin	Ireland	between September 19 and 25, 1847
Leary, Mary	40	Scotland	Cork	Ireland	between May 23 and 29, 1847
Leary, Mary	8	Scotland	Cork	Ireland	between June 6 and 12, 1847
Leary, Mary	31	Marinus	Dublin	Ireland	between August 15 and 21, 1847
Leary, Mary	9	Marinus	Dublin	Ireland	between September 19 and 25, 1847
Leary, Patrick	18	Bee	Cork	Ireland	between May 29 and June 5, 1847
Leary, Patrick	30	Bee	Cork	Ireland	between June 27 and July 3, 1847
Leary, Thomas	5	Minerva	Dublin	Ireland	between September 12 and 18, 1847
Lee, Ann	22	John Munn	Liverpool	England	1847/09/10
Lee, Ann	22	James Moran	Liverpool	England	between September 5 and 11, 1847
Lee, Ann	48	John Munn	Liverpool	England	between September 5 and 11, 1847
Lee, James	24	John Munn	Liverpool	England	between August 8 and 14, 1847
Leech, James	56	Free Trader	Liverpool	England	between September 5 and 11, 1847
Leehan, Margaret	6 months	Broom	Liverpool	England	between August 8 and 14, 1847
Leeson, Bridget	28	Aberdeen	Liverpool	England	between July 4 and 10, 1847
Legge, Edward		Lotus	Liverpool	England	
Leguire, Ann	30				1847/06/12
Lehan, Ann	25	Covenanter	Cork	Ireland	between August 29 and September 4, 1847
Lehan, Murty	7	Virginius	Liverpool	England	between August 8 and 14, 1847
Leland, Robert	45	Marchioness of Breadalbane	Sligo	Ireland	between August 8 and 14, 1847
Lemon, Ann	30	Triton	Liverpool	England	between August 22 and 28, 1847
Lemon, Catherine	50	Progress	New Ross	Ireland	between August 8 and 14, 1847
Lemon, Edward	50	Triton	Liverpool	England	between August 22 and 28, 1847
Lemon, James	12	Erin's Queen	Liverpool	England	between July 11 and 17, 1847
Lemon, Patrick	14	Erin's Queen	Liverpool	England	between July 18 and 24, 1847
Lemon, William	36	Royal Adelaide	Killala	Ireland	between August 8 and 14, 1847
Lenihan, Ellen	60	Jessie	Limerick	Ireland	between July 25 and 31, 1847
Lenihan, John	34	Wakefield	Cork	Ireland	between July 25 and 31, 1847
Lennon, Bridget		Progress	New Ross	Ireland	
Lennon, Martin	8	Progress	New Ross	Ireland	between August 8 and 14, 1847
Lennon, Patrick	46	John Munn	Liverpool	England	between September 19 and 25, 1847
Lennox, John	34	Eliza Morrison	Belfast	Ireland	between July 18 and 24, 1847
Leon, James	40	James Moran	Liverpool	England	between July 11 and 17, 1847
Leonard, Bridget	2	Greenock	Liverpool	England	between July 25 and 31, 1847
Leonard, Hugh	60	Goliah	Liverpool	England	between July 11 and 17, 1847
Leonard, J.	60				between July 11 and 17, 1847
Leonard, Mary	47	Covenanter	Cork	Ireland	between August 8 and 14, 1847
Leonard, Michael	47	Greenock	Liverpool	England	between July 25 and 31, 1847
Leonard, W.	45	Unicorn	Londonderry	Ireland	between July 11 and 17, 1847
Levy, Ann	34	Marinus	Dublin	Ireland	between October 3 and 9, 1847
Levy, Bridget	18	Marinus	Dublin	Ireland	between August 22 and 28, 1847
Levy, Michael	38	Marinus	Dublin	Ireland	between August 22 and 28, 1847
Lewis, John	26	John Francis	Cork	Ireland	between June 6 and 12, 1847
Leyden, Andrew		Argo			
Leyden, Ann	26	Avon	Cork	Ireland	between August 1 and 7, 1847
Leyden, James	14	Washington	Liverpool	England	between September 5 and 11, 1847
Leyden, Thomas	12	Washington	Liverpool	England	between September 5 and 11, 1847
Liddane, Patrick	60	Numa	Sligo	Ireland	between July 25 and 31, 1847
Liggett, George	1	Bee	Cork	Ireland	between May 29 and June 5, 1847
Liggett, George	1 year & 4 months	Bee	Cork	Ireland	1847/06/01

Lists of people who died and were buried on Grosse Île, in 1847

Name	Age	Vessel	Port	Country	Date of death
Linane, Michael	1	Jessie	Cork	Ireland	between July 25 and 31, 1847
Lindsay, Ann	20	Larch	Sligo	Ireland	1847/08/18
Lindsay, Maria	23	Virginius	Liverpool	England	1847/08/15
Lindsay, Robert	24	Yorkshire Lass	Killala	Ireland	1847/08/29
Linehan, Mary	1	Urania	Cork	Ireland	between June 13 and 19, 1847
Linehan, Patrick	35	Asia	Cork	Ireland	between September 26 and October 2, 1847
Linskey, John	23	Clarendon	Liverpool	England	between June 13 and 19, 1847
Lisk, Andrew	50	Dominica	Cork	Ireland	between June 13 and 19, 1847
Loftus, Catherine	14	Wolfville	Sligo	Ireland	between June 27 and July 3, 1847
Loftus, John	6	Royal Adelaide	Killala	Ireland	between August 15 and 21, 1847
Loftus, Martin	38	Abbeylands	Liverpool	England	between August 8 and 14, 1847
Loftus, Mrs	40	Independance	Belfast	Ireland	between July 25 and 31, 1847
Loftus, Thomas	26	Syria	Liverpool	England	between May 23 and 29, 1847
Loftus, William	39	Ann	Liverpool	England	between June 27 and July 3, 1847
Logan, Eliza	4	Greenock	Liverpool	England	between August 1 and 7, 1847
Lohan, Catherine	8	Greenock	Liverpool	England	between September 19 and 25, 1847
Lombard, Elisa		Lady Flora Hastings	Cork	Ireland	1847/07/08
Londrigan, Edward	22	Saguenay	Cork	Ireland	between August 29 and September 4, 1847
Long, Andrew	35	James Moran	Liverpool	England	between July 4 and 10, 1847
Long, Michael	7	James Moran	Liverpool	England	between July 18 and 24, 1847
Loughren, Patrick	2	Tay	Sligo	Ireland	between June 27 and July 3, 1847
Lowmann, Mary	1 year & 2 months				1847/08/09*
Lowry, Mary	25	Goliah	Liverpool	England	between July 11 and 17, 1847
Luby, John	29	Achilles	Liverpool	England	between June 6 and 12, 1847
Lundy, Margaret	23	John and Robert	Liverpool	England	between August 8 and 14, 1847
Lunny, Edward	18	Wandsworth	Dublin	Ireland	between June 13 and 19, 1847
Lunny, John	40	St. George			between June 27 and July 3, 1847
Lupton, Catherine	40	Odessa	Dublin	Ireland	between September 12 and 18, 1847
Lynch, Ann	50	Asia	Cork	Ireland	between October 3 and 9, 1847
Lynch, Bridget	7	Jessie	Cork	Ireland	between July 18 and 24, 1847
Lynch, Edward	40	Yorkshire Lass	Killala	Ireland	between August 8 and 14, 1847
Lynch, James	20	John Munn	Liverpool	England	between August 8 and 14, 1847
Lynch, James	20	John Munn	Liverpool	England	between August 15 and 21, 1847
Lynch, John	36	Eliza Caroline	Liverpool	England	between July 11 and 17, 1847
Lynch, Mary	3	James Moran	Liverpool	England	between September 5 and 11, 1847
Lynch, Mary	21	John Francis	Cork	Ireland	between June 27 and July 3, 1847
Lynch, Mary	38	Goliah	Liverpool	England	between July 11 and 17, 1847
Lynch, Mary A.	18	John Francis	Cork	Ireland	between June 27 and July 3, 1847
Lynch, Michael	19	Avon	Cork	Ireland	between July 18 and 24, 1847
Lyness, John	18	Saguenay	Cork	Ireland	1847/09/20
Lynn, John		Bee	Cork	Ireland	
Lynn, Margaret	23	Phoenix	Liverpool	England	between May 29 and June 5, 1847
Lynn, Mary	28	John Munn	Liverpool	England	between September 26 and October 2, 1847
Lyons, Eliza	21				between July 11 and 17, 1847
Lyons, Joseph	30	Avon	Cork	Ireland	between August 1 and 7, 1847
Lyons, Mary	10	Asia	Cork	Ireland	between August 15 and 21, 1847
Lyons, Mary	12	Virginius	Liverpool	England	between August 1 and 7, 1847
Lyons, Mary	2	Virginius	Liverpool	England	between August 15 and 21, 1847
Lyons, Mary	20	Agnes	Cork	Ireland	between July 4 and 10, 1847
Lyons, William	24	Lady Milton	Liverpool	England	between August 22 and 28, 1847
M___, E___					
M___, F___					
M___, S___					
MacFarlane, Andrew	20	Rose	Liverpool	England	between July 4 and 10, 1847
Mack, Mary	2	Wandsworth	Dublin	Ireland	1847/05/20
Mack, Mary Munro	50	Caithness-shire	Belfast	Ireland	1847/06/15
Mack, Michael	22	Yorkshire	Liverpool	England	between September 12 and 18, 1847
Mack, Thomas	35	Progress	New Ross	Ireland	between July 4 and 10, 1847
Macpherson, Ellen	1 year & 3 days				1847/05/21
Madden, Celia	51	John Munn	Liverpool	England	between September 5 and 11, 1847
Madden, Ellen	40	Larch	Sligo	Ireland	between August 22 and 28, 1847
Madden, John	22	John Munn	Liverpool	England	between September 26 and October 2, 1847
Madden, Mary	25	Argo	Liverpool	England	between August 15 and 21, 1847
Madden, Patrick	30	Scotland	Cork	Ireland	between May 23 and 29, 1847
Madden, Patrick	4	George	Liverpool	England	between June 6 and 12, 1847
Madigan, Daniel	22	Superior	Londonderry	Ireland	between September 12 and 18, 1847
Madigan, James	55	Wandsworth	Dublin	Ireland	between May 16 and 22, 1847
Madigan, John	35	Wandsworth	Dublin	Ireland	between June 6 and 12, 1847
Madigan, John	55	Wandsworth	Dublin	Ireland	between June 6 and 12, 1847
Madigan, John	21	Wandsworth	Dublin	Ireland	between May 29 and June 5, 1847
Magee, James		Superior	Londonderry	Ireland	
Maguire, Essey	16	Clarendon	Liverpool	England	between June 6 and 12, 1847
Maguire, Henry	30	Superior	Londonderry	Ireland	1847/09/26
Maguire, Honora	2	Gilmour	Cork	Ireland	between June 6 and 12, 1847
Maguire, James	50				1847/07/08
Maguire, James	45	Superior	Londonderry	Ireland	1847/09/15
Maguire, James	8	Clarendon	Liverpool	England	between June 13 and 19, 1847
Maguire, James	6	Naomi	Liverpool	England	between August 15 and 21, 1847
Maguire, Jane	13	Clarendon	Liverpool	England	between June 13 and 19, 1847

THE EMIGRANTS

Name	Age	Vessel	Port	Country	Date of death
Maguire, Mary	50	Gilmour	Cork	Ireland	between June 6 and 12, 1847
Maguire, Mary	40	Clarendon	Liverpool	England	between June 27 and July 3, 1847
Maguire, Michael	24	Scotland	Cork	Ireland	between July 4 and 10, 1847
Maguire, Sarah	50	Ganges	Liverpool	England	1847/08/14
Maher, Alice		Ann Kenny	Waterford	Ireland	
Maher, Catherine	37	Wellington	Liverpool	England	between October 3 and 9, 1847
Maher, John	30	Free Trader	Liverpool	England	between August 29 and September 4, 1847
Maher, John	6	Wm S. Hamilton	New Ross	Ireland	between August 1 and 7, 1847
Maher, Mary	8	Sir Henry Pottinger	Cork	Ireland	between August 15 and 21, 1847
Maher, Thomas	35	Wm S. Hamilton	New Ross	Ireland	between August 1 and 7, 1847
Mahon, Dolly	40	Phoenix	Liverpool	England	between May 29 and June 5, 1847
Mahon, Edward	18	John Munn	Liverpool	England	between September 19 and 25, 1847
Mahon, James	1	John Munn	Liverpool	England	between August 8 and 14, 1847
Mahon, James	3	Jessie	Limerick	Ireland	between August 1 and 7, 1847
Mahon, John	26	Agnes	Cork	Ireland	between May 29 and June 5, 1847
Mahon, Martin	25	Larch	Sligo	Ireland	between August 15 and 21, 1847
Mahon, Mary	40	Yorkshire Lass	Killala	Ireland	between July 18 and 24, 1847
Mahon, Robert	12	George	Liverpool	England	between May 30 and June 5, 1847
Mahon, Thomas	12	Naomi	Liverpool	England	between August 29 and September 4, 1847
Mahony, Ann	13	Jessie	Cork	Ireland	between August 1 and 7, 1847
Mahony, Bridget	35	Virginius	Liverpool	England	between August 15 and 21, 1847
Mahony, David	5	Asia	Cork	Ireland	between September 12 and 18, 1847
Mahony, Denis	24	Bee	Cork	Ireland	between July 25 and 31, 1847
Mahony, Ellen	45	Urania	Cork	Ireland	between June 20 and 26, 1847
Mahony, Helen	60	Marchioness of Breadalbane	Sligo	Ireland	between August 8 and 14, 1847
Mahony, Jeremiah	22	Asia	Cork	Ireland	between September 12 and 18, 1847
Mahony, Michael	16	Agnes	Cork	Ireland	between June 27 and July 3, 1847
Mahony, Patrick	25	Marinus	Dublin	Ireland	between August 15 and 21, 1847
Malcolm, Catherine	56	Pandora	New Ross	Ireland	between August 1 and 7, 1847
Malley, Eliza	1	Progress	New Ross	Ireland	between July 11 and 17, 1847
Malley, John	18	Scotland	Cork	Ireland	between June 13 and 19, 1847
Malley, Patrick	21	Henry	Donegal	Ireland	between June 20 and 26, 1847
Malley, Sarah	7	Progress	New Ross	Ireland	between July 18 and 24, 1847
Malone, Catherine	8 months	Royalist	Liverpool	England	between May 29 and June 5, 1847
Malone, Mary	36	Syria	Liverpool	England	between June 20 and 26, 1847
Malone, Michael	30	Aberdeen	Liverpool	England	between June 13 and 19, 1847
Malone, Patrick	25	Broom	Liverpool	England	between August 8 and 14, 1847
Malone, Thomas	33	Argyle	Newport	England	between September 26 and October 2, 1847
Maloney, Arthur	5	Naomi	Liverpool	England	between August 15 and 21, 1847
Maloney, Brady	16	Yeoman			between August 22 and 28, 1847
Maloney, Catherine	40	Virginius	Liverpool	England	between August 1 and 7, 1847
Maloney, Ellen	76	Goliah	Liverpool	England	between August 1 and 7, 1847
Maloney, John	30	Covenanter	Cork	Ireland	between August 8 and 14, 1847
Maloney, Mary	26	Aberdeen	Liverpool	England	between June 20 and 26, 1847
Maloney, Mary	26	Wolfville	Sligo	Ireland	between June 20 and 26, 1847
Mangan, Catherine	15	Wandsworth	Dublin	Ireland	between May 29 and June 5, 1847
Mangan, James	55	Wandsworth	Dublin	Ireland	1847/05/20
Mangan, John	27	Covenanter	Cork	Ireland	1847/08/18
Mangan, John	1	Champion	Liverpool	England	between September 12 and 18, 1847
Mangan, Michael	40	Champion	Liverpool	England	between September 26 and October 2, 1847
Mangan, Thomas	20	Wandsworth	Dublin	Ireland	between May 29 and June 5, 1847
Manley, Anthony		Ganges	Liverpool	England	
Mann, Mary	35	Free Trader	Liverpool	England	between August 15 and 21, 1847
Mann, William	30	Rankin	Liverpool	England	between June 27 and July 3, 1847
Mannin, Catherine	1 year & 6 months	Rankin	Liverpool	England	between June 13 and 19, 1847
Manning, John	12	Gilmour	Cork	Ireland	between June 13 and 19, 1847
Mannion, Bryan	38	Agnes	Cork	Ireland	between July 18 and 24, 1847
Mannion, Elizabeth	30	Sarah Milledge	Galway	Ireland	between October 17 and 23, 1847
Mannion, Mary	55	Virginius	Liverpool	England	between August 22 and 28, 1847
Mannis, Susan	40	Princess Royal	Liverpool	England	between June 27 and July 3, 1847
Manus, John	18	Avon	Cork	Ireland	between July 11 and 17, 1847
Mara, Michael	3				1847/05/15
Mark, Ellen	40	Free Trader	Liverpool	England	between September 12 and 18, 1847
Marken, Judith	8	Ganges	Liverpool	England	between August 22 and 28, 1847
Marr, Rose	30	Greenock	Liverpool	England	between August 8 and 14, 1847
Martin, Ann	28				1847/05/19
Martin, Henry	40	Bridgetown	Liverpool	England	between August 29 and September 4, 1847
Martin, Maria	26	Lady Milton	Liverpool	England	between June 27 and July 3, 1847
Martin, Mary	25	Covenanter	Cork	Ireland	between August 22 and 28, 1847
Mason, Charles	29	Bee	Cork	Ireland	between July 4 and 10, 1847
Mason, Helen	3 years & 6 months	Wandsworth	Dublin	Ireland	between June 13 and 19, 1847
Mason, Margaret					1847/09/27
Mason, Thomas	46				between July 11 and 17, 1847
Mason, William	2	Bee	Cork	Ireland	between June 13 and 19, 1847
Masters, Margaret	10	Tamarac	Liverpool	England	between July 18 and 24, 1847
Masterson, Bridget	40	Emigrant	Liverpool	England	between October 3 and 9, 1847

Lists of people who died and were buried on Grosse Île, in 1847

Name	Age	Vessel	Port	Country	Date of death
Masterson, Catherine	1	Emigrant	Liverpool	England	between October 10 and 16, 1847
Mathers, Margaret	30	Frankfield	Liverpool	England	between September 19 and 25, 1847
Mathews, Judith	20	Wakefield	Cork	Ireland	between September 26 and October 2, 1847
Mathews, Patrick	10	Saguenay	Cork	Ireland	between August 15 and 21, 1847
Mathewson, Donald	8	Virginius	Liverpool	England	1847/08/18
Mathewson, Flora	60	Eliza	Glasgow	Scotland	between September 19 and 25, 1847
Matthews, John	30	Frankfield	Liverpool	England	between August 1 and 7, 1847
McAllen, Hugh	10	George	Liverpool	England	between August 1 and 7, 1847
McAllister, Hugh	3	Superior	Londonderry	Ireland	between September 26 and October 2, 1847
McAllister, Martin					
McAllister, Mary		Superior	Londonderry	Ireland	
McAndrew, James	17	Numa	Sligo	Ireland	between August 22 and 28, 1847
McAndrew, Mary	6	James Moran	Liverpool	England	between July 18 and 24, 1847
McAndrew, Nancy	60	Numa	Sligo	Ireland	between August 29 and September 4, 1847
McAndrew, Richard	5	Numa	Sligo	Ireland	between August 8 and 14, 1847
McAndrew, Thomas	1	James Moran	Liverpool	England	between July 11 and 17, 1847
McAndrews, Margaret	10	James Moran	Liverpool	England	between July 25 and 31, 1847
McAuliffe, Denis	45	Bridgetown	Liverpool	England	between August 22 and 28, 1847
McAuliffe, H.	1	Champion	Liverpool	England	between September 12 and 18, 1847
McAuliffe, Helen	16	Saguenay	Cork	Ireland	between August 15 and 21, 1847
McAuliffe, Johana	26	Asia	Cork	Ireland	between July 25 and 31, 1847
McAuliffe, Patrick	2	Covenanter	Cork	Ireland	between August 1 and 7, 1847
McAvinny, Sarah		Pursuit	Liverpool	England	
McBride, Mary	40	Lotus	Liverpool	England	between June 20 and 26, 1847
McBride, Michael	1	Superior	Londonderry	Ireland	between September 12 and 18, 1847
McBride, Thomas	60	Superior	Londonderry	Ireland	between October 3 and 9, 1847
McBrien, Ann	30	George	Liverpool	England	between July 4 and 10, 1847
McBrien, Margaret					1847/06/09
McBurney, William	19	Caithness-shire	Belfast	Ireland	between July 25 and 31, 1847
McCabe, Alice		Superior	Londonderry	Ireland	
McCabe, Arnold	17	Aberdeen	Liverpool	England	between June 20 and 26, 1847
McCabe, Francis	6	Aberdeen	Liverpool	England	between June 20 and 26, 1847
McCabe, John	11	Superior	Londonderry	Ireland	between October 3 and 9, 1847
McCabe, John	21	Mail	Cork	Ireland	between June 27 and July 3, 1847
McCabe, Margaret	45	Lord Seaton	Belfast	Ireland	between June 20 and 26, 1847
McCabe, Margaret	40	John Bolton	Liverpool	England	between June 27 and July 3, 1847
McCabe, Mary		Superior	Londonderry	Ireland	
McCabe, Mary	30	Ganges	Liverpool	England	between August 22 and 28, 1847
McCabe, Owen	45	Superior	Londonderry	Ireland	between September 12 and 18, 1847
McCadden, James	38	Ganges	Liverpool	England	1847/08/18
McCafferty, Bridget	50	Unicorn	Londonderry	Ireland	between July 18 and 24, 1847
McCaffrey, Elizabeth	11	John and Robert	Liverpool	England	between August 22 and 28, 1847
McCaffrey, Ellen	42	Sisters	Liverpool	England	between June 27 and July 3, 1847
McCaffrey, Ellen	19	Asia	Cork	Ireland	between September 5 and 11, 1847
McCaffrey, James	25	Henry	Donegal	Ireland	between June 20 and 26, 1847
McCaffrey, James	14	John and Robert	Liverpool	England	between September 12 and 18, 1847
McCaffrey, Margaret	11	Sisters	Liverpool	England	between July 11 and 17, 1847
McCaffrey, Patrick					
McCaffrey, Peter	45	Maria Somes	Cork	Ireland	between September 12 and 18, 1847
McCaffrey, Phillip	22	Sisters	Liverpool	England	between June 27 and July 3, 1847
McCain, John	22	Eliza	Glasgow	Scotland	between September 12 and 18, 1847
McCall, Catherine	2	George	Liverpool	England	between July 4 and 10, 1847
McCall, John	15	Erin's Queen	Liverpool	England	1847/09/02
McCall, John	40	Erin's Queen	Liverpool	England	1847/08/22
McCall, Matthew	30	Erin's Queen	Liverpool	England	between September 5 and 11, 1847
McCall, Richard	19	George	Liverpool	England	between June 13 and 19, 1847
McCall, Thomas	4	George	Liverpool	England	between June 27 and July 3, 1847
McCallum, Archibald	1	Odessa	Dublin	Ireland	1847/08/23
McCallum, Margaret	23	Odessa	Dublin	Ireland	1847/08/22
McCarroll, Mary	40	Goliah	Liverpool	England	between July 18 and 24, 1847
McCarron, John	36	Royalist	Liverpool	England	between June 6 and 12, 1847
McCarron, William	49	Lord Seaton	Belfast	Ireland	between July 18 and 24, 1847
McCarry, John	30	Caithness-shire	Belfast	Ireland	between July 11 and 17, 1847
McCarry, Mary A.	10	Catherine	Sydney	Canada	between July 11 and 17, 1847
McCartan, Margaret	40	Superior	Londonderry	Ireland	between September 19 and 25, 1847
McCarter, Charles	37	Britannia	Greenock	Scotland	1847/08/29
McCarthy, Catherine	21	Roseanna	Cork	Ireland	between July 11 and 17, 1847
McCarthy, Catherine	5 months	Emigrant	Liverpool	England	between September 19 and 25, 1847
McCarthy, Catherine	22	Sisters	Liverpool	England	between June 27 and July 3, 1847
McCarthy, Charles	5	Numa	Sligo	Ireland	between August 15 and 21, 1847
McCarthy, Daniel	46	Julius Caesar	Liverpool	England	between September 19 and 25, 1847
McCarthy, Daniel	24	Agnes	Cork	Ireland	between August 15 and 21, 1847
McCarthy, Ellen	12	Wakefield	Cork	Ireland	between July 4 and 10, 1847
McCarthy, Flora	22	John Francis	Cork	Ireland	between May 29 and June 5, 1847
McCarthy, James	9	Wakefield	Cork	Ireland	between July 18 and 24, 1847
McCarthy, Jeremiah	9	Wakefield	Cork	Ireland	between July 11 and 17, 1847
McCarthy, Johanna	35	Wakefield	Cork	Ireland	between July 18 and 24, 1847
McCarthy, John	7	Pursuit	Liverpool	England	between July 4 and 10, 1847
McCarthy, John	60	Lively	Cork	Ireland	between July 11 and 17, 1847
McCarthy, John	1	Avon	Cork	Ireland	between July 25 and 31, 1847

The Emigrants

Name	Age	Vessel	Port	Country	Date of death
McCarthy, John	50	Emigrant	Liverpool	England	between September 26 and October 2, 1847
McCarthy, Judith	30	Bee	Cork	Ireland	between June 27 and July 3, 1847
McCarthy, M.					
McCarthy, Margaret	31	Avon	Cork	Ireland	between July 25 and 31, 1847
McCarthy, Margaret	21	Naomi	Liverpool	England	between August 8 and 14, 1847
McCarthy, Margaret	19	Avon	Cork	Ireland	between August 22 and 28, 1847
McCarthy, Michael	35	Jessie	Cork	Ireland	between August 1 and 7, 1847
McCarthy, Patrick	17	Champion	Liverpool	England	between September 26 and October 2, 1847
McCarthy, Thomas	7	Pursuit	Liverpool	England	between June 27 and July 3, 1847
McCarthy, Timothy	3	Wakefield	Cork	Ireland	between July 25 and 31, 1847
McCarthy, Timothy	3	Covenanter	Cork	Ireland	between August 1 and 7, 1847
McCarthy, Timothy	18	Gilmour	Cork	Ireland	between June 13 and 19, 1847
McCarty, Jeremiah		Bee	Cork	Ireland	
McCarty, Mary		Junior	Liverpool	England	
McCarty, Michael	25	Larch	Sligo	Ireland	between August 15 and 21, 1847
McCawell, Helen	25	Yorkshire	Liverpool	England	between August 22 and 28, 1847
McCawell, John	1	John Munn	Liverpool	England	between August 8 and 14, 1847
McClatchey, Mary		John Bolton	Liverpool	England	
McCleary, Margaret	50	Pursuit	Liverpool	England	between June 13 and 19, 1847
McClehaddy, Robert	23	Marchioness of Bute	Belfast	Ireland	between August 29 and September 4, 1847
McClintock, Margaret		Tamarac	Liverpool	England	1847/07/05
McClintock, Ruth		Tamarac	Liverpool	England	1847/07/05
McCloy, Honora	50	Odessa	Dublin	Ireland	between August 1 and 7, 1847
McClue, Mary J.	23	Scotland	Cork	Ireland	between July 4 and 10, 1847
McClung, James	50	Caithness-shire	Belfast	Ireland	between July 11 and 17, 1847
McCluskey, Catherine	27	Manchester	Liverpool	England	between August 1 and 7, 1847
McCluskey, Margaret	7	Manchester	Liverpool	England	between July 25 and 31, 1847
McCluskey, Patrick	22	Manchester	Liverpool	England	between October 3 and 9, 1847
McCluskey, Patrick	62	Manchester	Liverpool	England	between July 11 and 17, 1847
McComb, William	7 months	Constitution	Belfast	Ireland	1847/05/29
McConnell, Ellen	40	Wellington	Liverpool	England	1847/09/23
McConnon, Ellen	50	Huron	Belfast	Ireland	between July 18 and 24, 1847
McCormack, Catherine	25	Champion	Liverpool	England	between August 22 and 28, 1847
McCormack, John	64	Erin's Queen	Liverpool	England	between July 25 and 31, 1847
McCormack, Patrick	17	Avon	Cork	Ireland	between August 8 and 14, 1847
McCormack, Thomas	4	Washington	Liverpool	England	between August 22 and 28, 1847
McCormick, James	7	Washington	Liverpool	England	between October 3 and 9, 1847
McCormick, Mary	30	Superior	Londonderry	Ireland	between October 3 and 9, 1847
McCormick, Patrick	3	Lady Campbell	Dublin	Ireland	between September 12 and 18, 1847
McCoy, Ellen	13	Orlando	Newry	Ireland	between July 4 and 10, 1847
McCoy, James	25	Broom	Liverpool	England	1847/08/20
McCoy, M.	1 month	Orlando	Newry	Ireland	between July 18 and 24, 1847
McCoy, Mary	19	Yorkshire Lass	Killala	Ireland	between August 29 and September 4, 1847
McCracken, Mary	40	Free Trader	Liverpool	England	between August 22 and 28, 1847
McCraly, Francis	10	Triton	Liverpool	England	between August 1 and 7, 1847
McCrea, Alexander	11	Eliza	Glasgow	Scotland	between October 10 and 16, 1847
McCrea, Alexander	52	Eliza	Glasgow	Scotland	1847/10/07
McCrea, Donald	30	Eliza	Glasgow	Scotland	1847/09/17
McCrea, Finy	80	Eliza	Glasgow	Scotland	between September 5 and 11, 1847
McCrea, Flora	9	Eliza	Glasgow	Scotland	between September 12 and 18, 1847
McCrea, James	4	Eliza	Glasgow	Scotland	1847/09/25
McCrea, John		Eliza	Glasgow	Scotland	
McCrea, Margaret	42	Eliza	Glasgow	Scotland	1847/10/07
McCreed, Mary	16	Eliza Caroline	Liverpool	England	between July 18 and 24, 1847
McCreen, Mary	2	Sarah	Liverpool	England	between July 18 and 24, 1847
McCrone, Francis	55	Odessa	Dublin	Ireland	between August 8 and 14, 1847
McCuddy, C.	40	Naomi	Liverpool	England	between August 15 and 21, 1847
McCullen, Margaret	23	Odessa	Dublin	Ireland	between August 22 and 28, 1847
McCullough, Denis	20	Wellington	Liverpool	England	between September 19 and 25, 1847
McCullough, Jane	48	Virgilia	Liverpool	England	1847/09/27
McCullough, Margaret Armstrong	82	Lotus	Liverpool	England	1847/06/05
McCurley, James	25	Clarendon	Liverpool	England	between June 13 and 19, 1847
McCurley, James	45	Lotus	Liverpool	England	between June 20 and 26, 1847
McCurry, Kenneth	23	Wakefield	Cork	Ireland	between July 18 and 24, 1847
McDermott, Catherine	35	Ganges	Liverpool	England	between August 15 and 21, 1847
McDermott, Ellen	7	Naomi	Liverpool	England	between August 8 and 14, 1847
McDermott, Honora	70	Free Trader	Liverpool	England	between August 15 and 21, 1847
McDermott, Michael	16	Naomi	Liverpool	England	between September 5 and 11, 1847
McDermott, Timothy	4	Eliza Caroline	Liverpool	England	between June 20 and 26, 1847
McDolly, James	5	Erin's Queen	Liverpool	England	between August 1 and 7, 1847
McDonagh, Mary	24	Blonde	Liverpool	England	between June 20 and 26, 1847
McDonald, Alexander	34	Sobraon	Liverpool	England	between August 1 and 7, 1847
McDonald, Ann	26	Bridgetown	Liverpool	England	between September 5 and 11, 1847
McDonald, Ann	2	Bridgetown	Liverpool	England	1847/09/08
McDonald, Catherine	6	Erin's Queen	Liverpool	England	1847/09/04
McDonald, Christiana McGuinness					1847/08/09*
McDonald, Donald		Ann Rankin	Glasgow	Scotland	
McDonald, Hugh	1 month	Sir Henry Pottinger	Belfast	Ireland	1847/08/28
McDonald, James	2	Naomi	Liverpool	England	between August 15 and 21, 1847
McDonald, Margaret	8	Free Trader	Liverpool	England	between August 22 and 28, 1847
McDonald, Margaret	30	Ann Rankin	Glasgow	Scotland	1847/08/30
McDonald, Mark	26	Blonde	Liverpool	England	between June 6 and 12, 1847

43

Lists of people who died and were buried on Grosse Île, in 1847

Name	Age	Vessel	Port	Country	Date of death
McDonald, Mary	50	Royalist	Liverpool	England	between July 11 and 17, 1847
McDonald, Mary	4	Rankin	Liverpool	England	between August 8 and 14, 1847
McDonald, Mary	8	Free Trader	Liverpool	England	1847/08/25
McDonald, Matthew	16	John Bolton	Liverpool	England	between July 4 and 10, 1847
McDonald, Sally	1	Odessa	Dublin	Ireland	between August 8 and 14, 1847
McDonald, Sally	10 months	Ann Rankin	Glasgow	Scotland	1847/08/14
McDonald, Setina					1847/05/25
McDonnell, ___	22	John Bolton	Liverpool	England	between July 25 and 31, 1847
McDonnell, ___	9	Thistle	Liverpool	England	between August 1 and 7, 1847
McDonnell, Bridget	22	Lady Gordon	Belfast	Ireland	between July 4 and 10, 1847
McDonnell, Hannah	40	Lively	Cork	Ireland	between July 11 and 17, 1847
McDonnell, Honora	30	Ganges	Liverpool	England	between August 29 and September 4, 1847
McDonnell, Hugh	58	Bridgetown	Liverpool	England	between August 22 and 28, 1847
McDonnell, Jeremiah	6	Bridgetown	Liverpool	England	between August 29 and September 4, 1847
McDonnell, Jessica	32	Bridgetown	Liverpool	England	between August 29 and September 4, 1847
McDonnell, Patrick	4 months	Broom	Liverpool	England	1847/08/16
McDonnell, William	17	Progress	New Ross	Ireland	between July 11 and 17, 1847
McDonough, C.					
McDonough, Mary	19	Erin's Queen	Liverpool	England	between August 22 and 28, 1847
McDonough, Peter	28	Larch	Sligo	Ireland	between August 22 and 28, 1847
McDowell, Owen	35	Erin's Queen	Liverpool	England	between August 8 and 14, 1847
McDugall, Bridget	2	Erin's Queen	Liverpool	England	between August 1 and 7, 1847
McDunlief, Patrick	10	Naomi	Liverpool	England	between August 15 and 21, 1847
McDyke, Mary	20	Argyle	Newport	England	between September 19 and 25, 1847
McEnroe, Jane	40	Clarendon	Liverpool	England	between July 4 and 10, 1847
McEvoy, Ann	30	Coromandel	Dublin	Ireland	between July 25 and 31, 1847
McEvoy, James	22	Greenock	Liverpool	England	between July 25 and 31, 1847
McEvoy, James	43	George	Liverpool	England	between June 27 and July 3, 1847
McEvoy, Joseph	2 years & 6 months	Jane Black	Limerick	Ireland	between June 6 and 12, 1847
McFadden, A.		Sir Robert Peel	Liverpool	England	1847/09/30
McFadden, E.	34	Sir Robert Peel	Liverpool	England	between September 26 and October 2, 1847
McFadden, Emilia	10	Eliza	Glasgow	Scotland	between September 26 and October 2, 1847
McFadden, John	30	Eliza	Glasgow	Scotland	1847/09/18
McFahey, John	29	Christiana	Londonderry	Ireland	between June 13 and 19, 1847
McFarlane, Bernard	50	Broom	Liverpool	England	between August 1 and 7, 1847
McFarlane, Mary	14	Broom	Liverpool	England	1847/08/31
McFathum, Erson					1847/09/30
McGale, John	35	George	Liverpool	England	between June 13 and 19, 1847
McGee, Dennis	20	Lady Milton	Liverpool	England	between June 20 and 26, 1847
McGee, Jeremiah	30	Yorkshire Lass	Killala	Ireland	between July 25 and 31, 1847
McGee, John	26	Rose	Liverpool	England	between July 4 and 10, 1847
McGee, Margaret	20	Rose	Liverpool	England	between August 22 and 28, 1847
McGerity, Daniel	8	Julius Caesar	Liverpool	England	between October 10 and 16, 1847
McGillicuddy, Thomas	35	Virginius	Liverpool	England	between August 15 and 21, 1847
McGilly, P.					
McGirr, Edward	54	Broom	Liverpool	England	between August 22 and 28, 1847
McGirr, James	45	Superior	Londonderry	Ireland	between September 12 and 18, 1847
McGoldrick, James	17	Larch	Sligo	Ireland	between September 5 and 11, 1847
McGough, Margaret	45	Unicorn	Londonderry	Ireland	between July 11 and 17, 1847
McGourty, Patrick	11	Argo	Liverpool	England	between July 4 and 10, 1847
McGourty, Robert	9	Lady Milton	Liverpool	England	between July 4 and 10, 1847
McGovern, Bridget	6	Julius Caesar	Liverpool	England	between September 26 and October 2, 1847
McGovern, James	20	Free Trader	Liverpool	England	between September 26 and October 2, 1847
McGowan, Dominic	32	Naomi	Liverpool	England	between August 15 and 21, 1847
McGowan, Edward	45	Numa	Sligo	Ireland	between August 1 and 7, 1847
McGowan, Margaret	34	Ganges	Liverpool	England	between August 29 and September 4, 1847
McGowan, Patrick	9	Larch	Sligo	Ireland	between August 22 and 28, 1847
McGowan, Roger	33	Industry	Dublin	Ireland	between October 17 and 23, 1847
McGrady, Michael	30	Lotus	Liverpool	England	between July 18 and 24, 1847
McGrath, Andrew	31	John Munn	Liverpool	England	between August 8 and 14, 1847
McGrath, Andrew	34	Sir Henry Pottinger		Ireland	between August 8 and 14, 1847
McGrath, Ann	60	Manchester	Liverpool	England	between August 29 and September 4, 1847
McGrath, Bridget	60	Ajax	Liverpool	England	between July 18 and 24, 1847
McGrath, James	18	Araminta	Liverpool	England	between June 13 and 19, 1847
McGrath, James	20	Araminta	Liverpool	England	between June 13 and 19, 1847
McGrath, James	16	Numa	Sligo	Ireland	between September 5 and 11, 1847
McGrath, John	4	Manchester	Liverpool	England	between August 29 and September 4, 1847
McGrath, Mark	60	Manchester	Liverpool	England	between July 11 and 17, 1847
McGrath, Mary	30	Avon	Cork	Ireland	between July 25 and 31, 1847
McGrath, Michael	25	Hercules			between July 25 and 31, 1847
McGrath, P.					
McGrath, Patrick	1 year & 6 months	Araminta	Liverpool	England	between June 13 and 19, 1847
McGrath, Sally	28	Manchester	Liverpool	England	between September 5 and 11, 1847
McGregor, Amy					
McGuane, Bridget	40	Eliza Morrison	Belfast	Ireland	between July 11 and 17, 1847
McGuinn, William	4	Broom	Liverpool	England	between August 22 and 28, 1847

The Emigrants

Name	Age	Vessel	Port	Country	Date of death
McGuinness, Daniel	6	Free Trader	Liverpool	England	between August 8 and 14, 1847
McGuinness, Daniel	18	Sir Robert Peel	Liverpool	England	between September 19 and 25, 1847
McGuinness, Malcolm	2	Sir Robert Peel	Liverpool	England	between September 19 and 25, 1847
McGuinness, Malcom	4	Sir Robert Peel	Liverpool	England	1847/09/25
McGuinness, Thomas	16	Larch	Sligo	Ireland	between August 8 and 14, 1847
McGuinness, William	5	John Munn	Liverpool	England	between August 8 and 14, 1847
McGuire, Alexander	11	Champion	Liverpool	England	1847/08/27
McGuire, Ann	16	Maria Somes	Cork	Ireland	between September 5 and 11, 1847
McGuire, Bernard	57	Superior	Londonderry	Ireland	between September 12 and 18, 1847
McGuire, Catherine	55	Maria Somes	Cork	Ireland	between September 26 and October 2, 1847
McGuire, Connor	58	Larch	Sligo	Ireland	between August 8 and 14, 1847
McGuire, Duncan	50	Sir Robert Peel	Liverpool	England	1847/09/23
McGuire, Elizabeth	2	Maria Somes	Cork	Ireland	between September 12 and 18, 1847
McGuire, Henry	40	Superior	Londonderry	Ireland	between September 26 and October 2, 1847
McGuire, Jean	8	Henry	Donegal	Ireland	between June 6 and 12, 1847
McGuire, Mary	60	Courier			between August 8 and 14, 1847
McGuire, Mary					1847/06/29
McGuire, Mary	40	Royalist	Liverpool	England	between May 29 and June 5, 1847
McGuire, Mary	30	Sesostris	Londonderry	Ireland	between July 18 and 24, 1847
McGuire, Matthew	2	Clarendon	Liverpool	England	between May 29 and June 5, 1847
McGuire, Michael	16	Sesostris	Londonderry	Ireland	between July 18 and 24, 1847
McGuire, Patrick	26	John Munn	Liverpool	England	between September 12 and 18, 1847
McGuire, Peter	19	Superior	Londonderry	Ireland	between October 3 and 9, 1847
McGuire, Sally	28	Ganges	Liverpool	England	between September 12 and 18, 1847
McGuire, Sarah	26	Ganges	Liverpool	England	1847/09/18
McGuire, William	30	Superior	Londonderry	Ireland	1847/09/18
McHale, Margaret	30	Erin's Queen	Liverpool	England	between September 5 and 11, 1847
McHale, Thomas	22	Erin's Queen	Liverpool	England	between August 22 and 28, 1847
McHugh, Cyrus	8	Maria Somes	Cork	Ireland	between September 5 and 11, 1847
McHugh, Felix	26	Ganges	Liverpool	England	between September 19 and 25, 1847
McHugh, John	18	Isabella	Killala	Ireland	between September 19 and 25, 1847
McHugh, Margaret	9	Ganges	Liverpool	England	between August 22 and 28, 1847
McHugh, Nancy	24	John Munn	Liverpool	England	between September 26 and October 2, 1847
McHugh, Terrence	40	Maria Somes	Cork	Ireland	between August 29 and September 4, 1847
McIlwaine, Agnes	60	Lord Seaton	Belfast	Ireland	1847/05/28
McIlwaine, James	1 year & 6 months	Lord Seaton	Belfast	Ireland	1847/06/06
McInerney, Catherine	5	Jessie	Limerick	Ireland	between August 8 and 14, 1847
McInerney, Daniel	30	Ellen Simpson	Limerick	Ireland	between September 5 and 11, 1847
McInnis, John		Eliza	Glasgow	Scotland	
McIvor, Catherine	5	Lord Seaton	Belfast	Ireland	between June 6 and 12, 1847
McKay, Ellen		Orlando	Newry	Ireland	
McKay, James		Marchioness of Abercorn	Londonderry	Ireland	
McKay, James	25	Broom	Liverpool	England	between August 15 and 21, 1847
McKay, John	40	Orlando	Newry	Ireland	between June 27 and July 3, 1847
McKay, Mary Ann		Yorkshire	Liverpool	England	
McKay, Neil	1	Jamaica	Greenock	Scotland	1847/08/16
McKay, Neil	1	Tamarac	Liverpool	England	between August 15 and 21, 1847
McKeag, William	14	Lotus	Liverpool	England	between July 25 and 31, 1847
McKee, James	23	Superior	Londonderry	Ireland	1847/10/08
McKenna, Bridget	30	Lotus	Liverpool	England	between June 20 and 26, 1847
McKenna, Bridget	2	Sarah	Liverpool	England	between July 18 and 24, 1847
McKenna, Ellen	18	Lotus	Liverpool	England	between July 11 and 17, 1847
McKenna, Steven	40	Lord Seaton	Belfast	Ireland	between June 13 and 19, 1847
McKenzie, Charles		Gilmour	Cork	Ireland	
McKenzie, Donald	2	Eliza	Glasgow	Scotland	between September 12 and 18, 1847
McKenzie, William	15	John Munn	Liverpool	England	between August 8 and 14, 1847
McKiernan, Ellen	50	Christiana	Londonderry	Ireland	1847/06/06
McKiernan, Mary	26	Lord Seaton	Belfast	Ireland	between August 1 and 7, 1847
McKillan, Barney	40	John Munn	Liverpool	England	between October 3 and 9, 1847
McKillan, Mary	39	Tamarac	Liverpool	England	between July 11 and 17, 1847
McKinimon, Robert	3	Christiana	Londonderry	Ireland	1847/05/26
McKinley, Martin	3	Congress	Sligo	Ireland	between June 6 and 12, 1847
McKinnane, James	6	Sir Robert Peel	Liverpool	England	between September 19 and 25, 1847
McKinnane, Jannet	6	Sir Robert Peel	Liverpool	England	1847/09/19
McKinnane, John	58	Eliza	Glasgow	Scotland	between September 5 and 11, 1847
McKinnane, Michael	4	Eliza	Glasgow	Scotland	between September 12 and 18, 1847
McKinstry, James	25	Caithness-shire	Belfast	Ireland	1847/05/28
McKitterick, Eliza Ann	1	Washington	Liverpool	England	1847/08/25
McLaughlin, ___	32	Larch	Sligo	Ireland	between August 22 and 28, 1847
McLaughlin, Bridget	50	Emigrant	Liverpool	England	between October 3 and 9, 1847
McLaughlin, Catherine	4	Eliza Morrison	Belfast	Ireland	between July 18 and 24, 1847
McLaughlin, Catherine	50	Emigrant	Liverpool	England	between October 10 and 16, 1847
McLaughlin, John	3	Lady Milton	Liverpool	England	between July 4 and 10, 1847
McLaughlin, Sarah	34	Lady Milton	Liverpool	England	between September 12 and 18, 1847
McLaughlin, Sarah	30	Elizabeth	Liverpool	England	between June 27 and July 3, 1847
McLean, Catherine	8	Britannia	Greenock	Scotland	1847/08/18
McLean, Donald	25	Emigrant	Liverpool	England	1847/10/03
McLean, Hugh	25	Erin's Queen	Liverpool	England	between August 8 and 14, 1847
McLean, Jane	4 years & 6 months	Argo	Liverpool	England	1847/06/07
McLean, John	22	Eliza	Glasgow	Scotland	1847/09/13
McLean, Thomas	12	Maria Somes	Cork	Ireland	between August 29 and September 4, 1847
McMahon, Ann	17	Yorkshire	Liverpool	England	between August 15 and 21, 1847

LISTS OF PEOPLE WHO DIED AND WERE BURIED ON GROSSE ÎLE, IN 1847

Name	Age	Vessel	Port	Country	Date of death
McMahon, Ann	16	George	Liverpool	England	between July 11 and 17, 1847
McMahon, Bernard					
McMahon, Catherine	10	Yorkshire	Liverpool	England	between August 8 and 14, 1847
McMahon, Frank	30	George	Liverpool	England	between July 4 and 10, 1847
McMahon, Hugh	42	Free Trader	Liverpool	England	between September 12 and 18, 1847
McMahon, James	9	Free Trader	Liverpool	England	between August 22 and 28, 1847
McMahon, Jane	46	Free Trader	Liverpool	England	between September 19 and 25, 1847
McMahon, Jane	12	John Munn	Liverpool	England	between August 22 and 28, 1847
McMahon, John	45	Sir Henry Pottinger	Cork	Ireland	between August 8 and 14, 1847
McMahon, Margaret	9	Sarah	Liverpool	England	between August 15 and 21, 1847
McMahon, Mary	2	John Munn	Liverpool	England	between August 1 and 7, 1847
McMahon, Patrick	20	George	Liverpool	England	between July 11 and 17, 1847
McManamon, Judith	10	Triton	Liverpool	England	between August 8 and 14, 1847
McManamon, Mary	30	Rose	Liverpool	England	between June 20 and 26, 1847
McManus, Bridget	30	Pursuit	Liverpool	England	between June 13 and 19, 1847
McManus, Frank	40	Superior	Londonderry	Ireland	between September 19 and 25, 1847
McManus, Margaret	10	Pursuit	Liverpool	England	between June 20 and 26, 1847
McManus, Owen	48	Princess Royal	Liverpool	England	between July 4 and 10, 1847
McManus, Patrick	28	Princess Royal	Liverpool	England	between June 13 and 19, 1847
McMeeney, Catherine	5	Sir Henry Pottinger	Cork	Ireland	between August 8 and 14, 1847
McMichael, ___					
McMichael, Thomas	20	Jessie	Cork	Ireland	between July 18 and 24, 1847
McMichael, Thomas	34	Broom	Liverpool	England	between August 8 and 14, 1847
McMichael, William	22	Jessie	Cork	Ireland	between July 18 and 24, 1847
McMullen, Alexander	3	John Munn	Liverpool	England	1847/08/20
McMullen, Daniel	58	Bridgetown	Liverpool	England	1847/09/11
McMullen, Denis	58	Bridgetown	Liverpool	England	between September 5 and 11, 1847
McMullen, Eliza	34	John Munn	Liverpool	England	between August 22 and 28, 1847
McMullen, Eliza	4	John Munn	Liverpool	England	1847/08/31
McMullen, Elizabeth Swallow	34	John Munn	Liverpool	England	1847/08/23
McMullen, George	10	John Munn	Liverpool	England	1847/09/21
McMullen, John	32	Jamaica	Greenock	Scotland	1847/09/04
McMullen, Margaret	31	Bridgetown	Liverpool	England	between September 5 and 11, 1847
McMullen, Mary	60	Bridgetown	Liverpool	England	1847/09/05
McMullen, Roseanna	9	John Munn	Liverpool	England	1847/09/04
McNabb, Hugh	1	Euclid	Glasgow	Scotland	between July 25 and 31, 1847
McNabb, James	16	Jessie	Limerick	Ireland	between July 25 and 31, 1847
McNally, Frank	37	John Munn	Liverpool	England	between August 8 and 14, 1847
McNally, Philip	24	Sovereign	Limerick	Ireland	between June 20 and 26, 1847
McNamara, Mary	6 months	Covenanter	Cork	Ireland	between August 1 and 7, 1847
McNamara, Patrick	30	Broom	Liverpool	England	between August 8 and 14, 1847
McNeenan, Owen	13	Sarah	Liverpool	England	between August 1 and 7, 1847
McNeill, Catherine	30	Erin's Queen	Liverpool	England	between August 15 and 21, 1847
McNeill, Celia	45	Ayrshire	Newry	Ireland	between August 29 and September 4, 1847
McNeill, Ellen	45	Erin's Queen	Liverpool	England	between August 15 and 21, 1847
McNeill, John	17	Covenanter	Cork	Ireland	between August 8 and 14, 1847
McNeill, Martha	18	Erin's Queen	Liverpool	England	between August 1 and 7, 1847
McNeill, Martha	18	Junior	Liverpool	England	between August 1 and 7, 1847
McNeill, Mary	30	Virginius	Liverpool	England	between August 8 and 14, 1847
McNeill, Patrick	50	Virginius	Liverpool	England	between August 1 and 7, 1847
McNulty, Bridget	30	John Munn	Liverpool	England	between August 8 and 14, 1847
McNulty, Patrick	4	Naomi	Liverpool	England	between August 8 and 14, 1847
McNulty, Patrick	32	Triton	Liverpool	England	between July 25 and 31, 1847
McOwen, Mary	2 years & 2 months	Argo	Liverpool	England	1847/06/04
McPherson, Amelia	10	Eliza	Glasgow	Scotland	1847/09/27
McPherson, Janet	32	Eliza	Glasgow	Scotland	1847/10/10
McQuaid, Ann	40	Maria Somes	Cork	Ireland	between August 29 and September 4, 1847
McQuaid, Ann	16	Maria Somes	Cork	Ireland	between September 26 and October 2, 1847
McQuaid, George	2	Virgilia	Liverpool	England	1847/09/21
McVeigh, Patrick	45	Lord Seaton	Belfast	Ireland	between July 18 and 24, 1847
Meade, James	2	Jessie	Cork	Ireland	between July 18 and 24, 1847
Meade, Johanna		Ann Kenny	Waterford	Ireland	
Meade, John	24	Henry	Donegal	Ireland	between September 12 and 18, 1847
Meade, Joseph		Ann Kenny	Waterford	Ireland	
Meagher, Michael	65	Ganges	Liverpool	England	between September 5 and 11, 1847
Meany, Mary	1	Pursuit	Liverpool	England	between June 13 and 19, 1847
Mee, Catherine	2 years & 6 months				1847/05/19
Meehan, Ann	25	Larch	Sligo	Ireland	between August 15 and 21, 1847
Meehan, Catherine	11	Naomi	Liverpool	England	between August 22 and 28, 1847
Meehan, Ellen					
Meehan, Ellen	50	Numa	Sligo	Ireland	between August 1 and 7, 1847
Meehan, James	60	Superior	Londonderry	Ireland	between October 3 and 9, 1847
Meehan, John	16	Naomi	Liverpool	England	between August 22 and 28, 1847
Meehan, Mary	22	John Munn	Liverpool	England	between August 15 and 21, 1847
Meehan, Mary	40	Westmoreland	Sligo	Ireland	between August 29 and September 4, 1847
Meehan, Mary	26	Saguenay	Cork	Ireland	between August 15 and 21, 1847
Meehan, Michael	26	Greenock	Liverpool	England	between August 29 and September 4, 1847
Meehan, Peter	80				between August 8 and 14, 1847
Meehan, Richard		Covenanter	Cork	Ireland	

The emigrants

Name	Age	Vessel	Port	Country	Date of death
Meehan, Thomas	50	Free Trader	Liverpool	England	between August 15 and 21, 1847
Meek, Catherine	2	Jessie	Sligo	Ireland	1847/05/22
Melia, John	36	Argyle	Newport	England	between September 12 and 18, 1847
Mentz, Barbara	25	Henrietta Sophia	Hamburg	Germany	between July 25 and 31, 1847
Middleton, Robert	24	Yorkshire	Liverpool	England	1847/09/10
Miles, Charles	27	Dominica	Cork	Ireland	1847/06/10
Miles, Edward	23	Lively	Cork	Ireland	between August 8 and 14, 1847
Miles, James	24	Avon	Cork	Ireland	between August 1 and 7, 1847
Miller, Ann Eliza	1	Argo	Liverpool	England	1847/06/06
Miller, John	21	Champion	Liverpool	England	1847/09/02
Miller, John	40	Emigrant	Liverpool	England	between September 26 and October 2, 1847
Miller, Sarah	5	Argo	Liverpool	England	1847/06/01
Milligan, Mary	20	Greenock	Liverpool	England	between August 29 and September 4, 1847
Mills, Ann	55	Naparina	Dublin	Ireland	between August 8 and 14, 1847
Mills, George	4 years & 6 months	Ajax	Liverpool	England	1847/06/01
Milton, L.					1847/07/10
Milton, Sally	30	John Bolton	Liverpool	England	between June 20 and 26, 1847
Minihane, Cornelius	50	Agnes	Cork	Ireland	between May 23 and 29, 1847
Minihane, Eliza	20	Jessie	Cork	Ireland	between July 18 and 24, 1847
Minihane, Johanna	28	Agnes	Cork	Ireland	between May 23 and 29, 1847
Minihane, John	20	Agnes	Cork	Ireland	between May 29 and June 5, 1847
Minihane, Patrick	2	John Francis	Cork	Ireland	between June 6 and 12, 1847
Minihane, Thomas	24	George	Liverpool	England	between May 29 and June 5, 1847
Minnagh, John	27	John Munn	Liverpool	England	between August 29 and September 4, 1847
Mitchell, Andrew	60	Superior	Londonderry	Ireland	1847/09/10
Mitchell, Ann	40	Wellington	Liverpool	England	between October 10 and 16, 1847
Mitchell, James	25	Greenock	Liverpool	England	between July 25 and 31, 1847
Mitchell, John	30	Emigrant	Liverpool	England	1847/09/27
Mitchell, Patrick	35	Syria	Liverpool	England	between June 6 and 12, 1847
Mitchell, Thomas	30	Pursuit	Liverpool	England	between July 4 and 10, 1847
Mitchell, William	1	Superior	Londonderry	Ireland	1847/09/23
Molloy, Catherine	70	Triton	Liverpool	England	between August 1 and 7, 1847
Molloy, James	70	Triton	Liverpool	England	between August 1 and 7, 1847
Molloy, Patrick	30	Wolfville	Sligo	Ireland	between June 27 and July 3, 1847
Molloy, Patrick	15	Rose	Liverpool	England	between July 25 and 31, 1847
Molson, Michael		Eagle			1847/06/23*
Monaghan, Bridget	3	Wandsworth	Dublin	Ireland	1847/05/22
Monaghan, John	40	Virgilia	Liverpool	England	between September 19 and 25, 1847
Monaghan, John		Syria	Liverpool	England	
Monaghan, Michael	14	Virginius	Liverpool	England	between September 5 and 11, 1847
Monaghan, Nancy	35	Virginius	Liverpool	England	between August 15 and 21, 1847
Monaghan, Peter	40	Westmoreland	Sligo	Ireland	between August 8 and 14, 1847
Monday, Catherine	23	Maria Somes	Cork	Ireland	between August 29 and September 4, 1847
Monday, Patrick	54	Colonist	New Ross	Ireland	between August 29 and September 4, 1847
Montgomery, Main	3	Pursuit	Liverpool	England	between June 13 and 19, 1847
Montgomery, Mary	30	Odessa	Dublin	Ireland	1847/08/16
Montgomery, Samuel	35	Royal Adelaide	Killala	Ireland	1847/08/16
Moody, Robert	22	Argo	Liverpool	England	1847/06/05
Mooney, John	38	Woodbine	Londonderry	Ireland	between July 11 and 17, 1847
Mooney, John	11 months	Rankin	Liverpool	England	1847/05/30
Mooney, Mary	10	Rose	Liverpool	England	between June 20 and 26, 1847
Mooney, Michael	29	George	Liverpool	England	between June 13 and 19, 1847
Mooney, Patrick	52	Rose	Liverpool	England	between July 11 and 17, 1847
Mooney, Patrick	50	Rose	Liverpool	England	between July 11 and 17, 1847
Mooney, Rachel	45	Horatio	Limerick	Ireland	between September 5 and 11, 1847
Mooney, Sarah	30	Industry	Sligo	Ireland	between September 12 and 18, 1847
Moore, Anastasia	47	Avon	Cork	Ireland	between August 1 and 7, 1847
Moore, Catherine	9	Triton	Liverpool	England	between August 22 and 28, 1847
Moore, James	27	James Moran	Liverpool	England	between August 8 and 14, 1847
Moore, Mary	22	Larch	Sligo	Ireland	between August 15 and 21, 1847
Moore, Mary	3	John Munn	Liverpool	England	between August 1 and 7, 1847
Moore, Patrick	46	Highland Mary	Cork	Ireland	between July 4 and 10, 1847
Moore, Patrick	20	Triton	Liverpool	England	between August 15 and 21, 1847
Moore, Thomas	26	Highland Mary	Cork	Ireland	between July 4 and 10, 1847
Moore, Timothy	35	Avon	Cork	Ireland	between August 1 and 7, 1847
Moore, William	30	Syria	Liverpool	England	between June 13 and 19, 1847
Moran, Ann	29	Virginius	Liverpool	England	between August 15 and 21, 1847
Moran, Bridget	46	Goliah	Liverpool	England	between July 11 and 17, 1847
Moran, Bridget	5	James Moran	Liverpool	England	between July 4 and 10, 1847
Moran, Bridget	3	Virginius	Liverpool	England	between August 15 and 21, 1847
Moran, Francis	55	Naomi	Liverpool	England	between August 8 and 14, 1847
Moran, James	6	Goliah	Liverpool	England	between July 11 and 17, 1847
Moran, James	50	Sesostris	Londonderry	Ireland	between July 11 and 17, 1847
Moran, James	40	John Bolton	Liverpool	England	between July 11 and 17, 1847
Moran, James	30	Erin's Queen	Liverpool	England	between August 22 and 28, 1847
Moran, Maria	5	Emigrant	Liverpool	England	between September 26 and October 2, 1847
Moran, Mary	50	Emigrant	Liverpool	England	between September 26 and October 2, 1847
Moran, Mary	6 months	Washington	Liverpool	England	between September 5 and 11, 1847
Moran, Michael	50	Superior	Londonderry	Ireland	between September 26 and October 2, 1847

Lists of people who died and were buried on Grosse Île, in 1847

Name	Age	Vessel	Port	Country	Date of death
Moran, Michael	8	Emigrant	Liverpool	England	between October 3 and 9, 1847
Moran, Michael	40	Emigrant	Liverpool	England	between October 3 and 9, 1847
Moran, Nancy	30	Lotus	Liverpool	England	between August 8 and 14, 1847
Moran, Patrick	35	Naomi	Liverpool	England	between September 5 and 11, 1847
Moran, Patrick	2 years & 6 months	Emigrant	Liverpool	England	between September 26 and October 2, 1847
Moran, Patrick	22	Wandsworth	Dublin	Ireland	between June 6 and 12, 1847
Moran, Patrick	1	Covenanter	Cork	Ireland	between August 1 and 7, 1847
Moran, William	60	Bridgetown	Liverpool	England	between August 29 and September 4, 1847
Moriarty, John	27	Sir Henry Pottinger	Cork	Ireland	between August 1 and 7, 1847
Moriarty, Judith	10	Yorkshire	Liverpool	England	between August 15 and 21, 1847
Moriarty, Timothy	43	Bee	Cork	Ireland	between May 29 and June 5, 1847
Morley, Anthony	27	Ganges	Liverpool	England	between August 29 and September 4, 1847
Morley, John	18	Clarendon	Liverpool	England	between June 13 and 19, 1847
Moroney, Patrick	60	Hibernia			between June 6 and 12, 1847
Morris, Ann	10	George	Liverpool	England	between July 18 and 24, 1847
Morris, Bridget	40	George	Liverpool	England	between June 6 and 12, 1847
Morris, John	40	St. George			between June 27 and July 3, 1847
Morrison, John	30	Constitution	Belfast	Ireland	1847/07/14
Morrison, William	5 months	Constitution	Belfast	Ireland	1847/06/05
Morrow, John	48	Julius Caesar	Liverpool	England	1847/09/19
Morrow, John	5 months	Champion	Liverpool	England	between August 29 and September 4, 1847
Morrow, Judith	3	Champion	Liverpool	England	between August 29 and September 4, 1847
Morrow, Mary Tolarton	54	Lord Seaton	Belfast	Ireland	1847/06/11
Moss, Charles	23	Lotus	Liverpool	England	between July 25 and 31, 1847
Mossip, Jane	5	Ninian	Limerick	Ireland	1847/06/02
Mowatt, Henry	20	James Moran	Liverpool	England	between August 1 and 7, 1847
Moylan, Philip	23	Free Trader	Liverpool	England	between August 22 and 28, 1847
Mulcahey, Mary		John Bolton	Liverpool	England	
Muldoon, John	7	John Munn	Liverpool	England	between August 8 and 14, 1847
Mulhall, Catherine	22	Aberdeen	Liverpool	England	between July 18 and 24, 1847
Mulhall, James	30	Eliza Caroline	Liverpool	England	between July 11 and 17, 1847
Mulhall, James	12	Aberdeen	Liverpool	England	between July 4 and 10, 1847
Mulhern, Thomas	9	Henry	Donegal	Ireland	between June 20 and 26, 1847
Mulholland, Catherine		Syria	Liverpool	England	
Mulholland, Catherine	4	Yorkshire	Liverpool	England	between August 8 and 14, 1847
Mulholland, Catherine	30	Lord Seaton	Belfast	Ireland	between June 13 and 19, 1847
Mulholland, Mary	30	Naomi	Liverpool	England	between August 8 and 14, 1847
Mulholland, Mary	12	John Munn	Liverpool	England	between August 15 and 21, 1847
Mulkeen, Mary	60	Wolfville	Sligo	Ireland	between May 29 and June 5, 1847
Mullaney, Hugh	36	Sarah Maria	Sligo	Ireland	between June 27 and July 3, 1847
Mullaney, John	20	Junior	Liverpool	England	between June 27 and July 3, 1847
Mullany, Catherine	30	George	Liverpool	England	between May 23 and 29, 1847
Mullarkey, Austin	22	Eliza Caroline	Liverpool	England	between August 1 and 7, 1847
Mullen, Bridget	24	Wolfville	Sligo	Ireland	between June 27 and July 3, 1847
Mullen, Bridget	20	Free Trader	Liverpool	England	between September 5 and 11, 1847
Mullen, John	60	Bridgetown	Liverpool	England	between September 12 and 18, 1847
Mullen, Mary	21	Naomi	Liverpool	England	between August 29 and September 4, 1847
Mullen, Mary	25	Naomi	Liverpool	England	between August 15 and 21, 1847
Mullen, May	40	Covenanter	Cork	Ireland	between August 8 and 14, 1847
Mullen, Michael	35	Gilmour	Cork	Ireland	between June 13 and 19, 1847
Mullen, Patrick	10	Virginius	Liverpool	England	between August 8 and 14, 1847
Mulligan, Catherine	60	Scotland	Cork	Ireland	between August 8 and 14, 1847
Mulligan, Elizabeth	14	Avon	Cork	Ireland	between August 15 and 21, 1847
Mulligan, John	20	Eliza Morrison	Belfast	Ireland	between August 22 and 28, 1847
Mulligan, Judith	6	Greenock	Liverpool	England	between August 8 and 14, 1847
Mulligan, Mary	12	Congress	Sligo	Ireland	between July 11 and 17, 1847
Mulligan, Thomas	28	Coromandel	Dublin	Ireland	between July 25 and 31, 1847
Mulroney, James	35	Avon	Cork	Ireland	between August 15 and 21, 1847
Mulroy, Honora	17	George	Liverpool	England	between August 8 and 14, 1847
Mulry, Owen	60	Free Trader	Liverpool	England	between August 15 and 21, 1847
Mulvey, Bridget	19	Wm S. Hamilton	New Ross	Ireland	between August 8 and 14, 1847
Mulvey, Mary	22	Messenger	Liverpool	England	between October 10 and 16, 1847
Mulvihill, Patrick	3	George	Liverpool	England	between May 29 and June 5, 1847
Mulvochery, Catherine	8	George	Liverpool	England	between May, 29 and June 5, 1847
Mulvochery, M.	6	Urania	Cork	Ireland	between May 29 and June 5, 1847
Murnane, Francis		Bee	Cork	Ireland	
Murphy, Austin	26	Ganges	Liverpool	England	between September 19 and 25, 1847
Murphy, Bridget	12	Naomi	Liverpool	England	between August 8 and 14, 1847
Murphy, Catherine	17	Margaret	New Ross	Ireland	between July 11 and 17, 1847
Murphy, Charles	30	Avon	Cork	Ireland	between September 5 and 11, 1847
Murphy, Ellen	3	Coromandel	Dublin	Ireland	between July 25 and 31, 1847
Murphy, Helen	22	Agamemnon	Liverpool	England	between August 8 and 14, 1847
Murphy, James	45	Coromandel	Dublin	Ireland	between July 4 and 10, 1847
Murphy, James	20	Margaret	New Ross	Ireland	between July 4 and 10, 1847
Murphy, James	12	Wolfville	Sligo	Ireland	between June 13 and 19, 1847
Murphy, Jane	4	Naomi	Liverpool	England	between August 8 and 14, 1847

The emigrants

Name	Age	Vessel	Port	Country	Date of death
Murphy, Johanna	22	Agnes	Cork	Ireland	between July 4 and 10, 1847
Murphy, John	17	Agnes	Cork	Ireland	between May 29 and June 5, 1847
Murphy, John	27	Wolfville	Sligo	Ireland	between May 29 and June 5, 1847
Murphy, John	50	Ganges	Liverpool	England	between August 22 and 28, 1847
Murphy, John	20	Thistle	Liverpool	England	between July 18 and 24, 1847
Murphy, John	10	Rose	Liverpool	England	between June 27 and July 3, 1847
Murphy, John	1 year & 6 months				1847/05/18
Murphy, Margaret	42	Clarendon	Liverpool	England	between May 29 and June 5, 1847
Murphy, Martin	7	Asia	Cork	Ireland	between August 1 and 7, 1847
Murphy, Mary	8	Virginius	Liverpool	England	between August 15 and 21, 1847
Murphy, Mary	21	Broom	Liverpool	England	between August 8 and 14, 1847
Murphy, Mary	40	George	Liverpool	England	between July 11 and 17, 1847
Murphy, Mary	22	Avon	Cork	Ireland	between July 18 and 24, 1847
Murphy, Mary	27	Naomi	Liverpool	England	between August 22 and 28, 1847
Murphy, Mary	9 months	Lord Sandon	Cork	Ireland	between June 20 and 26, 1847
Murphy, Mary	35	Lord Sandon	Cork	Ireland	between June 20 and 26, 1847
Murphy, Mary	6	George	Liverpool	England	between July 11 and 17, 1847
Murphy, Mary	20	Rose	Liverpool	England	between August 22 and 28, 1847
Murphy, Michael	1	Isabella	Killala	Ireland	between September 19 and 25, 1847
Murphy, Michael	24	Avon	Cork	Ireland	between October 10 and 16, 1847
Murphy, Patrick	30	George	Liverpool	England	between June 27 and July 3, 1847
Murphy, Patrick	40	George	Liverpool	England	between June 6 and 12, 1847
Murphy, Patrick	1	Sir Henry Pottinger	Cork	Ireland	between August 1 and 7, 1847
Murphy, Rose	30	Rose	Liverpool	England	between August 8 and 14, 1847
Murphy, Susan	25	Marchioness of Breadalbane	Sligo	Ireland	between August 8 and 14, 1847
Murphy, Susan	9	John Munn	Liverpool	England	between August 15 and 21, 1847
Murphy, Sybil	30	Naomi	Liverpool	England	between August 22 and 28, 1847
Murphy, Thomas	25	Erin's Queen	Liverpool	England	between September 5 and 11, 1847
Murphy, Thomas	28	Free Trader	Liverpool	England	between August 15 and 21, 1847
Murphy, Thomas	26	Wandsworth	Dublin	Ireland	between June 27 and July 3, 1847
Murphy, Thomas	50	Odessa	Dublin	Ireland	between August 22 and 28, 1847
Murphy, Thomas	25	Argyle	Newport	England	between September 26 and October 2, 1847
Murphy, Timothy	24	Margaret	New Ross	Ireland	between June 27 and July 3, 1847
Murray, Ann	5	Bridgetown	Liverpool	England	between September 19 and 25, 1847
Murray, Ann	3	Naomi	Liverpool	England	between August 8 and 14, 1847
Murray, Anthony	1	Triton	Liverpool	England	between July 18 and 24, 1847
Murray, Catherine	38	Jessie	Cork	Ireland	between July 4 and 10, 1847
Murray, Charles	40	Pursuit	Liverpool	England	between August 1 and 7, 1847
Murray, Daniel	22	John Francis	Cork	Ireland	between May 23 and 29, 1847
Murray, Denis	27	Marchioness of Abercorn	Londonderry	Ireland	between August 1 and 7, 1847
Murray, Eliza	35	Pursuit	Liverpool	England	between July 18 and 24, 1847
Murray, Ellen	60	John Francis	Cork	Ireland	between June 20 and 26, 1847
Murray, George	11	Naomi	Liverpool	England	between August 22 and 28, 1847
Murray, John	1	Bridgetown	Liverpool	England	between September 5 and 11, 1847
Murray, Luke	8	Naomi	Liverpool	England	between August 8 and 14, 1847
Murray, Margaret	11	James Moran	Liverpool	England	between July 11 and 17, 1847
Murray, Margaret	16	Broom	Liverpool	England	between August 1 and 7, 1847
Murray, Mary	38	Virginius	Liverpool	England	between August 22 and 28, 1847
Murray, Michael	5	John Munn	Liverpool	England	between September 5 and 11, 1847
Murray, Michael	3	Erin's Queen	Liverpool	England	between July 25 and 31, 1847
Murray, Michael	50	Washington	Liverpool	England	between August 22 and 28, 1847
Murray, Patrick	24	Agnes	Cork	Ireland	between June 6 and 12, 1847
Murray, Thomas	50	George	Liverpool	England	between May 29 and June 5, 1847
Murtagh, Ellen	46	Perseverance	Dublin	Ireland	1847/05/22
Murtagh, Ellen	50	Perseverance	Dublin	Ireland	1847/05/20
Murtagh, Margaret	5	Perseverance	Dublin	Ireland	between May 30 and June 5, 1847
Mylan, Ann		Free Trader	Liverpool	England	
Myland, Harry	5	Syria	Liverpool	England	between May 29 and June 5, 1847
N___, I___					
N___, J___					
N___, P___					
Nagle, Garrett	26	Bee	Cork	Ireland	between May 29 and June 5, 1847
Naughton, A.					
Naughton, Bridget	22	Naparina	Dublin	Ireland	between August 15 and 21, 1847
Naughton, Bridget	20	Eliza Caroline	Liverpool	England	between July 11 and 17, 1847
Naughton, John	40	Covenanter	Cork	Ireland	between August 8 and 14, 1847
Naughton, Nancy	3	Triton	Liverpool	England	between July 25 and 31, 1847
Naylor, Bridget	30	Progress	New Ross	Ireland	between July 25 and 31, 1847
Naylor, Michael	28	Saguenay	Cork	Ireland	between August 29 and September 4, 1847
Neal, Mary	30	Progress	New Ross	Ireland	between July 25 and 31, 1847
Neary, Mary	30	Dykes	Sligo	Ireland	between July 11 and 17, 1847
Negro, John	14				1847/08/08
Neil, Darby	30	Sir Henry Pottinger	Belfast	Ireland	between August 29 and September 4, 1847
Neil, George	1	Lord Seaton	Belfast	Ireland	1847/05/22
Neil, Michael	50	Wandsworth	Dublin	Ireland	between June 6 and 12, 1847
Neil, Peter	40	Progress	New Ross	Ireland	between July 11 and 17, 1847
Neilan, John	35	Virginius	Liverpool	England	between August 15 and 21, 1847

Lists of people who died and were buried on Grosse Île, in 1847

Name	Age	Vessel	Port	Country	Date of death
Neilan, Judith	28	Cape Breton	Dublin	Ireland	between June 20 and 26, 1847
Nelis, Catherine	1	Numa	Sligo	Ireland	between July 25 and 31, 1847
Nelis, Isabella	24	Superior	Londonderry	Ireland	between September 26 and October 2, 1847
Nelis, Mary	35	Numa	Sligo	Ireland	between July 18 and 24, 1847
Nelligan, Margaret Jane	1 year & 4 months	Christiana	Londonderry	Ireland	1847/06/06
Nelligan, Mary	20	Erin's Queen	Liverpool	England	between July 18 and 24, 1847
Nelligan, Morris	4	Triton	Liverpool	England	between July 25 and 31, 1847
Neville, Ann	22	Wandsworth	Dublin	Ireland	between May 23 and 29, 1847
Neville, John	1	Saguenay	Cork	Ireland	between August 15 and 21, 1847
Neville, Mary	1 year & 6 months	Bee	Cork	Ireland	between June 13 and 19, 1847
Neville, William	4	Free Trader	Liverpool	England	between August 15 and 21, 1847
Newell, Catherine	4	Minerva	Galway	Ireland	between September 19 and 25, 1847
Newell, Margaret	4	Minerva	Dublin	Ireland	between September 12 and 18, 1847
Newman, Thomas		Wandsworth	Dublin	Ireland	
Newman, Thomas	26	Perseverance	Dublin	Ireland	between May 29 and June 5, 1847
Newman, William	39	Wandsworth	Dublin	Ireland	between May 29 and June 5, 1847
Nicolson, Daniel	4	Caithness-shire	Belfast	Ireland	between June 6 and 12, 1847
Nicolson, John	36	Caithness-shire	Belfast	Ireland	1847/06/09
Nilan, Anna	30	Free Trader	Liverpool	England	between September 12 and 18, 1847
Nochtin, Anthony	40	Eliza Caroline	Liverpool	England	between June 6 and 12, 1847
Nolan, Daniel	7	Wandsworth	Dublin	Ireland	between June 13 and 19, 1847
Nolan, Daniel	40	Wandsworth	Dublin	Ireland	between May 29 and June 5, 1847
Nolan, James	9	Charles Walton	Killala	Ireland	between August 1 and 7, 1847
Nolan, Johanna	47	Rankin	Liverpool	England	between July 25 and 31, 1847
Nolan, Margaret	30	Standard	New Ross	Ireland	between July 18 and 24, 1847
Nolan, Mary	21	Lady Campbell	Dublin	Ireland	between September 5 and 11, 1847
Nolan, Mary	20	Margaret	New Ross	Ireland	between July 25 and 31, 1847
Nolan, Michael	24	Jessie	Limerick	Ireland	between August 29 and September 4, 1847
Noon, John	35	Virginius	Liverpool	England	between August 22 and 28, 1847
Noonan, Alexander	20	Erin's Queen	Liverpool	England	between August 8 and 14, 1847
Noonan, Catherine	40	Free Trader	Liverpool	England	between August 8 and 14, 1847
Noonan, Catherine	40	John Munn	Liverpool	England	between August 8 and 14, 1847
Noonan, Ellen	13	Odessa	Dublin	Ireland	between September 12 and 18, 1847
Noonan, John	5	Odessa	Dublin	Ireland	between August 29 and September 4, 1847
Noonan, Joseph	10	Odessa	Dublin	Ireland	between August 22 and 28, 1847
Noonan, Margaret	7	George	Liverpool	England	between June 6 and 12, 1847
Noonan, Mary	40	Odessa	Dublin	Ireland	between August 29 and September 4, 1847
Noonan, Patrick	40	Odessa	Dublin	Ireland	between August 22 and 28, 1847
Noonan, Patrick	25	Minerva	Dublin	Ireland	between September 26 and October 2, 1847
Norton, James	4	Blonde	Liverpool	England	between May 29 and June 5, 1847
Norton, Mary	4	Blonde	Liverpool	England	between June 13 and 19, 1847
Norton, Patrick	8	Blonde	Liverpool	England	between June 6 and 12, 1847
Nowlan, Mary		Goliah	Liverpool	England	
Nugent, Ellen	6	Virgilia	Liverpool	England	between September 12 and 18, 1847
Nugent, George	40	Virgilia	Liverpool	England	between September 12 and 18, 1847
Nugent, James	10	Naomi	Liverpool	England	between August 8 and 14, 1847
Nugent, John	50	John Munn	Liverpool	England	between August 1 and 7, 1847
O'Brien, Eliza	17	Free Trader	Liverpool	England	between May 23 and 29, 1847
O'Brien, James	25	Junior	Liverpool	England	between August 1 and 7, 1847
O'Brien, John	26	Odessa	Dublin	Ireland	between August 8 and 14, 1847
O'Brien, Joseph		Junior	Liverpool	England	
O'Brien, Margaret	38	Junior	Liverpool	England	between July 4 and 10, 1847
O'Brien, Mary	28	Eliza Caroline	Liverpool	England	between July 11 and 17, 1847
O'Brien, Michael		Tamarac	Liverpool	England	
O'Brien, Patrick	34	James Moran	Liverpool	England	between August 8 and 14, 1847
O'Brien, Timothy	43	Jane Black	Limerick	Ireland	between May 23 and 29, 1847
O'Connell, Dominick	26	John Munn	Liverpool	England	between August 22 and 28, 1847
O'Donnell, Helen	2	Agnes	Cork	Ireland	between May 23 and 29, 1847
O'Donnell, Hugh	3	Free Trader	Liverpool	England	between August 15 and 21, 1847
O'Donnell, Sydney	5	Sarah	Liverpool	England	between August 15 and 21, 1847
O'Donoghue, Michael		Pandora	New Ross	Ireland	
O'Dowd, James	30	Sarah	Liverpool	England	between July 18 and 24, 1847
O'Hara, Ann	24	Virginius	Liverpool	England	between August 8 and 14, 1847
O'Hara, Barnet	14	John Munn	Liverpool	England	between August 8 and 14, 1847
O'Hara, Michael	2 months	Constitution	Belfast	Ireland	between June 13 and 19, 1847
O'Hara, Nelly	5	John and Robert	Liverpool	England	between August 8 and 14, 1847
O'Hara, Thomas	2 years & 6 months	Aberdeen	Liverpool	England	between June 20 and 26, 1847
O'Hare, Sarah	48	Sir Henry Pottinger	Belfast	Ireland	1847/09/14
O'Hart, Margaret	24	Aberdeen	Liverpool	England	between June 20 and 26, 1847
O'Hart, Rose	25	Aberdeen	Liverpool	England	between June 27 and July 3, 1847
O'Hoy, Catherine	3 months	Numa	Sligo	Ireland	between August 29 and September 4, 1847
O'Leary, Mary	2 years & 6 months	Agnes	Cork	Ireland	between June 6 and 12, 1847
O'Leary, Thomas	44	George	Liverpool	England	between June 6 and 12, 1847
O'Malley, Bridget		Erin's Queen	Liverpool	England	
O'Malley, John	30	Erin's Queen	Liverpool	England	between August 15 and 21, 1847
O'Neill, Catherine	5	Triton	Liverpool	England	between July 25 and 31, 1847

The Emigrants

Name	Age	Vessel	Port	Country	Date of death
O'Neill, John	26	Avon	Cork	Ireland	between July 25 and 31, 1847
O'Neill, Mary	24	John Munn	Liverpool	England	between August 15 and 21, 1847
O'Neill, Mary	10	Wandsworth	Dublin	Ireland	between June 6 and 12, 1847
O'Neill, Mary	20	Marinus	Dublin	Ireland	between September 19 and 25, 1847
O'Neill, Stephen	30	Covenanter	Cork	Ireland	between September 12 and 18, 1847
O'Neill, William	40	Triton	Liverpool	England	between July 25 and 31, 1847
O'Reilly, Edward	30				1847/05/18
O'Reilly, Patrick		Syria	Liverpool	England	
O'Shaughnessy, Ellen	22	Naomi	Liverpool	England	between September 12 and 18, 1847
O'Shaughnessy, Thomas	22	Naomi	Liverpool	England	between September 26 and October 2, 1847
Oates, Dominic	30	Clarendon	Liverpool	England	between May 29 and June 5, 1847
Oates, Donald	32	Clarendon	Liverpool	England	between June 20 and 26, 1847
Oniov, Jacob	8	Wellington	Liverpool	England	1847/09/23
Orr, Alexander	17	Yorkshire	Liverpool	England	1847/08/17
Orr, Dorothy	11	Yorkshire	Liverpool	England	1847/09/16
Orr, John		Westmoreland	Sligo	Ireland	1847/09/12
Orr, Mary	40	Yorkshire	Liverpool	England	1847/08/22
Osborne, Ann	40	Emily	Cork	Ireland	between August 8 and 14, 1847
Owen, Mary	48	Yorkshire	Liverpool	England	between August 15 and 21, 1847
Owen, Sally	14	Yorkshire	Liverpool	England	between August 22 and 28, 1847
Owen, Thomas	3 months	Yorkshire Lass	Killala	Ireland	1847/08/08
P___, ___					
Park, Joseph	30	Emigrant	Liverpool	England	1847/09/27
Parsons, Samuel	30	Eliza Caroline	Liverpool	England	1847/08/20
Patterson, John	60	Ganges	Liverpool	England	between August 29 and September 4, 1847
Patterson, John	45	Superior	Londonderry	Ireland	1847/10/03
Patterson, Thomas	15	Ganges	Liverpool	England	1847/08/29
Patterson, William	60	Ganges	Liverpool	England	1847/08/29
Patton, Mary	9	Goliah	Liverpool	England	1847/07/21
Patton, Thomas	55	Phoenix	Liverpool	England	between May 29 and June 5, 1847
Patton, William	50	Goliah	Liverpool	England	between August 8 and 14, 1847
Paul, Agnes	28	Sobraon	Liverpool	England	1847/07/12
Pearson, Henry	3	Triton	Liverpool	England	between July 11 and 17, 1847
Peel, Mary	26	Pursuit	Liverpool	England	between June 20 and 26, 1847
Peoples, Thomas	25	Apollo	Halifax	Canada	between July 18 and 24, 1847
Perry, Charles	21	Wakefield	Cork	Ireland	between July 4 and 10, 1847
Perry, William					1847/07/10
Peters, Philip	1 year & 6 months	Araminta	Liverpool	England	between August 8 and 14, 1847
Phelan, Bridget	17	Dominica	Cork	Ireland	between June 13 and 19, 1847
Phelan, Edward	35	Odessa	Dublin	Ireland	between August 1 and 7, 1847
Phelan, John	17	Aberdeen	Liverpool	England	between June 6 and 12, 1847
Phelan, John	23	Royalist	Liverpool	England	between May 29 and June 5, 1847
Picken, Catherine	83	Gilmour	Cork	Ireland	between July 24 and 31, 1847
Pickering, Sarah	13	Goliah	Liverpool	England	between July 18 and 24, 1847
Pierce, Edward	20	Larch	Sligo	Ireland	between August 15 and 21, 1847
Pierce, Margaret	28	Jessie	Limerick	Ireland	between August 1 and 7, 1847
Pierce, Mary	6	Naomi	Liverpool	England	between August 15 and 21, 1847
Pierce, William	30	Jessie	Cork	Ireland	1847/07/26
Pigott, Ann	60	Wakefield	Cork	Ireland	between July 18 and 24, 1847
Pigott, John	5 months	John Francis	Cork	Ireland	between May 29 and June 5, 1847
Pigott, Mary	30	Elizabeth	Liverpool	England	between August 29 and September 4, 1847
Pigott, William	36	John Francis	Cork	Ireland	between June 6 and 12, 1847
Pinu, Alexander	15	Aberdeen	Liverpool	England	between June 27 and July 3, 1847
Polk, John	36	Junior	Liverpool	England	between July 4 and 10, 1847
Polk, Joseph	20	Araminta	Liverpool	England	between August 15 and 21, 1847
Pollock, Isaac	6	Yorkshire Lass	Killala	Ireland	between August 1 and 7, 1847
Potter, Thomas	24	Minerva	Galway	Ireland	between August 22 and 28, 1847
Powell, John	28	Virginius	Liverpool	England	between August 29 and September 4, 1847
Powell, Mary	32	Avon	Cork	Ireland	between August 8 and 14, 1847
Power, Carroll	35	Araminta	Liverpool	England	between June 27 and July 3, 1847
Power, Catherine	50	Erin's Queen	Liverpool	England	between August 1 and 7, 1847
Power, George	27	Free Trader	Liverpool	England	1847/08/22
Power, Honora					
Power, John	38	Lord Sandon	Cork	Ireland	between June 20 and 26, 1847
Power, Mary	19	Dominica	Cork	Ireland	between June 13 and 19, 1847
Power, Mary	22	Avon	Cork	Ireland	between August 22 and 28, 1847
Power, Patrick	12	Erin's Queen	Liverpool	England	between July 25 and 31, 1847
Power, Patrick	4 months	Columbia	Sligo	Ireland	between August 8 and 14, 1847
Prendergast, Catherine	5	Avon	Cork	Ireland	between August 22 and 28, 1847
Prendergast, Timothy	30	Avon	Cork	Ireland	between July 18 and 24, 1847
Prestage, Ellen	2	Aberdeen	Liverpool	England	1847/05/30
Price, Edward					
Price, James	27	Wellington	Liverpool	England	between September 26 and October 2, 1847
Price, Thomas	36				between July 25 and 31, 1847
Pritchard, William	27				between July 18 and 24, 1847
Pugh, Catherine	10	Free Trader	Liverpool	England	between August 8 and 14, 1847
Purcell, Alexander	2	Perseverance	Dublin	Ireland	1847/05/21
Purcell, Ellen	50	Brothers	Dublin	Ireland	between August 29 and September 4, 1847
Purcell, Hugh	30	Jessie	Limerick	Ireland	between August 8 and 14, 1847
Quane, B.	12	John Bolton	Liverpool	England	between June 6 and 12, 1847
Quigley, Edward		Lotus	Liverpool	England	
Quigley, Joseph	50	Odessa	Dublin	Ireland	between August 29 and September 4, 1847
Quigley, Mary	26	Wandsworth	Dublin	Ireland	between June 6 and 12, 1847

Lists of people who died and were buried on Grosse Île, in 1847

Name	Age	Vessel	Port	Country	Date of death
Quigley, Michael	52	James Moran	Liverpool	England	between August 29 and September 4, 1847
Quigley, Thomas	2	Wandsworth	Dublin	Ireland	between May 23 and 29, 1847
Quigley, Thomas	25	James Moran	Liverpool	England	between July 25 and 31, 1847
Quigley, William	46	Virgilia	Liverpool	England	between September 19 and 25, 1847
Quilligan, Martin	10	Triton	Liverpool	England	between August 8 and 14, 1847
Quiltey, Johanna	26	John Munn	Liverpool	England	between September 5 and 11, 1847
Quines, Mary	48	Clarendon	Liverpool	England	between May 29 and June 5, 1847
Quinlan, Ann	30	Agnes	Cork	Ireland	between July 4 and 10, 1847
Quinlan, Ellen	20	Agnes	Cork	Ireland	between June 27 and July 3, 1847
Quinlan, Margaret	21	John Francis	Cork	Ireland	between June 13 and 19, 1847
Quinlan, Mary	1	Virgilia	Liverpool	England	between September 26 and October 2, 1847
Quinn, Catherine	1	Naomi	Liverpool	England	between August 8 and 14, 1847
Quinn, Catherine	2	Sir Robert Peel	Liverpool	England	between September 19 and 25, 1847
Quinn, Charles	20	Independance	Belfast	Ireland	between August 8 and 14, 1847
Quinn, Edward	7	Independance	Belfast	Ireland	between August 22 and 28, 1847
Quinn, George	5 months	Emigrant	Liverpool	England	between September 26 and October 2, 1847
Quinn, James	45	Naomi	Liverpool	England	between August 22 and 28, 1847
Quinn, James	18	Sisters	Liverpool	England	between July 25 and 31, 1847
Quinn, James	19	Independance	Belfast	Ireland	between August 1 and 7, 1847
Quinn, Mary	40	Naomi	Liverpool	England	between August 8 and 14, 1847
Quinn, Mary	80	Odessa	Dublin	Ireland	between August 8 and 14, 1847
Quinn, Mary	12	Independance	Belfast	Ireland	between August 1 and 7, 1847
Quinn, Mary	9	Naomi	Liverpool	England	between August 22 and 28, 1847
Quinn, Mary	28	Naomi	Liverpool	England	between September 19 and 25, 1847
Quinn, Robert	3	Independance	Belfast	Ireland	between July 25 and 31, 1847
Quinn, Roger	55	Virginius	Liverpool	England	between August 15 and 21, 1847
Quinn, Thomas	40	Independance	Belfast	Ireland	between July 25 and 31, 1847
Quinn, Timothy	35	James Moran	Liverpool	England	between July 11 and 17, 1847
Quinn, William	56	Odessa	Dublin	Ireland	between August 1 and 7, 1847
Quinton, Ann	35	Agnes	Cork	Ireland	between May 23 and 29, 1847
Quirke, Margaret	4 months	Lord Sandon	Cork	Ireland	between July 4 and 10, 1847
Quirke, Mary	23	Jessie	Cork	Ireland	between July 18 and 24, 1847
R___, Mary		Albion			
Rafferty, Mary	26	Wolfville	Sligo	Ireland	between June 20 and 26, 1847
Rahilly, James	1	Araminta	Liverpool	England	between June 20 and 26, 1847
Ray, Eliza	25	Prince George			between June 20 and 26, 1847
Ray, George		John Jardine	Liverpool	England	
Reaburn, Henry	19	John and Robert	Liverpool	England	between September 12 and 18, 1847
Reaburn, Henry	19	John and Robert	Liverpool	England	1847/09/13
Reaburn, Mary	24	Triton	Liverpool	England	between July 18 and 24, 1847
Reddy, Ann	2	Wolfville	Sligo	Ireland	between May 29 and June 5, 1847
Reddy, Bryan	23	Larch	Sligo	Ireland	between August 29 and September 4, 1847
Reddy, Bryan	23	Greenock	Liverpool	England	between August 29 and September 4, 1847
Reddy, John	35	Ocean Queen	Cork	Ireland	between August 15 and 21, 1847
Reddy, Mary	14	Greenock	Liverpool	England	between August 15 and 21, 1847
Reddy, Mary	45	Greenock	Liverpool	England	between August 29 and September 4, 1847
Reddy, Rose	16	Greenock	Liverpool	England	between July 25 and 31, 1847
Reddy, Thomas	55	Greenock	Liverpool	England	between July 25 and 31, 1847
Redmond, John	26	Lady Gordon	Belfast	Ireland	between June 13 and 19, 1847
Regan, Cornelius	2	Pursuit	Liverpool	England	between June 27 and July 3, 1847
Regan, Denis	22	Lady Flora Hastings	Cork	Ireland	between August 22 and 28, 1847
Regan, Donald	16	Triton	Liverpool	England	between August 1 and 7, 1847
Regan, Helen	6	Rankin	Liverpool	England	between August 8 and 14, 1847
Regan, John	30	Gilmour	Cork	Ireland	between June 13 and 19, 1847
Regan, John	36	Jessie	Cork	Ireland	between July 25 and 31, 1847
Regan, M.					
Regan, Mary	22	Ganges	Liverpool	England	between August 15 and 21, 1847
Regan, Matthew	3	James Moran	Liverpool	England	between July 11 and 17, 1847
Regan, Patrick	40	Virginius	Liverpool	England	between August 29 and September 4, 1847
Reid, Elisa	5 years & 6 months				1847/06/07
Reid, James	57	Marchioness of Bute	Belfast	Ireland	between August 1 and 7, 1847
Reilly, Catherine	4	Argo	Liverpool	England	between June 13 and 19, 1847
Reilly, Catherine	1	Courier			between August 22 and 28, 1847
Reilly, Catherine	21	Corea	Liverpool	England	between September 12 and 18, 1847
Reilly, Catherine	24	Superior	Londonderry	Ireland	between September 26 and October 2, 1847
Reilly, Edward	30	Syria	Liverpool	England	1847/05/19
Reilly, Edward	30	Free Trader	Liverpool	England	between August 8 and 14, 1847
Reilly, John	9 months	George	Liverpool	England	between June 13 and 19, 1847
Reilly, Joshua	8	George	Liverpool	England	between June 20 and 26, 1847
Reilly, M.					
Reilly, Margaret	27	Ajax	Liverpool	England	between July 18 and 24, 1847
Reilly, Margaret	22	Gilmour	Cork	Ireland	between July 4 and 10, 1847
Reilly, Margaret Barry	32	Avon	Cork	Ireland	between July 18 and 24, 1847
Reilly, Mary	31	George	Liverpool	England	between June 20 and 26, 1847

The emigrants

Name	Age	Vessel	Port	Country	Date of death
Reilly, Mary	3	Corea	Liverpool	England	between August 29 and September 4, 1847
Reilly, Mary	24	Junior	Liverpool	England	between June 27 and July 3, 1847
Reilly, Mary	5	Naomi	Liverpool	England	between August 15 and 21, 1847
Reilly, Michael	25	Gilmour	Cork	Ireland	between July 11 and 17, 1847
Reilly, Michael	40	Superior	Londonderry	Ireland	between September 19 and 25, 1847
Reilly, Michael	1	Gilmour	Cork	Ireland	between June 6 and 12, 1847
Reilly, Nancy		John Bolton	Liverpool	England	
Reilly, Nancy	24	Syria	Liverpool	England	1847/05/20
Reilly, Patrick	30	Corea	Liverpool	England	between September 12 and 18, 1847
Reilly, Patrick	3	Triton	Liverpool	England	between August 8 and 14, 1847
Reilly, Philip	1 month	Argo	Liverpool	England	between June 27 and July 3, 1847
Reilly, T.	30	Agnes	Cork	Ireland	between May 23 and 29, 1847
Renney, Thomas	40	Covenanter	Cork	Ireland	between August 15 and 21, 1847
Reynolds, Alexander	4	Rankin	Liverpool	England	between June 13 and 19, 1847
Reynolds, Alice	50	Rankin	Liverpool	England	between July 4 and 10, 1847
Reynolds, Ellen	36	Champion	Liverpool	England	between September 5 and 11, 1847
Reynolds, Hugh	10	Rankin	Liverpool	England	between July 4 and 10, 1847
Reynolds, James	24	Ann	Liverpool	England	between July 4 and 10, 1847
Reynolds, John	24	Larch	Sligo	Ireland	between August 29 and September 4, 1847
Reynolds, Margaret	6	Rankin	Liverpool	England	1847/06/02
Reynolds, Mary	11	Virginius	Liverpool	England	between August 8 and 14, 1847
Reynolds, Mary		Princess Royal	Liverpool	England	
Reynolds, Mary	11	Naomi	Liverpool	England	between August 15 and 21, 1847
Reynolds, Patrick	20	Ganges	Liverpool	England	between August 15 and 21, 1847
Rice, Charles	40	Orlando	Newry	Ireland	between June 27 and July 3, 1847
Rice, Edward	18	Caithness-shire	Belfast	Ireland	between June 13 and 19, 1847
Rice, Elizabeth	55	Caithness-shire	Belfast	Ireland	1847/06/07
Rice, William	18	Junior	Liverpool	England	between June 27 and July 3, 1847
Richardson, John	23	Eliza	Glasgow	Scotland	1847/09/19
Rigney, Bridget	43	Clarendon	Liverpool	England	between June 13 and 19, 1847
Rigney, John	3	Clarendon	Liverpool	England	between May 23 and 29, 1847
Rigney, Thadeus		Clarendon	Liverpool	England	
Riordan, Bridget	17	Sobraon	Liverpool	England	between July 25 and 31, 1847
Riordan, Daniel	55	John Munn	Liverpool	England	between August 8 and 14, 1847
Riordan, John	23	John Francis	Cork	Ireland	between May 29 and June 5, 1847
Riordan, Margaret	16	Jessie	Cork	Ireland	between July 18 and 24, 1847
Ritchie, Jane	1	Rose	Liverpool	England	between June 27 and July 3, 1847
Ritchie, Thomas	2 years & 6 months	Constitution	Belfast	Ireland	between July 11 and 17, 1847
Rivlachen, Andrew	50	Jessie	Sligo	Ireland	between May 23 and 29, 1847
Roach, James	20	Scotland	Cork	Ireland	between July 18 and 24, 1847
Roach, Martha	30	Aberdeen	Liverpool	England	between July 4 and 10, 1847
Robb, Eliza	12	Rose	Liverpool	England	1847/06/15
Roberts, Margaret	6 months				1847/06/19
Robinson, Alex	20	Clarendon	Liverpool	England	between May 29 and June 5, 1847
Robinson, George	48	Rankin	Liverpool	England	1847/06/04
Robinson, James	21	Coromandel	Dublin	Ireland	between August 15 and 21, 1847
Robinson, Jane	9	Christiana	Londonderry	Ireland	between June 13 and 19, 1847
Robinson, John	34	Agnes	Cork	Ireland	between June 6 and 12, 1847
Robinson, John	22	Virginius	Liverpool	England	1847/08/23
Robinson, Mary	28	Naomi	Liverpool	England	between August 15 and 21, 1847
Robinson, Mary	36	Yorkshire	Liverpool	England	1847/08/19
Robinson, Thomas	36	Yorkshire	Liverpool	England	1847/08/22
Robinson, William	18				1847/06/28
Roche, Allison	60	John Munn	Liverpool	England	between August 8 and 14, 1847
Roche, John	24	Agnes	Cork	Ireland	between July 4 and 10, 1847
Rock, James	34	Industry	Dublin	Ireland	between September 19 and 25, 1847
Rodden, John	44	Marinus	Dublin	Ireland	1847/08/20
Rodden, John	40	Broom	Liverpool	England	between August 15 and 21, 1847
Rodgers, Francis	4	Margaret	New Ross	Ireland	between August 8 and 14, 1847
Rodgers, Mary	5	Greenock	Liverpool	England	between August 15 and 21, 1847
Rogers, Ellen	35	Eliza Caroline	Liverpool	England	between July 18 and 24, 1847
Rogers, Mary	38	Aberdeen	Liverpool	England	between June 20 and 26, 1847
Rogers, Matthew	3	James Moran	Liverpool	England	between July 11 and 17, 1847
Rogers, Michael	1	Sarah	Liverpool	England	between August 8 and 14, 1847
Rogers, Patrick	33	John Bolton	Liverpool	England	between August 1 and 7, 1847
Rohan, Elizabeth	33	Greenock	Liverpool	England	between July 25 and 31, 1847
Ronan, Margaret	13	Saguenay	Cork	Ireland	between August 15 and 21, 1847
Ronan, Mary	2	Saguenay	Cork	Ireland	between August 15 and 21, 1847
Ronan, Mary A.	31	Saguenay	Cork	Ireland	between August 15 and 21, 1847
Ronayne, Maurice	25	Euclid	Glasgow	Scotland	between August 15 and 21, 1847
Rooney, Bridget	40	Araminta	Liverpool	England	between June 27 and July 3, 1847
Rooney, Mary	50	Superior	Londonderry	Ireland	between October 3 and 9, 1847
Rooney, Mary	21	Emigrant	Liverpool	England	between October 17 and 23, 1847
Rooney, Patrick	45	Syria	Liverpool	England	between June 6 and 12, 1847
Ross, Alexander	19	Agnes	Cork	Ireland	between May 23 and 29, 1847
Ross, Catherine	1	Saguenay	Cork	Ireland	between August 22 and 28, 1847
Ross, Emma	1 year & 2 months	Ganges	Liverpool	England	1847/08/24
Ross, Esther	20	Lillias	Dublin	Ireland	between August 15 and 21, 1847
Ross, John	28	Saguenay	Cork	Ireland	between September 26 and October 2, 1847
Ross, Patrick	1	Lillias	Dublin	Ireland	between August 29 and September 4, 1847

Lists of people who died and were buried on Grosse Île, in 1847

Name	Age	Vessel	Port	Country	Date of death
Rossiter, Mary	36	Covenanter	Cork	Ireland	between August 15 and 21, 1847
Roth, John	40				1847/06/16*
Rourke, Farrel					
Rourke, John	35	Ganges	Liverpool	England	between August 22 and 28, 1847
Rourke, John	43	Yorkshire Lass	Killala	Ireland	between August 8 and 14, 1847
Rourke, Michael	19	Saguenay	Cork	Ireland	between September 5 and 11, 1847
Rourke, Thomas	3	Syria	Liverpool	England	between June 6 and 12, 1847
Rowan, Luke	30	John Munn	Liverpool	England	between September 19 and 25, 1847
Ruane, John	32	John Munn	Liverpool	England	between August 29 and September 4, 1847
Ruane, Luke	3	John Munn	Liverpool	England	between August 22 and 28, 1847
Ruane, Patrick	21	Washington	Liverpool	England	between September 12 and 18, 1847
Rush, Mary					
Rush, Patrick	60	Covenanter	Cork	Ireland	between August 8 and 14, 1847
Rush, Peter	3	Naomi	Liverpool	England	between August 8 and 14, 1847
Russell, Margaret	30	Bee	Cork	Ireland	between June 6 and 12, 1847
Rutledge, Ann	13	Ajax	Liverpool	England	between August 1 and 7, 1847
Rutledge, Catherine	44	Ajax	Liverpool	England	between June 20 and 26, 1847
Rutledge, Francis	10	Ajax	Liverpool	England	between July 4 and 10, 1847
Rutledge, J.					
Ryan, ___					
Ryan, Andrew	25	Avon	Cork	Ireland	between September 19 and 25, 1847
Ryan, Ann	2	Syria	Liverpool	England	between May 30 and June 5, 1847
Ryan, Anthony	31	Brothers	Dublin	Ireland	between September 26 and October 2, 1847
Ryan, Bridget	25	Greenock	Liverpool	England	between August 1 and 7, 1847
Ryan, Catherine	7	Virgilia	Liverpool	England	between October 17 and 23, 1847
Ryan, Cornelius	38	Greenock	Liverpool	England	between July 25 and 31, 1847
Ryan, Denis	23	Lady Flora Hastings	Cork	Ireland	between August 1 and 7, 1847
Ryan, Edward	40	Jessie	Limerick	Ireland	between August 8 and 14, 1847
Ryan, Helen	25	Sarah	Liverpool	England	between August 8 and 14, 1847
Ryan, James	40	Jane Black	Limerick	Ireland	between June 6 and 12, 1847
Ryan, John	4 months	Lord Seaton	Belfast	Ireland	between June 6 and 12, 1847
Ryan, John	6 months	Try Again	Cork	Ireland	between June 6 and 12, 1847
Ryan, John	55	Scotland	Cork	Ireland	between June 20 and 26, 1847
Ryan, Martin	30	Ann Kenny	Waterford	Ireland	between August 22 and 28, 1847
Ryan, Martin	1 year & 6 months	John Munn	Liverpool	England	between August 22 and 28, 1847
Ryan, Mary	26	Avon	Cork	Ireland	between July 18 and 24, 1847
Ryan, Mary	24	Scotland	Cork	Ireland	between June 20 and 26, 1847
Ryan, Mary	20	Ajax	Liverpool	England	between June 20 and 26, 1847
Ryan, Mary	29	Syria	Liverpool	England	between May 29 and June 5, 1847
Ryan, Michael	6 months	Try Again	Cork	Ireland	between June 6 and 12, 1847
Ryan, Noreen	50	Goliah	Liverpool	England	between July 25 and 31, 1847
Ryan, Patrick	30	Avon	Cork	Ireland	between July 18 and 24, 1847
Ryan, Patrick	55	Brothers	Dublin	Ireland	between August 22 and 28, 1847
Ryan, Philip	27	Free Trader	Liverpool	England	between September 12 and 18, 1847
Ryan, Thomas	25	Caithness-shire	Belfast	Ireland	between July 11 and 17, 1847
Ryan, William	32	George	Liverpool	England	between May 29 and June 5, 1847
Ryan, William	24	Free Trader	Liverpool	England	between August 22 and 28, 1847
S___, J___					
Saul, William	38	Jessie	Cork	Ireland	between July 4 and 10, 1847
Saunders, Owen	4	Naomi	Liverpool	England	between August 8 and 14, 1847
Scanlan, Bridget	24	Free Trader	Liverpool	England	between August 22 and 28, 1847
Scanlan, Rose	3	Greenock	Liverpool	England	between August 1 and 7, 1847
Scanlan, Thadeus	18	Broom	Liverpool	England	between August 15 and 21, 1847
Scott, Eliza	1	Triton	Liverpool	England	between August 15 and 21, 1847
Scott, Eliza	3	Avon	Cork	Ireland	between August 8 and 14, 1847
Scott, Foster	36	Champion	Liverpool	England	1847/09/09
Scott, George	2	Virginius	Liverpool	England	between August 8 and 14, 1847
Scott, George	31	Ganges	Liverpool	England	1847/09/09
Scott, George	1	Ann	Liverpool	England	between June 27 and July 3, 1847
Scott, M.A.	4	Superior	Londonderry	Ireland	between October 17 and 23, 1847
Scott, Mary	35	Douce Davie	Sligo	Ireland	1847/10/11
Scott, Mary	25	Ayrshire	Newry	Ireland	between August 15 and 21, 1847
Scott, Robert	28	Congress	Sligo	Ireland	1847/07/05
Scott, Thomas	50	Ajax	Liverpool	England	1847/05/29
Scott, Thomas	25	John Munn	Liverpool	England	1847/08/25
Scully, Jeremiah	23	Agnes	Cork	Ireland	between May 29 and June 5, 1847
Scully, John	23	Agnes	Cork	Ireland	between July 4 and 10, 1847
Scully, Michael	50	Agnes	Cork	Ireland	between June 6 and 12, 1847
Seery, Margaret	50	Covenanter	Cork	Ireland	between August 8 and 14, 1847
Selby, James Hall	30	Ajax	Liverpool	England	1847/06/18
Sewell, Edward	26	Gilmour	Cork	Ireland	between June 13 and 19, 1847
Sewell, Edward		Syria	Liverpool	England	
Sewell, Patrick		Syria	Liverpool	England	
Seymour, Margaret	3				1847/08/09*
Shanahan, Catherine	9	Sarah	Liverpool	England	between August 8 and 14, 1847
Shanahan, Daniel	24	Sir Henry Pottinger	Belfast	Ireland	between August 29 and September 4, 1847
Shanahan, Eliza	14	John and Robert	Liverpool	England	between August 8 and 14, 1847
Shanahan, Honora	20	Odessa	Dublin	Ireland	between September 12 and 18, 1847
Shanahan, Susan	2	Bridgetown	Liverpool	England	between August 22 and 28, 1847
Shanahan, William	3	Washington	Liverpool	England	between August 29 and September 4, 1847
Shanahy, Felix	35	George	Liverpool	England	between July 11 and 17, 1847

The emigrants

Name	Age	Vessel	Port	Country	Date of death
Shane, George		Ann			
Shanks, William	4	Independance	Belfast	Ireland	1847/07/23
Shanley, Joseph	9	Virginius	Liverpool	England	between September 5 and 11, 1847
Shanley, Mary	40	Covenanter	Cork	Ireland	between August 8 and 14, 1847
Shannon, Andrew	44	Elizabeth	Liverpool	England	between July 18 and 24, 1847
Shannon, Andrew		Lady Flora Hastings	Cork	Ireland	
Shannon, Daniel		Sir Henry Pottinger	Belfast	Ireland	1847/08/29
Shannon, Patrick	23	Naparina	Dublin	Ireland	between August 22 and 28, 1847
Sharkey, Judith	19	Greenock	Liverpool	England	between August 29 and September 4, 1847
Sharkey, Patrick	29	Greenock	Liverpool	England	between September 5 and 11, 1847
Shaughnessy, Catherine	8	Argo	Liverpool	England	between August 15 and 21, 1847
Shaw, Cornelius	21	Wakefield	Cork	Ireland	between July 11 and 17, 1847
Shaw, John	4				1847/06/29
Shea, Bridget	16	Wakefield	Cork	Ireland	between July 18 and 24, 1847
Shea, Daniel	38	Sir Henry Pottinger	Cork	Ireland	between August 1 and 7, 1847
Shea, Denis	40	Henrietta Mary	Cork	Ireland	between October 3 and 9, 1847
Shea, Thomas	30	Bee	Cork	Ireland	between June 6 and 12, 1847
Shea, Thomas	27	Bridgetown	Liverpool	England	between August 22 and 28, 1847
Shea, Timothy	22	Free Briton	Cork	Ireland	between August 1 and 7, 1847
Sheedy, John	14	Ann	Liverpool	England	between June 27 and July 3, 1847
Sheehan, Ann	14	Naomi	Liverpool	England	between August 8 and 14, 1847
Sheehan, Catherine	11	Colonist	New Ross	Ireland	between September 5 and 11, 1847
Sheehan, John	23	Saguenay	Cork	Ireland	between September 5 and 11, 1847
Sheehan, Patrick	44	Champion	Liverpool	England	between August 22 and 28, 1847
Sheehan, Patrick	18	Asia	Cork	Ireland	between August 1 and 7, 1847
Sheehan, Patrick		John and Robert	Liverpool	England	
Shelly, Bridget	3 months	Champion	Liverpool	England	between August 29 and September 4, 1847
Shelly, Denis	30	Sir Henry Pottinger	Belfast	Ireland	between August 29 and September 4, 1847
Shelly, John	30	Jessie	Cork	Ireland	between July 4 and 10, 1847
Shelly, John	35	John Francis	Cork	Ireland	between May 29 and June 5, 1847
Shelly, Mary	16	Champion	Liverpool	England	between September 26 and October 2, 1847
Shelly, Mary	32	Champion	Liverpool	England	between September 5 and 11, 1847
Shelly, Patrick	6	Champion	Liverpool	England	between September 5 and 11, 1847
Sheridan, Anna	10	Rose	Liverpool	England	between August 8 and 14, 1847
Sheridan, Bernard	50	Triton	Liverpool	England	between August 1 and 7, 1847
Sheridan, Catherine	36	Champion	Liverpool	England	between August 22 and 28, 1847
Sheridan, Darby	30	Greenock	Liverpool	England	between August 1 and 7, 1847
Sheridan, John	52	Wellington	Liverpool	England	between October 3 and 9, 1847
Sheridan, John	42	Junior	Liverpool	England	between July 11 and 17, 1847
Sheridan, Joseph	6	Greenock	Liverpool	England	between August 15 and 21, 1847
Sheridan, Margaret	16	Triton	Liverpool	England	between August 1 and 7, 1847
Sheridan, Mary	60	Naomi	Liverpool	England	between August 22 and 28, 1847
Sheridan, Mary	35	James Moran	Liverpool	England	between August 22 and 28, 1847
Sheridan, Patrick	19	Rose	Liverpool	England	between July 4 and 10, 1847
Sheridan, Patrick	30	Lady Flora Hastings	Cork	Ireland	between July 4 and 10, 1847
Sherman, Daniel	47	Sir Robert Peel	Liverpool	England	between September 19 and 25, 1847
Sherry, Ann	12	George	Liverpool	England	between June 6 and 12, 1847
Sherry, Anthony	23	George	Liverpool	England	between May 23 and 29, 1847
Sherry, Bridget	30	George	Liverpool	England	between May 23 and 29, 1847
Sherry, Mary	6	George	Liverpool	England	between May 23 and 29, 1847
Sherry, Richard	50	Lively	Cork	Ireland	between July 25 and 31, 1847
Shiel, John	13	Rose	Liverpool	England	between August 1 and 7, 1847
Shiel, Judith	35	Virginius	Liverpool	England	between August 8 and 14, 1847
Shields, Edward	2	Rose	Liverpool	England	between June 27 and July 3, 1847
Shields, William	1 year & 6 months	Constitution	Belfast	Ireland	1847/05/28
Shields, William	2	Maria Somes	Cork	Ireland	between September 5 and 11, 1847
Shirley, Patrick	13	George	Liverpool	England	between June 20 and 26, 1847
Shirley, Peter	30	Larch	Sligo	Ireland	between September 19 and 25, 1847
Short, William	32	Broom	Liverpool	England	1847/09/21
Silke, Frances	26	Dominica	Cork	Ireland	between July 11 and 17, 1847
Silke, John	34	Ganges	Liverpool	England	between September 19 and 25, 1847
Simpson, D.	26	George	Liverpool	England	between June 13 and 19, 1847
Simpson, John	30	Erin's Queen	Liverpool	England	between August 8 and 14, 1847
Sinclair, Edward	55	Scotland	Cork	Ireland	between July 11 and 17, 1847
Skews, Jane Moore	26	Agnes	Cork	Ireland	1847/05/28
Skews, John	1 year & 6 months	Agnes	Cork	Ireland	1847/06/01
Slaney, Catherine	14	William Pirie	Belfast	Ireland	between August 8 and 14, 1847
Slaney, James	13	Lively	Cork	Ireland	between August 22 and 28, 1847
Slaney, Mary	7	Lively	Cork	Ireland	between July 11 and 17, 1847
Slattery, Bridget	60	Hercules			between June 13 and 19, 1847
Slattery, James	55	Samson			between October 3 and 9, 1847
Slattery, John	40	Champion	Liverpool	England	between August 29 and September 4, 1847
Slattery, Mary	14	Champion	Liverpool	England	between August 22 and 28, 1847
Slevin, Thomas	2	Odessa	Dublin	Ireland	between August 22 and 28, 1847
Sloane, Michael	23	Julius Caesar	Liverpool	England	between September 19 and 25, 1847
Small, James		John Bolton	Liverpool	England	
Small, James	50	Clarendon	Liverpool	England	between June 13 and 19, 1847
Smith, Alexander	3	Tamarac	Liverpool	England	between July 18 and 24, 1847

LISTS OF PEOPLE WHO DIED AND WERE BURIED ON GROSSE ÎLE, IN 1847

Name	Age	Vessel	Port	Country	Date of death
Smith, Alice	3	Syria	Liverpool	England	between June 13 and 19, 1847
Smith, Ann	20	Minerva	Dublin	Ireland	between October 3 and 9, 1847
Smith, Arthur	11	Achilles	Liverpool	England	between August 1 and 7, 1847
Smith, Catherine	19	Sarah	Liverpool	England	between July 25 and 31, 1847
Smith, Eliza	3	Tamarac	Liverpool	England	between July 18 and 24, 1847
Smith, George	55	Independance	Belfast	Ireland	between July 11 and 17, 1847
Smith, Hugh	19	Lady Milton	Liverpool	England	between August 1 and 7, 1847
Smith, James	30	Margaret	New Ross	Ireland	between July 18 and 24, 1847
Smith, John	40	Sir Henry Pottinger	Cork	Ireland	between August 1 and 7, 1847
Smith, John	40	John Munn	Liverpool	England	between August 22 and 28, 1847
Smith, John	22	Agnes	Cork	Ireland	between June 6 and 12, 1847
Smith, John	4	Yorkshire Lass	Killala	Ireland	between August 1 and 7, 1847
Smith, John	50	John Munn	Liverpool	England	between August 8 and 14, 1847
Smith, John	5	Argo	Liverpool	England	between August 1 and 7, 1847
Smith, John	18	Saguenay	Cork	Ireland	between September 19 and 25, 1847
Smith, John Jr	10	Achilles	Liverpool	England	between June 13 and 19, 1847
Smith, John Sr	20	Achilles	Liverpool	England	between June 13 and 19, 1847
Smith, Mary	23	Free Trader	Liverpool	England	between August 8 and 14, 1847
Smith, Michael	10	John Bolton	Liverpool	England	between June 6 and 12, 1847
Smith, Michael	3	Argo	Liverpool	England	between August 8 and 14, 1847
Smith, Michael	17	Virginius	Liverpool	England	between August 8 and 14, 1847
Smith, Nicholas	45	Triton	Liverpool	England	between August 15 and 21, 1847
Smith, Nicolas		Yorkshire	Liverpool	England	
Smith, Patrick	8	Sir Henry Pottinger	Cork	Ireland	between August 8 and 14, 1847
Smith, Robert	2	Sir Robert Peel	Liverpool	England	between October 3 and 9, 1847
Smith, Thomas	18	Free Trader	Liverpool	England	between August 15 and 21, 1847
Smylie, James	14	Ayrshire	Newry	Ireland	1847/08/30
Smylie, Samuel	14	Ayrshire	Newry	Ireland	between August 29 and September 4, 1847
Smyth, Ann	20	Minerva		Ireland	1847/10/03
Smyth, Robert	2	Sir Henry Pottinger		Ireland	1847/10/06
Sool, Catherine		Lady Campbell	Dublin	Ireland	
Sool, Ellen		Lady Campbell	Dublin	Ireland	
Spellman, Mary	1	Greenock	Liverpool	England	between August 8 and 14, 1847
Spellman, Mary	34	Odessa	Dublin	Ireland	between August 22 and 28, 1847
Spellman, Patrick	2	Sir Robert Peel	Liverpool	England	between September 12 and 18, 1847
Spellman, William	18	Avon	Cork	Ireland	between July 25 and 31, 1847
Spencer, Elizabeth	40	Brothers	Dublin	Ireland	between September 19 and 25, 1847
Spillane, Catherine	8	Agnes	Cork	Ireland	between May 29 and June 5, 1847
Spillane, Edward	40	Agnes	Cork	Ireland	between June 6 and 12, 1847
Spillane, Morris	45	Scotland	Cork	Ireland	between June 13 and 19, 1847
Spillane, Nanny	45	Agnes	Cork	Ireland	between June 20 and 26, 1847
Spillane, Nicholas	50	Agnes	Cork	Ireland	between June 6 and 12, 1847
Spillane, William	10	Agnes	Cork	Ireland	between June 6 and 12, 1847
Stanton, Mary	30	Junior	Liverpool	England	between August 1 and 7, 1847
Stanton, Philip	22	Unicorn	Londonderry	Ireland	between August 8 and 14, 1847
Stanwicks, James	40	Independance	Belfast	Ireland	between July 4 and 10, 1847
Stapleton, Elizabeth	60	Lady Campbell	Dublin	Ireland	between August 8 and 14, 1847
Stapleton, William	19	Argo	Liverpool	England	between July 4 and 10, 1847
Steele, John		Araminta	Liverpool	England	1847/06/08
Steele, John	50	Araminta	Liverpool	England	1847/05/31
Steele, Margaret Cook	42	Araminta	Liverpool	England	1847/06/01
Stephens, Patrick	80	Minerva	Galway	Ireland	between August 8 and 14, 1847
Stewart, Elizabeth	19	Naomi	Liverpool	England	between August 29 and September 4, 1847
Stewart, John	3	Avon	Cork	Ireland	between August 8 and 14, 1847
Stewart, Margaret	20	William Pirie	Belfast	Ireland	between September 19 and 25, 1847
Stobo, William	36	Lady Milton	Liverpool	England	1847/07/10
Stokes, Mary	2	Independance	Belfast	Ireland	between August 1 and 7, 1847
Storey, Ellen	24	Lillias	Dublin	Ireland	between September 5 and 11, 1847
Sturgeon, Cumberland	5	Lord Seaton	Belfast	Ireland	1847/05/28
Sullivan, Alexander	29	Agnes	Cork	Ireland	between June 6 and 12, 1847
Sullivan, Alice	37	Scotland	Cork	Ireland	between May 23 and 29, 1847
Sullivan, Bartholomew	50	Agnes King	Limerick	Ireland	between July 11 and 17, 1847
Sullivan, Bartholomew	30	Agnes	Cork	Ireland	between June 13 and 19, 1847
Sullivan, Bridget	28	Odessa	Dublin	Ireland	between August 15 and 21, 1847
Sullivan, Catherine	50	Gilmour	Cork	Ireland	between June 27 and July 3, 1847
Sullivan, Catherine	40	Agnes	Cork	Ireland	between June 20 and 26, 1847
Sullivan, Daniel	5	Saguenay	Cork	Ireland	between August 15 and 21, 1847
Sullivan, Daniel	60	Manchester	Liverpool	England	between August 8 and 14, 1847
Sullivan, Daniel	40	Urania	Cork	Ireland	between May 29 and June 5, 1847
Sullivan, Darby	22	Bridgetown	Liverpool	England	between August 29 and September 4, 1847
Sullivan, Denis	10	Jessie	Limerick	Ireland	between September 5 and 11, 1847
Sullivan, Eliza	1 year & 9 months	Wakefield	Cork	Ireland	between July 18 and 24, 1847
Sullivan, Elizabeth	20	Wakefield	Cork	Ireland	between July 18 and 24, 1847
Sullivan, Ellen	1	Bee	Cork	Ireland	between May 29 and June 5, 1847
Sullivan, Ellen	47	Washington	Liverpool	England	between August 22 and 28, 1847
Sullivan, Flora	26	Bridgetown	Liverpool	England	between September 12 and 18, 1847
Sullivan, Florence	50	Covenanter	Cork	Ireland	between August 22 and 28, 1847
Sullivan, Honora	19	Triton	Liverpool	England	between October 3 and 9, 1847

The Emigrants

Name	Age	Vessel	Port	Country	Date of death
Sullivan, Honora	23	Wellington	Liverpool	England	between September 19 and 25, 1847
Sullivan, Honora	28	Henrietta Mary	Cork	Ireland	between October 10 and 16, 1847
Sullivan, James	19	Junior	Liverpool	England	between July 11 and 17, 1847
Sullivan, Jeremiah	13	Triton	Liverpool	England	between August 22 and 28, 1847
Sullivan, Jeremiah	26	Bridgetown	Liverpool	England	between September 26 and October 2, 1847
Sullivan, Jeremiah	13	Virginius	Liverpool	England	between September 5 and 11, 1847
Sullivan, Johanna	2	Covenanter	Cork	Ireland	between August 22 and 28, 1847
Sullivan, John	18	Agnes	Cork	Ireland	between June 6 and 12, 1847
Sullivan, John	30	Jessie	Cork	Ireland	between July 18 and 24, 1847
Sullivan, John	24	Saguenay	Cork	Ireland	between September 5 and 11, 1847
Sullivan, John	1	Wandsworth	Dublin	Ireland	between June 13 and 19, 1847
Sullivan, John	35	Rose	Liverpool	England	between June 27 and July 3, 1847
Sullivan, Judith	2	Washington	Liverpool	England	between August 22 and 28, 1847
Sullivan, Justin	30	Bee	Cork	Ireland	between June 6 and 12, 1847
Sullivan, Margaret	7	John Francis	Cork	Ireland	between May 29 and June 5, 1847
Sullivan, Margaret	24	John Munn	Liverpool	England	between August 15 and 21, 1847
Sullivan, Margaret	30				1847/05/15
Sullivan, Martin		Sir Henry Pottinger		Ireland	
Sullivan, Mary	15	Pursuit	Liverpool	England	between June 27 and July 3, 1847
Sullivan, Mary	13	Jessie	Limerick	Ireland	between September 5 and 11, 1847
Sullivan, Mary	6	Covenanter	Cork	Ireland	between August 22 and 28, 1847
Sullivan, Mary	13	Larch	Sligo	Ireland	between September 19 and 25, 1847
Sullivan, Michael	2	Saguenay	Cork	Ireland	between August 15 and 21, 1847
Sullivan, Michael	3	Covenanter	Cork	Ireland	between August 1 and 7, 1847
Sullivan, Michael	30	Sir Henry Pottinger	Belfast	Ireland	between September 19 and 25, 1847
Sullivan, Patrick	50	Triton	Liverpool	England	between July 8 and 14, 1847
Sullivan, Patrick	22	Virginius	Liverpool	England	between August 15 and 21, 1847
Sullivan, Patrick	23	Eliza Caroline	Liverpool	England	between August 15 and 21, 1847
Sullivan, Patrick	30	John Francis	Cork	Ireland	between May 29 and June 5, 1847
Sullivan, Robert	30	Scotland	Cork	Ireland	between July 4 and 10, 1847
Sullivan, Samuel	45				between August 29 and September 4, 1847
Sullivan, Thadeus	20	Triton	Liverpool	England	between July 25 and 31, 1847
Sullivan, Thadeus	2	Henrietta Mary	Cork	Ireland	between October 10 and 16, 1847
Sullivan, Timothy	30	Covenanter	Cork	Ireland	between August 29 and September 4, 1847
Supple, Thomas	23	Jessie	Cork	Ireland	between July 25 and 31, 1847
Sutton, Catherine	4	Odessa	Dublin	Ireland	between August 22 and 28, 1847
Swan, Thomas	20	Ajax	Liverpool	England	between June 20 and 26, 1847
Swanton, Ann	17	Lady Flora Hastings	Cork	Ireland	between June 27 and July 3, 1847
Swanton, Eliza	18	Argo	Liverpool	England	between June 27 and July 3, 1847
Swanton, George	11	Rose	Liverpool	England	1847/06/28
Sweade, Alicia Henry		Broom	Liverpool	England	1847/08/05
Sweade, Robert	34	Broom	Liverpool	England	1847/09/01
Sweade, Robert W.	1 year & 6 months	Ganges	Liverpool	England	1847/08/18
Sweeney, Cornelius	23	Bridgetown	Liverpool	England	between September 26 and October 2, 1847
Sweeney, Dolly	15	Wolfville	Sligo	Ireland	between June 13 and 19, 1847
Sweeney, Eliza	14	Wolfville	Sligo	Ireland	between June 20 and 26, 1847
Sweeney, Eliza	7	Agnes	Cork	Ireland	between June 13 and 19, 1847
Sweeney, Honora	2	Washington	Liverpool	England	between August 29 and September 4, 1847
Sweeney, Mary	18	Wolfville	Sligo	Ireland	between June 13 and 19, 1847
Sweeney, Mary	9	Washington	Liverpool	England	between September 19 and 25, 1847
Sweeney, Nancy	4	Jessie	Cork	Ireland	between July 18 and 24, 1847
Sweeney, Patrick	10	Rose	Liverpool	England	between July 4 and 10, 1847
Sweeney, Patrick	8	Rose	Liverpool	England	between July 4 and 10, 1847
Sweeney, Patrick	36	Lively	Cork	Ireland	between August 1 and 7, 1847
T___, J___					
T___, T___					
Taaffe, Ellen	14	Free Trader	Liverpool	England	1847/08/22
Taaffe, Mary	22	Venilia	Limerick	Ireland	between July 11 and 17, 1847
Taaffe, Susan	35	Ganges	Liverpool	England	between August 15 and 21, 1847
Tangney, Patrick	19	Odessa	Dublin	Ireland	between August 8 and 14, 1847
Taylor, Daniel	1	Euclid	Glasgow	Scotland	between August 1 and 7, 1847
Taylor, Edward	30	Westmoreland	Sligo	Ireland	1847/09/25
Taylor, Eliza	22	Maria Somes	Cork	Ireland	1847/10/05
Taylor, Frances	5	Broom	Liverpool	England	1847/08/14
Taylor, Henry	63	Junior	Liverpool	England	between July 4 and 10, 1847
Taylor, Henry	14	Jessie	Cork	Ireland	between July 18 and 24, 1847
Taylor, John	61	Maria Somes	Cork	Ireland	1847/10/04
Taylor, Margaret	45	Jessie	Cork	Ireland	between July 11 and 17, 1847
Taylor, Margaret	23	Maria Somes	Cork	Ireland	1847/10/07
Taylor, Sarah		Westmoreland	Sligo	Ireland	
Taylor, William	8	Jessie	Cork	Ireland	1847/07/21
Taylor, William	20	Aberdeen	Liverpool	England	between June 13 and 19, 1847
Teahan, Daniel	60	Saguenay	Cork	Ireland	between August 15 and 21, 1847
Teahan, Mary	14	Yorkshire	Liverpool	England	between June 20 and 26, 1847
Terry, Ann M.	63	Junior	Liverpool	England	between July 11 and 17, 1847
Thomas, William	1	Rankin	Liverpool	England	between June 13 and 19, 1847
Thompson, David	6	Rankin	Liverpool	England	between June 20 and 26, 1847
Thompson, Elizabeth		Araminta	Liverpool	England	
Thompson, Elizabeth	50	Asia	Cork	Ireland	1847/08/10
Thompson, John	17	Erin's Queen	Liverpool	England	between August 29 and September 4, 1847

LISTS OF PEOPLE WHO DIED AND WERE BURIED ON GROSSE ÎLE, IN 1847

Name	Age	Vessel	Port	Country	Date of death
Thompson, John	2	Maria Somes	Cork	Ireland	1847/09/12
Thompson, Joseph	25	Wm S. Hamilton	New Ross	Ireland	between August 29 and September 4, 1847
Thompson, Joseph	24	Rankin	Liverpool	England	between July 25 and 31, 1847
Thompson, Margaret	15	Rankin	Liverpool	England	between July 4 and 10, 1847
Thompson, Robert	30	Yorkshire Lass	Killala	Ireland	between August 1 and 7, 1847
Thompson, William	55	Rankin	Liverpool	England	1847/06/15
Thompson, William	44	Maria Somes	Cork	Ireland	1847/09/02
Thomson, Elizabeth		Rankin	Liverpool	England	
Thorne, Isabella		Sir Robert Peel	Liverpool	England	
Thornton, Catherine	30	Emigrant	Liverpool	England	between September 26 and October 2, 1847
Thornton, M.A.	29	Yorkshire	Liverpool	England	between September 12 and 18, 1847
Thornton, Margaret	60	Scotland	Cork	Ireland	between May 23 and 29, 1847
Thornton, Mary	22	Yorkshire	Liverpool	England	between August 15 and 21, 1847
Thorpe, Ellen	14	Free Trader	Liverpool	England	between August 22 and 28, 1847
Tierney, Jeremiah	35	Rose	Liverpool	England	between June 27 and July 3, 1847
Tighe, Nancy	60	John Munn	Liverpool	England	between August 22 and 28, 1847
Tighe, Thomas	45	Sarah	Liverpool	England	between July 18 and 24, 1847
Timberman, Mary	58	Saguenay	Cork	Ireland	between August 29 and September 4, 1847
Timberman, Michael	50	Washington	Liverpool	England	between September 5 and 11, 1847
Timlin, John		Eliza Caroline	Liverpool	England	1847/06/01
Timlin, Thomas	6	Emigrant	Liverpool	England	between October 10 and 16, 1847
Timony, James	22	Rankin	Liverpool	England	between July 4 and 10, 1847
Timony, John	1	Rankin	Liverpool	England	between June 27 and July 3, 1847
Tobin, Michael	16	Saguenay	Cork	Ireland	between August 15 and 21, 1847
Tobin, Michael	6	Agnes	Cork	Ireland	between May 29 and June 5, 1847
Tobin, Patrick	12	Saguenay	Cork	Ireland	between September 12 and 18, 1847
Tolan, James	18	Free Trader	Liverpool	England	between August 22 and 28, 1847
Tolan, James	22	Lady Campbell	Dublin	Ireland	between August 15 and 21, 1847
Tolan, Margaret	24	Yorkshire	Liverpool	England	between August 8 and 14, 1847
Tombs, Bella	51	Sir Robert Peel	Liverpool	England	1847/09/27
Tonra, Honora	45	John and Robert	Liverpool	England	between August 22 and 28, 1847
Toolan, Michael	21	James Moran	Liverpool	England	between July 25 and 31, 1847
Toole, Hugh	55	Rose	Liverpool	England	between June 27 and July 3, 1847
Toole, Margaret	16	Lady Campbell	Dublin	Ireland	between September 12 and 18, 1847
Toole, Mary	1	Constitution	Belfast	Ireland	between June 6 and 12, 1847
Toole, Michael	2	Progress	New Ross	Ireland	between July 11 and 17, 1847
Toole, Robert	17	Saguenay	Cork	Ireland	between September 5 and 11, 1847
Tormey, Edward	60	Agnes	Cork	Ireland	between May 29 and June 5, 1847
Tougher, Hugh	50	Larch	Sligo	Ireland	between August 15 and 21, 1847
Tougher, Philip	70	Yorkshire Lass	Killala	Ireland	between July 18 and 24, 1847
Toukere, Mary	50	Jessie	Cork	Ireland	between August 1 and 7, 1847
Towey, Thomas	2	Broom	Liverpool	England	between August 1 and 7, 1847
Towhey, Mary	18	Asia	Cork	Ireland	between August 22 and 28, 1847
Towhey, Matthew	50	Numa	Sligo	Ireland	between August 1 and 7, 1847
Townley, Michael	16	Odessa	Dublin	Ireland	between August 15 and 21, 1847
Tracey, ___		Ann Kenny	Waterford	Ireland	
Tracey, Ann	40	Larch	Sligo	Ireland	between August 15 and 21, 1847
Tracey, Daniel	15				between August 15 and 21, 1847
Tracey, John	31	Scotland	Cork	Ireland	between May 29 and June 5, 1847
Tracey, Michael	40	Aberdeen	Liverpool	England	between July 25 and 31, 1847
Tracey, Michael	22	Lillias	Dublin	Ireland	between August 15 and 21, 1847
Tracey, Patrick	30	Scotland	Cork	Ireland	between May 23 and 29, 1847
Tracey, William	30	Bolton	Dublin	Ireland	between May 29 and June 5, 1847
Trainor, Peter	40	Sisters	Liverpool	England	between July 11 and 17, 1847
Travers, Michael	39	Ellen	Sligo	Ireland	between July 25 and 31, 1847
Trimble, Charles	50	Ayrshire	Newry	Ireland	1847/09/03
Trimble, Hall	23	Maria Somes	Cork	Ireland	1847/09/19
Trimble, Isabella	25	Ayrshire	Newry	Ireland	1847/08/26
Trimble, Jane	62	Maria Somes	Cork	Ireland	1847/09/22
Trimble, Joseph	25	Yorkshire	Liverpool	England	1847/09/10
Trimble, Thomas	25	Maria Somes	Cork	Ireland	1847/09/26
Trotter, Moses		Tamarac	Liverpool	England	1847/07/05
Troy, Edward					
Troy, Judith	36	John and Robert	Liverpool	England	between August 22 and 28, 1847
Trunnell, William	60	Maria Somes	Cork	Ireland	between August 22 and 28, 1847
Tucker, Honora	27	Avon	Cork	Ireland	between August 8 and 14, 1847
Tucker, Joseph		Larch	Sligo	Ireland	
Tufts, Daniel	32	Jane Black	Limerick	Ireland	between July 11 and 17, 1847
Tufts, Michael	6	Jane Black	Limerick	Ireland	between July 11 and 17, 1847
Tweedy, Eliza	31	Broom	Liverpool	England	between August 1 and 7, 1847
Tweedy, Robert	34	Broom	Liverpool	England	between August 29 and September 4, 1847
Tweedy, Robert H.	1 year & 6 months	Larch	Sligo	Ireland	between August 15 and 21, 1847
Tweedy, Samuel	5	Larch	Sligo	Ireland	between August 8 and 14, 1847
Tweedy, Sarah	31	Virgilia	Liverpool	England	1847/09/22
Twohig, Richard	26	Yorkshire	Liverpool	England	between September 5 and 11, 1847
Tyrrell, Catherine	15	Syria	Liverpool	England	between May 23 and 29, 1847
Tyrrell, Catherine	26	Syria	Liverpool	England	between July 4 and 10, 1847
Tyrrell, Mary	5	Syria	Liverpool	England	between June 13 and 19, 1847
Tyrrell, Patrick	40	Syria	Liverpool	England	between June 27 and July 3, 1847
Unknown					
Unknown					
Unknown					
Unknown					1847/08/03*

The emigrants

Name	Age	Vessel	Port	Country	Date of death
Unknown					1847/08/03*
Unknown					1847/08/03*
Unknown					1847/08/03*
Unknown					1847/08/03*
Unknown					1847/08/03*
Unknown, Boy	14	Naomi	Liverpool	England	between August 15 and 21, 1847
Unknown, Child	1				between August 29 and September 4, 1847
Unknown, Dutchman	20	Free Trader	Liverpool	England	between August 22 and 28, 1847
Unknown, Man	50	Saguenay	Cork	Ireland	between August 22 and 28, 1847
Unknown, Man	45				between August 22 and 28, 1847
Unknown, Woman	20	Saguenay	Cork	Ireland	between August 15 and 21, 1847
Unknown, Woman	50				between August 22 and 28, 1847
Vallelly, Ann	3	Blenheim	Cork	Ireland	between August 8 and 14, 1847
Vaughan, John	23	Emigrant	Liverpool	England	between October 3 and 9, 1847
Vaughan, John Henry					1847/05/26
Vaux, James	40	Larch	Sligo	Ireland	1847/08/16
Verdon, James	23	Sarah Maria	Sligo	Ireland	between June 27 and July 3, 1847
Waddell, James	28	Virginius	Liverpool	England	between August 8 and 14, 1847
Walker, Ann	55	Lotus	Liverpool	England	between July 18 and 24, 1847
Walker, James	5	Lord Seaton	Belfast	Ireland	1847/05/31
Walker, W.H.	21	Saguenay	Cork	Ireland	between September 12 and 18, 1847
Wall, Catherine	30	Try Again	Cork	Ireland	between May 29 and June 5, 1847
Wallace, Bridget		Virginius	Liverpool	England	
Wallace, Charles	27	Covenanter	Cork	Ireland	between August 1 and 7, 1847
Wallace, Eliza	25	Triton	Liverpool	England	between August 8 and 14, 1847
Wallace, Margaret	20	John Munn	Liverpool	England	between August 8 and 14, 1847
Wallace, Samuel	28	Sarah	Liverpool	England	between July 25 and 31, 1847
Wallace, Thomas	50	Virginius	Liverpool	England	between August 8 and 14, 1847
Walsh, Bridget	4	Lady Campbell	Dublin	Ireland	between August 1 and 7, 1847
Walsh, Bridget	16	Sarah	Liverpool	England	between August 1 and 7, 1847
Walsh, Bridget	25	Royal Adelaide	Killala	Ireland	between September 19 and 25, 1847
Walsh, Bridget	22	Yorkshire Lass	Killala	Ireland	between July 4 and 10, 1847
Walsh, Catherine	40	Ganges	Liverpool	England	between August 22 and 28, 1847
Walsh, Darby	6	Triton	Liverpool	England	between July 25 and 31, 1847
Walsh, Edmund	50	John and Robert	Liverpool	England	between August 8 and 14, 1847
Walsh, Ellen	60	Bee	Cork	Ireland	between June 27 and July 3, 1847
Walsh, James	25	Champion	Liverpool	England	between August 29 and September 4, 1847
Walsh, John	19	Minerva	Galway	Ireland	between August 22 and 28, 1847
Walsh, John	2	Yorkshire Lass	Killala	Ireland	between July 25 and 31, 1847
Walsh, John	25	Yorkshire Lass	Killala	Ireland	between July 25 and 31, 1847
Walsh, John	20	George	Liverpool	England	between July 18 and 24, 1847
Walsh, John	22	Triton	Liverpool	England	between July 11 and 17, 1847
Walsh, John	21	Junior	Liverpool	England	between July 18 and 24, 1847
Walsh, John	24	Scotland	Cork	Ireland	between May 29 and June 5, 1847
Walsh, Judith	1	Gilmour	Cork	Ireland	between June 13 and 19, 1847
Walsh, Mary	20	Asia	Cork	Ireland	between August 1 and 7, 1847
Walsh, Mary		Avon	Cork	Ireland	
Walsh, Mary	35	Sarah	Liverpool	England	between July 25 and 31, 1847
Walsh, Patrick	25	Royal Adelaide	Killala	Ireland	between September 5 and 11, 1847
Walsh, Patrick	11	Brothers	Dublin	Ireland	between August 15 and 21, 1847
Walsh, Patrick	57	X.L.	Galway	Ireland	between August 1 and 7, 1847
Walsh, Patrick	16	Ajax	Liverpool	England	between August 22 and 28, 1847
Walsh, Patrick	26	Sir Robert Peel	Liverpool	England	between October 10 and 16, 1847
Walsh, Patrick Owen	75	Oregon	Killala	Ireland	between August 1 and 7, 1847
Walsh, Patrick Owen	6	Sarah	Liverpool	England	between August 1 and 7, 1847
Walsh, Peter	24	Free Trader	Liverpool	England	between September 19 and 25, 1847
Walsh, Richard	50	Progress	New Ross	Ireland	between July 11 and 17, 1847
Walsh, Thomas	24	Minerva	Galway	Ireland	between August 22 and 28, 1847
Ward, Charles	30	Charles Richard	Sligo	Ireland	between July 18 and 24, 1847
Ward, Daniel	15	Odessa	Dublin	Ireland	between August 8 and 14, 1847
Ward, Eliza	6	Christiana	Londonderry	Ireland	between July 4 and 10, 1847
Ward, James	7	Charles Richard	Sligo	Ireland	between August 22 and 28, 1847
Ward, John	60	Bridgetown	Liverpool	England	between August 29 and September 4, 1847
Ward, John	18	Charles Richard	Sligo	Ireland	between August 1 and 7, 1847
Ward, Margaret	40	James Moran	Liverpool	England	between July 25 and 31, 1847
Ward, Margaret	5	Champion	Liverpool	England	between September 26 and October 2, 1847
Ward, Martin	9	Champion	Liverpool	England	between September 12 and 18, 1847
Ward, Phoebe	13	James Moran	Liverpool	England	between July 11 and 17, 1847
Ward, Rebecca	21	Lord Seaton	Belfast	Ireland	between June 13 and 19, 1847
Ward, Sarah	50	Charles Richard	Sligo	Ireland	between July 11 and 17, 1847
Wasson, Margaret	8	Syria	Liverpool	England	between September 26 and October 2, 1847
Wasson, Sarah	42				1847/06/29
Watson, Andrew		Sarah	Liverpool	England	between July 4 and 10, 1847
Watson, James	30	Unicorn	Londonderry	Ireland	between July 4 and 10, 1847
Watson, James					1847/07/08
Watson, Sarah	49	Syria	Liverpool	England	between June 27 and July 3, 1847
Watt, Barbara	25	Bridgetown	Liverpool	England	between October 10 and 16, 1847
Watters, Michael	50	John Munn	Liverpool	England	between August 8 and 14, 1847
Watters, Patrick	18	Numa	Sligo	Ireland	between August 22 and 28, 1847

Lists of people who died and were buried on Grosse Île, in 1847

Name	Age	Vessel	Port	Country	Date of death
Watters, William	49	Virgilia	Liverpool	England	between September 26 and October 2, 1847
Watts, Catherine					
Watts, Ellen					
Watts, James	9	Bridgetown	Liverpool	England	between September 19 and 25, 1847
Watts, James	55	Bridgetown	Liverpool	England	between September 5 and 11, 1847
Watts, Mary	5	Bridgetown	Liverpool	England	between August 29 and September 4, 1847
Watts, Mary	40	Bridgetown	Liverpool	England	between August 22 and 28, 1847
Waugh, James	25	Jessie	Limerick	Ireland	between September 19 and 25, 1847
Webb, Ann	47	Bridgetown	Liverpool	England	between September 5 and 11, 1847
Webb, John	18	Bridgetown	Liverpool	England	between August 29 and September 4, 1847
Westland, George	20	Rose	Liverpool	England	between August 1 and 7, 1847
Westman, Matthew	40	Clarendon	Liverpool	England	1847/06/19
Weston, William Thomas	1				1847/06/19
Whelan, Ann	55	Bridgetown	Liverpool	England	between August 22 and 28, 1847
Whelan, Ann	7				1847/06/19*
Whelan, Denis	40	Progress	New Ross	Ireland	between July 18 and 24, 1847
Whelan, Elizabeth	3	Wandsworth	Dublin	Ireland	1847/05/22
Whelan, John	4	Wandsworth	Dublin	Ireland	1847/05/22
Whelan, Mary	20	Progress	New Ross	Ireland	between August 1 and 7, 1847
Whelan, Mary	18	Bryan Abbs	Limerick	Ireland	between June 6 and 12, 1847
Whelan, Timothy	8 months	Larch	Sligo	Ireland	between August 15 and 21, 1847
Whelan, William	25	Progress	New Ross	Ireland	between July 11 and 17, 1847
Whelehan, Matthew	30	Emigrant	Liverpool	England	between September 26 and October 2, 1847
White, Andrew		Bee	Cork	Ireland	
White, Ann	6	Champion	Liverpool	England	between September 12 and 18, 1847
White, Darby	8	Bee	Cork	Ireland	between June 13 and 19, 1847
White, Edmund	40	Saguenay	Cork	Ireland	between August 22 and 28, 1847
White, Elizabeth	63	Emigrant	Liverpool	England	1847/10/07
White, Ellen	30	Bee	Cork	Ireland	between June 6 and 12, 1847
White, John	30	Jessie	Cork	Ireland	between July 18 and 24, 1847
White, Jude	2	Bee	Cork	Ireland	between May 29 and June 5, 1847
White, Mary	9	Pursuit	Liverpool	England	between June 13 and 19, 1847
White, Patrick	7	Bee	Cork	Ireland	between June 20 and 26, 1847
White, Thomas	32	Yorkshire	Liverpool	England	between August 8 and 14, 1847
White, William	40	Pursuit	Liverpool	England	between June 13 and 19, 1847
Whittaker, Ann	20				between July 18 and 24, 1847
Whittaker, Jane	20	Dunbrody	New Ross	Ireland	between July 18 and 24, 1847
Wiggins, Eliza	60	Sobraon	Liverpool	England	between July 25 and 31, 1847
Wilcock, Thomas James					
Wilkinson, Sarah		Wakefield	Cork	Ireland	1847/07/04
Williams, Anne Banniford	35	Free Trader	Liverpool	England	1847/09/07
Williams, Daniel	14				1847/09/03
Williams, Eliza	11	Free Trader	Liverpool	England	between August 8 and 14, 1847
Williams, Johanna	4	Naomi	Liverpool	England	between August 8 and 14, 1847
Williams, John	54	Free Trader	Liverpool	England	between August 15 and 21, 1847
Williams, Martha	14	Free Trader	Liverpool	England	between August 22 and 28, 1847
Williams, Mary	10	Free Trader	Liverpool	England	1847/09/15
Williams, Owen	14	Wakefield	Cork	Ireland	between August 15 and 21, 1847
Williams, Patrick	6	Odessa	Dublin	Ireland	between August 15 and 21, 1847
Williams, Sarah	3	Free Trader	Liverpool	England	between August 15 and 21, 1847
Williams, William	44	Free Trader	Liverpool	England	1847/07/21
Williamson, Daniel	65	Emigrant	Liverpool	England	between October 3 and 9, 1847
Williamson, Rose	19	Emigrant	Liverpool	England	between October 10 and 16, 1847
Willis, Mary A.	17	Jessie	Cork	Ireland	between June 27 and July 3, 1847
Wilson, Ann	3	Washington	Liverpool	England	between August 29 and September 4, 1847
Wilson, J.	35	Coromandel	Dublin	Ireland	between July 4 and 10, 1847
Wilson, Mary	54	Achilles	Liverpool	England	1847/06/04
Wilson, Seth	1 year & 6 months	Argo	Liverpool	England	1847/06/07
Wise, Michael	18	Yorkshire Lass	Killala	Ireland	between July 25 and 31, 1847
Wood, Owen	2 weeks	Syria	Liverpool	England	between May 23 and 29, 1847
Woodburn, D.					
Woodlock, Mary	33	Larch	Sligo	Ireland	between August 22 and 28, 1847
Woods, Ann	40	Erin's Queen	Liverpool	England	between July 25 and 31, 1847
Woods, Catherine	3	Yorkshire Lass	Killala	Ireland	between August 1 and 7, 1847
Woods, Francis	32	Yorkshire	Liverpool	England	between August 22 and 28, 1847
Woodside, John	5 months	Constitution	Belfast	Ireland	1847/06/07
Woolrich, Thomas	28	Triton	Liverpool	England	between July 18 and 24, 1847
Wren, Patrick	18	John Munn	Liverpool	England	between August 15 and 21, 1847
Wright, David	22	John Bolton	Liverpool	England	between July 25 and 31, 1847
Wright, Ellen	26	Larch	Sligo	Ireland	between August 29 and September 4, 1847
Wright, Margaret	21	John Bolton	Liverpool	England	between August 1 and 7, 1847
Wright, Margaret	5	Sisters	Liverpool	England	1847/06/03
Wright, Patrick	30	Larch	Sligo	Ireland	between September 12 and 18, 1847
Wright, Thomas	6 months	Larch	Sligo	Ireland	between August 22 and 28, 1847
Wynne, Cornelius	29	Agnes	Cork	Ireland	between May 29 and June 5, 1847
Young, Edward	30	Clarendon	Liverpool	England	between June 6 and 12, 1847
Young, John	20	Ganges	Liverpool	England	between June 13 and 19, 1847
Young, Mary	35	Urania	Cork	Ireland	between June 13 and 19, 1847
Young, Richard	21	Wandsworth	Dublin	Ireland	1847/06/13

LISTS OF PEOPLE WHO DIED AND WERE BURIED ON GROSSE ÎLE, IN 1847

b. *The employees of the Quarantine Station*

Name	Age	Trade	Date of death
Andrews, Vincent	34	Nurse	1847/07/23
Ferguson, Hugh	43	Hospital Steward	1847/09/15
Garneau, ___		Nurse	1847/07/13
Hobbs, Margaret	29	Nurse	1847/08/15
Kenny, James	36	Nurse Attendant	between September 19 and 25, 1847
Lindsay, William	24	Policeman	between October 17 and 23, 1847
Maxwell, Elizabeth	30	Nurse	1847/07/01
McConaty, Catherine	32	Nurse	between August 8 and 14, 1847
McGaracher, Catherine		Nurse	
McKay, ___		Wife or child of the chief hospitals steward	1847/07/05
Palmer, Samuel	46	Policeman	1847/10/06
Pinet, Alexis Albert	22	Physician	1847/07/24
Plante, Alexis	19	Baker	1847/09/12
Polk, William	22	Sutler's Clerk	between October 10 and 16, 1847
Stanley, Ellen	30	Nurse	between August 8 and 14, 1847

c. The sailors

Name	Age	Trade	Vessel	Port	Country	Date of death
Adamson, James	24	Seaman	Argo	Liverpool	England	1847/06/15
Andrews, James	18	Seaman	Gilmour	Cork	Ireland	1847/06/10
Andrews, William	36	Seaman	Abbotsford	Dublin	Ireland	1847/06/10
Angells, Argus	40	Seaman	Emigrant	Liverpool	England	1847/09/24
Banks, Abraham	22	Seaman	Sir Henry Pottinger	Belfast	Ireland	1847/08/19
Benger, John	42	Seaman	Broom	Liverpool	England	1847/09/15
Bonney, William	20	Seaman	James Moran	Liverpool	England	1847/07/05
Boucher, Martin		Seaman	Aberdeen	Liverpool	England	
Bowes, Richard	48	Seaman	Lord Seaton	Belfast	Ireland	1847/06/19
Boyce, John	21	Seaman	Scotland	Cork	Ireland	1847/06/06
Boyd, Charles	27	Seaman Carpenter	Marchioness of Bute	Belfast	Ireland	1847/08/07
Buchanan, James	25	Seaman Cook	Ajax	Liverpool	England	1847/08/08
Crowell, George	18		Sir Henry Pottinger	Belfast	Ireland	1847/08/15
Davis, John	50	Seaman Cook	Agnes	Cork	Ireland	1847/05/31
Edwards, John	26	Seaman	Ganges	Liverpool	England	1847/08/30
Eelbeck, John	33	Seaman	George	Liverpool	England	
English, James	16	Seaman	Coromandel	Dublin	Ireland	1847/09/04
Evans, Benjamin	20	Seaman	Goliah	Liverpool	England	1847/09/27
Fisher, Randolph	29	Cook	Constitution	Belfast	Ireland	1847/06/02
Fletcher, Richard	22	Seaman	Dykes	Sligo	Ireland	1847/06/07
Gordon, George	32	Seaman	Saguenay	Cork	Ireland	1847/09/10
Hare, Bartholomew	24	Seaman	Saguenay	Cork	Ireland	1847/08/15
Hertle, ___		Seaman	Abbotsford	Dublin	Ireland	1847/06/16
Jacques, John	22	Seaman	Elizabeth			1847/06/12
Kant, Peter		Seaman				1847/09/11
Knight, Frederick	12	Seaman	Zealous	London	England	1847/09/08
Leven, George	20	Seaman	Gilmour	Cork	Ireland	1847/06/15
Long, Samuel		Seaman	Rankin	Liverpool	England	beetwen July 4 and 10, 1847
McLean, James	24	Seaman	Brothers	Dublin	Ireland	1847/09/08
Pyne, Alexander	19	Seaman	Aberdeen	Liverpool	England	
Reid, John	52	Master	Marchioness of Bute	Belfast	Ireland	1847/08/06
Robinson, John	21	Seaman Carpenter	Agnes	Cork	Ireland	1847/06/09
Staunton, William		Seaman	Marchioness of Breadalbane	Sligo	Ireland	1847/08/05
Stobo, Robert		Seaman	Lady Milton	Liverpool	England	
Sutherland, Alexander	35	Seaman	Agnes	Cork	Ireland	1847/06/10
Sutherland, William	17	Seaman	Blenheim	Cork	Ireland	1847/08/24
Tyson, William	17	Seaman	Saguenay	Cork	Ireland	1847/08/30
Unknown	40	Seaman	Dunbrody	New Ross	Ireland	between July 18 and 24, 1847

2

List of people who died on ship at sea or in quarantine at Grosse Île, in 1847

The Irish Cemetery of Grosse Île as it appeared at the beginning of the 20th century.
(ANQQ, P560, S2, D677705, P5.)

LIST OF PEOPLE WHO DIED ON SHIPS AT SEA OR IN QUARANTINE AT GROSSE ÎLE, IN 1847

Name	Age	Vessel	Port	Country	Embarkation	Qc Arrival
Abbott, Margaret	18	Jessie	Limerick	Ireland	1847/04/18	1847/06/26
Adair, Thomas	2	Corea	Liverpool	England	1847/07/02	1847/08/14
Agnew, Alexander	4	Goliah	Liverpool	England	1847/05/21	1847/07/18
Ahern, Margaret	62	Aberdeen	Liverpool	England	1847/05/01	1847/06/13
Alary, Margaret	70	Larch	Sligo	Ireland	1847/07/11	1847/08/20
Alexander, Ann	31	Royal Adelaide	Killala	Ireland	1847/06/09	1847/08/09
Alexander, Sarah		Sobraon	Liverpool	England	1847/05/08	1847/06/29
Allen, Martha	7	Triton	Liverpool	England	1847/05/14	1847/07/24
Allen, Mary	20	Bridgetown	Liverpool	England	1847/07/03	1847/08/29
Allen, Thomas	3	Nelson's Village	Belfast	Ireland	1847/05/10	1847/06/26
Allison, John	1	Washington	Liverpool	England	1847/07/09	1847/08/26
Anderson, Jane	60	Christiana	Londonderry	Ireland	1847/04/08	1847/06/10
Andrews, Mary	13	Lord Ashburton	Liverpool	England	1847/09/13	1847/11/01
Araright, Maria		Leontine	Bremen	Germany	1847/05/28	1847/07/28
Armstrong, Ann	4	Christiana	Londonderry	Ireland	1847/04/08	1847/06/10
Armstrong, Ann	14	Christiana	Londonderry	Ireland	1847/04/08	1847/06/10
Armstrong, Ann		John Munn	Liverpool	England	1847/06/16	1847/08/13
Armstrong, Elizabeth	50	Free Trader	Liverpool	England	1847/06/22	1847/08/14
Armstrong, Mary A.	2	Yorkshire	Liverpool	England	1847/06/09	1847/08/10
Armstrong, Mrs.	27	John Munn	Liverpool	England	1847/06/16	1847/08/13
Armstrong, Sarah	65	Marchioness of Bute	Belfast	Ireland	1847/06/10	1847/07/31
Arnold, Dorothy	2	Leontine	Bremen	Germany	1847/05/28	1847/07/28
Arnold, Hannah		Leontine	Bremen	Germany	1847/05/28	1847/07/28
Ashe, Richard	50	Colonist	New Ross	Ireland	1847/07/13	1847/08/29
Atkinson, Bridget	3	Wolfville	Sligo	Ireland	1847/04/25	1847/06/10
Atkinson, Martha	65	Broom	Liverpool	England	1847/06/13	1847/08/06
Atkinson, Thomas	5	Wolfville	Sligo	Ireland	1847/04/25	1847/06/10
Aylward, James	3	Agnes	Cork	Ireland	1847/04/10	1847/06/10
Aylward, James	88	Ann Kenny	Waterford	Ireland	1847/06/27	1847/08/05
Bachus, George	3	Juliet	London	England	1847/07/03	1847/08/28
Bailey, Ann	16	Ajax	Liverpool	England	1847/04/16	1847/06/23
Bailey, Ann	21	Ajax	Liverpool	England	1847/04/16	1847/06/23
Bailey, George	26	Broom	Liverpool	England	1847/06/13	1847/08/06
Bailey, Mary	3	Wakefield	Cork	Ireland	1847/05/28	1847/07/12
Baker, Catherine	25	Sir Henry Pottinger	Cork	Ireland	1847/05/29	1847/08/07
Baker, George	1	Sir Henry Pottinger	Cork	Ireland	1847/05/29	1847/08/07
Baker, Mr.	40	Lady Flora Hastings	Cork	Ireland	1847/05/11	1847/06/26
Baker, Mrs.	38	Lady Flora Hastings	Cork	Ireland	1847/05/11	1847/06/26
Baldwin, John	2	Free Trader	Liverpool	England	1847/06/22	1847/08/14
Bamford, Margaret	1	Tamarac	Liverpool	England	1847/05/26	1847/07/11
Bane, William	2	Ajax	Liverpool	England	1847/04/16	1847/06/23
Banks, Ellen	2	Mary	Sligo	Ireland	1847/05/24	1847/07/27
Banks, John	45	Mary	Sligo	Ireland	1847/05/24	1847/07/27
Bannon, James	3	Bee	Cork	Ireland	1847/04/17	1847/06/12
Bannon, Martha	63	Naparina	Dublin	Ireland	1847/06/17	1847/08/23
Barber, James	42	Sarah Maria	Sligo	Ireland	1847/05/07	1847/06/28
Barnes, Ellen		Eliza Caroline	Liverpool	England	1847/05/03	1847/06/14
Barnes, William	2	Ajax	Liverpool	England	1847/04/16	1847/06/23
Barrett, Bridget	1	Larch	Sligo	Ireland	1847/07/11	1847/08/20
Barrett, Catherine	34	Larch	Sligo	Ireland	1847/07/11	1847/08/20
Barrett, Catherine	3	Larch	Sligo	Ireland	1847/07/11	1847/08/20
Barrett, Catherine	28	Sir Henry Pottinger	Cork	Ireland	1847/05/29	1847/08/07
Barrett, Catherine		Larch	Sligo	Ireland	1847/07/11	1847/08/20
Barrett, Edward	1	Lady Flora Hastings	Cork	Ireland	1847/05/11	1847/06/26
Barrett, Honora		X.L.	Galway	Ireland	1847/06/10	1847/08/01
Barrett, John	20	Isabella	Killala	Ireland	1847/07/17	1847/09/17
Barrett, John		Larch	Sligo	Ireland	1847/07/11	1847/08/20
Barrett, Kate	1	Sir Henry Pottinger	Cork	Ireland	1847/05/29	1847/08/07
Barrett, Margaret	45	Scotland	Cork	Ireland	1847/04/13	1847/06/08
Barrett, Margaret	54	Scotland	Cork	Ireland	1847/04/13	1847/06/08
Barrett, Mary		Larch	Sligo	Ireland	1847/07/11	1847/08/20
Barrett, Mary	6	Larch	Sligo	Ireland	1847/07/11	1847/08/20
Barrett, Mary	9	Larch	Sligo	Ireland	1847/07/11	1847/08/20
Barrett, Michael	6	John Bolton	Liverpool	England	1847/04/13	1847/06/10
Barrett, Michael	25	Bee	Cork	Ireland	1847/04/17	1847/06/12
Barrett, Michael	29	Bee	Cork	Ireland	1847/04/17	1847/06/12
Barrett, Robert	2	Rose	Liverpool	England	1847/04/19	1847/07/01
Barrett, Sarah	3	Larch	Sligo	Ireland	1847/07/11	1847/08/20
Barrett, Thomas		Larch	Sligo	Ireland	1847/07/11	1847/08/20
Barrett, Thomas	3	Larch	Sligo	Ireland	1847/07/11	1847/08/20
Barrett, Thomas	36	Larch	Sligo	Ireland	1847/07/11	1847/08/20
Barrett, William	1	Sir Henry Pottinger	Cork	Ireland	1847/05/29	1847/08/07
Barry, Abby	15	Mail	Cork	Ireland	1847/04/25	1847/06/19
Barry, Ann	30	Jessie	Cork	Ireland	1847/06/03	1847/07/24
Barry, Bartholomew	30	Sir Henry Pottinger	Cork	Ireland	1847/05/29	1847/08/07
Barry, Dennis	2	Lord Sandon	Cork	Ireland	1847/05/11	1847/06/26
Barry, Ellen	30	Jessie	Cork	Ireland	1847/06/03	1847/07/24
Barry, Hanna		Royal Adelaide	Killala	Ireland	1847/06/09	1847/08/09
Barry, Hannah	38	Sir Henry Pottinger	Cork	Ireland	1847/05/29	1847/08/07
Barry, J.		Sir Henry Pottinger	Cork	Ireland	1847/05/29	1847/08/07
Barry, J.		Sir Henry Pottinger	Cork	Ireland	1847/05/29	1847/08/07
Barry, J.		Lady Campbell	Dublin	Ireland	1847/06/03	1847/08/05
Barry, James		Sir Henry Pottinger	Cork	Ireland	1847/05/29	1847/08/07
Barry, James	9	Jessie	Cork	Ireland	1847/06/03	1847/07/24
Barry, James	27	Avon	Cork	Ireland	1847/05/19	1847/07/26
Barry, Jennifer	40	Lady Flora Hastings	Cork	Ireland	1847/05/11	1847/06/26
Barry, Johanna		Eliza Caroline	Liverpool	England	1847/05/03	1847/06/14
Barry, John	30	Agnes	Cork	Ireland	1847/04/10	1847/06/10
Barry, John	45	Scotland	Cork	Ireland	1847/04/13	1847/06/08
Barry, John	45	Lady Flora Hastings	Cork	Ireland	1847/05/11	1847/06/26
Barry, John		Jessie	Limerick	Ireland	1847/04/18	1847/06/26
Barry, John	3	Sir Henry Pottinger	Cork	Ireland	1847/05/29	1847/08/07
Barry, Margaret	25	Mail	Cork	Ireland	1847/04/25	1847/06/19
Barry, Margaret	20	Larch	Sligo	Ireland	1847/07/11	1847/08/20
Barry, Mary	6	Lord Sandon	Cork	Ireland	1847/05/11	1847/06/26
Barry, Michael	1	Jessie	Cork	Ireland	1847/06/03	1847/07/24
Barry, Mr.	25	Larch	Sligo	Ireland	1847/07/11	1847/08/20

LIST OF PEOPLE WHO DIED ON SHIPS AT SEA OR IN QUARANTINE AT GROSSE ÎLE, IN 1847

Name	Age	Vessel	Port	Country	Embarkation	Qc Arrival
Barry, Patrick	50	Agnes	Cork	Ireland	1847/04/10	1847/06/10
Barry, Patrick	2	Aberfoyle	Waterford	Ireland	1847/05/27	1847/07/04
Barry, Patrick	22	Avon	Cork	Ireland	1847/05/19	1847/07/26
Barry, Patrick	52	Saguenay	Cork	Ireland	1847/06/05	1847/08/22
Barry, Thomas	10	Lady Flora Hastings	Cork	Ireland	1847/05/11	1847/06/26
Bartley, Catherine		Virgilia	Liverpool	England	1847/07/22	1847/09/20
Bateman, Mary	3	Avon	Cork	Ireland	1847/05/19	1847/07/26
Bates, Robert	4	Progress	New Ross	Ireland	1847/05/05	1847/07/14
Bath, Catherine		Julius Caesar	Liverpool	England	1847/07/13	1847/09/05
Bean, James		George	Liverpool	England	1847/04/13	1847/06/12
Beatty, Ellen	32	Mary Brack	Limerick	Ireland	1847/05/03	1847/06/12
Beatty, Hugh	6	Eliza Caroline	Liverpool	England	1847/05/03	1847/06/14
Beatty, Sarah	2	Emigrant	Liverpool	England	1847/08/11	1847/10/03
Beck, Margaret		New Zealand	Newry	Ireland	1847/05/20	1847/07/03
Bedford, Thomas	1	Ajax	Liverpool	England	1847/04/16	1847/06/23
Bedford, Thomas	30	Ajax	Liverpool	England	1847/04/16	1847/06/23
Bedford, Thomas	2	Ajax	Liverpool	England	1847/04/16	1847/06/23
Beggs, Wilson	1	Lord Ashburton	Liverpool	England	1847/09/13	1847/11/01
Begley, John	17	Emigrant	Liverpool	England	1847/08/11	1847/10/03
Begley, M.	50	Wakefield	Cork	Ireland	1847/05/28	1847/07/12
Begley, Margaret	3	Marinus	Dublin	Ireland	1847/06/05	1847/08/13
Begley, Michael	40	Bridgetown	Liverpool	England	1847/07/03	1847/08/29
Begley, Robert	10	Marinus	Dublin	Ireland	1847/06/05	1847/08/13
Behan, Abraham	50	Margrette	New Ross	Ireland	1847/05/02	1847/07/08
Behan, Abraham	5	Margrette	New Ross	Ireland	1847/05/02	1847/07/08
Behan, Eliza		Lotus	Liverpool	England	1847/04/15	1847/06/24
Behan, Michael	25	Emily	Cork	Ireland	1847/05/12	1847/07/06
Bell, Alexander	8	Westmoreland	Sligo	Ireland	1847/06/12	1847/08/10
Bell, Ann	40	Sir Henry Pottinger	Belfast	Ireland	1847/07/09	1847/08/29
Bell, Francis	3	Wellington	Liverpool	England	1847/07/29	1847/09/20
Bell, John	11	Caithness-shire	Belfast	Ireland	1847/04/10	1847/06/12
Bell, Mary		New York Packet	Liverpool	England	1847/04/24	1847/06/29
Bell, Sarah	24	Independance	Belfast	Ireland	1847/05/23	1847/07/07
Bennett, Bridget	2	Sir Robert Peel	Liverpool	England	1847/07/26	1847/09/19
Bennett, Michael	35	Bee	Cork	Ireland	1847/04/17	1847/06/12
Bennett, Michael	29	Bee	Cork	Ireland	1847/04/17	1847/06/12
Bennett, William	2	Sir Henry Pottinger	Cork	Ireland	1847/05/29	1847/08/07
Benning, Edward	6	Naomi	Liverpool	England	1847/06/15	1847/08/10
Bentley, Joseph	3	Sir Robert Peel	Liverpool	England	1847/07/26	1847/09/19
Bergin, John	2	Columbia	Sligo	Ireland	1847/05/01	1847/06/10
Bergin, Joseph	6	Abbotsford	Dublin	Ireland	1847/04/23	1847/06/21
Berkley, Eliza	5	Goliah	Liverpool	England	1847/05/21	1847/07/18
Berry, James	46	Lady Flora Hastings	Cork	Ireland	1847/05/11	1847/06/26
Berry, John	4	Eliza Caroline	Liverpool	England	1847/05/03	1847/06/14
Berry, John	30	Agnes	Cork	Ireland	1847/04/10	1847/06/10
Berry, Thomas	11	Caithness-shire	Belfast	Ireland	1847/04/10	1847/06/12
Berryment, Mary		Constitution	Belfast	Ireland	1847/04/21	1847/06/08
Bevel, Catherine	6	Avon	Cork	Ireland	1847/05/19	1847/07/26
Bevel, Ellen	45	Avon	Cork	Ireland	1847/05/19	1847/07/26
Bevel, Michael	60	Avon	Cork	Ireland	1847/05/19	1847/07/26
Bingham, John	3	Yorkshire	Liverpool	England	1847/06/09	1847/08/10
Bingham, John		Yorkshire	Liverpool	England	1847/06/09	1847/08/10
Bink, Maria	11	John Bolton	Liverpool	England	1847/04/13	1847/06/10
Birch, Barbara	2	Juliet	London	England	1847/07/03	1847/08/28
Birch, John		Juliet	London	England	1847/07/03	1847/08/28
Birch, Maria	1	Juliet	London	England	1847/07/03	1847/08/28
Birch, Martin	1	Juliet	London	England	1847/07/03	1847/08/28
Bird, Jane		Herald	Dublin	Ireland	1847/05/20	1847/06/26
Bird, Jane	8	Sarah Maria	Sligo	Ireland	1847/05/07	1847/06/28
Bird, Thomas	30	Emigrant	Liverpool	England	1847/08/11	1847/10/03
Birmingham, Daniel	2	Columbia	Sligo	Ireland	1847/05/01	1847/06/10
Birmingham, Patrick	33	Abbotsford	Dublin	Ireland	1847/04/23	1847/06/21
Birney, Andrew	7	Yorkshire	Liverpool	England	1847/06/09	1847/08/10
Birney, Berkley	4	Lotus	Liverpool	England	1847/04/15	1847/06/24
Birney, Bridget		Lotus	Liverpool	England	1847/04/15	1847/06/24
Birney, Catherine	4	Sobraon	Liverpool	England	1847/05/08	1847/06/29
Birney, Charles	22	Agent	New Ross	Ireland	1847/05/20	1847/07/02
Birney, Charles	12	Lotus	Liverpool	England	1847/04/15	1847/06/24
Birney, Ellen	10	Lotus	Liverpool	England	1847/04/15	1847/06/24
Birney, John	3	Wolfville	Sligo	Ireland	1847/04/25	1847/06/10
Birney, John	60	Pandora	New Ross	Ireland	1847/06/11	1847/08/04
Birney, Mary	63	Progress	New Ross	Ireland	1847/05/05	1847/07/14
Birney, Michael	4	Eliza Caroline	Liverpool	England	1847/05/03	1847/06/14
Birney, Michael		Progress	New Ross	Ireland	1847/05/05	1847/07/14
Birney, Peter	70	Bridgetown	Liverpool	England	1847/07/03	1847/08/29
Birney, Richard	16	Colonist	New Ross	Ireland	1847/07/13	1847/08/29
Birney, Rose	60	Lady Milton	Liverpool	England	1847/05/05	1847/06/26
Birney, Thomas	44	Yorkshire	Liverpool	England	1847/06/09	1847/08/10
Birney, Thomas	4	Columbia	Sligo	Ireland	1847/05/01	1847/06/10
Birney, William	4	Colonist	New Ross	Ireland	1847/07/13	1847/08/29
Bishop, Charles	5	Free Trader	Liverpool	England	1847/06/22	1847/08/14
Bisner, Daniel		Henrietta Mary	Cork	Ireland	1847/08/18	1847/09/29
Bisner, Jeremiah	2	Henrietta Mary	Cork	Ireland	1847/08/18	1847/09/29
Bisner, Johanna	30	Henrietta Mary	Cork	Ireland	1847/08/18	1847/09/29
Black, Judith	5	Minerva	Galway	Ireland	1847/06/17	1847/08/14
Black, Margaret	5	Ann	Liverpool	England	1847/05/16	1847/06/30
Black, Maria	3	Ann	Liverpool	England	1847/05/16	1847/06/30
Black, Patrick		Ann	Liverpool	England	1847/05/16	1847/06/30
Black, Richard	4	John Bolton	Liverpool	England	1847/04/13	1847/06/10
Black, Sarah	1	Constitution	Belfast	Ireland	1847/04/21	1847/06/08
Blake, Mary		Standard	New Ross	Ireland	1847/04/22	1847/06/19
Blake, Mary		Standard	New Ross	Ireland	1847/04/22	1847/06/19
Blake, Richard	60	Avon	Cork	Ireland	1847/05/19	1847/07/26
Blakley, Francis	16	Christiana	Londonderry	Ireland	1847/04/08	1847/06/10
Blaney, Margaret	85	Charlotte Harrison	Greenock	Scotland	1847/05/14	1847/06/18
Bodkin, James		Naomi	Liverpool	England	1847/06/15	1847/08/10
Bohan, John	18	Colonist	New Ross	Ireland	1847/07/13	1847/08/29
Bohan, Philip		John Bell	New Ross	Ireland	1847/05/10	1847/06/29
Bonar, Patrick		Venilia	Limerick	Ireland	1847/05/28	1847/07/11
Bonar, Timothy	65	Bee	Cork	Ireland	1847/04/17	1847/06/12
Booth, John	5	Julius Caesar	Liverpool	England	1847/07/13	1847/09/05
Booth, Robert	60	Elliotts	Dublin	Ireland	1847/05/14	1847/06/30
Bourke, Mary	40	Sir Henry Pottinger	Cork	Ireland	1847/05/29	1847/08/07
Bourke, Michael	16	Sir Henry Pottinger	Cork	Ireland	1847/05/29	1847/08/07
Bourke, Patrick	4	Colonist	New Ross	Ireland	1847/07/13	1847/08/29
Bourke, William	55	Triton	Liverpool	England	1847/05/14	1847/07/24
Bowe, Margaret	8	Jessie	Limerick	Ireland	1847/04/18	1847/06/26
Bowlan, Johanna	22	Venilia	Limerick	Ireland	1847/05/28	1847/07/11
Bowles, John	2	Lotus	Liverpool	England	1847/04/15	1847/06/24
Boyd, Widow	50	Lady Campbell	Dublin	Ireland	1847/06/03	1847/08/05
Boyle, Allison	45	Margaret	New Ross	Ireland	1847/05/19	1847/07/02
Boyle, Catherine	7	Tamarac	Liverpool	England	1847/05/26	1847/07/11
Boyle, Eliza	1	Constitution	Belfast	Ireland	1847/04/21	1847/06/08
Boyle, Mary	50	Eliza Caroline	Liverpool	England	1847/05/03	1847/06/14
Boyle, Mary		Albion	Limerick	Ireland	1847/04/19	1847/06/18
Boyle, Stephen	1	Abbotsford	Dublin	Ireland	1847/04/23	1847/06/21
Boyne, John	3	Bee	Cork	Ireland	1847/04/17	1847/06/12
Brabazon, John	80	Dykes	Sligo	Ireland	1847/04/23	1847/06/10
Bradley, Alexander	9	Eagle	Dublin	Ireland	1847/05/12	1847/06/25
Bradley, Andrew	2	Nelson's Village	Belfast	Ireland	1847/05/10	1847/06/26
Bradley, Ann	27	Pursuit	Liverpool	England	1847/05/04	1847/06/23
Bradley, Catherine	20	Eagle	Dublin	Ireland	1847/05/12	1847/06/25
Bradley, John		George	Liverpool	England	1847/04/13	1847/06/12
Bradley, Philip		George	Liverpool	England	1847/04/13	1847/06/12

LIST OF PEOPLE WHO DIED ON SHIPS AT SEA OR IN QUARANTINE AT GROSSE ÎLE, IN 1847

Name	Age	Vessel	Port	Country	Embarkation	Qc Arrival
Bradley, Philip	2	Pursuit	Liverpool	England	1847/05/04	1847/06/23
Bradley, Thomas	3	Pursuit	Liverpool	England	1847/05/04	1847/06/23
Brady, Catherine	2	Wellington	Liverpool	England	1847/07/29	1847/09/20
Branagan, Edmund	3	Saguenay	Cork	Ireland	1847/06/05	1847/08/22
Branagan, Thomas	3	Saguenay	Cork	Ireland	1847/06/05	1847/08/22
Breadon, Mary	13	Gilmour	Cork	Ireland	1847/04/24	1847/06/18
Breen, Edwin	1	Argo	Liverpool	England	1847/05/04	1847/06/12
Breen, James	40	Avon	Cork	Ireland	1847/05/19	1847/07/26
Breen, Johanna	3	Jessie	Cork	Ireland	1847/06/03	1847/07/24
Breen, John	50	Avon	Cork	Ireland	1847/05/19	1847/07/26
Breen, Julia	7	Avon	Cork	Ireland	1847/05/19	1847/07/26
Breen, Margaret	30	Avon	Cork	Ireland	1847/05/19	1847/07/26
Breen, Mary	26	Primrose	Limerick	Ireland	1847/04/07	1847/06/18
Breen, Mary	32	Avon	Cork	Ireland	1847/05/19	1847/07/26
Breen, Matthew	1	Jessie	Cork	Ireland	1847/06/03	1847/07/24
Breen, Noreen		Avon	Cork	Ireland	1847/05/19	1847/07/26
Brennan, Ann	60	Elliotts	Dublin	Ireland	1847/05/14	1847/06/30
Brennan, Anthony	18	Odessa	Dublin	Ireland	1847/06/09	1847/08/09
Brennan, Bernard	23	Virginius	Liverpool	England	1847/05/28	1847/08/12
Brennan, Bernard	13	Virginius	Liverpool	England	1847/05/28	1847/08/12
Brennan, Bridget	2	John Bolton	Liverpool	England	1847/04/13	1847/06/10
Brennan, Bridget	8	Virginius	Liverpool	England	1847/05/28	1847/08/12
Brennan, Bridget	37	Virginius	Liverpool	England	1847/05/28	1847/08/12
Brennan, Catherine	1	Larch	Sligo	Ireland	1847/07/11	1847/08/20
Brennan, Eliza		Elliotts	Dublin	Ireland	1847/05/14	1847/06/30
Brennan, Elizabeth	2	Virginius	Liverpool	England	1847/05/28	1847/08/12
Brennan, Ellen	13	Columbia	Sligo	Ireland	1847/05/01	1847/06/10
Brennan, James	18	Virginius	Liverpool	England	1847/05/28	1847/08/12
Brennan, James	1	Sir Henry Pottinger	Cork	Ireland	1847/05/29	1847/08/07
Brennan, John	3	Elliotts	Dublin	Ireland	1847/05/14	1847/06/30
Brennan, John		Virginius	Liverpool	England	1847/05/28	1847/08/12
Brennan, Judith	4	Abbotsford	Dublin	Ireland	1847/04/23	1847/06/21
Brennan, Margaret	16	Virginius	Liverpool	England	1847/05/28	1847/08/12
Brennan, Margaret	20	Virginius	Liverpool	England	1847/05/28	1847/08/12
Brennan, Margaret	30	Virginius	Liverpool	England	1847/05/28	1847/08/12
Brennan, Martin	7	Virginius	Liverpool	England	1847/05/28	1847/08/12
Brennan, Mary	36	Elliotts	Dublin	Ireland	1847/05/14	1847/06/30
Brennan, Mary	2	Virginius	Liverpool	England	1847/05/28	1847/08/12
Brennan, Mary	34	Emigrant	Liverpool	England	1847/08/11	1847/10/03
Brennan, Mary	2	Georgiana	Dublin	Ireland	1847/05/16	1847/06/29
Brennan, Mary	46	Odessa	Dublin	Ireland	1847/06/09	1847/08/09
Brennan, Mary	2	Odessa	Dublin	Ireland	1847/06/09	1847/08/09
Brennan, Michael	4	Virginius	Liverpool	England	1847/05/28	1847/08/12
Brennan, Michael	3	Larch	Sligo	Ireland	1847/07/11	1847/08/20
Brennan, Patrick	34	Dykes	Sligo	Ireland	1847/04/23	1847/06/10
Brennan, Patrick	3	Jane Avery	Dublin	Ireland	1847/05/09	1847/06/25
Brennan, Patrick	3	Naomi	Liverpool	England	1847/06/15	1847/08/10
Brennan, Patrick	10	Virginius	Liverpool	England	1847/05/28	1847/08/12
Brennan, Rose	7	Elliotts	Dublin	Ireland	1847/05/14	1847/06/30
Brennan, Thadeus	20	Columbia	Sligo	Ireland	1847/05/01	1847/06/10
Brennan, Thomas	40	Virginius	Liverpool	England	1847/05/28	1847/08/12
Brennan, William	6	Odessa	Dublin	Ireland	1847/06/09	1847/08/09
Brennan, Winifred	28	Elliotts	Dublin	Ireland	1847/05/14	1847/06/30
Breslin, James	1	Louisa	Limerick	Ireland	1847/05/08	1847/06/25
Brett, Bridget	4	John Bolton	Liverpool	England	1847/04/13	1847/06/10
Brett, Edward	11	John Bolton	Liverpool	England	1847/04/13	1847/06/10
Brett, Mary	3	Jane Avery	Dublin	Ireland	1847/05/09	1847/06/25
Brickley, John		Avon	Cork	Ireland	1847/05/19	1847/07/26
Brickley, Thomas	45	Naparina	Dublin	Ireland	1847/06/17	1847/08/23
Brien, Bridget	32	Scotland	Cork	Ireland	1847/04/13	1847/06/08
Brien, Catherine	54	Scotland	Cork	Ireland	1847/04/13	1847/06/08
Brien, Catherine	5	Avon	Cork	Ireland	1847/05/19	1847/07/26
Brien, Cornelius	2	Bee	Cork	Ireland	1847/04/17	1847/06/12
Brien, Cornelius	20	Scotland	Cork	Ireland	1847/04/13	1847/06/08
Brien, David	5	Avon	Cork	Ireland	1847/05/19	1847/07/26
Brien, Eliza	2	Ajax	Liverpool	England	1847/04/16	1847/06/23
Brien, Elizabeth	45	Mail	Cork	Ireland	1847/04/25	1847/06/19
Brien, Honora	6	Albion	Cork	Ireland	1847/08/13	1847/09/29
Brien, Jeremiah	30	Mail	Cork	Ireland	1847/04/25	1847/06/19
Brien, John	23	Scotland	Cork	Ireland	1847/04/13	1847/06/08
Brien, John	70	Scotland	Cork	Ireland	1847/04/13	1847/06/08
Brien, John	12	Jessie	Limerick	Ireland	1847/04/18	1847/06/26
Brien, John	40	Gilmour	Cork	Ireland	1847/04/24	1847/06/18
Brien, John	50	Jessie	Limerick	Ireland	1847/04/18	1847/06/26
Brien, John	30	Scotland	Cork	Ireland	1847/04/13	1847/06/08
Brien, Margaret	3	Wakefield	Cork	Ireland	1847/05/28	1847/07/12
Brien, Margaret	4	Avon	Cork	Ireland	1847/05/19	1847/07/26
Brien, Margaret	30	Gilmour	Cork	Ireland	1847/04/24	1847/06/18
Brien, Mary	23	Scotland	Cork	Ireland	1847/04/13	1847/06/08
Brien, Mary	65	Lady Milton	Liverpool	England	1847/05/05	1847/06/26
Brien, Mary	23	Jessie	Limerick	Ireland	1847/04/18	1847/06/26
Brien, Mary	7	Minerva	Galway	Ireland	1847/06/17	1847/08/14
Brien, Mary	3	Avon	Cork	Ireland	1847/05/19	1847/07/26
Brien, Mary	29	Lady Flora Hastings	Cork	Ireland	1847/05/11	1847/06/26
Brien, Mary	5	Avon	Cork	Ireland	1847/05/19	1847/07/26
Brien, Mary S.	1	Scotland	Cork	Ireland	1847/04/13	1847/06/08
Brien, Michael	6	Avon	Cork	Ireland	1847/05/19	1847/07/26
Brien, Noreen	6	Avon	Cork	Ireland	1847/05/19	1847/07/26
Brien, Patrick	15	Jessie	Limerick	Ireland	1847/04/18	1847/06/26
Brien, Patrick	50	Scotland	Cork	Ireland	1847/04/13	1847/06/08
Brien, Robert	35	Free Trader	Liverpool	England	1847/06/22	1847/08/14
Brien, Rodger	5	Wakefield	Cork	Ireland	1847/05/28	1847/07/12
Brien, Thomas	3	Scotland	Cork	Ireland	1847/04/13	1847/06/08
Brien, Winifred	48	Jessie	Limerick	Ireland	1847/04/18	1847/06/26
Brigham, Louis	9	Leontine	Bremen	Germany	1847/05/28	1847/07/28
Britton, Ann	25	Rose	Liverpool	England	1847/04/19	1847/07/01
Britton, Richard	2	Rose	Liverpool	England	1847/04/19	1847/07/01
Brock, Michael	45	George	Liverpool	England	1847/04/13	1847/06/12
Broderick, Catherine	69	Alert	Waterford	Ireland	1847/06/05	1847/07/15
Broderick, Edmond	4	John Bolton	Liverpool	England	1847/04/13	1847/06/10
Broderick, John	1	Bee	Cork	Ireland	1847/04/17	1847/06/12
Broderick, John	1	Bee	Cork	Ireland	1847/04/17	1847/06/12
Broderick, John	75	Alert	Waterford	Ireland	1847/06/05	1847/07/15
Broderick, Mary	20	Sisters	Liverpool	England	1847/04/22	1847/06/20
Brogan, Catherine	2	John Bolton	Liverpool	England	1847/04/13	1847/06/10
Brophy, Margaret	50	Columbia	Sligo	Ireland	1847/05/01	1847/06/10
Brosnan, Bridget	6	Sir Robert Peel	Liverpool	England	1847/07/26	1847/09/19
Brosnan, Jane	3	Sir Robert Peel	Liverpool	England	1847/07/26	1847/09/19
Brosnan, Thomas	9	Saguenay	Cork	Ireland	1847/06/05	1847/08/22
Brosnan, Timothy	3	Sir Robert Peel	Liverpool	England	1847/07/26	1847/09/19
Brown, Eliza	3	Nelson's Village	Belfast	Ireland	1847/05/10	1847/06/26
Brown, James	50	Covenanter	Liverpool	England	1847/06/24	1847/08/09
Brown, Jane	1	Agamemnon	Liverpool	England	1847/06/24	1847/07/31
Brown, John	57	Sobraon	Liverpool	England	1847/05/08	1847/06/29
Brown, John		Sir Henry Pottinger	Cork	Ireland	1847/05/29	1847/08/07
Brown, John	2	Lady Flora Hastings	Cork	Ireland	1847/05/11	1847/06/26
Brown, John		Virgilia	Liverpool	England	1847/07/22	1847/09/20
Brown, John	11	Larch	Sligo	Ireland	1847/07/11	1847/08/20
Brown, Margaret	24	Avon	Cork	Ireland	1847/05/19	1847/07/26
Brown, Maria	2	Julius Caesar	Liverpool	England	1847/07/13	1847/09/05
Brown, Mary	32	Sir Henry Pottinger	Cork	Ireland	1847/05/29	1847/08/07
Brown, Mary Ann	3	Tamarac	Liverpool	England	1847/05/26	1847/07/11
Brown, Patrick	2	John Bolton	Liverpool	England	1847/04/13	1847/06/10
Brown, Rachel		Nelson's Village	Belfast	Ireland	1847/05/10	1847/06/26
Brown, Richard	13	Gilmour	Cork	Ireland	1847/04/24	1847/06/18
Brown, Susan	2	Gilmour	Cork	Ireland	1847/04/24	1847/06/18

LIST OF PEOPLE WHO DIED ON SHIPS AT SEA OR IN QUARANTINE AT GROSSE ÎLE, IN 1847

Name	Age	Vessel	Port	Country	Embarkation	Qc Arrival
Brown, Thomas	3	Wolfville	Sligo	Ireland	1847/04/25	1847/06/10
Brown, Thomas	4	John Bolton	Liverpool	England	1847/04/13	1847/06/10
Brown, William	25	Avon	Cork	Ireland	1847/05/19	1847/07/26
Brown, William	1	Sir Henry Pottinger	Cork	Ireland	1847/05/29	1847/08/07
Brown, William	30	Sir Henry Pottinger	Cork	Ireland	1847/05/29	1847/08/07
Brown, William		Avon	Cork	Ireland	1847/05/19	1847/07/26
Brown, Winifred	45	Royal Adelaide	Killala	Ireland	1847/06/09	1847/08/09
Bruce, Catherine	54	Scotland	Cork	Ireland	1847/04/13	1847/06/08
Bryan, Catherine	30	Ajax	Liverpool	England	1847/04/16	1847/06/23
Bryan, Cornelius	2	Lady Flora Hastings	Cork	Ireland	1847/05/11	1847/06/26
Bryan, Dennis	60	Achsah	Limerick	Ireland	1847/05/11	1847/06/23
Bryan, Elizabeth	2	Araminta	Liverpool	England	1847/05/01	1847/06/20
Bryan, Elizabeth	1	Aberdeen	Liverpool	England	1847/05/01	1847/06/13
Bryan, James	40	Bee	Cork	Ireland	1847/04/17	1847/06/12
Bryan, James	24	Jessie	Limerick	Ireland	1847/04/18	1847/06/26
Bryan, John	54	Scotland	Cork	Ireland	1847/04/13	1847/06/08
Bryan, John		Junior	Liverpool	England	1847/05/10	1847/07/03
Bryan, John	4	Coromandel	Dublin	Ireland	1847/05/13	1847/07/02
Bryan, Lawrence	40	Wakefield	Cork	Ireland	1847/05/28	1847/07/12
Bryan, Margaret	1	Jessie	Cork	Ireland	1847/06/03	1847/07/24
Bryan, Mary	60	Coromandel	Dublin	Ireland	1847/05/13	1847/07/02
Bryan, Matthew	25	Aberfoyle	Waterford	Ireland	1847/05/27	1847/07/04
Bryan, Patrick	7	Coromandel	Dublin	Ireland	1847/05/13	1847/07/02
Bryan, Thomas	20	Lady Flora Hastings	Cork	Ireland	1847/05/11	1847/06/26
Bryan, Thomas	4	Lady Flora Hastings	Cork	Ireland	1847/05/11	1847/06/26
Bryan, Thomas	24	Scotland	Cork	Ireland	1847/04/13	1847/06/08
Bryson, Cornelius	2	Bee	Cork	Ireland	1847/04/17	1847/06/12
Bryson, Patrick	3	Saguenay	Cork	Ireland	1847/06/05	1847/08/22
Buckland, Augustina	1	General Hewitt	Bremen	Germany	1847/07/22	1847/09/12
Buckley, Denis	30	Avon	Cork	Ireland	1847/05/19	1847/07/26
Buckley, Donald		Goliah	Liverpool	England	1847/05/21	1847/07/18
Buckley, Johanna	22	Emily	Cork	Ireland	1847/05/12	1847/07/06
Buckley, John	30	Covenanter	Cork	Ireland	1847/06/17	1847/08/09
Bullman, Catherine	8	Avon	Cork	Ireland	1847/05/19	1847/07/26
Bullman, John	30	Avon	Cork	Ireland	1847/05/19	1847/07/26
Bullman, Margaret		Avon	Cork	Ireland	1847/05/19	1847/07/26
Burchill, John		George	Liverpool	England	1847/04/13	1847/06/12
Burke, Bridget	40	Lord Ashburton	Liverpool	England	1847/09/13	1847/11/01
Burke, Catherine	20	Lord Sandon	Cork	Ireland	1847/05/11	1847/06/26
Burke, H.	20	Lady Milton	Liverpool	England	1847/05/05	1847/06/26
Burke, James	1	Jane Black	Limerick	Ireland	1847/08/10	1847/09/17
Burke, James	8	Goliah	Liverpool	England	1847/05/21	1847/07/18
Burke, John	25	Sir Henry Pottinger	Cork	Ireland	1847/05/29	1847/08/07
Burke, Margaret	60	Virginius	Liverpool	England	1847/05/28	1847/08/12
Burke, Maria	2	Virgilia	Liverpool	England	1847/07/22	1847/09/20
Burke, Mary	2	Argo	Liverpool	England	1847/05/04	1847/06/12
Burke, Mary	17	Scotland	Cork	Ireland	1847/04/13	1847/06/08
Burke, Mary		Lord Sandon	Cork	Ireland	1847/05/11	1847/06/26
Burke, Mary	51	Asia	Cork	Ireland	1847/06/02	1847/07/27
Burke, Mary	6	Abbotsford	Dublin	Ireland	1847/04/23	1847/06/21
Burke, Mary	2	Scotland	Cork	Ireland	1847/04/13	1847/06/08
Burke, Patrick	3	Avon	Cork	Ireland	1847/05/19	1847/07/26
Burke, Patrick	1	Columbia	Sligo	Ireland	1847/05/01	1847/06/10
Burke, Thomas	27	John Bolton	Liverpool	England	1847/04/13	1847/06/10
Burke, Thomas	27	Lord Sandon	Cork	Ireland	1847/05/11	1847/06/26
Burke, Thomas	1	Primrose	Limerick	Ireland	1847/04/07	1847/06/18
Burke, Thomas	70	Asia	Cork	Ireland	1847/06/02	1847/07/27
Burns, Ann	1	Pandora	New Ross	Ireland	1847/06/11	1847/08/04
Burns, Catherine	50	Triton	Liverpool	England	1847/05/14	1847/07/24
Burns, Catherine	53	Virginius	Liverpool	England	1847/05/28	1847/08/12
Burns, Denis	6	Covenanter	Cork	Ireland	1847/06/17	1847/08/09
Burns, Elizabeth	55	Naomi	Liverpool	England	1847/06/15	1847/08/10
Burns, Elizabeth	60	Scotland	Cork	Ireland	1847/04/13	1847/06/08
Burns, Elizabeth	15	Pandora	New Ross	Ireland	1847/06/11	1847/08/04
Burns, James	22	Scotland	Cork	Ireland	1847/04/13	1847/06/08
Burns, James	46	Lady Campbell	Dublin	Ireland	1847/06/03	1847/08/05
Burns, Jannet	20	Avon	Cork	Ireland	1847/05/19	1847/07/26
Burns, John	2	John Munn	Liverpool	England	1847/06/16	1847/08/13
Burns, John	12	Margaret	New Ross	Ireland	1847/05/19	1847/07/02
Burns, John	10	Champion	Liverpool	England	1847/07/13	1847/08/28
Burns, John	45	Wellington	Liverpool	England	1847/07/29	1847/09/20
Burns, John	24	Avon	Cork	Ireland	1847/05/19	1847/07/26
Burns, John	55	Naomi	Liverpool	England	1847/06/15	1847/08/10
Burns, Lucy	1	Avon	Cork	Ireland	1847/05/19	1847/07/26
Burns, Lucy	22	Avon	Cork	Ireland	1847/05/19	1847/07/26
Burns, Mary	4	Champion	Liverpool	England	1847/07/13	1847/08/28
Burns, Mary	46	Pandora	New Ross	Ireland	1847/06/11	1847/08/04
Burns, Mary	60	Naomi	Liverpool	England	1847/06/15	1847/08/10
Burns, Mary	65	Pandora	New Ross	Ireland	1847/06/11	1847/08/04
Burns, Patrick	16	Triton	Liverpool	England	1847/05/14	1847/07/24
Burns, Patrick	7	Champion	Liverpool	England	1847/07/13	1847/08/28
Burns, Thomas	4	Avon	Cork	Ireland	1847/05/19	1847/07/26
Burns, Thomas	40	Bridgetown	Liverpool	England	1847/07/03	1847/08/29
Burns, Timothy	65	Bee	Cork	Ireland	1847/04/17	1847/06/12
Burns, Winford	23	Aberdeen	Liverpool	England	1847/05/01	1847/06/13
Burns, Winford	23	Araminta	Liverpool	England	1847/05/01	1847/06/20
Butler, Ann	2	John Munn	Liverpool	England	1847/06/16	1847/08/13
Butler, Ellen	2	Alert	Waterford	Ireland	1847/06/05	1847/07/15
Butler, James	4	Wolfville	Sligo	Ireland	1847/04/25	1847/06/10
Butler, Margaret	60	Wolfville	Sligo	Ireland	1847/04/25	1847/06/10
Butler, Mrs.	60	John Munn	Liverpool	England	1847/06/16	1847/08/13
Byers, William	1	Sesostris	Londonderry	Ireland	1847/05/14	1847/06/24
Byers, William		Herald	Dublin	Ireland	1847/05/20	1847/06/26
Byrne, Mary	7	Lady Milton	Liverpool	England	1847/05/05	1847/06/26
Byrne, Mary	13	Lotus	Liverpool	England	1847/04/15	1847/06/24
Caffrey, Peter		Lillias	Dublin	Ireland	1847/07/01	1847/08/16
Cahill, Catherine	32	Mary Brack	Limerick	Ireland	1847/05/03	1847/06/12
Cahill, Catherine	5	Emily	Cork	Ireland	1847/05/12	1847/07/06
Cahill, Charles	1	Sir Henry Pottinger	Cork	Ireland	1847/05/29	1847/08/07
Cahill, John	21	Yorkshire	Liverpool	England	1847/06/09	1847/08/10
Cahill, Martin	40	Yorkshire	Liverpool	England	1847/06/09	1847/08/10
Cahill, Michael	50	John Francis	Cork	Ireland	1847/04/10	1847/06/10
Cahill, Patrick	5	Saguenay	Cork	Ireland	1847/06/05	1847/08/22
Cahir, John	3	Agent	New Ross	Ireland	1847/05/20	1847/07/02
Cain, Anthony	8	Wolfville	Sligo	Ireland	1847/04/25	1847/06/10
Cain, Jane		Rose	Liverpool	England	1847/04/19	1847/07/01
Cain, Jeremiah	2	Scotland	Cork	Ireland	1847/04/13	1847/06/08
Cain, Jeremiah	24	Scotland	Cork	Ireland	1847/04/13	1847/06/08
Cain, John	1	Sir Henry Pottinger	Belfast	Ireland	1847/07/09	1847/08/29
Cain, John	2	Champion	Liverpool	England	1847/07/13	1847/08/28
Cain, Mary	21	Scotland	Cork	Ireland	1847/04/13	1847/06/08
Cain, Mary	21	Scotland	Cork	Ireland	1847/04/13	1847/06/08
Cain, Mary	1	Tamarac	Liverpool	England	1847/05/26	1847/07/11
Cain, Owen	24	New York Packet	Liverpool	England	1847/04/24	1847/06/29
Cain, Patrick	2	Scotland	Cork	Ireland	1847/04/13	1847/06/08
Cain, Patrick	3	Scotland	Cork	Ireland	1847/04/13	1847/06/08
Cain, Patrick		Rose	Liverpool	England	1847/04/19	1847/07/01
Cain, Peter	8	Tamarac	Liverpool	England	1847/05/26	1847/07/11
Cain, Peter	7	Rose	Liverpool	England	1847/04/19	1847/07/01
Callaghan, Allison	8	Eliza Caroline	Liverpool	England	1847/05/03	1847/06/14
Callaghan, Bridget	39	Avon	Cork	Ireland	1847/05/19	1847/07/26
Callaghan, Catherine	25	Venilia	Limerick	Ireland	1847/05/28	1847/07/11

LIST OF PEOPLE WHO DIED ON SHIPS AT SEA OR IN QUARANTINE AT GROSSE ÎLE, IN 1847

Name	Age	Vessel	Port	Country	Embarkation	Qc Arrival
Callaghan, Daniel	25	Triton	Liverpool	England	1847/05/14	1847/07/24
Callaghan, Ellen		Lady Flora Hastings	Cork	Ireland	1847/05/11	1847/06/26
Callaghan, James	6	Avon	Cork	Ireland	1847/05/19	1847/07/26
Callaghan, James	40	Avon	Cork	Ireland	1847/05/19	1847/07/26
Callaghan, Johanna		Avon	Cork	Ireland	1847/05/19	1847/07/26
Callaghan, John	70	Covenanter	Cork	Ireland	1847/06/17	1847/08/09
Callaghan, Julia	40	Triton	Liverpool	England	1847/05/14	1847/07/24
Callaghan, Martin	4	George	Liverpool	England	1847/04/13	1847/06/12
Callaghan, Michael		Ninian	Limerick	Ireland	1847/04/13	1847/06/12
Callaghan, William	40	Unicorn	Londonderry	Ireland	1847/05/23	1847/07/09
Cameron, Donald	60	Eliza	Glasgow	Scotland	1847/07/17	1847/09/17
Cameron, Duncan		Eliza	Glasgow	Scotland	1847/07/17	1847/09/17
Cameron, S.	64	Ann	Liverpool	England	1847/05/16	1847/06/30
Campbell, Agnes	21	Marchioness of Bute	Belfast	Ireland	1847/06/10	1847/07/31
Campbell, Catherine		Greenock	Liverpool	England	1847/06/19	1847/07/29
Campbell, James	52	Sobraon	Liverpool	England	1847/05/08	1847/06/29
Campbell, John	40	Christiana	Londonderry	Ireland	1847/04/08	1847/06/10
Campbell, Malcolm	3	Ann Rankin	Glasgow	Scotland	1847/06/27	1847/08/09
Campbell, Margaret	2	Tamarac	Liverpool	England	1847/05/26	1847/07/11
Campbell, Margaret	49	Virginius	Liverpool	England	1847/05/28	1847/08/12
Campbell, Mary	1	Tamarac	Liverpool	England	1847/05/26	1847/07/11
Campbell, Mary Ann	1	Sir Robert Peel	Liverpool	England	1847/07/26	1847/09/19
Campbell, William	26	Virginius	Liverpool	England	1847/05/28	1847/08/12
Canny, Bridget		George	Liverpool	England	1847/04/13	1847/06/12
Canny, Mary		Gilmour	Cork	Ireland	1847/04/24	1847/06/18
Canny, Patrick	10	Ajax	Liverpool	England	1847/04/16	1847/06/23
Carey, Bartholomew	25	Larch	Sligo	Ireland	1847/07/11	1847/08/20
Carey, Bridget	21	Larch	Sligo	Ireland	1847/07/11	1847/08/20
Carey, Peter	20	Bee	Cork	Ireland	1847/04/17	1847/06/12
Carey, Peter	20	Bee	Cork	Ireland	1847/04/17	1847/06/12
Carmody, Ellen		Lord Sandon	Cork	Ireland	1847/05/11	1847/06/26
Carney, Catherine	50	Wolfville	Sligo	Ireland	1847/04/25	1847/06/10
Carney, Catherine	13	John Munn	Liverpool	England	1847/06/16	1847/08/13
Carney, Dennis	50	Progress	New Ross	Ireland	1847/05/05	1847/07/14
Carney, John	45	Independance	Belfast	Ireland	1847/05/23	1847/07/07
Carney, John		Goliah	Liverpool	England	1847/05/21	1847/07/18
Carney, John	40	Jessie	Cork	Ireland	1847/06/03	1847/07/24
Carney, John	30	Larch	Sligo	Ireland	1847/07/11	1847/08/20
Carney, Lawrence	25	Eliza Caroline	Liverpool	England	1847/05/03	1847/06/14
Carney, Margaret	30	Jessie	Cork	Ireland	1847/06/03	1847/07/24
Carney, Mary	4	Lady Milton	Liverpool	England	1847/05/05	1847/06/26
Carney, Matthew	2	Goliah	Liverpool	England	1847/05/21	1847/07/18
Carney, Patrick	60	Wolfville	Sligo	Ireland	1847/04/25	1847/06/10
Carney, Peter	40	Ann	Liverpool	England	1847/05/16	1847/06/30
Carney, Peter	3	Ann	Liverpool	England	1847/05/16	1847/06/30
Caroline, Jane		Sobraon	Liverpool	England	1847/05/08	1847/06/29
Caroline, Mary	1	Allan Kerr	Sligo	Ireland	1847/06/23	1847/08/04
Carpenter, Sally	40	Lord Ashburton	Liverpool	England	1847/09/13	1847/11/01
Carpenter, Thomas	5	Lord Ashburton	Liverpool	England	1847/09/13	1847/11/01
Carpenter, William	12	Lord Ashburton	Liverpool	England	1847/09/13	1847/11/01
Carr, John	24	Agent	New Ross	Ireland	1847/05/20	1847/07/02
Carr, Joseph		Charlotte	Plymouth	England	1847/06/02	1847/07/13
Carr, Mary	1	Margrette	New Ross	Ireland	1847/05/02	1847/07/08
Carr, Samuel	24	Sir Robert Peel	Liverpool	England	1847/07/26	1847/09/19
Carrigan, Bridget	7	Virginius	Liverpool	England	1847/05/28	1847/08/12
Carrigan, Eliza	6	Rose	Liverpool	England	1847/04/19	1847/07/01
Carrigan, James	45	Rose	Liverpool	England	1847/04/19	1847/07/01
Carrigan, John	40	Sarah	Liverpool	England	1847/05/29	1847/07/19
Carrigan, John	3	Rose	Liverpool	England	1847/04/19	1847/07/01
Carrigan, Mary	2	Virginius	Liverpool	England	1847/05/28	1847/08/12
Carrigan, Mary J.		Ann	Liverpool	England	1847/05/16	1847/06/30
Carrigan, Michael	3	Virginius	Liverpool	England	1847/05/28	1847/08/12
Carrigan, Mrs.	45	Sarah	Liverpool	England	1847/05/29	1847/07/19
Carrigan, Patrick	2	Rose	Liverpool	England	1847/04/19	1847/07/01
Carrigan, Patrick	10	Sarah	Liverpool	England	1847/05/29	1847/07/19
Carroll, Bridget		Sisters	Liverpool	England	1847/04/22	1847/06/20
Carroll, Catherine	1	Douce Davie	Sligo	Ireland	1847/08/11	1847/09/30
Carroll, Charles		George	Liverpool	England	1847/04/13	1847/06/12
Carroll, Henry	13	Eliza Caroline	Liverpool	England	1847/05/03	1847/06/14
Carroll, James	25	Saguenay	Cork	Ireland	1847/06/05	1847/08/22
Carroll, John	2	Sisters	Liverpool	England	1847/04/22	1847/06/20
Carroll, John	74	Greenock	Liverpool	England	1847/06/19	1847/07/29
Carroll, Mary	60	Sisters	Liverpool	England	1847/04/22	1847/06/20
Carroll, Mary	20	Bridgetown	Liverpool	England	1847/07/03	1847/08/29
Carroll, Mary	46	Naparina	Dublin	Ireland	1847/06/17	1847/08/23
Carroll, Mary	35	Bridgetown	Liverpool	England	1847/07/03	1847/08/29
Carroll, Mary	2	Erin's Queen	Liverpool	England	1847/06/01	1847/07/23
Carroll, Mary		Avon	Cork	Ireland	1847/05/19	1847/07/26
Carroll, Mary		George	Liverpool	England	1847/04/13	1847/06/12
Carroll, Michael	16	Odessa	Dublin	Ireland	1847/06/09	1847/08/09
Carroll, Mrs.	35	Princess Royal	Liverpool	England	1847/05/05	1847/06/16
Carroll, Mrs.	53	Saguenay	Cork	Ireland	1847/06/05	1847/08/22
Carroll, Owen	70	Bridgetown	Liverpool	England	1847/07/03	1847/08/29
Carroll, Patrick	63	Sisters	Liverpool	England	1847/04/22	1847/06/20
Carroll, Patrick	1	Jane Black	Limerick	Ireland	1847/08/10	1847/09/17
Carrothers, James	2	Triton	Liverpool	England	1847/05/14	1847/07/24
Carrothers, Mary	3	Triton	Liverpool	England	1847/05/14	1847/07/24
Cart, James		Goliah	Liverpool	England	1847/05/21	1847/07/18
Carter, Ellen		Asia	Cork	Ireland	1847/06/02	1847/07/27
Carton, Richard	70	Camillia	Sligo	Ireland	1847/05/19	1847/07/07
Carton, Richard	4	Sisters	Liverpool	England	1847/04/22	1847/06/20
Carty, Catherine	3	Pursuit	Liverpool	England	1847/05/04	1847/06/23
Carty, Catherine	80	Atalanta	Dublin	Ireland	1847/07/30	1847/09/12
Carty, Daniel	26	Jessie	Limerick	Ireland	1847/04/18	1847/06/26
Carty, Daniel	16	Pursuit	Liverpool	England	1847/05/04	1847/06/23
Carty, Ellen	2	Dominica	Cork	Ireland	1847/05/01	1847/06/14
Carty, Helen	18	Lady Flora Hastings	Cork	Ireland	1847/05/11	1847/06/26
Carty, Jeremiah	28	Lady Flora Hastings	Cork	Ireland	1847/05/11	1847/06/26
Carty, John	30	Scotland	Cork	Ireland	1847/04/13	1847/06/08
Carty, John	40	Scotland	Cork	Ireland	1847/04/13	1847/06/08
Carty, Mary	6	Pursuit	Liverpool	England	1847/05/04	1847/06/23
Carty, Thomas		George	Liverpool	England	1847/04/13	1847/06/12
Casey, Bridget		Julius Caesar	Liverpool	England	1847/07/13	1847/09/05
Casey, Catherine	32	Sir Robert Peel	Liverpool	England	1847/07/26	1847/09/19
Casey, Daniel	3	Henrietta Mary	Cork	Ireland	1847/08/18	1847/09/29
Casey, Dennis	1	Sir Henry Pottinger	Cork	Ireland	1847/05/29	1847/08/07
Casey, James	7	Wolfville	Sligo	Ireland	1847/04/25	1847/06/10
Casey, James	50	Erin's Queen	Liverpool	England	1847/06/01	1847/07/23
Casey, Margaret	40	Wolfville	Sligo	Ireland	1847/04/25	1847/06/10
Casey, Martha	3	Lotus	Liverpool	England	1847/04/15	1847/06/24
Casey, Mary	15	Erin's Queen	Liverpool	England	1847/06/01	1847/07/23
Casey, Mary	5	Wolfville	Sligo	Ireland	1847/04/25	1847/06/10
Casey, Patrick	45	Lady Flora Hastings	Cork	Ireland	1847/05/11	1847/06/26
Casey, Patrick	12	Ganges	Liverpool	England	1847/06/16	1847/08/21
Casey, Peter	35	Naomi	Liverpool	England	1847/06/15	1847/08/10
Cash, John	45	John Bolton	Liverpool	England	1847/04/13	1847/06/10
Cash, William	4	John Bolton	Liverpool	England	1847/04/13	1847/06/10
Cashel, John	4	Argo	Liverpool	England	1847/05/04	1847/06/12
Cashman, Bridget	20	Avon	Cork	Ireland	1847/05/19	1847/07/26
Cashman, Francis	23	Avon	Cork	Ireland	1847/05/19	1847/07/26
Cashman, Mary	28	Bee	Cork	Ireland	1847/04/17	1847/06/12
Cashman, Mary	28	Bee	Cork	Ireland	1847/04/17	1847/06/12
Cassidy, Barney	1	Tamarac	Liverpool	England	1847/05/26	1847/07/11
Cassidy, Daniel	2	Standard	New Ross	Ireland	1847/04/22	1847/06/19
Cassidy, John	6	Tamarac	Liverpool	England	1847/05/26	1847/07/11

LIST OF PEOPLE WHO DIED ON SHIPS AT SEA OR IN QUARANTINE AT GROSSE ÎLE, IN 1847

Name	Age	Vessel	Port	Country	Embarkation	Qc Arrival
Cassidy, William		Lady Campbell	Dublin	Ireland	1847/06/03	1847/08/05
Caulfield, Lawrence	42	George	Liverpool	England	1847/04/13	1847/06/12
Caulfield, Nancy	50	Jessie	Limerick	Ireland	1847/04/18	1847/06/26
Caulfield, Rose	11	George	Liverpool	England	1847/04/13	1847/06/12
Caulfield, Thomas	13	George	Liverpool	England	1847/04/13	1847/06/12
Caulfield, Thomas		George	Liverpool	England	1847/04/13	1847/06/12
Cavanagh, Ann	1	Ajax	Liverpool	England	1847/04/16	1847/06/23
Cavanagh, Bridget	70	Triton	Liverpool	England	1847/05/14	1847/07/24
Cavanagh, Bridget	3	Triton	Liverpool	England	1847/05/14	1847/07/24
Cavanagh, Edward	6	Primrose	Limerick	Ireland	1847/04/07	1847/06/18
Cavanagh, Ellen	1	Washington	Liverpool	England	1847/07/09	1847/08/26
Cavanagh, John	60	Wakefield	Cork	Ireland	1847/05/28	1847/07/12
Cavanagh, John	1	Triton	Liverpool	England	1847/05/14	1847/07/24
Cavanagh, Mary	9	Primrose	Limerick	Ireland	1847/04/07	1847/06/18
Cavanagh, Michael		Progress	New Ross	Ireland	1847/05/05	1847/07/14
Cavanagh, Michael	12	Primrose	Limerick	Ireland	1847/04/07	1847/06/18
Cavanagh, Patrick	3	Triton	Liverpool	England	1847/05/14	1847/07/24
Cavanagh, Robert	3	John Bolton	Liverpool	England	1847/04/13	1847/06/10
Cavanagh, William	16	John Bolton	Liverpool	England	1847/04/13	1847/06/10
Cavanagh, Winifred	5	Yorkshire	Liverpool	England	1847/06/09	1847/08/10
Cawley, Ellen	1	Emigrant	Liverpool	England	1847/08/11	1847/10/03
Cawley, Francis	6	Wolfville	Sligo	Ireland	1847/04/25	1847/06/10
Cawley, John	3	Wolfville	Sligo	Ireland	1847/04/25	1847/06/10
Chambers, Ann	80	Nelson's Village	Belfast	Ireland	1847/05/10	1847/06/26
Chambers, Daniel	1	Ajax	Liverpool	England	1847/04/16	1847/06/23
Cheasty, Elizabeth		Sobraon	Liverpool	England	1847/05/08	1847/06/29
Chisholm, Isabella	52	Sesostris	Londonderry	Ireland	1847/05/14	1847/06/24
Chisholm, Isabella		Herald	Dublin	Ireland	1847/05/20	1847/06/26
Chittick, Mary	23	Yorkshire	Liverpool	England	1847/06/09	1847/08/10
Chittick, Stewart	10	Yorkshire	Liverpool	England	1847/06/09	1847/08/10
Chittick, Thomas	60	Yorkshire	Liverpool	England	1847/06/09	1847/08/10
Christie, Bridget	6	Richard Watson	Sligo	Ireland	1847/09/13	1847/11/08
Cinnamon, Henry	38	Lotus	Liverpool	England	1847/04/15	1847/06/24
Cinnamon, Matthew	5	Lotus	Liverpool	England	1847/04/15	1847/06/24
Clancy, Ellen	15	Lord Sandon	Cork	Ireland	1847/05/11	1847/06/26
Clancy, Ellen	15	John Bolton	Liverpool	England	1847/04/13	1847/06/10
Clancy, Margaret	1	Albion	Limerick	Ireland	1847/04/19	1847/06/18
Clancy, Mary	5	Albion	Limerick	Ireland	1847/04/19	1847/06/18
Clancy, Mrs.	45	Albion	Limerick	Ireland	1847/04/19	1847/06/18
Clark, Bell	2	Frankfield	Liverpool	England	1847/06/29	1847/08/09
Clark, Helen	2	John Munn	Liverpool	England	1847/06/16	1847/08/13
Clark, James	6	John Munn	Liverpool	England	1847/06/16	1847/08/13
Clark, John	10	John Bolton	Liverpool	England	1847/04/13	1847/06/10
Clark, John		Goliah	Liverpool	England	1847/05/21	1847/07/18
Clark, Mary	30	John Munn	Liverpool	England	1847/06/16	1847/08/13
Clark, Mary Ann	3	Eliza Caroline	Liverpool	England	1847/05/03	1847/06/14
Clark, Michael	5	John Munn	Liverpool	England	1847/06/16	1847/08/13
Clark, Michael	11	John Munn	Liverpool	England	1847/06/16	1847/08/13
Clark, Patrick	15	Julius Caesar	Liverpool	England	1847/07/13	1847/09/05
Clark, Patrick		Julius Caesar	Liverpool	England	1847/07/13	1847/09/05
Clark, Susan	2	Champion	Liverpool	England	1847/07/13	1847/08/28
Clark, Thomas	13	Goliah	Liverpool	England	1847/05/21	1847/07/18
Clark, Thomas		Goliah	Liverpool	England	1847/05/21	1847/07/18
Clark, Thomas	27	John Munn	Liverpool	England	1847/06/16	1847/08/13
Cleary, Ann	3	Albion	Limerick	Ireland	1847/04/19	1847/06/18
Cleary, Ann	3	Albion	Limerick	Ireland	1847/04/19	1847/06/18
Cleary, Thomas	2	Allan Kerr	Sligo	Ireland	1847/06/23	1847/08/04
Cleary, William	4	Collingwood	Londonderry	Ireland	1847/05/27	1847/07/13
Cleary, William	26	Yorkshire	Liverpool	England	1847/06/09	1847/08/10
Clegg, Edward	84	Free Trader	Liverpool	England	1847/06/22	1847/08/14
Clifford, Jennifer	25	Bee	Cork	Ireland	1847/04/17	1847/06/12
Clifford, Thomas	3	Princess Royal	Liverpool	England	1847/05/05	1847/06/16
Clifford, Thomas	35	Princess Royal	Liverpool	England	1847/05/05	1847/06/16
Closkey, Margaret	13	Sisters	Liverpool	England	1847/04/22	1847/06/20
Cluff, Ann	19	Free Trader	Liverpool	England	1847/06/22	1847/08/14
Cluff, Richard	40	Josepha	Belfast	Ireland	1847/05/09	1847/06/18
Clune, Ellen	1	Agnes	Cork	Ireland	1847/04/10	1847/06/10
Clyne, John	23	Virginius	Liverpool	England	1847/05/28	1847/08/12
Clyne, Margaret	47	George	Liverpool	England	1847/04/13	1847/06/12
Clyne, Michael		Naomi	Liverpool	England	1847/06/15	1847/08/10
Clyne, Patrick	65	Naomi	Liverpool	England	1847/06/15	1847/08/10
Clyne, Percy	35	Naomi	Liverpool	England	1847/06/15	1847/08/10
Clynes, Mary	60	Virginius	Liverpool	England	1847/05/28	1847/08/12
Coakley, Mary	18	Agnes	Cork	Ireland	1847/04/10	1847/06/10
Coakley, Thomas	24	Agnes	Cork	Ireland	1847/04/10	1847/06/10
Cochrane, Catherine	44	Lady Milton	Liverpool	England	1847/05/05	1847/06/26
Cochrane, John		Lady Milton	Liverpool	England	1847/05/05	1847/06/26
Cochrane, John	1	Argo	Liverpool	England	1847/05/04	1847/06/12
Cochrane, Michael	23	Jessie	Limerick	Ireland	1847/04/18	1847/06/26
Cochrane, Nancy	4	Bee	Cork	Ireland	1847/04/17	1847/06/12
Cody, James	20	Saguenay	Cork	Ireland	1847/06/05	1847/08/22
Cody, Margaret		John Munn	Liverpool	England	1847/06/16	1847/08/13
Cody, Michael	1	Rose	Liverpool	England	1847/04/19	1847/07/01
Coen, Bridget	30	Abbotsford	Dublin	Ireland	1847/04/23	1847/06/21
Coen, Thomas	2	Allan Kerr	Sligo	Ireland	1847/06/23	1847/08/04
Coffey, Honora	15	Saguenay	Cork	Ireland	1847/06/05	1847/08/22
Coffey, James	4	Washington	Liverpool	England	1847/07/09	1847/08/26
Coffey, John	4	Washington	Liverpool	England	1847/07/09	1847/08/26
Cogan, Mrs.	75	Coromandel	Dublin	Ireland	1847/05/13	1847/07/02
Coggins, Luke	3	Virginius	Liverpool	England	1847/05/28	1847/08/12
Coghlan, Ellen	30	Mail	Cork	Ireland	1847/04/25	1847/06/19
Coghlan, Mary		Gilmour	Cork	Ireland	1847/04/24	1847/06/18
Colbert, Grace		Goliah	Liverpool	England	1847/05/21	1847/07/18
Colclough, Margaret	82	Lotus	Liverpool	England	1847/04/15	1847/06/24
Coleman, Maria	1	Tay	Sligo	Ireland	1847/05/05	1847/06/09
Coleman, Thomas	23	Avon	Cork	Ireland	1847/05/19	1847/07/26
Colgan, Catherine	1	Virginius	Liverpool	England	1847/05/28	1847/08/12
Collins, Bridget	26	George	Liverpool	England	1847/04/13	1847/06/12
Collins, Dennis	30	Avon	Cork	Ireland	1847/05/19	1847/07/26
Collins, Mary	65	Goliah	Liverpool	England	1847/05/21	1847/07/18
Collins, Mary	3	Avon	Cork	Ireland	1847/05/19	1847/07/26
Collins, Matthew	20	Saguenay	Cork	Ireland	1847/06/05	1847/08/22
Collins, Theodore	50	Jessie	Cork	Ireland	1847/06/03	1847/07/24
Collough, Jane Ann		Lotus	Liverpool	England	1847/04/15	1847/06/24
Colter, Margaret	56	Avon	Cork	Ireland	1847/05/19	1847/07/26
Colter, Richard	60	Avon	Cork	Ireland	1847/05/19	1847/07/26
Commerford, Michael		Wellington	Liverpool	England	1847/07/29	1847/09/20
Conaty, Judith	24	Bee	Cork	Ireland	1847/04/17	1847/06/12
Conaty, Mary	10	Bee	Cork	Ireland	1847/04/17	1847/06/12
Condon, Honora	30	Saguenay	Cork	Ireland	1847/06/05	1847/08/22
Condon, James	3	Eliza Caroline	Liverpool	England	1847/05/03	1847/06/14
Condon, James	22	Avon	Cork	Ireland	1847/05/19	1847/07/26
Condon, James	3	Eliza Caroline	Liverpool	England	1847/05/03	1847/06/14
Condon, James	3	Pacha	Cork	Ireland	1847/05/03	1847/06/14
Condon, Johanna	24	Avon	Cork	Ireland	1847/05/19	1847/07/26
Condon, John	1	Wellington	Liverpool	England	1847/07/29	1847/09/20
Condon, John	2	Jessie	Cork	Ireland	1847/06/03	1847/07/24
Condon, Margaret	14	Avon	Cork	Ireland	1847/05/19	1847/07/26
Condon, Patrick	6	Avon	Cork	Ireland	1847/05/19	1847/07/26
Condon, Patrick	21	Avon	Cork	Ireland	1847/05/19	1847/07/26
Condon, Patrick	5	Avon	Cork	Ireland	1847/05/19	1847/07/26
Condon, Thomas	15	Saguenay	Cork	Ireland	1847/06/05	1847/08/22
Conegan, Thomas	24	John Bolton	Liverpool	England	1847/04/13	1847/06/10
Conlan, Bridget	67	New Zealand	Newry	Ireland	1847/05/20	1847/07/03
Conlan, Bridget	1	Sisters	Liverpool	England	1847/04/22	1847/06/20
Conlan, Catherine	10	Sisters	Liverpool	England	1847/04/22	1847/06/20
Conlan, Daniel		Mail	Cork	Ireland	1847/04/25	1847/06/19
Conlan, Jeremiah	24	Avon	Cork	Ireland	1847/05/19	1847/07/26
Conlan, John	25	Charles Richard	Sligo	Ireland	1847/05/27	1847/07/16
Conlan, Lawrence	50	John Francis	Cork	Ireland	1847/04/10	1847/06/10

List of people who died on ships at sea or in quarantine at Grosse Île, in 1847

Name	Age	Vessel	Port	Country	Embarkation	Qc Arrival
Conlan, Peter	5	Camillia	Sligo	Ireland	1847/05/19	1847/07/07
Conlan, Rose	45	Free Trader	Liverpool	England	1847/06/22	1847/08/14
Connaughton, Honora		Agnes	Cork	Ireland	1847/04/10	1847/06/10
Connaughton, Patrick	2	Triton	Liverpool	England	1847/05/14	1847/07/24
Connaughton, Peter	23	Aberdeen	Liverpool	England	1847/05/01	1847/06/13
Connaughton, Peter	23	Araminta	Liverpool	England	1847/05/01	1847/06/20
Connell, Ann	25	Mail	Cork	Ireland	1847/04/25	1847/06/19
Connell, Bridget	4	Julius Caesar	Liverpool	England	1847/07/13	1847/09/05
Connell, Catherine	60	John Francis	Cork	Ireland	1847/04/10	1847/06/10
Connell, Daniel	4	Bee	Cork	Ireland	1847/04/17	1847/06/12
Connell, Daniel	2	Bee	Cork	Ireland	1847/04/17	1847/06/12
Connell, Ellen	30	Urania	Cork	Ireland	1847/04/09	1847/06/10
Connell, Ellen	40	Yorkshire	Liverpool	England	1847/06/09	1847/08/10
Connell, Jane	9	Standard	New Ross	Ireland	1847/04/22	1847/06/19
Connell, Jeremy	8	Julius Caesar	Liverpool	England	1847/07/13	1847/09/05
Connell, John	2	Bee	Cork	Ireland	1847/04/17	1847/06/12
Connell, John	5	Bee	Cork	Ireland	1847/04/17	1847/06/12
Connell, John	5	Bee	Cork	Ireland	1847/04/17	1847/06/12
Connell, John	4	Bee	Cork	Ireland	1847/04/17	1847/06/12
Connell, Mary	5	John Bolton	Liverpool	England	1847/04/13	1847/06/10
Connell, Mary		Ann	Liverpool	England	1847/05/16	1847/06/30
Connell, Michael	8	John Bolton	Liverpool	England	1847/04/13	1847/06/10
Connell, Patrick	47	Champion	Liverpool	England	1847/07/13	1847/08/28
Connell, Richard	6	John Bolton	Liverpool	England	1847/04/13	1847/06/10
Conners, Christopher	50	Blenheim	Cork	Ireland	1847/06/16	1847/07/29
Conners, John	60	Albion	Limerick	Ireland	1847/04/19	1847/06/18
Conners, Mary	32	John Bell	New Ross	Ireland	1847/05/10	1847/06/29
Conners, Michael	65	Mary	Sligo	Ireland	1847/05/24	1847/07/27
Conners, Nathaniel	27	Standard	New Ross	Ireland	1847/04/22	1847/06/19
Conners, Owen	84	Margaret	New Ross	Ireland	1847/05/19	1847/07/02
Connolly, Catherine	15	John Bolton	Liverpool	England	1847/04/13	1847/06/10
Connolly, Catherine	2	Tamarac	Liverpool	England	1847/05/26	1847/07/11
Connolly, Johanna	1	Rose	Liverpool	England	1847/04/19	1847/07/01
Connolly, John		Rose	Liverpool	England	1847/04/19	1847/07/01
Connolly, Julia	1	Albion	Cork	Ireland	1847/08/13	1847/09/29
Connolly, Margaret	1	Wilhelmina	Belfast	Ireland	1847/05/08	1847/06/20
Connolly, Martin	30	Ann	Liverpool	England	1847/05/16	1847/06/30
Connolly, Michael	1	Venilia	Limerick	Ireland	1847/05/28	1847/07/11
Connolly, Nelly	5	John and Robert	Liverpool	England	1847/06/09	1847/08/06
Connolly, Timothy	2	Yorkshire	Liverpool	England	1847/06/09	1847/08/10
Connoly, Daniel	30	Sisters	Liverpool	England	1847/04/22	1847/06/20
Connor, Ann	40	Julius Caesar	Liverpool	England	1847/07/13	1847/09/05
Connor, Bridget	2	Covenanter	Cork	Ireland	1847/06/17	1847/08/09
Connor, Bryan		Yorkshire	Liverpool	England	1847/06/09	1847/08/10
Connor, Catherine	3	Pacha	Cork	Ireland	1847/05/05	1847/06/14
Connor, Catherine	26	Sir Henry Pottinger	Cork	Ireland	1847/05/29	1847/08/07
Connor, Catherine	18	Sir Henry Pottinger	Cork	Ireland	1847/05/29	1847/08/07
Connor, Catherine	70	Julius Caesar	Liverpool	England	1847/07/13	1847/09/05
Connor, Daniel	21	Julius Caesar	Liverpool	England	1847/07/13	1847/09/05
Connor, Denis	60	Pursuit	Liverpool	England	1847/05/04	1847/06/23
Connor, Ellen	1	John Jardine	Liverpool	England	1847/06/04	1847/07/16
Connor, Ellen	32	Sir Henry Pottinger	Cork	Ireland	1847/05/29	1847/08/07
Connor, George		Sobraon	Liverpool	England	1847/05/08	1847/06/29
Connor, Jane	1	Thetis	Limerick	Ireland	1847/05/10	1847/06/20
Connor, John	1	Virgilia	Liverpool	England	1847/07/22	1847/09/20
Connor, John	40	Champion	Liverpool	England	1847/07/13	1847/08/28
Connor, John	1	Triton	Liverpool	England	1847/05/14	1847/07/24
Connor, John		Avon	Cork	Ireland	1847/05/19	1847/07/26
Connor, Margaret	4	Eliza Caroline	Liverpool	England	1847/05/03	1847/06/14
Connor, Mary	50	Agent	New Ross	Ireland	1847/05/20	1847/07/02
Connor, Mary	30	Wakefield	Cork	Ireland	1847/05/28	1847/07/12
Connor, Mary	22	Sir Henry Pottinger	Cork	Ireland	1847/05/29	1847/08/07
Connor, Maurice	3	Triton	Liverpool	England	1847/05/14	1847/07/24
Connor, Michael	4	Avon	Cork	Ireland	1847/05/19	1847/07/26
Connor, Michael	3	Wakefield	Cork	Ireland	1847/05/28	1847/07/12
Connor, Owen		Margaret	New Ross	Ireland	1847/05/19	1847/07/02
Connor, Patrick	32	Mary Brack	Limerick	Ireland	1847/05/03	1847/06/12
Connor, Timothy	2	Sir Henry Pottinger	Cork	Ireland	1847/05/29	1847/08/07
Constantine, Bridget		Horatio	Limerick	Ireland	1847/07/18	1847/09/03
Convey, James	15	Larch	Sligo	Ireland	1847/07/11	1847/08/20
Conway, Ann	30	Larch	Sligo	Ireland	1847/07/11	1847/08/20
Conway, Bernard	48	George	Liverpool	England	1847/04/13	1847/06/12
Conway, Bridget	2	Sisters	Liverpool	England	1847/04/22	1847/06/20
Conway, Catherine		Larch	Sligo	Ireland	1847/07/11	1847/08/20
Conway, Donald	56	George	Liverpool	England	1847/04/13	1847/06/12
Conway, James	28	Larch	Sligo	Ireland	1847/07/11	1847/08/20
Conway, James		Triton	Liverpool	England	1847/05/14	1847/07/24
Conway, Jane	9	George	Liverpool	England	1847/04/13	1847/06/12
Conway, Johanna	50	Saguenay	Cork	Ireland	1847/06/05	1847/08/22
Conway, John	48	Triton	Liverpool	England	1847/05/14	1847/07/24
Conway, John	33	Manchester	Liverpool	England	1847/06/05	1847/07/17
Conway, John	6	Triton	Liverpool	England	1847/05/14	1847/07/24
Conway, John	18	Numa	Sligo	Ireland	1847/06/02	1847/07/27
Conway, John	15	George	Liverpool	England	1847/04/13	1847/06/12
Conway, Mary	3	John Bolton	Liverpool	England	1847/04/13	1847/06/10
Conway, Patrick	13	Pursuit	Liverpool	England	1847/05/04	1847/06/23
Conway, Patrick	3	Larch	Sligo	Ireland	1847/07/11	1847/08/20
Conway, Patrick	4	John Bolton	Liverpool	England	1847/04/13	1847/06/10
Conway, Richard	5	George	Liverpool	England	1847/04/13	1847/06/12
Conway, Timothy	5	George	Liverpool	England	1847/04/13	1847/06/12
Coogan, James	15	Lady Flora Hastings	Cork	Ireland	1847/05/11	1847/06/26
Coogan, John		Abbotsford	Dublin	Ireland	1847/04/23	1847/06/21
Coogan, Judith	7	Columbia	Sligo	Ireland	1847/05/01	1847/06/10
Coogan, Mary	1	Bee	Cork	Ireland	1847/04/17	1847/06/12
Cook, James	6	Rose	Liverpool	England	1847/04/19	1847/07/01
Cook, Jane		Lady Gordon	Belfast	Ireland	1847/04/14	1847/06/20
Cook, Mary	1	Rose	Liverpool	England	1847/04/19	1847/07/01
Cook, Mary	45	Sir Henry Pottinger	Cork	Ireland	1847/05/29	1847/08/07
Cook, Patrick	5	Rose	Liverpool	England	1847/04/19	1847/07/01
Coolahan, Maria	7	George	Liverpool	England	1847/04/13	1847/06/12
Cooley, Bryan	12	Wolfville	Sligo	Ireland	1847/04/25	1847/06/10
Cooley, Francis	11	Lotus	Liverpool	England	1847/04/15	1847/06/24
Cooley, John	13	Lotus	Liverpool	England	1847/04/15	1847/06/24
Cooley, Sarah	9	Lotus	Liverpool	England	1847/04/15	1847/06/24
Cooney, Ann	4	Triton	Liverpool	England	1847/05/14	1847/07/24
Cooney, Edward	2	Triton	Liverpool	England	1847/05/14	1847/07/24
Cooney, Margaret	8	Triton	Liverpool	England	1847/05/14	1847/07/24
Cootes, Francis	7	Odessa	Dublin	Ireland	1847/06/09	1847/08/09
Coppinger, Thomas	30	Saguenay	Cork	Ireland	1847/06/05	1847/08/22
Corbett, Bridget	1	Broom	Liverpool	England	1847/06/13	1847/08/06
Corbett, Bridget		Rose	Liverpool	England	1847/04/19	1847/07/01
Corbett, John	44	Rose	Liverpool	England	1847/04/19	1847/07/01
Corbett, Margaret	5	Rose	Liverpool	England	1847/04/19	1847/07/01
Corbett, Mary	35	Rose	Liverpool	England	1847/04/19	1847/07/01
Corcoran, Bridget	3	Virginius	Liverpool	England	1847/05/28	1847/08/12
Corcoran, Dennis	22	Wellington	Liverpool	England	1847/07/29	1847/09/20
Corcoran, John	28	Bee	Cork	Ireland	1847/04/17	1847/06/12
Corcoran, Mary	43	Virginius	Liverpool	England	1847/05/28	1847/08/12
Corcoran, Nancy	70	Isabella	Killala	Ireland	1847/07/17	1847/09/17
Corcoran, William	28	Virginius	Liverpool	England	1847/05/28	1847/08/12
Corish, Catherine		Corea	Liverpool	England	1847/07/02	1847/08/14
Corkery, John	2	John Munn	Liverpool	England	1847/06/16	1847/08/13
Corkery, Mary	4	John Bolton	Liverpool	England	1847/04/13	1847/06/10
Cormick, James	15	Pandora	New Ross	Ireland	1847/06/11	1847/08/04
Cornell, Daniel	28	John Francis	Cork	Ireland	1847/04/10	1847/06/10

LIST OF PEOPLE WHO DIED ON SHIPS AT SEA OR IN QUARANTINE AT GROSSE ÎLE, IN 1847

Name	Age	Vessel	Port	Country	Embarkation	Qc Arrival
Corrigan, Catherine	6	Broom	Liverpool	England	1847/06/13	1847/08/06
Corrigan, John	1	Avon	Cork	Ireland	1847/05/19	1847/07/26
Corrigan, Mrs.	50	John Munn	Liverpool	England	1847/06/16	1847/08/13
Corrigan, Owen	7	Broom	Liverpool	England	1847/06/13	1847/08/06
Cosgrove, Patrick	18	Sarah	Liverpool	England	1847/05/29	1847/07/19
Cosgrove, Patrick	30	Larch	Sligo	Ireland	1847/07/11	1847/08/20
Costello, Bryan	8	Sisters	Liverpool	England	1847/04/22	1847/06/20
Costello, John	10	Sisters	Liverpool	England	1847/04/22	1847/06/20
Costello, Michael	2	John Jardine	Liverpool	England	1847/06/04	1847/07/16
Costello, Michael	3	John and Robert	Liverpool	England	1847/06/09	1847/08/06
Coughlan, Catherine	12	Sir Robert Peel	Liverpool	England	1847/07/26	1847/09/19
Coughlan, Denis	25	Sir Henry Pottinger	Cork	Ireland	1847/05/29	1847/08/07
Coughlan, Dennis	3	Avon	Cork	Ireland	1847/05/19	1847/07/26
Coughlan, Eliza	25	Sir Henry Pottinger	Cork	Ireland	1847/05/29	1847/08/07
Coulter, Ann	2	Wolfville	Sligo	Ireland	1847/04/25	1847/06/10
Courtney, John	22	Wakefield	Cork	Ireland	1847/05/28	1847/07/12
Courtney, John	45	Free Trader	Liverpool	England	1847/06/22	1847/08/14
Courtney, Michael	60	Herald	Dublin	Ireland	1847/05/20	1847/06/26
Courtney, P.		Mary	Sligo	Ireland	1847/05/24	1847/07/27
Courtney, Patrick	2	Wakefield	Cork	Ireland	1847/05/28	1847/07/12
Courtney, Patrick	2	Covenanter	Cork	Ireland	1847/06/17	1847/08/09
Courtney, Patrick	7	Covenanter	Cork	Ireland	1847/06/17	1847/08/09
Coveny, Mary	30	Avon	Cork	Ireland	1847/05/19	1847/07/26
Coveny, Thomas	30	Avon	Cork	Ireland	1847/05/19	1847/07/26
Cox, Ann	19	Lillias	Dublin	Ireland	1847/07/01	1847/08/16
Cox, Bridget	36	Lord Ashburton	Liverpool	England	1847/09/13	1847/11/01
Cox, Catherine	3	Charles Walton	Killala	Ireland	1847/06/24	1847/08/05
Cox, Catherine	14	Virginius	Liverpool	England	1847/05/28	1847/08/12
Cox, Catherine	25	Virginius	Liverpool	England	1847/05/28	1847/08/12
Cox, Catherine	7	Virginius	Liverpool	England	1847/05/28	1847/08/12
Cox, Darby	50	Virginius	Liverpool	England	1847/05/28	1847/08/12
Cox, Dolly	35	Naomi	Liverpool	England	1847/06/15	1847/08/10
Cox, Ellen	16	Virginius	Liverpool	England	1847/05/28	1847/08/12
Cox, James	35	Erin's Queen	Liverpool	England	1847/06/01	1847/07/23
Cox, Martin	20	Virginius	Liverpool	England	1847/05/28	1847/08/12
Cox, Michael	47	Virginius	Liverpool	England	1847/05/28	1847/08/12
Cox, Patrick	45	Oregon	Killala	Ireland	1847/06/09	1847/08/02
Cox, Patrick	5	Oregon	Killala	Ireland	1847/06/09	1847/08/02
Cox, Patrick		Naomi	Liverpool	England	1847/06/15	1847/08/10
Cox, Thomas	18	Virginius	Liverpool	England	1847/05/28	1847/08/12
Cox, Thomas	7	Naomi	Liverpool	England	1847/06/15	1847/08/10
Coyle, Bridget	10	Emigrant	Liverpool	England	1847/08/11	1847/10/03
Coyle, Bridget	24	Lord Ashburton	Liverpool	England	1847/09/13	1847/11/01
Coyle, James	3	Julius Caesar	Liverpool	England	1847/07/13	1847/09/05
Coyle, Michael	5	Emigrant	Liverpool	England	1847/08/11	1847/10/03
Coyle, Thomas	1	Emigrant	Liverpool	England	1847/08/11	1847/10/03
Crane, Edward		Corea	Liverpool	England	1847/07/02	1847/08/14
Crane, Helen	2	Argo	Liverpool	England	1847/05/04	1847/06/12
Crane, James	5	Argo	Liverpool	England	1847/05/04	1847/06/12
Crane, John	3	Argo	Liverpool	England	1847/05/04	1847/06/12
Crane, Michael	6	Argo	Liverpool	England	1847/05/04	1847/06/12
Crane, T.	1	Agnes	Cork	Ireland	1847/04/10	1847/06/10
Crane, Thomas	9	Argo	Liverpool	England	1847/05/04	1847/06/12
Cranny, Thomas	30	Lady Campbell	Dublin	Ireland	1847/06/03	1847/08/05
Crawford, Ann	18	Lord Ashburton	Liverpool	England	1847/09/13	1847/11/01
Crawford, James	60	Lord Ashburton	Liverpool	England	1847/09/13	1847/11/01
Crawley, Judith	24	Bee	Cork	Ireland	1847/04/17	1847/06/12
Crawley, Nancy	10	Bee	Cork	Ireland	1847/04/17	1847/06/12
Creary, Ann		Herald	Dublin	Ireland	1847/05/20	1847/06/26
Creed, Michael	7	Elliotts	Dublin	Ireland	1847/05/14	1847/06/30
Creed, Patrick	43	Bridgetown	Liverpool	England	1847/07/03	1847/08/29
Creen, Andrew	30	Bridgetown	Liverpool	England	1847/07/03	1847/08/29
Creen, Bridget		Thompson	Sligo	Ireland	1847/05/05	1847/06/14
Cregan, John	56	Eliza Caroline	Liverpool	England	1847/05/03	1847/06/14
Cregan, Patrick	7	Eliza Caroline	Liverpool	England	1847/05/03	1847/06/14
Creighton, Sarah Jane	1	Marchioness of Abercorn	Londonderry	Ireland	1847/06/15	1847/08/05
Creikimize, Johann	65	Henrietta Sophia	Hamburg	Germany	1847/05/12	1847/07/21
Cremin, Ellen	37	Odessa	Dublin	Ireland	1847/06/09	1847/08/09
Cremin, John	37	Progress	New Ross	Ireland	1847/05/05	1847/07/14
Cremin, Mary	2	Odessa	Dublin	Ireland	1847/06/09	1847/08/09
Croker, James	23	Horatio	Limerick	Ireland	1847/07/18	1847/09/03
Cromie, Winifred	2	Larch	Sligo	Ireland	1847/07/11	1847/08/20
Cronin, James	30	Wakefield	Cork	Ireland	1847/05/28	1847/07/12
Cronin, John	10	Agnes	Cork	Ireland	1847/04/10	1847/06/10
Cronin, John	35	Saguenay	Cork	Ireland	1847/06/05	1847/08/22
Cronin, John	35	Saguenay	Cork	Ireland	1847/06/05	1847/08/22
Cronin, Julia	20	Bee	Cork	Ireland	1847/04/17	1847/06/12
Cronin, Julia	20	Bee	Cork	Ireland	1847/04/17	1847/06/12
Crooks, Catherine	1	Free Trader	Liverpool	England	1847/06/22	1847/08/14
Crosby, John	35	Dykes	Sligo	Ireland	1847/04/23	1847/06/10
Crosby, John	27	Dykes	Sligo	Ireland	1847/04/23	1847/06/10
Crossan, Bernard	3	Goliah	Liverpool	England	1847/05/21	1847/07/18
Crowe, Mrs.	28	Saguenay	Cork	Ireland	1847/06/05	1847/08/22
Crowley, John	3	Mail	Cork	Ireland	1847/04/25	1847/06/19
Crowley, Mary	21	Avon	Cork	Ireland	1847/05/19	1847/07/26
Crowley, Mary	6	Saguenay	Cork	Ireland	1847/06/05	1847/08/22
Crowley, Thomas	30	Avon	Cork	Ireland	1847/05/19	1847/07/26
Cuffe, Catherine		Thompson	Sligo	Ireland	1847/05/05	1847/06/14
Cuffe, Mary	30	Thompson	Sligo	Ireland	1847/05/05	1847/06/14
Cuffe, Patrick	46	Standard	New Ross	Ireland	1847/04/22	1847/06/19
Culkin, Michael	32	John Jardine	Liverpool	England	1847/06/04	1847/07/16
Cullen, Ann	3	Ajax	Liverpool	England	1847/04/16	1847/06/23
Cullen, Francis	39	Free Trader	Liverpool	England	1847/06/22	1847/08/14
Cullen, Johanna	43	Lady Flora Hastings	Cork	Ireland	1847/05/11	1847/06/26
Cullen, Mary	60	Wolfville	Sligo	Ireland	1847/04/25	1847/06/10
Cullen, Mary	2	Sisters	Liverpool	England	1847/04/22	1847/06/20
Cullen, Michael	4	Sisters	Liverpool	England	1847/04/22	1847/06/20
Cullen, Susan	45	Ajax	Liverpool	England	1847/04/16	1847/06/23
Culligan, Barney	24	Ajax	Liverpool	England	1847/04/16	1847/06/23
Culligan, Francis		Goliah	Liverpool	England	1847/05/21	1847/07/18
Cummings, Bridget	3	Covenanter	Cork	Ireland	1847/06/17	1847/08/09
Cummings, Bridget		Covenanter	Cork	Ireland	1847/06/17	1847/08/09
Cummins, James	43	Thetis	Limerick	Ireland	1847/05/10	1847/06/20
Cummins, John	1	Sisters	Liverpool	England	1847/04/22	1847/06/20
Cummins, Mary	2	Covenanter	Cork	Ireland	1847/06/17	1847/08/09
Cummins, Michael	5	Sisters	Liverpool	England	1847/04/22	1847/06/20
Cummins, Peter	7	Sisters	Liverpool	England	1847/04/22	1847/06/20
Cunnane, Bridget		Wakefield	Cork	Ireland	1847/05/28	1847/07/12
Cunnane, Ellen	3	John Bolton	Liverpool	England	1847/04/13	1847/06/10
Cunneen, John	28	Bee	Cork	Ireland	1847/04/17	1847/06/12
Cunningham, Alex		Sesostris	Londonderry	Ireland	1847/05/14	1847/06/24
Cunningham, Alex		Herald	Dublin	Ireland	1847/05/20	1847/06/26
Cunningham, Catherine	14	John Bolton	Liverpool	England	1847/04/13	1847/06/10
Cunningham, Catherine	20	John Bolton	Liverpool	England	1847/04/13	1847/06/10
Cunningham, Catherine	20	John Bolton	Liverpool	England	1847/04/13	1847/06/10
Cunningham, David	26	Triton	Liverpool	England	1847/05/14	1847/07/24
Cunningham, Ellen		Yorkshire	Liverpool	England	1847/06/09	1847/08/10
Cunningham, George		Frankfield	Liverpool	England	1847/06/29	1847/08/09
Cunningham, Hannah	60	John Francis	Cork	Ireland	1847/04/10	1847/06/10
Cunningham, J.	16	Columbia	Sligo	Ireland	1847/05/01	1847/06/10
Cunningham, John	7	Rose	Liverpool	England	1847/04/19	1847/07/01
Cunningham, Joseph	2	Argo	Liverpool	England	1847/05/04	1847/06/12
Cunningham, Margaret	2	Frankfield	Liverpool	England	1847/06/29	1847/08/09
Cunningham, Mary	7	Albion	Limerick	Ireland	1847/04/19	1847/06/18

LIST OF PEOPLE WHO DIED ON SHIPS AT SEA OR IN QUARANTINE AT GROSSE ÎLE, IN 1847

Name	Age	Vessel	Port	Country	Embarkation	Qc Arrival
Cunningham, Patrick	4	John Bolton	Liverpool	England	1847/04/13	1847/06/10
Cunningham, Patrick	1	Triton	Liverpool	England	1847/05/14	1847/07/24
Curley, Ellen	1	Yorkshire	Liverpool	England	1847/06/09	1847/08/10
Curley, James		Junior	Liverpool	England	1847/05/10	1847/07/03
Curley, John	1	John Jardine	Liverpool	England	1847/06/04	1847/07/16
Curley, John	5	Yorkshire	Liverpool	England	1847/06/09	1847/08/10
Curley, John	70	Emigrant	Liverpool	England	1847/08/11	1847/10/03
Curley, John		Yorkshire	Liverpool	England	1847/06/09	1847/08/10
Curley, Judith	60	Yorkshire	Liverpool	England	1847/06/09	1847/08/10
Curley, Matthew	4	Free Trader	Liverpool	England	1847/06/22	1847/08/14
Curley, Patrick	5	Yorkshire	Liverpool	England	1847/06/09	1847/08/10
Curley, Patrick		Yorkshire	Liverpool	England	1847/06/09	1847/08/10
Curley, Susan	1	Emigrant	Liverpool	England	1847/08/11	1847/10/03
Curran, Catherine	6	John and Robert	Liverpool	England	1847/06/09	1847/08/06
Curran, Margaret	2	Wakefield	Cork	Ireland	1847/05/28	1847/07/12
Curran, Mary	32	John and Robert	Liverpool	England	1847/06/09	1847/08/06
Curran, Nancy	6	John and Robert	Liverpool	England	1847/06/09	1847/08/06
Curran, Patrick	55	Lady Campbell	Dublin	Ireland	1847/06/03	1847/08/05
Curry, Catherine	5	John Bolton	Liverpool	England	1847/04/13	1847/06/10
Curry, Patrick	35	Jessie	Limerick	Ireland	1847/04/18	1847/06/26
Curry, Patrick	14	John Bolton	Liverpool	England	1847/04/13	1847/06/10
Curtin, Daniel	3	Jessie	Cork	Ireland	1847/06/03	1847/07/24
Curtin, Ellen	16	Saguenay	Cork	Ireland	1847/06/05	1847/08/22
Curtin, George	2	Jessie	Cork	Ireland	1847/06/03	1847/07/24
Curtin, John		Henrietta Mary	Cork	Ireland	1847/08/18	1847/09/29
Curtin, Philip	3	Avon	Cork	Ireland	1847/05/19	1847/07/26
Curtin, William	4	Avon	Cork	Ireland	1847/05/19	1847/07/26
Cussen, James	28	Jane Black	Limerick	Ireland	1847/08/10	1847/09/17
Cussen, John	28	Virgilia	Liverpool	England	1847/07/22	1847/09/20
Dahill, Catherine	4	Lord Seaton	Belfast	Ireland	1847/04/12	1847/06/10
Dahill, Rose	1	Lord Seaton	Belfast	Ireland	1847/04/12	1847/06/10
Daley, Ellen	1	Bee	Cork	Ireland	1847/04/17	1847/06/12
Daley, John	40	Champion	Liverpool	England	1847/07/13	1847/08/28
Daley, Michael	60	Avon	Cork	Ireland	1847/05/19	1847/07/26
Dalton, James	69	Georgiana	Dublin	Ireland	1847/05/16	1847/06/29
Dalton, Johanna	8	John Bolton	Liverpool	England	1847/04/13	1847/06/10
Dalton, John	7	John Bolton	Liverpool	England	1847/04/13	1847/06/10
Dalton, Mary	24	John Bolton	Liverpool	England	1847/04/13	1847/06/10
Dalton, Mary	1	Erin's Queen	Liverpool	England	1847/06/01	1847/07/23
Dalton, Sarah	18	Wakefield	Cork	Ireland	1847/05/28	1847/07/12
Dalton, William	6	John Bolton	Liverpool	England	1847/04/13	1847/06/10
Daly, David	6	Mail	Cork	Ireland	1847/04/25	1847/06/19
Daly, Eliza	9	Urania	Cork	Ireland	1847/04/09	1847/06/10
Daly, Ellen	30	Bee	Cork	Ireland	1847/04/17	1847/06/12
Daly, Margaret	2	Covenanter	Cork	Ireland	1847/06/17	1847/08/09
Daly, Margaret	61	Avon	Cork	Ireland	1847/05/19	1847/07/26
Daly, Mary		Avon	Cork	Ireland	1847/05/19	1847/07/26
Daly, Mary	29	Sir Henry Pottinger	Cork	Ireland	1847/05/29	1847/08/07
Daly, Michael	4	Avon	Cork	Ireland	1847/05/19	1847/07/26
Daly, Michael	36	Marinus	Dublin	Ireland	1847/06/05	1847/08/13
Daly, Nancy	28	Covenanter	Cork	Ireland	1847/06/17	1847/08/09
Daly, Patrick		Henrietta Mary	Cork	Ireland	1847/08/18	1847/09/29
Daly, Thomas	7	Margrette	New Ross	Ireland	1847/05/02	1847/07/08
Darby, Daniel	3	Bee	Cork	Ireland	1847/04/17	1847/06/12
Darby, John	40	Abbotsford	Dublin	Ireland	1847/04/23	1847/06/21
Darcey, Margaret	45	Albion	Limerick	Ireland	1847/04/19	1847/06/18
Dargan, Margaret	3	Caithness-shire	Belfast	Ireland	1847/04/10	1847/06/12
Darmody, Ann	2	Erin's Queen	Liverpool	England	1847/06/01	1847/07/23
Darmody, Mary	4	Erin's Queen	Liverpool	England	1847/06/01	1847/07/23
Darmody, Michael	6	Erin's Queen	Liverpool	England	1847/06/01	1847/07/23
Darmody, Timothy	2	Bridgetown	Liverpool	England	1847/07/03	1847/08/29
Davey, Ann	30	James Moran	Liverpool	England	1847/05/22	1847/07/11
Davey, Michael	46	Albion	Limerick	Ireland	1847/04/19	1847/06/18
Davidson, Walter	5	Rosalinda	Belfast	Ireland	1847/06/22	1847/08/07
Davitt, Catherine	3	Lady Milton	Liverpool	England	1847/05/05	1847/06/26
Davitt, Catherine	8	Larch	Sligo	Ireland	1847/07/11	1847/08/20
Davitt, Mary	7	Lady Milton	Liverpool	England	1847/05/05	1847/06/26
Davitt, Thomas		Lady Milton	Liverpool	England	1847/05/05	1847/06/26
Dawley, Catherine	5	Wakefield	Cork	Ireland	1847/05/28	1847/07/12
Dawson, John	35	Bee	Cork	Ireland	1847/04/17	1847/06/12
Dawson, Margaret	40	Wakefield	Cork	Ireland	1847/05/28	1847/07/12
Dawson, William	60	Erin's Queen	Liverpool	England	1847/06/01	1847/07/23
Dean, Patrick		Naomi	Liverpool	England	1847/06/15	1847/08/10
Deasy, Mary	2	Sir Henry Pottinger	Cork	Ireland	1847/05/29	1847/08/07
Deasy, Michael	18	Gilmour	Cork	Ireland	1847/04/24	1847/06/18
Deegan, Denis	7	Pandora	New Ross	Ireland	1847/06/11	1847/08/04
Deegan, Elizabeth	5	John Bolton	Liverpool	England	1847/04/13	1847/06/10
Deegan, Elizabeth	3	Pandora	New Ross	Ireland	1847/06/11	1847/08/04
Deegan, Jack	50	George	Liverpool	England	1847/04/13	1847/06/12
Deegan, James		George	Liverpool	England	1847/04/13	1847/06/12
Deegan, John		George	Liverpool	England	1847/04/13	1847/06/12
Deegan, John	5	George	Liverpool	England	1847/04/13	1847/06/12
Deegan, Mary	56	Eagle	Dublin	Ireland	1847/05/12	1847/06/25
Deenan, Denis	1	Agnes	Cork	Ireland	1847/04/10	1847/06/10
Deenan, Timothy	36	Agnes	Cork	Ireland	1847/04/10	1847/06/10
Deery, Catherine	1	Sir Henry Pottinger	Cork	Ireland	1847/05/29	1847/08/07
Deery, Mary	24	Sir Henry Pottinger	Cork	Ireland	1847/05/29	1847/08/07
Deery, Peter	26	Ellen	Sligo	Ireland	1847/05/27	1847/07/10
Deevy, John	34	Sir Henry Pottinger	Cork	Ireland	1847/05/29	1847/08/07
Delahunt, Paul	27	Lady Milton	Liverpool	England	1847/05/05	1847/06/26
Delaney, Ann	3	Jane Avery	Dublin	Ireland	1847/05/09	1847/06/25
Delaney, Bridget	4	Rose	Liverpool	England	1847/04/19	1847/07/01
Delaney, Hugh	1	Argo	Liverpool	England	1847/05/04	1847/06/12
Delaney, John	4	John Bolton	Liverpool	England	1847/04/13	1847/06/10
Delaney, Michael	5	Covenanter	Cork	Ireland	1847/06/17	1847/08/09
Delmage, Bridget	30	Marinus	Dublin	Ireland	1847/06/05	1847/08/13
Delmage, Bridget	30	Sir Henry Pottinger	Cork	Ireland	1847/05/29	1847/08/07
Delmage, Catherine	55	Free Trader	Liverpool	England	1847/06/22	1847/08/14
Delmage, Michael	37	Sir Henry Pottinger	Cork	Ireland	1847/05/29	1847/08/07
Delmage, Zariah	19	Sir Henry Pottinger	Cork	Ireland	1847/05/29	1847/08/07
Demon, Crimmon	2	Diamond	Bremerhaven	Germany	1847/06/08	1847/07/31
Dempsey, Bridget	2	Sisters	Liverpool	England	1847/04/22	1847/06/20
Dempsey, Bryan	37	Lady Campbell	Dublin	Ireland	1847/06/03	1847/08/05
Dempsey, Catherine	22	Gilmour	Cork	Ireland	1847/04/24	1847/06/18
Dempsey, Margaret	6	Abbotsford	Dublin	Ireland	1847/04/23	1847/06/21
Dempsey, Mary	52	Naomi	Liverpool	England	1847/06/15	1847/08/10
Dempsey, Patrick		Naomi	Liverpool	England	1847/06/15	1847/08/10
Dempsey, Thomas	2	Naomi	Liverpool	England	1847/06/15	1847/08/10
Denney, Margaret		Lotus	Liverpool	England	1847/04/15	1847/06/24
Derbyshire, George	32	Sir Robert Peel	Liverpool	England	1847/07/26	1847/09/19
Dermott, Mary		John and Robert	Liverpool	England	1847/06/09	1847/08/06
Derry, Jerry	1	Lady Flora Hastings	Cork	Ireland	1847/05/11	1847/06/26
Derry, John	3	Lady Flora Hastings	Cork	Ireland	1847/05/11	1847/06/26
Desmond, Catherine	4	John Bolton	Liverpool	England	1847/04/13	1847/06/10
Desmond, Margaret	2	John Bolton	Liverpool	England	1847/04/13	1847/06/10
Devaney, Bridget	8	Lotus	Liverpool	England	1847/04/15	1847/06/24
Devaney, John	12	Lotus	Liverpool	England	1847/04/15	1847/06/24
Devaney, Mary	4	Lotus	Liverpool	England	1847/04/15	1847/06/24
Devaney, Michael	35	Lotus	Liverpool	England	1847/04/15	1847/06/24
Devaney, Thomas	6	Lotus	Liverpool	England	1847/04/15	1847/06/24
Devine, Bridget	52	Larch	Sligo	Ireland	1847/07/11	1847/08/20
Devine, James	30	Argo	Sligo	Ireland	1847/06/11	1847/07/31

List of people who died on ships at sea or in quarantine at Grosse Île, in 1847

Name	Age	Vessel	Port	Country	Embarkation	Qc Arrival
Devine, John	4	Larch	Sligo	Ireland	1847/07/11	1847/08/20
Devine, Margaret	1	Ninian	Limerick	Ireland	1847/04/13	1847/06/12
Devine, Morris	1	Ninian	Limerick	Ireland	1847/04/13	1847/06/12
Devine, Patrick	35	Saguenay	Cork	Ireland	1847/06/05	1847/08/22
Devlin, Arthur		Lady Gordon	Belfast	Ireland	1847/04/14	1847/06/20
Devlin, Mary	7	Eliza Caroline	Liverpool	England	1847/05/03	1847/06/14
Devlin, Mrs.	60	Agnes and Ann	Newry	Ireland	1847/05/15	1847/07/02
Dickson, Margaret	2	Allan Kerr	Sligo	Ireland	1847/06/23	1847/08/04
Dignan, Patrick	26	Progress	New Ross	Ireland	1847/05/05	1847/07/14
Dignan, William	5	Progress	New Ross	Ireland	1847/05/05	1847/07/14
Dillon, Catherine	1	Frankfield	Liverpool	England	1847/06/29	1847/08/09
Dillon, Timothy	20	John Francis	Cork	Ireland	1847/04/10	1847/06/10
Dineen, Catherine	14	Covenanter	Cork	Ireland	1847/06/17	1847/08/09
Dineen, John		Covenanter	Cork	Ireland	1847/06/17	1847/08/09
Dineen, John	3	Covenanter	Cork	Ireland	1847/06/17	1847/08/09
Dingel, Bandudor		Diamond	Bremerhaven	Germany	1847/06/08	1847/07/31
Dinsmore, Jane	1	Rosalinda	Belfast	Ireland	1847/06/22	1847/08/07
Dirrane, John	4	Greenock	Liverpool	England	1847/06/19	1847/07/29
Dirrane, Joseph	24	Lord Ashburton	Liverpool	England	1847/09/13	1847/11/01
Dixon, Ellen	5	Allan Kerr	Sligo	Ireland	1847/06/23	1847/08/04
Dixon, William	3	Eliza Caroline	Liverpool	England	1847/05/03	1847/06/14
Dobbin, Bridget	2	Rose	Liverpool	England	1847/04/19	1847/07/01
Dobbin, Christopher	2	Primrose	Limerick	Ireland	1847/04/07	1847/06/18
Dobbin, John	1	Bee	Cork	Ireland	1847/04/17	1847/06/12
Dobbins, B.	25	Bee	Cork	Ireland	1847/04/17	1847/06/12
Dobbins, J.	3	Bee	Cork	Ireland	1847/04/17	1847/06/12
Dobbins, John	4	Bee	Cork	Ireland	1847/04/17	1847/06/12
Dobsin, Alexander		Lady Gordon	Belfast	Ireland	1847/04/14	1847/06/20
Dobson, Bridget	8	Sisters	Liverpool	England	1847/04/22	1847/06/20
Dodds, Fanny	11	Lord Seaton	Belfast	Ireland	1847/04/12	1847/06/10
Dodds, Hugh	4	Lord Seaton	Belfast	Ireland	1847/04/12	1847/06/10
Dodds, Thomas	3	Lord Seaton	Belfast	Ireland	1847/04/12	1847/06/10
Doherty, Ann	1	New York Packet	Liverpool	England	1847/04/24	1847/06/29
Doherty, Barbara	4	Sisters	Liverpool	England	1847/04/22	1847/06/20
Doherty, Bridget	1	Sisters	Liverpool	England	1847/04/22	1847/06/20
Doherty, Catherine	7	Sisters	Liverpool	England	1847/04/22	1847/06/20
Doherty, Ellen	3	Isabella	Killala	Ireland	1847/07/17	1847/09/17
Doherty, Mary	7	Sisters	Liverpool	England	1847/04/22	1847/06/20
Doherty, Mary	24	Marinus	Dublin	Ireland	1847/06/05	1847/08/13
Doherty, Mary	50	Charles Walton	Killala	Ireland	1847/06/24	1847/08/05
Doherty, Patrick	18	Sisters	Liverpool	England	1847/04/22	1847/06/20
Doherty, Sarah	35	Christiana	Londonderry	Ireland	1847/04/08	1847/06/10
Dolan, Daniel	5	Agamemnon	Liverpool	England	1847/06/24	1847/07/31
Dolan, Elizabeth	40	Lord Ashburton	Liverpool	England	1847/09/13	1847/11/01
Dolan, Henry	40	Primrose	Limerick	Ireland	1847/04/07	1847/06/18
Dolan, Michael	3	Goliah	Liverpool	England	1847/05/21	1847/07/18
Dolan, Michael	50	Free Trader	Liverpool	England	1847/06/22	1847/08/14
Dolan, Sally	6	Lord Ashburton	Liverpool	England	1847/09/13	1847/11/01
Dolan, Thomas	76	Standard	New Ross	Ireland	1847/04/22	1847/06/19
Donaghy, Susan		Tamarac	Liverpool	England	1847/05/26	1847/07/11
Donald, Mary	2	Sarah	Liverpool	England	1847/05/29	1847/07/19
Donald, Mary	8	Eliza Caroline	Liverpool	England	1847/05/03	1847/06/14
Donegan, Margaret	5	Corea	Liverpool	England	1847/07/02	1847/08/14
Donegan, Mary	25	John and Robert	Liverpool	England	1847/06/09	1847/08/06
Donegan, William	2	Emigrant	Liverpool	England	1847/08/11	1847/10/03
Donelan, Michael	50	Virginius	Liverpool	England	1847/05/28	1847/08/12
Donelan, Winford	40	Virginius	Liverpool	England	1847/05/28	1847/08/12
Donnelly, Catherine	27	Free Trader	Liverpool	England	1847/06/22	1847/08/14
Donnelly, J.		Sir Henry Pottinger	Cork	Ireland	1847/05/29	1847/08/07
Donnelly, James	60	Progress	New Ross	Ireland	1847/05/05	1847/07/14
Donnelly, James	2	Eliza Caroline	Liverpool	England	1847/05/03	1847/06/14
Donnelly, Nancy	25	Energy	Limerick	Ireland	1847/05/28	1847/07/05
Donoghue, Catherine	26	John Francis	Cork	Ireland	1847/04/10	1847/06/10
Donoghue, Frederick	1	Wilhelmina	Belfast	Ireland	1847/05/08	1847/06/20
Donoghue, Judith	70	Scotland	Cork	Ireland	1847/04/13	1847/06/08
Donoghue, Judith	45	Scotland	Cork	Ireland	1847/04/13	1847/06/08
Donoghue, Noreen	22	Avon	Cork	Ireland	1847/05/19	1847/07/26
Donoghue, Philip		Covenanter	Cork	Ireland	1847/06/17	1847/08/09
Donohoe, Cornelius	3	Covenanter	Cork	Ireland	1847/06/17	1847/08/09
Donohoe, Patrick	2	John Munn	Liverpool	England	1847/06/16	1847/08/13
Donohue, Ann		Triton	Liverpool	England	1847/05/14	1847/07/24
Donohue, Bridget	60	Colonist	New Ross	Ireland	1847/07/13	1847/08/29
Donohue, Johanna	2	Triton	Liverpool	England	1847/05/14	1847/07/24
Donohue, Mary	50	Avon	Cork	Ireland	1847/05/19	1847/07/26
Donovan, Ann		Naomi	Liverpool	England	1847/06/15	1847/08/10
Donovan, Bridget	45	Scotland	Cork	Ireland	1847/04/13	1847/06/08
Donovan, Bridget	5	Tay	Liverpool	England	1847/05/22	1847/06/23
Donovan, Catherine	3	Scotland	Cork	Ireland	1847/04/13	1847/06/08
Donovan, Catherine	3	Scotland	Cork	Ireland	1847/04/13	1847/06/08
Donovan, Daniel	23	Agnes	Cork	Ireland	1847/04/10	1847/06/10
Donovan, James	19	Margrette	New Ross	Ireland	1847/05/02	1847/07/08
Donovan, James	2	Rose	Liverpool	England	1847/04/19	1847/07/01
Donovan, Jeremiah	40	Scotland	Cork	Ireland	1847/04/13	1847/06/08
Donovan, Jerry	50	Scotland	Cork	Ireland	1847/04/13	1847/06/08
Donovan, Johanna	35	Jessie	Cork	Ireland	1847/06/03	1847/07/24
Donovan, John	30	Agnes	Cork	Ireland	1847/04/10	1847/06/10
Donovan, John	1	Free Briton	Cork	Ireland	1847/05/25	1847/07/10
Donovan, John		Margrette	New Ross	Ireland	1847/05/02	1847/07/08
Donovan, John	43	Jessie	Cork	Ireland	1847/06/03	1847/07/24
Donovan, John	43	Jessie	Cork	Ireland	1847/06/03	1847/07/24
Donovan, John	24	Julius Caesar	Liverpool	England	1847/07/13	1847/09/05
Donovan, Julia	11	Bee	Cork	Ireland	1847/04/17	1847/06/12
Donovan, Julia	10	Bee	Cork	Ireland	1847/04/17	1847/06/12
Donovan, Mary	27	Urania	Cork	Ireland	1847/04/09	1847/06/10
Donovan, Mary	60	Bee	Cork	Ireland	1847/04/17	1847/06/12
Donovan, Mary	30	Bee	Cork	Ireland	1847/04/17	1847/06/12
Donovan, Mary	30	Bee	Cork	Ireland	1847/04/17	1847/06/12
Donovan, Mary	60	Bee	Cork	Ireland	1847/04/17	1847/06/12
Donovan, Mary	1	Scotland	Cork	Ireland	1847/04/13	1847/06/08
Donovan, Mary		Naomi	Liverpool	England	1847/06/15	1847/08/10
Donovan, Mary	25	Scotland	Cork	Ireland	1847/04/13	1847/06/08
Donovan, Mary		Tay	Liverpool	England	1847/05/22	1847/06/23
Donovan, Maurice	22	Scotland	Cork	Ireland	1847/04/13	1847/06/08
Donovan, Michael	4	Wakefield	Cork	Ireland	1847/05/28	1847/07/12
Donovan, Patrick	4	Lady Flora Hastings	Cork	Ireland	1847/05/11	1847/06/26
Donovan, Patrick	4	Wakefield	Cork	Ireland	1847/05/28	1847/07/12
Donovan, Patrick	28	Agnes	Cork	Ireland	1847/04/10	1847/06/10
Donovan, Richard	70	Washington	Liverpool	England	1847/07/09	1847/08/26
Donovan, Thomas		John Munn	Liverpool	England	1847/06/16	1847/08/13
Donovan, Timothy	3	Scotland	Cork	Ireland	1847/04/13	1847/06/08
Doody, Daniel	3	Bee	Cork	Ireland	1847/04/17	1847/06/12
Doogan, Thadeus	3	Horatio	Limerick	Ireland	1847/07/18	1847/09/03
Doohan, Patrick	65	Triton	Liverpool	England	1847/05/14	1847/07/24
Doolan, Bridget		Pandora	New Ross	Ireland	1847/06/11	1847/08/04
Doolan, John	2	Broom	Liverpool	England	1847/06/13	1847/08/06
Doolan, Patrick	15	Pandora	New Ross	Ireland	1847/06/11	1847/08/04
Dooley, Mary	3	John Munn	Liverpool	England	1847/06/16	1847/08/13
Dooley, Patrick	35	John Munn	Liverpool	England	1847/06/16	1847/08/13
Dooley, Patrick	60	Champion	Liverpool	England	1847/07/13	1847/08/28
Doolin, Mary		Eliza Caroline	Liverpool	England	1847/05/03	1847/06/14
Doran, Daniel	30	Medusa	Cork	Ireland	1847/06/03	1847/07/16
Doran, Denis	2	Abbotsford	Dublin	Ireland	1847/04/23	1847/06/21
Doran, James	7	Rose	Liverpool	England	1847/04/19	1847/07/01
Doran, John	60	Columbia	Sligo	Ireland	1847/05/01	1847/06/10
Doran, William	19	Sarah	Liverpool	England	1847/05/29	1847/07/19
Douglas, William	2	Goliah	Liverpool	England	1847/05/21	1847/07/18
Dowell, Mary	14	Lady Flora Hastings	Cork	Ireland	1847/05/11	1847/06/26
Downes, Thomas	1	Argo	Liverpool	England	1847/05/04	1847/06/12

LIST OF PEOPLE WHO DIED ON SHIPS AT SEA OR IN QUARANTINE AT GROSSE ÎLE, IN 1847

Name	Age	Vessel	Port	Country	Embarkation	Qc Arrival
Downes, William	2	Argo	Liverpool	England	1847/05/04	1847/06/12
Downey, Archibald		Douce Davie	Sligo	Ireland	1847/08/11	1847/09/30
Downey, Donald	3	Ninian	Limerick	Ireland	1847/04/13	1847/06/12
Downey, Edward	65	Abbotsford	Dublin	Ireland	1847/04/23	1847/06/21
Downey, Hugh	50	Tamarac	Liverpool	England	1847/05/26	1847/07/11
Downey, James	1	Urania	Cork	Ireland	1847/04/09	1847/06/10
Downey, James	6	Tamarac	Liverpool	England	1847/05/26	1847/07/11
Downey, John	25	Bee	Cork	Ireland	1847/04/17	1847/06/12
Downey, Margaret	64	Columbia	Sligo	Ireland	1847/05/01	1847/06/10
Downey, Mary		Julius Caesar	Liverpool	England	1847/07/13	1847/09/05
Downey, Mary	26	Julius Caesar	Liverpool	England	1847/07/13	1847/09/05
Downey, Mary		Sobraon	Liverpool	England	1847/05/08	1847/06/29
Downey, William	1	Sobraon	Liverpool	England	1847/05/08	1847/06/29
Downing, Peter	8	Erin's Queen	Liverpool	England	1847/06/01	1847/07/23
Doyle, Barney		Naomi	Liverpool	England	1847/06/15	1847/08/10
Doyle, Catherine	7	Progress	New Ross	Ireland	1847/05/05	1847/07/14
Doyle, Catherine	28	Naomi	Liverpool	England	1847/06/15	1847/08/10
Doyle, Honora	5	Progress	New Ross	Ireland	1847/05/05	1847/07/14
Doyle, Margaret	1	Sarah Maria	Sligo	Ireland	1847/05/07	1847/06/28
Doyle, Michael	26	Sarah	Liverpool	England	1847/05/29	1847/07/19
Doyle, Michael	7	Progress	New Ross	Ireland	1847/05/05	1847/07/14
Doyle, Patrick		Jessie	Limerick	Ireland	1847/04/18	1847/06/26
Drain, Michael	8	Erin's Queen	Liverpool	England	1847/06/01	1847/07/23
Drew, John	30	Lord Ashburton	Liverpool	England	1847/09/13	1847/11/01
Driscoll, Daniel	6	Gilmour	Cork	Ireland	1847/04/24	1847/06/18
Driscoll, Daniel	50	Covenanter	Cork	Ireland	1847/06/17	1847/08/09
Driscoll, Daniel	24	Bridgetown	Liverpool	England	1847/07/03	1847/08/29
Driscoll, Ellen	27	Urania	Cork	Ireland	1847/04/09	1847/06/10
Driscoll, Mary	2	Gilmour	Cork	Ireland	1847/04/24	1847/06/18
Driscoll, Mary	2	Covenanter	Cork	Ireland	1847/06/17	1847/08/09
Driscoll, Mary	30	Lord Ashburton	Liverpool	England	1847/09/13	1847/11/01
Driscoll, Patrick	11	Gilmour	Cork	Ireland	1847/04/24	1847/06/18
Driscoll, Patrick	45	Covenanter	Cork	Ireland	1847/06/17	1847/08/09
Driscoll, Patrick	1.5	Lord Ashburton	Liverpool	England	1847/09/13	1847/11/01
Driscoll, Theodore		Agnes	Cork	Ireland	1847/04/10	1847/06/10
Driscoll, Timothy	30	Agnes	Cork	Ireland	1847/04/10	1847/06/10
Drohan, Alice	6	Rose	Liverpool	England	1847/04/19	1847/07/01
Drohan, Ann	4	Rose	Liverpool	England	1847/04/19	1847/07/01
Drohan, Catherine	36	Rose	Liverpool	England	1847/04/19	1847/07/01
Drohan, John	7	Rose	Liverpool	England	1847/04/19	1847/07/01
Drum, Charles	5	Rose	Liverpool	England	1847/04/19	1847/07/01
Drum, Eliza	1	Rose	Liverpool	England	1847/04/19	1847/07/01
Drummy, Ellen	35	Naomi	Liverpool	England	1847/06/15	1847/08/10
Duff, John	40	Rose	Liverpool	England	1847/04/19	1847/07/01
Duff, Mary Ann		Naomi	Liverpool	England	1847/06/15	1847/08/10
Duff, Thomas	6	Tay	Liverpool	England	1847/05/22	1847/06/23
Duffy, Hugh	40	Ann	Liverpool	England	1847/05/16	1847/06/30
Duffy, John	40	Virginius	Liverpool	England	1847/05/28	1847/08/12
Duffy, John	19	Sarah	Liverpool	England	1847/05/29	1847/07/19
Duffy, Lackey	18	Virginius	Liverpool	England	1847/05/28	1847/08/12
Duffy, Robert	20	Yorkshire	Liverpool	England	1847/06/09	1847/08/10
Duggan, Bernard	15	Rose	Liverpool	England	1847/04/19	1847/07/01
Duggan, Cornelius	8	Covenanter	Cork	Ireland	1847/06/17	1847/08/09
Duggan, John	7	Covenanter	Cork	Ireland	1847/06/17	1847/08/09
Duggan, Mary		Horatio	Limerick	Ireland	1847/07/18	1847/09/03
Duggan, Michael	2	Blenheim	Cork	Ireland	1847/06/16	1847/07/29
Duggan, Michael		Covenanter	Cork	Ireland	1847/06/17	1847/08/09
Duggan, Patrick	1	Covenanter	Cork	Ireland	1847/06/17	1847/08/09
Duggan, Theodore	35	Covenanter	Cork	Ireland	1847/06/17	1847/08/09
Duggan, Timothy	10	Covenanter	Cork	Ireland	1847/06/17	1847/08/09
Duggan, Timothy	1	Covenanter	Cork	Ireland	1847/06/17	1847/08/09
Duignan, Ann	7	Dykes	Sligo	Ireland	1847/04/23	1847/06/10
Dunbar, Bridget	1	Venilia	Limerick	Ireland	1847/05/28	1847/07/11
Duncan, Catherine	60	Asia	Cork	Ireland	1847/06/02	1847/07/27
Duncan, John		Asia	Cork	Ireland	1847/06/02	1847/07/27
Duncan, John	35	Asia	Cork	Ireland	1847/06/02	1847/07/27
Duncan, Patrick	24	George	Liverpool	England	1847/04/13	1847/06/12
Dunlief, Bridget	3	Admiral	Waterford	Ireland	1847/06/01	1847/07/07
Dunlop, John	1	Constitution	Belfast	Ireland	1847/04/21	1847/06/08
Dunn, David	12	Saguenay	Cork	Ireland	1847/06/05	1847/08/22
Dunn, James	9	Elliotts	Dublin	Ireland	1847/05/14	1847/06/30
Dunn, John	1	Elliotts	Dublin	Ireland	1847/05/14	1847/06/30
Dunn, Mary	10	Saguenay	Cork	Ireland	1847/06/05	1847/08/22
Dunn, Michael	22	Jessie	Limerick	Ireland	1847/04/18	1847/06/26
Dunn, Michael	2	Emigrant	Liverpool	England	1847/08/11	1847/10/03
Dunn, Owen	24	Scotland	Cork	Ireland	1847/04/13	1847/06/08
Dunn, Owen	24	Scotland	Cork	Ireland	1847/04/13	1847/06/08
Dunn, Thomas	56	John Jardine	Liverpool	England	1847/06/04	1847/07/16
Dunn, William	23	Naparina	Dublin	Ireland	1847/06/17	1847/08/23
Dunn, Winford		Emigrant	Liverpool	England	1847/08/11	1847/10/03
Dunnigan, Mary	3	Marchioness of Breadalbane	Sligo	Ireland	1847/06/11	1847/08/12
Durkin, Luke	25	Westmoreland	Sligo	Ireland	1847/06/12	1847/08/10
Durkin, Michael	28	John Munn	Liverpool	England	1847/06/16	1847/08/13
Durkin, Mrs.	70	John Munn	Liverpool	England	1847/06/16	1847/08/13
Durnin, John	2	Wilhelmina	Belfast	Ireland	1847/05/08	1847/06/20
Dwyer, Catherine	2	Free Trader	Liverpool	England	1847/06/22	1847/08/14
Dwyer, Cornelius	6	Virgilia	Liverpool	England	1847/07/22	1847/09/20
Dwyer, Daniel	1	John Jardine	Liverpool	England	1847/06/04	1847/07/16
Dwyer, Daniel	1	Sir Henry Pottinger	Cork	Ireland	1847/05/29	1847/08/07
Dwyer, Ellen		Louisa	Limerick	Ireland	1847/05/08	1847/06/25
Dwyer, Humphrey	2	Wakefield	Cork	Ireland	1847/05/28	1847/07/12
Dwyer, Judith	5	Free Trader	Liverpool	England	1847/06/22	1847/08/14
Dwyer, Margaret	9	Virgilia	Liverpool	England	1847/07/22	1847/09/20
Early, Catherine	18	Sarah	Liverpool	England	1847/05/29	1847/07/19
Early, Hugh	7	Triton	Liverpool	England	1847/05/14	1847/07/24
Early, Patrick	4	Triton	Liverpool	England	1847/05/14	1847/07/24
Edwards, Ann		Ann	Liverpool	England	1847/05/16	1847/06/30
Egan, Bridget	22	Bee	Cork	Ireland	1847/04/17	1847/06/12
Egan, Bridget	22	Bee	Cork	Ireland	1847/04/17	1847/06/12
Egan, Bridget	50	Charles Walton	Killala	Ireland	1847/06/24	1847/08/05
Egan, Daniel	1	Agamemnon	Liverpool	England	1847/06/24	1847/07/31
Egan, John	20	Free Trader	Liverpool	England	1847/06/22	1847/08/14
Egan, Joseph		Wellington	Liverpool	England	1847/07/29	1847/09/20
Egan, Lawrence	45	Larch	Sligo	Ireland	1847/07/11	1847/08/20
Egan, Margaret	45	Larch	Sligo	Ireland	1847/07/11	1847/08/20
Egan, Maria	5	Mary Brack	Limerick	Ireland	1847/05/03	1847/06/12
Egan, Mary	22	Free Trader	Liverpool	England	1847/06/22	1847/08/14
Egan, Michael	44	Wave	Dublin	Ireland	1847/04/30	1847/06/09
Egan, Nancy	18	Larch	Sligo	Ireland	1847/07/11	1847/08/20
Egan, Peter	24	Larch	Sligo	Ireland	1847/07/11	1847/08/20
Egan, Robert	25	Triton	Liverpool	England	1847/05/14	1847/07/24
Egan, William	17	Ann Kenny	Waterford	Ireland	1847/06/27	1847/08/05
Egerton, Jacob	1	Juliet	London	England	1847/07/03	1847/08/28
Egerton, John	4	Champion	Liverpool	England	1847/07/13	1847/08/28
Egerton, Mary	3	Champion	Liverpool	England	1847/07/13	1847/08/28
Eichner, Patite	1	Canton	Bremen	Germany	1847/06/20	1847/08/07
Elliott, James	1	Tamarac	Liverpool	England	1847/05/26	1847/07/11
Elliott, Mary	60	Lady Milton	Liverpool	England	1847/05/05	1847/06/26
Elliott, Mary Ann		Lady Milton	Liverpool	England	1847/05/05	1847/06/26
Elliott, William		Thistle	Liverpool	England	1847/06/01	1847/07/18
English, William	6	Scotland	Cork	Ireland	1847/04/13	1847/06/08
English, William	23	Scotland	Cork	Ireland	1847/04/13	1847/06/08
Ennis, Ellen		Jane Avery	Dublin	Ireland	1847/05/09	1847/06/25
Enrian, Johanna Alias	1	Leontine	Bremen	Germany	1847/05/28	1847/07/28
Eustace, James		Margaret	New Ross	Ireland	1847/05/19	1847/07/02
Evans, Davis	27	Vesta	Limerick	Ireland	1847/06/21	1847/08/09
Evans, Eliza	2	Emigrant	Liverpool	England	1847/08/11	1847/10/03
Evans, John	13	Emigrant	Liverpool	England	1847/08/11	1847/10/03

LIST OF PEOPLE WHO DIED ON SHIPS AT SEA OR IN QUARANTINE AT GROSSE ÎLE, IN 1847

Name	Age	Vessel	Port	Country	Embarkation	Qc Arrival
Evans, Mary	38	Rose	Liverpool	England	1847/04/19	1847/07/01
Evans, Mary Jane	16	Aberdeen	Liverpool	England	1847/05/01	1847/06/13
Evans, Mary Jane	15	Araminta	Liverpool	England	1847/05/01	1847/06/20
Evans, Thomas	1	Triton	Liverpool	England	1847/05/14	1847/07/24
Fadden, John	28	X.L.	Galway	Ireland	1847/06/10	1847/08/01
Fagan, Edward	37	Sobraon	Liverpool	England	1847/05/08	1847/06/29
Fagan, Mary	44	Wave	Dublin	Ireland	1847/04/30	1847/06/09
Fagan, Patrick	56	Wave	Dublin	Ireland	1847/04/30	1847/06/09
Fagan, Richard	4	Sir Robert Peel	Liverpool	England	1847/07/26	1847/09/19
Fagan, Robert	2	Nelson's Village	Belfast	Ireland	1847/05/10	1847/06/26
Fagan, Robert		Sobraon	Liverpool	England	1847/05/08	1847/06/29
Fahey, Bridget	22	Argo	Liverpool	England	1847/05/04	1847/06/12
Fahey, Catherine	35	Abbotsford	Dublin	Ireland	1847/04/23	1847/06/21
Fahey, John	64	Sarah Maria	Sligo	Ireland	1847/05/07	1847/06/28
Fahey, Maria		Naomi	Liverpool	England	1847/06/15	1847/08/10
Fahey, Thomas	6	John Francis	Cork	Ireland	1847/04/10	1847/06/10
Fallon, Andrew		Sisters	Liverpool	England	1847/04/22	1847/06/20
Fallon, Bridget	1	Numa	Sligo	Ireland	1847/06/02	1847/07/27
Fallon, James	2	Virginius	Liverpool	England	1847/05/28	1847/08/12
Fallon, John	42	Virginius	Liverpool	England	1847/05/28	1847/08/12
Fallon, John	9	Virginius	Liverpool	England	1847/05/28	1847/08/12
Fallon, John	40	Virginius	Liverpool	England	1847/05/28	1847/08/12
Fallon, Mary	16	Virginius	Liverpool	England	1847/05/28	1847/08/12
Fallon, Mary	35	Virginius	Liverpool	England	1847/05/28	1847/08/12
Fallon, Mary	34	Virginius	Liverpool	England	1847/05/28	1847/08/12
Fallon, Mary	3	Pacha	Cork	Ireland	1847/05/05	1847/06/14
Fallon, Patrick	35	Sisters	Liverpool	England	1847/04/22	1847/06/20
Fallon, Patrick	50	Virginius	Liverpool	England	1847/05/28	1847/08/12
Falloon, Luke	1	Naomi	Liverpool	England	1847/06/15	1847/08/10
Falvey, Johanna	28	Julius Caesar	Liverpool	England	1847/07/13	1847/09/05
Fanning, Bridget		Avon	Cork	Ireland	1847/05/19	1847/07/26
Farlane, Judith	40	Free Trader	Liverpool	England	1847/06/22	1847/08/14
Farlane, Judith	26	Free Trader	Liverpool	England	1847/06/22	1847/08/14
Farlane, Peter	40	Free Trader	Liverpool	England	1847/06/22	1847/08/14
Farley, Bridget		Minerva	Galway	Ireland	1847/06/17	1847/08/14
Farley, Dominick	60	George	Liverpool	England	1847/04/13	1847/06/12
Farley, George	23	Sobraon	Liverpool	England	1847/05/08	1847/06/29
Farley, George		George	Liverpool	England	1847/04/13	1847/06/12
Farley, Mrs.	26	Ajax	Liverpool	England	1847/04/16	1847/06/23
Farley, Mrs.		Ajax	Liverpool	England	1847/04/16	1847/06/23
Farmer, John	40	Larch	Sligo	Ireland	1847/07/11	1847/08/20
Farrell, Anthony		Charles Walton	Killala	Ireland	1847/06/24	1847/08/05
Farrell, James	3	Naomi	Liverpool	England	1847/06/15	1847/08/10
Farrell, James	2	Naomi	Liverpool	England	1847/06/15	1847/08/10
Farrell, James	1	John Munn	Liverpool	England	1847/06/16	1847/08/13
Farrell, Luke	40	John Munn	Liverpool	England	1847/06/16	1847/08/13
Farrell, Margaret	37	Lady Milton	Liverpool	England	1847/05/05	1847/06/26
Farrell, Martin	45	Charles Walton	Killala	Ireland	1847/06/24	1847/08/05
Farrell, Mary	40	Naomi	Liverpool	England	1847/06/15	1847/08/10
Farrell, Mary		Virginius	Liverpool	England	1847/05/28	1847/08/12
Farrell, Mary	2	Charles Walton	Killala	Ireland	1847/06/24	1847/08/05
Farrell, Mary	26	Larch	Sligo	Ireland	1847/07/11	1847/08/20
Farrell, Michael	10	Naomi	Liverpool	England	1847/06/15	1847/08/10
Farrell, Patrick	2	Champion	Liverpool	England	1847/07/13	1847/08/28
Farrell, Timothy	52	Odessa	Dublin	Ireland	1847/06/09	1847/08/09
Farren, Catherine	2	Jane Avery	Dublin	Ireland	1847/05/09	1847/06/25
Farry, Daniel	28	Swallow	Limerick	Ireland	1847/05/15	1847/06/25
Fay, Dennis	16	John Bolton	Liverpool	England	1847/04/13	1847/06/10
Fay, Hugh	40	Blenheim	Cork	Ireland	1847/06/16	1847/07/29
Fay, James		Princess Royal	Liverpool	England	1847/05/05	1847/06/16
Fay, John		Princess Royal	Liverpool	England	1847/05/05	1847/06/16
Fay, Luke		George	Liverpool	England	1847/04/13	1847/06/12
Fay, Mary	7	Pursuit	Liverpool	England	1847/05/04	1847/06/23
Fay, Michael	41	Princess Royal	Liverpool	England	1847/05/05	1847/06/16
Fee, Patrick	3	Wolfville	Sligo	Ireland	1847/04/25	1847/06/10
Feeney, Catherine	10	Virginius	Liverpool	England	1847/05/28	1847/08/12
Feeney, Ellen	55	Naomi	Liverpool	England	1847/06/15	1847/08/10
Feeney, James	70	Naomi	Liverpool	England	1847/06/15	1847/08/10
Feeney, James		Naomi	Liverpool	England	1847/06/15	1847/08/10
Feeney, Mary	2	Dykes	Sligo	Ireland	1847/04/23	1847/06/10
Feeney, Mary	15	Virginius	Liverpool	England	1847/05/28	1847/08/12
Feeney, Michael	28	Virginius	Liverpool	England	1847/05/28	1847/08/12
Feeney, Patrick	42	Virginius	Liverpool	England	1847/05/28	1847/08/12
Feeney, Patrick	50	Virginius	Liverpool	England	1847/05/28	1847/08/12
Feeney, Thomas	18	Naomi	Liverpool	England	1847/06/15	1847/08/10
Fenlon, Celia	1	Emigrant	Liverpool	England	1847/08/11	1847/10/03
Fennely, Edward	2	Admiral	Waterford	Ireland	1847/06/01	1847/07/07
Fennerty, Mary	2	Avon	Cork	Ireland	1847/05/19	1847/07/26
Fenton, James	30	Gilmour	Cork	Ireland	1847/04/24	1847/06/18
Fenton, Johanna	2	Lord Sandon	Cork	Ireland	1847/05/11	1847/06/26
Fenton, John	25	Scotland	Cork	Ireland	1847/04/13	1847/06/08
Fenton, Mary	24	Agnes	Cork	Ireland	1847/04/10	1847/06/10
Fergus, Susan	32	John and Robert	Liverpool	England	1847/06/09	1847/08/06
Ferguson, Alexander	12	Euclid	Glasgow	Scotland	1847/06/01	1847/07/29
Ferris, Patrick	20	Covenanter	Cork	Ireland	1847/06/17	1847/08/09
Ferriter, Manus	25	Lord Sandon	Cork	Ireland	1847/05/11	1847/06/26
Finaghy, Dennis	45	Lady Milton	Liverpool	England	1847/05/05	1847/06/26
Finch, Maria	1	Juliet	London	England	1847/07/03	1847/08/28
Finlay, Bridget	5	Eliza Caroline	Liverpool	England	1847/05/03	1847/06/14
Finlay, Margaret	2	Agnes	Cork	Ireland	1847/04/10	1847/06/10
Finn, Ann	70	Colonist	New Ross	Ireland	1847/07/13	1847/08/29
Finn, Augustin	60	Champion	Liverpool	England	1847/07/13	1847/08/28
Finn, Catherine	40	Lady Flora Hastings	Cork	Ireland	1847/05/11	1847/06/26
Finn, Donald	25	Agnes	Cork	Ireland	1847/04/10	1847/06/10
Finn, Edward	10	Lady Flora Hastings	Cork	Ireland	1847/05/11	1847/06/26
Finn, Finton	5	Odessa	Dublin	Ireland	1847/06/09	1847/08/09
Finn, Hodly	3	Agnes	Cork	Ireland	1847/04/10	1847/06/10
Finn, James	30	Agnes	Cork	Ireland	1847/04/10	1847/06/10
Finn, John	2	Sir Henry Pottinger	Cork	Ireland	1847/05/29	1847/08/07
Finn, John	16	Lady Flora Hastings	Cork	Ireland	1847/05/11	1847/06/26
Finn, Julia	35	Sir Henry Pottinger	Cork	Ireland	1847/05/29	1847/08/07
Finn, Mary		Lady Flora Hastings	Cork	Ireland	1847/05/11	1847/06/26
Finn, Mary	4	Larch	Sligo	Ireland	1847/07/11	1847/08/20
Finn, Michael	1	Agnes	Cork	Ireland	1847/04/10	1847/06/10
Finn, Michael	1	Bee	Cork	Ireland	1847/04/17	1847/06/12
Finn, Michael	16	Lady Flora Hastings	Cork	Ireland	1847/05/11	1847/06/26
Finn, Theodore		Agnes	Cork	Ireland	1847/04/10	1847/06/10
Finnegan, Ann	5	Lotus	Liverpool	England	1847/04/15	1847/06/24
Finnegan, James	50	Sobraon	Liverpool	England	1847/05/08	1847/06/29
Finnegan, James	2	Lotus	Liverpool	England	1847/04/15	1847/06/24
Finnegan, Patrick	60	Princess Royal	Liverpool	England	1847/05/05	1847/06/16
Finnegan, Richard		Princess Royal	Liverpool	England	1847/05/05	1847/06/16
Finneran, James	8	Larch	Sligo	Ireland	1847/07/11	1847/08/20
Finnerty, Anthony	50	Marchioness of Breadalbane	Sligo	Ireland	1847/06/11	1847/08/12
Finnerty, Anthony	50	Marchioness of Breadalbane	Sligo	Ireland	1847/06/11	1847/08/12
Finnerty, Bridget		Tom	Dublin	Ireland	1847/05/26	1847/07/12
Finnerty, Dennis	1	Avon	Cork	Ireland	1847/05/19	1847/07/26
Finnerty, Ellen	60	Marchioness of Breadalbane	Sligo	Ireland	1847/06/11	1847/08/12
Finnerty, John	4	Goliah	Liverpool	England	1847/05/21	1847/07/18
Finnerty, John		Goliah	Liverpool	England	1847/05/21	1847/07/18
Finnerty, Margaret	32	Avon	Cork	Ireland	1847/05/19	1847/07/26
Finnerty, Thomas	30	Avon	Cork	Ireland	1847/05/19	1847/07/26
Fisher, Andrew	1	Lord Ashburton	Liverpool	England	1847/09/13	1847/11/01

List of people who died on ships at sea or in quarantine at Grosse Île, in 1847

Name	Age	Vessel	Port	Country	Embarkation	Qc Arrival
Fitzgerald, Catherine	30	Lady Flora Hastings	Cork	Ireland	1847/05/11	1847/06/26
Fitzgerald, James	30	Sir Henry Pottinger	Cork	Ireland	1847/05/29	1847/08/07
Fitzgerald, John	30	Avon	Cork	Ireland	1847/05/19	1847/07/26
Fitzgerald, John	1	Wellington	Liverpool	England	1847/07/29	1847/09/20
Fitzgerald, Mary	6	Wakefield	Cork	Ireland	1847/05/28	1847/07/12
Fitzgerald, Mary	20	Saguenay	Cork	Ireland	1847/06/05	1847/08/22
Fitzgerald, Mary	1	Washington	Liverpool	England	1847/07/09	1847/08/26
Fitzgerald, Patrick	17	Sir Henry Pottinger	Cork	Ireland	1847/05/29	1847/08/07
Fitzgerald, Thomas	30	Saguenay	Cork	Ireland	1847/06/05	1847/08/22
Fitzgerald, William	20	Avon	Cork	Ireland	1847/05/19	1847/07/26
Fitzpatrick, Bridget	50	Minerva	Galway	Ireland	1847/06/17	1847/08/14
Fitzpatrick, Dennis	2	John Francis	Cork	Ireland	1847/04/10	1847/06/10
Fitzpatrick, Eliza		Emigrant	Liverpool	England	1847/08/11	1847/10/03
Fitzpatrick, Eliza	14	Progress	New Ross	Ireland	1847/05/05	1847/07/14
Fitzpatrick, James	14	John Bolton	Liverpool	England	1847/04/13	1847/06/10
Fitzpatrick, James		Odessa	Dublin	Ireland	1847/06/09	1847/08/09
Fitzpatrick, Jeremy	5	John Francis	Cork	Ireland	1847/04/10	1847/06/10
Fitzpatrick, John	50	Minerva	Galway	Ireland	1847/06/17	1847/08/14
Fitzpatrick, John		Wellington	Liverpool	England	1847/07/29	1847/09/20
Fitzpatrick, Mary	6	John Francis	Cork	Ireland	1847/04/10	1847/06/10
Fitzpatrick, Mary	3	Odessa	Dublin	Ireland	1847/06/09	1847/08/09
Fitzsimmons, Catherine	3	Agamemnon	Liverpool	England	1847/06/24	1847/07/31
Fitzsimmons, Eleanor	4	Tamarac	Liverpool	England	1847/05/26	1847/07/11
Flahy, Margaret	13	John Bolton	Liverpool	England	1847/04/13	1847/06/10
Flahy, Thomas	5	John Bolton	Liverpool	England	1847/04/13	1847/06/10
Flanagan, Bridget	16	Virginius	Liverpool	England	1847/05/28	1847/08/12
Flanagan, Catherine	2	Tay	Liverpool	England	1847/05/22	1847/06/23
Flanagan, James	16	Virginius	Liverpool	England	1847/05/28	1847/08/12
Flanagan, John	10	Virginius	Liverpool	England	1847/05/28	1847/08/12
Flanagan, John	6	Rose	Liverpool	England	1847/04/19	1847/07/01
Flanagan, John	22	Larch	Sligo	Ireland	1847/07/11	1847/08/20
Flanagan, Mary	15	Virginius	Liverpool	England	1847/05/28	1847/08/12
Flanagan, Timothy	9	Virginius	Liverpool	England	1847/05/28	1847/08/12
Flanagan, William		Rose	Liverpool	England	1847/04/19	1847/07/01
Flannelly, Anthony	40	Charles Walton	Killala	Ireland	1847/06/24	1847/08/05
Flannelly, Anthony	4	Charles Walton	Killala	Ireland	1847/06/24	1847/08/05
Flannelly, Eleanor	3	Charles Walton	Killala	Ireland	1847/06/24	1847/08/05
Flannelly, Margaret	9	Charles Walton	Killala	Ireland	1847/06/24	1847/08/05
Flannelly, Mary	40	Charles Walton	Killala	Ireland	1847/06/24	1847/08/05
Flannery, Patrick	2	Ganges	Liverpool	England	1847/06/16	1847/08/21
Fleming, Alexander	5	Lord Seaton	Belfast	Ireland	1847/04/12	1847/06/10
Fleming, Bridget		Sisters	Liverpool	England	1847/04/22	1847/06/20
Fleming, Dennis	5	Sisters	Liverpool	England	1847/04/22	1847/06/20
Fleming, Edward	53	Aberfoyle	Waterford	Ireland	1847/05/27	1847/07/04
Fleming, James	24	Sisters	Liverpool	England	1847/04/22	1847/06/20
Fleming, James		Herald	Dublin	Ireland	1847/05/20	1847/06/26
Fleming, Jane		Sesostris	Londonderry	Ireland	1847/05/14	1847/06/24
Fleming, John	7	Sisters	Liverpool	England	1847/04/22	1847/06/20
Fleming, John	3	Sisters	Liverpool	England	1847/04/22	1847/06/20
Fleming, Mary	5	Sisters	Liverpool	England	1847/04/22	1847/06/20
Flood, Bridget	19	Virginius	Liverpool	England	1847/05/28	1847/08/12
Flood, Edward	15	Virginius	Liverpool	England	1847/05/28	1847/08/12
Flood, Mary	15	Virginius	Liverpool	England	1847/05/28	1847/08/12
Flore, Matthew	22	Maria and Elizabeth	Liverpool	England	1847/05/06	1847/06/24
Flynn, Bridget	3	John Bolton	Liverpool	England	1847/04/13	1847/06/10
Flynn, David	24	Gilmour	Cork	Ireland	1847/04/24	1847/06/18
Flynn, John	4	John Bolton	Liverpool	England	1847/04/13	1847/06/10
Flynn, John	24	Jessie	Cork	Ireland	1847/06/03	1847/07/24
Flynn, John		Lord Glenelg	Limerick	Ireland	1847/05/06	1847/06/19
Flynn, John	34	Larch	Sligo	Ireland	1847/07/11	1847/08/20
Flynn, Martin	28	Coromandel	Dublin	Ireland	1847/05/13	1847/07/02
Flynn, Mary	6	Rose	Liverpool	England	1847/04/19	1847/07/01
Flynn, Michael		Princess Royal	Liverpool	England	1847/05/05	1847/06/16
Flynn, Michael	6	John Bolton	Liverpool	England	1847/04/13	1847/06/10
Flynn, Patrick	8	John Bolton	Liverpool	England	1847/04/13	1847/06/10
Flynn, Patrick	1	Allan Kerr	Sligo	Ireland	1847/06/23	1847/08/04
Flynn, Thomas	40	John Bolton	Liverpool	England	1847/04/13	1847/06/10
Fogarty, Ann	2	Margrette	New Ross	Ireland	1847/05/02	1847/07/08
Fogarty, Catherine	8	Free Trader	Liverpool	England	1847/06/22	1847/08/14
Fogarty, Daniel	2	Free Trader	Liverpool	England	1847/06/22	1847/08/14
Fogarty, Daniel	9	Avon	Cork	Ireland	1847/05/19	1847/07/26
Fogarty, Ellen	1	Avon	Cork	Ireland	1847/05/19	1847/07/26
Fogarty, Ellen	1	Avon	Cork	Ireland	1847/05/19	1847/07/26
Fogarty, John	65	Avon	Cork	Ireland	1847/05/19	1847/07/26
Fogarty, Michael	2	Margrette	New Ross	Ireland	1847/05/02	1847/07/08
Fogarty, Patrick	4	Free Trader	Liverpool	England	1847/06/22	1847/08/14
Foley, Daniel	1	Wakefield	Cork	Ireland	1847/05/28	1847/07/12
Foley, Mary	1	Free Briton	Cork	Ireland	1847/05/25	1847/07/10
Foley, Michael	40	Pursuit	Liverpool	England	1847/05/04	1847/06/23
Foran, James	51	Rose	Liverpool	England	1847/04/19	1847/07/01
Foran, John	4	Rose	Liverpool	England	1847/04/19	1847/07/01
Forbes, Jane	25	Goliah	Liverpool	England	1847/05/21	1847/07/18
Forbes, John	1	Goliah	Liverpool	England	1847/05/21	1847/07/18
Forbes, Samuel	26	Erin's Queen	Liverpool	England	1847/06/01	1847/07/23
Ford, Ann		Nelson's Village	Belfast	Ireland	1847/05/10	1847/06/26
Ford, Daniel	40	Bee	Cork	Ireland	1847/04/17	1847/06/12
Ford, Elizabeth	3	Nelson's Village	Belfast	Ireland	1847/05/10	1847/06/26
Ford, Jennifer	45	Bee	Cork	Ireland	1847/04/17	1847/06/12
Ford, Jennifer	3	Bee	Cork	Ireland	1847/04/17	1847/06/12
Ford, John	4	Nelson's Village	Belfast	Ireland	1847/05/10	1847/06/26
Forkin, Barbara	3	City of Derry	London	England	1847/05/23	1847/07/04
Forrestall, Thomas	75	Scotland	Cork	Ireland	1847/04/13	1847/06/08
Forster, Wilhelmine	2	Canton	Bremen	Germany	1847/06/20	1847/08/07
Foster, Ann	2	Ajax	Liverpool	England	1847/04/16	1847/06/23
Foster, Mary	3	Virgilia	Liverpool	England	1847/07/22	1847/09/20
Foster, Richard		Goliah	Liverpool	England	1847/05/21	1847/07/18
Foster, Robert	60	Wellington	Liverpool	England	1847/07/29	1847/09/20
Fox, Ann	5	Lotus	Liverpool	England	1847/04/15	1847/06/24
Fox, Elizabeth	14	Rose	Liverpool	England	1847/04/19	1847/07/01
Fox, Ewing	4	Lotus	Liverpool	England	1847/04/15	1847/06/24
Fox, James		Lotus	Liverpool	England	1847/04/15	1847/06/24
Fox, Mary	2	Lotus	Liverpool	England	1847/04/15	1847/06/24
Fox, Mary		Larch	Sligo	Ireland	1847/07/11	1847/08/20
Fox, Mary		Bridgetown	Liverpool	England	1847/07/03	1847/08/29
Fox, Michael	7	Bridgetown	Liverpool	England	1847/07/03	1847/08/29
Fox, Thomas	50	Bridgetown	Liverpool	England	1847/07/03	1847/08/29
Fox, William	26	Larch	Sligo	Ireland	1847/07/11	1847/08/20
Foy, Michael		Goliah	Liverpool	England	1847/05/21	1847/07/18
Foy, Richard	4	Goliah	Liverpool	England	1847/05/21	1847/07/18
Framer, Frank	45	Bridgetown	Liverpool	England	1847/07/03	1847/08/29
Francis, Mary	60	Lord Seaton	Belfast	Ireland	1847/04/12	1847/06/10
Francis, Mary	2	Lord Seaton	Belfast	Ireland	1847/04/12	1847/06/10
Fraser, Catherine	56	Broom	Liverpool	England	1847/06/13	1847/08/06
Fraser, James		Argo	Sligo	Ireland	1847/06/11	1847/07/31
Fraser, Robert	51	Broom	Liverpool	England	1847/06/13	1847/08/06
Frost, Thomas	23	Larch	Sligo	Ireland	1847/07/11	1847/08/20
Fuller, Mary	19	Princess Royal	Liverpool	England	1847/05/05	1847/06/16
Furlong, Peter	30	Bridgetown	Liverpool	England	1847/07/03	1847/08/29
Gaffney, N.	65	Pandora	New Ross	Ireland	1847/06/11	1847/08/04
Gagan, James	30	Scotland	Cork	Ireland	1847/04/13	1847/06/08
Gahan, Judith	2	Margrette	New Ross	Ireland	1847/05/02	1847/07/08
Galbraith, Alexander	2	Ann Rankin	Glasgow	Scotland	1847/06/27	1847/08/09
Gallaghan, Anthony	45	Erin's Queen	Liverpool	England	1847/06/01	1847/07/23
Gallaghan, Bridget	4	Triton	Liverpool	England	1847/05/14	1847/07/24
Gallaghan, Bridget	1	Triton	Liverpool	England	1847/05/14	1847/07/24

List of people who died on ships at sea or in quarantine at Grosse Île, in 1847

Name	Age	Vessel	Port	Country	Embarkation	Qc Arrival
Gallaghan, Bridget	57	Countess of Arran	Donegal	Ireland	1847/06/30	1847/08/10
Gallaghan, Mary	10	Erin's Queen	Liverpool	England	1847/06/01	1847/07/23
Gallaghan, Richard	25	Avon	Cork	Ireland	1847/05/19	1847/07/26
Gallagher, Catherine	11	Robert Newton	Limerick	Ireland	1847/07/18	1847/08/29
Gallagher, Edward	15	Aberdeen	Liverpool	England	1847/05/01	1847/06/13
Gallagher, Edward	20	Araminta	Liverpool	England	1847/05/01	1847/06/20
Gallagher, Francis	30	Larch	Sligo	Ireland	1847/07/11	1847/08/20
Gallagher, Johanna		Mail	Cork	Ireland	1847/04/25	1847/06/19
Gallagher, John	4	George	Liverpool	England	1847/04/13	1847/06/12
Gallagher, Martin	22	Ganges	Liverpool	England	1847/06/16	1847/08/21
Gallagher, Mary	4	Mail	Cork	Ireland	1847/04/25	1847/06/19
Gallagher, Mary	10	John and Robert	Liverpool	England	1847/06/09	1847/08/06
Gallagher, Peter	1	Christiana	Londonderry	Ireland	1847/04/08	1847/06/10
Gallagher, Selby	30	Lotus	Liverpool	England	1847/04/15	1847/06/24
Gallivan, Edward	45	Lord Sandon	Cork	Ireland	1847/05/11	1847/06/26
Gallivan, James	2	Sir Henry Pottinger	Cork	Ireland	1847/05/29	1847/08/07
Gallivan, John		Sir Henry Pottinger	Cork	Ireland	1847/05/29	1847/08/07
Gallivan, Julia	1	Sir Henry Pottinger	Cork	Ireland	1847/05/29	1847/08/07
Gallivan, Morris	22	Covenanter	Cork	Ireland	1847/06/17	1847/08/09
Galvin, Nancy	50	Virgilia	Liverpool	England	1847/07/22	1847/09/20
Galway, Patrick		Isabella	Killala	Ireland	1847/07/17	1847/09/17
Gamble, Ann	4	Tamarac	Liverpool	England	1847/05/26	1847/07/11
Ganley, William	5	Yorkshire	Liverpool	England	1847/06/09	1847/08/10
Gannon, Frank	10	Isabella	Killala	Ireland	1847/07/17	1847/09/17
Gannon, John	1	Larch	Sligo	Ireland	1847/07/11	1847/08/20
Gannon, John	3	Isabella	Killala	Ireland	1847/07/17	1847/09/17
Gannon, Mary	3	George	Liverpool	England	1847/04/13	1847/06/12
Gannon, Michael	60	Isabella	Killala	Ireland	1847/07/17	1847/09/17
Gannon, Patrick	30	Bridgetown	Liverpool	England	1847/07/03	1847/08/29
Gannon, William	2	Isabella	Killala	Ireland	1847/07/17	1847/09/17
Gansen, Rose		Lotus	Liverpool	England	1847/04/15	1847/06/24
Garrett, Owen	7	Goliah	Liverpool	England	1847/05/21	1847/07/18
Garrigle, Ann	4	Virginius	Liverpool	England	1847/05/28	1847/08/12
Garrigle, Elizabeth		Eliza Caroline	Liverpool	England	1847/05/03	1847/06/14
Garry, David	30	Scotland	Cork	Ireland	1847/04/13	1847/06/08
Garry, David	27	Scotland	Cork	Ireland	1847/04/13	1847/06/08
Garry, John	25	Sir Henry Pottinger	Cork	Ireland	1847/05/29	1847/08/07
Garry, William	16	Sir Henry Pottinger	Cork	Ireland	1847/05/29	1847/08/07
Gaughan, Michael	6	George	Liverpool	England	1847/04/13	1847/06/12
Gaughan, Patrick	15	Lady Milton	Liverpool	England	1847/05/05	1847/06/26
Gaughran, Bridget	21	Ann	Liverpool	England	1847/05/16	1847/06/30
Gaughran, Catherine	25	Ann	Liverpool	England	1847/05/16	1847/06/30
Gaughran, John	5	Ann	Liverpool	England	1847/05/16	1847/06/30
Gault, Margaret	6	Ajax	Liverpool	England	1847/04/16	1847/06/23
Gault, Robert	6	Ajax	Liverpool	England	1847/04/16	1847/06/23
Gault, Robert	5	Ajax	Liverpool	England	1847/04/16	1847/06/23
Gault, Samuel		Ajax	Liverpool	England	1847/04/16	1847/06/23
Gault, Sarah	6	Ajax	Liverpool	England	1847/04/16	1847/06/23
Gavaghan, Timothy	67	Ajax	Liverpool	England	1847/04/16	1847/06/23
Gavin, Ann	37	Sisters	Liverpool	England	1847/04/22	1847/06/20
Gavin, Ann	8	Sisters	Liverpool	England	1847/04/22	1847/06/20
Gavin, Peter	35	Sisters	Liverpool	England	1847/04/22	1847/06/20
Gawley, Mary	1	Yorkshire	Liverpool	England	1847/06/09	1847/08/10
Gaynor, Edward	1	Lord Ashburton	Liverpool	England	1847/09/13	1847/11/01
Gaynor, Mary	24	Jessie	Cork	Ireland	1847/06/03	1847/07/24
Geary, Ellen	22	Sir Henry Pottinger	Cork	Ireland	1847/05/29	1847/08/07
Geary, John	2	Sir Henry Pottinger	Cork	Ireland	1847/05/29	1847/08/07
Geehan, Bridget	17	Bridgetown	Liverpool	England	1847/07/03	1847/08/29
Geehan, Elizabeth	1	Allan Kerr	Sligo	Ireland	1847/06/23	1847/08/04
Geraghty, Ellen	13	Naomi	Liverpool	England	1847/06/15	1847/08/10
Gerald, Johanna	3	Bridgetown	Liverpool	England	1847/07/03	1847/08/29
Gettins, Bridget		Avon	Cork	Ireland	1847/05/19	1847/07/26
Gettins, John	8	Avon	Cork	Ireland	1847/05/19	1847/07/26
Gettins, Nancy	38	Avon	Cork	Ireland	1847/05/19	1847/07/26
Getty, Edmund		Sir Robert Peel	Liverpool	England	1847/07/26	1847/09/19
Gibb, Mary	32	Virgilia	Liverpool	England	1847/07/22	1847/09/20
Gibbon, Joseph	1	Admiral	Waterford	Ireland	1847/06/01	1847/07/07
Gibbon, William		Goliah	Liverpool	England	1847/05/21	1847/07/18
Gibbons, Margaret	1	Lady Milton	Liverpool	England	1847/05/05	1847/06/26
Gibbons, Mary	40	Lady Milton	Liverpool	England	1847/05/05	1847/06/26
Gibbons, Patrick	3	Lady Milton	Liverpool	England	1847/05/05	1847/06/26
Gibbons, Sarah	7	Lady Milton	Liverpool	England	1847/05/05	1847/06/26
Gibney, Catherine	2	Lotus	Liverpool	England	1847/04/15	1847/06/24
Gibney, Richard		Aberdeen	Liverpool	England	1847/05/01	1847/06/13
Gibney, Richard		Araminta	Liverpool	England	1847/05/01	1847/06/20
Giles, Enoch	2	Rosalinda	Belfast	Ireland	1847/06/22	1847/08/07
Gill, Ann		Sisters	Liverpool	England	1847/04/22	1847/06/20
Gill, Michael	8	Sisters	Liverpool	England	1847/04/22	1847/06/20
Gill, Patrick	24	Columbia	Sligo	Ireland	1847/05/01	1847/06/10
Gillan, Alexander	50	Marchioness of Bute	Belfast	Ireland	1847/06/10	1847/07/31
Gillan, John	4	Numa	Sligo	Ireland	1847/06/02	1847/07/27
Gilleroy, John	2	Dykes	Sligo	Ireland	1847/04/23	1847/06/10
Gilligan, Thomas	30	Lotus	Liverpool	England	1847/04/15	1847/06/24
Gilloway, Barbara		George	Liverpool	England	1847/04/13	1847/06/12
Gilmartin, Michael	65	Numa	Sligo	Ireland	1847/06/02	1847/07/27
Gilmartin, Nancy	80	Charles Walton	Killala	Ireland	1847/06/24	1847/08/05
Gilmour, Bridget	1	Tay	Sligo	Ireland	1847/05/05	1847/06/09
Gilmour, Ellen	20	Agent	New Ross	Ireland	1847/05/20	1847/07/02
Ginley, Thomas	12	Pursuit	Liverpool	England	1847/05/04	1847/06/23
Gleeson, Mary Ann	4	Sisters	Liverpool	England	1847/04/22	1847/06/20
Gleeson, Michael	55	Jane Avery	Dublin	Ireland	1847/05/09	1847/06/25
Glenny, Eliza	25	Dykes	Sligo	Ireland	1847/04/23	1847/06/10
Glenny, Mary J.		Eliza Caroline	Liverpool	England	1847/05/03	1847/06/14
Glenny, William	2	Eliza Caroline	Liverpool	England	1847/05/03	1847/06/14
Glynn, Ann	2	Manchester	Liverpool	England	1847/06/05	1847/07/17
Glynn, Bridget		Lord Glenelg	Limerick	Ireland	1847/05/06	1847/06/19
Glynn, James		Tom	Dublin	Ireland	1847/05/26	1847/07/12
Glynn, John	2	Dykes	Sligo	Ireland	1847/04/23	1847/06/10
Goen, Ann	20	Colonist	New Ross	Ireland	1847/07/13	1847/08/29
Gogan, Betsy	35	Virginius	Liverpool	England	1847/05/28	1847/08/12
Gogan, James	54	Scotland	Cork	Ireland	1847/04/13	1847/06/08
Gogan, William	5	Pandora	New Ross	Ireland	1847/06/11	1847/08/04
Goggin, Michael	9	Virginius	Liverpool	England	1847/05/28	1847/08/12
Golding, John	40	Eliza Caroline	Liverpool	England	1847/05/03	1847/06/14
Golding, Michael	2	Jane Avery	Dublin	Ireland	1847/05/09	1847/06/25
Golding, Patrick		Goliah	Liverpool	England	1847/05/21	1847/07/18
Gordon, Austin	44	Yorkshire	Liverpool	England	1847/06/09	1847/08/10
Gordon, Wilson		Lady Gordon	Belfast	Ireland	1847/04/14	1847/06/20
Gorman, Bridget	12	Progress	New Ross	Ireland	1847/05/05	1847/07/14
Gorman, Catherine	20	Bridgetown	Liverpool	England	1847/07/03	1847/08/29
Gorman, Catherine	35	Yorkshire	Liverpool	England	1847/06/09	1847/08/10
Gorman, Gerard	26	Yorkshire	Liverpool	England	1847/06/09	1847/08/10
Gorman, Margaret		John Munn	Liverpool	England	1847/06/16	1847/08/13
Gorman, Patrick	1	Albion	Limerick	Ireland	1847/04/19	1847/06/18
Gorman, Richard		John Munn	Liverpool	England	1847/06/16	1847/08/13
Gracey, John	2	New Zealand	Newry	Ireland	1847/05/20	1847/07/03
Grady, Ellen	40	Jessie	Limerick	Ireland	1847/04/18	1847/06/26
Grady, John	3	Saguenay	Cork	Ireland	1847/06/05	1847/08/22
Grady, John	45	Saguenay	Cork	Ireland	1847/06/05	1847/08/22
Grady, Michael	45	Albion	Limerick	Ireland	1847/04/19	1847/06/18
Grady, Patrick	10	Saguenay	Cork	Ireland	1847/06/05	1847/08/22
Grady, Patrick	10	Saguenay	Cork	Ireland	1847/06/05	1847/08/22
Grady, Thomas	45	Jessie	Limerick	Ireland	1847/04/18	1847/06/26

List of people who died on ships at sea or in quarantine at Grosse Île, in 1847

Name	Age	Vessel	Port	Country	Embarkation	Qc Arrival
Grady, William	48	Saguenay	Cork	Ireland	1847/06/05	1847/08/22
Graham, Catherine	18	Canada	Glasgow	Scotland	1847/07/14	1847/09/04
Graham, Edmond	50	John Francis	Cork	Ireland	1847/04/10	1847/06/10
Graham, John	2	Larch	Sligo	Ireland	1847/07/11	1847/08/20
Graham, Martha	23	Lord Ashburton	Liverpool	England	1847/09/13	1847/11/01
Graham, Mary	2	Canada	Glasgow	Scotland	1847/07/14	1847/09/04
Graham, Mary	18	Lord Ashburton	Liverpool	England	1847/09/13	1847/11/01
Graham, Timothy	67	Ajax	Liverpool	England	1847/04/16	1847/06/23
Grannan, Judith	13	Lady Flora Hastings	Cork	Ireland	1847/05/11	1847/06/26
Grant, James	2	Lord Seaton	Belfast	Ireland	1847/04/12	1847/06/10
Grant, James	10	Agamemnon	Liverpool	England	1847/06/24	1847/07/31
Graves, Margaret	34	Larch	Sligo	Ireland	1847/07/11	1847/08/20
Graves, Michael	2	New York Packet	Liverpool	England	1847/04/24	1847/06/29
Gray, Bridget	10	John Bolton	Liverpool	England	1847/04/13	1847/06/10
Gray, Michael	4	John Bolton	Liverpool	England	1847/04/13	1847/06/10
Gray, Richard	3	Goliah	Liverpool	England	1847/05/21	1847/07/18
Greally, Bridget	22	Rose	Liverpool	England	1847/04/19	1847/07/01
Greany, Daniel	30	Pacha	Cork	Ireland	1847/05/05	1847/06/14
Greany, James	4	Goliah	Liverpool	England	1847/05/21	1847/07/18
Green, Bernard	2	Lady Milton	Liverpool	England	1847/05/05	1847/06/26
Green, James	11	Virginius	Liverpool	England	1847/05/28	1847/08/12
Green, John	60	Virginius	Liverpool	England	1847/05/28	1847/08/12
Green, John	43	Sir Robert Peel	Liverpool	England	1847/07/26	1847/09/19
Green, Luke	8	Virginius	Liverpool	England	1847/05/28	1847/08/12
Green, Margaret	12	Virginius	Liverpool	England	1847/05/28	1847/08/12
Green, Martin	29	Virginius	Liverpool	England	1847/05/28	1847/08/12
Green, Mary	30	Virginius	Liverpool	England	1847/05/28	1847/08/12
Green, Michael	2	Lady Milton	Liverpool	England	1847/05/05	1847/06/26
Green, Naples	48	Naomi	Liverpool	England	1847/06/15	1847/08/10
Green, Patrick	6	Lady Milton	Liverpool	England	1847/05/05	1847/06/26
Green, Sarah	2	Lord Seaton	Belfast	Ireland	1847/04/12	1847/06/10
Green, Thomas	2	Virginius	Liverpool	England	1847/05/28	1847/08/12
Green, W.J.	2	Lord Seaton	Belfast	Ireland	1847/04/12	1847/06/10
Gregory, Andrew		Junior	Liverpool	England	1847/05/10	1847/07/03
Griffin, Catherine	50	Rose	Liverpool	England	1847/04/19	1847/07/01
Griffin, Charles	23	Caithness-shire	Belfast	Ireland	1847/04/10	1847/06/12
Griffin, Elizabeth	3	Jessie	Cork	Ireland	1847/06/03	1847/07/24
Griffin, Henry	30	Caithness-shire	Belfast	Ireland	1847/04/10	1847/06/12
Griffin, James		Junior	Liverpool	England	1847/05/10	1847/07/03
Griffin, Patrick	25	Saguenay	Cork	Ireland	1847/06/05	1847/08/22
Grimason, Eliza	1	Sisters	Liverpool	England	1847/04/22	1847/06/20
Grimes, Joseph	3	Lord Seaton	Belfast	Ireland	1847/04/12	1847/06/10
Grimes, Sarah	35	Sisters	Liverpool	England	1847/04/22	1847/06/20
Grimley, Patrick	17	Rose	Liverpool	England	1847/04/19	1847/07/01
Groarke, James		Princess Royal	Liverpool	England	1847/05/05	1847/06/16
Grogan, John	3	Agamemnon	Liverpool	England	1847/06/24	1847/07/31
Grunnile, Margaret	1	General Hewitt	Bremen	Germany	1847/07/22	1847/09/12
Guerin, John	40	Sisters	Liverpool	England	1847/04/22	1847/06/20
Guerin, John	3	Lord Glenelg	Limerick	Ireland	1847/05/06	1847/06/19
Guerin, Mary	10	Sisters	Liverpool	England	1847/04/22	1847/06/20
Guerin, Michael		Lotus	Liverpool	England	1847/04/15	1847/06/24
Guinan, Bridget	2	Wolfville	Sligo	Ireland	1847/04/25	1847/06/10
Guiney, Catherine	1.5	Richard Watson	Sligo	Ireland	1847/09/13	1847/11/08
Gunning, Catherine	38	Thompson	Sligo	Ireland	1847/05/05	1847/06/14
Gunning, Eleanor	3	Thompson	Sligo	Ireland	1847/05/05	1847/06/14
Gunning, Rose	60	Wilhelmina	Belfast	Ireland	1847/05/08	1847/06/20
Haddock, Rodger	1	Washington	Liverpool	England	1847/07/09	1847/08/26
Haddon, Bridget	13	John Bolton	Liverpool	England	1847/04/13	1847/06/10
Haddon, John B.	21	Sir Robert Peel	Liverpool	England	1847/07/26	1847/09/19
Hagan, Alex	6	Tay	Sligo	Ireland	1847/05/05	1847/06/09
Hagan, Alice	2	Rose	Liverpool	England	1847/04/19	1847/07/01
Hagan, Catherine	3	Virginius	Liverpool	England	1847/05/28	1847/08/12
Hagan, Charles	10	Rosalinda	Belfast	Ireland	1847/06/22	1847/08/07
Hagan, Elizabeth	3	Rose	Liverpool	England	1847/04/19	1847/07/01
Hagan, James	22	Free Trader	Liverpool	England	1847/06/22	1847/08/14
Hagan, James	2	Naomi	Liverpool	England	1847/06/15	1847/08/10
Hagan, Maria	25	Virginius	Liverpool	England	1847/05/28	1847/08/12
Hagan, Michael	40	Marchioness of Abercorn	Londonderry	Ireland	1847/06/15	1847/08/05
Hagan, Owen	14	Naomi	Liverpool	England	1847/06/15	1847/08/10
Hagan, William	7	Rose	Liverpool	England	1847/04/19	1847/07/01
Hagert, Edward	3	Frankfield	Liverpool	England	1847/06/29	1847/08/09
Haines, Mary	16	Ellen	Sligo	Ireland	1847/05/27	1847/07/10
Haines, R.		Junior	Liverpool	England	1847/05/10	1847/07/03
Haines, William	12	Jessie	Limerick	Ireland	1847/04/18	1847/06/26
Haley, Mary	4	Argo	Liverpool	England	1847/05/04	1847/06/12
Haley, Patrick	59	Avon	Cork	Ireland	1847/05/19	1847/07/26
Haley, Patrick	28	Avon	Cork	Ireland	1847/05/19	1847/07/26
Hall, George	48	Broom	Liverpool	England	1847/06/13	1847/08/06
Hall, James	28	Agnes	Cork	Ireland	1847/04/10	1847/06/10
Hallahan, Julia	2	Lord Sandon	Cork	Ireland	1847/05/11	1847/06/26
Halligan, Ann		Ajax	Liverpool	England	1847/04/16	1847/06/23
Halligan, James	31	Lady Flora Hastings	Cork	Ireland	1847/05/11	1847/06/26
Halligan, Jessie	3	Rose	Liverpool	England	1847/04/19	1847/07/01
Halligan, John	22	Ajax	Liverpool	England	1847/04/16	1847/06/23
Halligan, John	19	Ajax	Liverpool	England	1847/04/16	1847/06/23
Halligan, Mary	5	Rose	Liverpool	England	1847/04/19	1847/07/01
Halligan, Richard	30	Ajax	Liverpool	England	1847/04/16	1847/06/23
Halligan, Thomas	14	Rose	Liverpool	England	1847/04/19	1847/07/01
Halton, Casper	2	Juliet	London	England	1847/07/03	1847/08/28
Hamburg, Simon		Juliet	London	England	1847/07/03	1847/08/28
Hamel, Catherine		Lady Gordon	Belfast	Ireland	1847/04/14	1847/06/20
Hamel, Elizabeth	8	Marchioness of Bute	Belfast	Ireland	1847/06/10	1847/07/31
Hamel, Margaret		Lady Gordon	Belfast	Ireland	1847/04/14	1847/06/20
Hamel, Maria	4	Marchioness of Bute	Belfast	Ireland	1847/06/10	1847/07/31
Hamel, Mary	6	John Bolton	Liverpool	England	1847/04/13	1847/06/10
Hamel, Mary	62	Marchioness of Bute	Belfast	Ireland	1847/06/10	1847/07/31
Hamilton, Barry	15	John Bolton	Liverpool	England	1847/04/13	1847/06/10
Hamilton, Mary	5	John Munn	Liverpool	England	1847/06/16	1847/08/13
Hamilton, Mary J.	4	Argo	Liverpool	England	1847/05/04	1847/06/12
Hamilton, Mrs.	30	Eliza Caroline	Liverpool	England	1847/05/03	1847/06/14
Hamilton, William		Sobraon	Liverpool	England	1847/05/08	1847/06/29
Hammond, Michael	1	John and Robert	Liverpool	England	1847/06/09	1847/08/06
Hammond, William	10	John and Robert	Liverpool	England	1847/06/09	1847/08/06
Handy, Catherine	4	Sisters	Liverpool	England	1847/04/22	1847/06/20
Handy, John	8	Sisters	Liverpool	England	1847/04/22	1847/06/20
Handy, Mary	35	Sisters	Liverpool	England	1847/04/22	1847/06/20
Hanifin, Daniel	65	Venilia	Limerick	Ireland	1847/05/28	1847/07/11
Hanifin, Timothy	50	Wakefield	Cork	Ireland	1847/05/28	1847/07/12
Hanley, Ann	75	Lotus	Liverpool	England	1847/04/15	1847/06/24
Hanley, Bridget	13	Virginius	Liverpool	England	1847/05/28	1847/08/12
Hanley, Catherine	2	Marchioness of Breadalbane	Sligo	Ireland	1847/06/11	1847/08/12
Hanley, Catherine	17	Virginius	Liverpool	England	1847/05/28	1847/08/12
Hanley, Edward	34	Virginius	Liverpool	England	1847/05/28	1847/08/12
Hanley, Elizabeth	1	Naomi	Liverpool	England	1847/06/15	1847/08/10
Hanley, Ellen	1	Virgilia	Liverpool	England	1847/07/22	1847/09/20
Hanley, James		Sisters	Liverpool	England	1847/04/22	1847/06/20
Hanley, Mary	26	Virginius	Liverpool	England	1847/05/28	1847/08/12
Hanley, Mary	1	Emigrant	Liverpool	England	1847/08/11	1847/10/03
Hanley, Mary		Virginius	Liverpool	England	1847/05/28	1847/08/12
Hanley, Michael	37	Sisters	Liverpool	England	1847/04/22	1847/06/20
Hanley, Nancy	3	Virginius	Liverpool	England	1847/05/28	1847/08/12
Hanley, Patrick		Naomi	Liverpool	England	1847/06/15	1847/08/10
Hanley, Phelim	40	Virginius	Liverpool	England	1847/05/28	1847/08/12

List of people who died on ships at sea or in quarantine at Grosse Île, in 1847

Name	Age	Vessel	Port	Country	Embarkation	Qc Arrival
Hanley, William	5	Sisters	Liverpool	England	1847/04/22	1847/06/20
Hanlon, James	30	Caithness-shire	Belfast	Ireland	1847/04/10	1847/06/12
Hanna, Catherine	40	Independance	Belfast	Ireland	1847/05/23	1847/07/07
Hanna, James	6	Naomi	Liverpool	England	1847/06/15	1847/08/10
Hanna, John		Nelson's Village	Belfast	Ireland	1847/05/10	1847/06/26
Hanna, John	45	Naomi	Liverpool	England	1847/06/15	1847/08/10
Hanna, Mrs.	55	Agnes and Ann	Newry	Ireland	1847/05/15	1847/07/02
Hanna, William	2	John Bolton	Liverpool	England	1847/04/13	1847/06/10
Hannigan, James		Ferald	Dublin	Ireland	1847/05/20	1847/06/26
Hannigan, James	70	Sesostris	Londonderry	Ireland	1847/05/14	1847/06/24
Hannon, Joseph	6	Diamond	Bremerhaven	Germany	1847/06/08	1847/07/31
Hannon, Margaret	23	Larch	Sligo	Ireland	1847/07/11	1847/08/20
Hannon, Patrick		Larch	Sligo	Ireland	1847/07/11	1847/08/20
Harding, Mary	11	Rose	Liverpool	England	1847/04/19	1847/07/01
Hardy, Michael	40	Lord Ashburton	Liverpool	England	1847/09/13	1847/11/01
Hare, Rose	1	Sisters	Liverpool	England	1847/04/22	1847/06/20
Harkin, Bridget	52	Wolfville	Sligo	Ireland	1847/04/25	1847/06/10
Harkin, Catherine	2	Charles Richard	Sligo	Ireland	1847/05/27	1847/07/16
Harkin, James	12	Wolfville	Sligo	Ireland	1847/04/25	1847/06/10
Harkin, James		Wellington	Liverpool	England	1847/07/29	1847/09/20
Harkin, James	55	Charles Richard	Sligo	Ireland	1847/05/27	1847/07/16
Harkin, Patrick	25	Wolfville	Sligo	Ireland	1847/04/25	1847/06/10
Harkin, Sarah	50	Charles Richard	Sligo	Ireland	1847/05/27	1847/07/16
Harkness, Jane	1	Rosalinda	Belfast	Ireland	1847/06/22	1847/08/07
Harley, Patrick	21	Greenock	Liverpool	England	1847/06/19	1847/07/29
Harold, Eliza	18	Henrietta Mary	Cork	Ireland	1847/08/18	1847/09/29
Harold, Ellen	25	Avon	Cork	Ireland	1847/05/19	1847/07/26
Harrell, Sarah	40	Lotus	Liverpool	England	1847/04/15	1847/06/24
Harrigan, Catherine	5	Free Briton	Cork	Ireland	1847/05/25	1847/07/10
Harrigan, James	9	Free Briton	Cork	Ireland	1847/05/25	1847/07/10
Harrigan, Jerry	40	Free Briton	Cork	Ireland	1847/05/25	1847/07/10
Harrigan, John	32	Scotland	Cork	Ireland	1847/04/13	1847/06/08
Harrington, James	25	Trade	Waterford	Ireland	1847/04/17	1847/06/26
Harrington, Mary	1	Urania	Cork	Ireland	1847/04/09	1847/06/10
Harrington, Michael	28	John Francis	Cork	Ireland	1847/04/10	1847/06/10
Harrison, Daniel	1	Urania	Cork	Ireland	1847/04/09	1847/06/10
Hart, Daniel	2	Agnes	Cork	Ireland	1847/04/10	1847/06/10
Hart, Daniel	35	Emigrant	Liverpool	England	1847/08/11	1847/10/03
Hart, Elizabeth	7	Bridgetown	Liverpool	England	1847/07/03	1847/08/29
Hart, Francis	5	Pacha	Cork	Ireland	1847/05/05	1847/06/14
Hart, Francis	30	Pacha	Cork	Ireland	1847/05/05	1847/06/14
Hart, John	3	Bridgetown	Liverpool	England	1847/07/03	1847/08/29
Hart, John	1	Bridgetown	Liverpool	England	1847/07/03	1847/08/29
Hart, Matthew	4	Gilmour	Cork	Ireland	1847/04/24	1847/06/18
Hart, Michael	1	Agnes	Cork	Ireland	1847/04/10	1847/06/10
Hart, Michael		Agnes	Cork	Ireland	1847/04/10	1847/06/10
Hart, Michael	7	Eliza Caroline	Liverpool	England	1847/05/03	1847/06/14
Hart, Michael	48	Triton	Liverpool	England	1847/05/14	1847/07/24
Hart, Michael	4	Bridgetown	Liverpool	England	1847/07/03	1847/08/29
Hartigan, Mary	1	Nerio	Limerick	Ireland	1847/08/05	1847/09/28
Hartinfeld, Andrew	5	Canton	Bremen	Germany	1847/06/20	1847/08/07
Hartman, Eliza	2	Juliet	London	England	1847/07/03	1847/08/28
Hartnett, Mary	29	Lotus	Liverpool	England	1847/04/15	1847/06/24
Hartnett, Nora		Margrette	New Ross	Ireland	1847/05/02	1847/07/08
Harty, Thomas	4	Lord Ashburton	Liverpool	England	1847/09/13	1847/11/01
Hassett, Marcus	14	Wakefield	Cork	Ireland	1847/05/28	1847/07/12
Hawe, Margaret	60	Aberfoyle	Waterford	Ireland	1847/05/27	1847/07/04
Hawkins, Bridget	3	John Bolton	Liverpool	England	1847/04/13	1847/06/10
Hawkins, Eliza	11	John Bolton	Liverpool	England	1847/04/13	1847/06/10
Hawthorn, Hugh	78	Emigrant	Liverpool	England	1847/08/11	1847/10/03
Hayes, Ann	17	Jessie	Limerick	Ireland	1847/04/18	1847/06/26
Hayes, Bridget	68	Lord Glenelg	Limerick	Ireland	1847/05/06	1847/06/19
Hayes, David	30	Saguenay	Cork	Ireland	1847/06/05	1847/08/22
Hayes, David	30	Saguenay	Cork	Ireland	1847/06/05	1847/08/22
Hayes, Harriett	3	Margrette	New Ross	Ireland	1847/05/02	1847/07/08
Hayes, James	22	Primrose	Limerick	Ireland	1847/04/07	1847/06/18
Hayes, Judith		Albion	Limerick	Ireland	1847/04/19	1847/06/18
Hayes, M.	50	Bridgetown	Liverpool	England	1847/07/03	1847/08/29
Hayes, Margaret	39	Scotland	Cork	Ireland	1847/04/13	1847/06/08
Hayes, Mary	4	Pacha	Cork	Ireland	1847/05/05	1847/06/14
Hayes, Mary	1	Washington	Liverpool	England	1847/07/09	1847/08/26
Hayes, Roddy	24	Primrose	Limerick	Ireland	1847/04/07	1847/06/18
Hayes, Susana		Champion	Liverpool	England	1847/07/13	1847/08/28
Hayes, William	30	Saguenay	Cork	Ireland	1847/06/05	1847/08/22
Hayes, William	35	Saguenay	Cork	Ireland	1847/06/05	1847/08/22
Headon, James	4	Larch	Sligo	Ireland	1847/07/11	1847/08/20
Healy, Ann	7	Oregon	Killala	Ireland	1847/06/09	1847/08/02
Healy, Bridget	8	Princess Royal	Liverpool	England	1847/05/05	1847/06/16
Healy, James	2	Avon	Cork	Ireland	1847/05/19	1847/07/26
Healy, Margaret	30	Avon	Cork	Ireland	1847/05/19	1847/07/26
Healy, Margaret	7	Saguenay	Cork	Ireland	1847/06/05	1847/08/22
Healy, Owen	15	Larch	Sligo	Ireland	1847/07/11	1847/08/20
Healy, Patrick	1	Julius Caesar	Liverpool	England	1847/07/13	1847/09/05
Healy, William	40	Avon	Cork	Ireland	1847/05/19	1847/07/26
Hegarty, Ann	5	John Munn	Liverpool	England	1847/06/16	1847/08/13
Hegarty, Denis	43	Pursuit	Liverpool	England	1847/05/04	1847/06/23
Hegarty, Mary	50	Bridgetown	Liverpool	England	1847/07/03	1847/08/29
Hegarty, Mrs.	18	Bridgetown	Liverpool	England	1847/07/03	1847/08/29
Hegarty, Patrick	17	Saguenay	Cork	Ireland	1847/06/05	1847/08/22
Henderson, James	1	Lord Seaton	Belfast	Ireland	1847/04/12	1847/06/10
Henderson, Thomas	11	Aberdeen	Liverpool	England	1847/05/01	1847/06/13
Henderson, Thomas	11	Araminta	Liverpool	England	1847/05/01	1847/06/20
Henderson, Thomas	28	Bee	Cork	Ireland	1847/04/17	1847/06/12
Hendrick, Edward	7	Margrette	New Ross	Ireland	1847/05/02	1847/07/08
Hendrick, Honora	36	Margrette	New Ross	Ireland	1847/05/02	1847/07/08
Henehan, James	27	Admiral	Waterford	Ireland	1847/06/01	1847/07/07
Hennessy, Eliza	50	Progress	New Ross	Ireland	1847/05/05	1847/07/14
Hennessy, Eliza	3	Washington	Liverpool	England	1847/07/09	1847/08/26
Hennessy, John		Washington	Liverpool	England	1847/07/09	1847/08/26
Hennessy, Michael	75	Naparina	Dublin	Ireland	1847/06/17	1847/08/23
Hennessy, Michael	3	Nerio	Limerick	Ireland	1847/08/05	1847/09/28
Henrick, Mary	6	Argo	Liverpool	England	1847/05/04	1847/06/12
Henry, Ann	42	Erin's Queen	Liverpool	England	1847/06/01	1847/07/23
Henry, Catherine		Greenock	Liverpool	England	1847/06/19	1847/07/29
Henry, Hugh	8	Standard	New Ross	Ireland	1847/04/22	1847/06/19
Henry, James	2	Ajax	Liverpool	England	1847/04/16	1847/06/23
Henry, John	3	Argo	Liverpool	England	1847/05/04	1847/06/12
Henry, John	7	Ajax	Liverpool	England	1847/04/16	1847/06/23
Henry, Lawrence	60	John Francis	Cork	Ireland	1847/04/10	1847/06/10
Henry, Margaret	11	Caithness-shire	Belfast	Ireland	1847/04/10	1847/06/12
Henry, Margaret	12	Erin's Queen	Liverpool	England	1847/06/01	1847/07/23
Henry, Mr.	80	Rosalinda	Belfast	Ireland	1847/06/22	1847/08/07
Henry, Neill		Sobraon	Liverpool	England	1847/05/08	1847/06/29
Henry, Patrick	4	Sobraon	Liverpool	England	1847/05/08	1847/06/29
Henry, Patrick	9	Erin's Queen	Liverpool	England	1847/06/01	1847/07/23
Henry, Patrick	26	Agnes	Cork	Ireland	1847/04/10	1847/06/10
Henry, Samuel	40	Lotus	Liverpool	England	1847/04/15	1847/06/24
Henry, Thomas	2	Sobraon	Liverpool	England	1847/05/08	1847/06/29
Henshaw, Michael	27	Greenock	Liverpool	England	1847/06/19	1847/07/29
Heron, Ann	11	Venilia	Limerick	Ireland	1847/05/28	1847/07/11
Heron, Mary	13	Venilia	Limerick	Ireland	1847/05/28	1847/07/11
Hession, Michael	26	Triton	Liverpool	England	1847/05/14	1847/07/24
Hetherington, Jane	2	Dykes	Sligo	Ireland	1847/04/23	1847/06/10
Hetherington, John	2	Dykes	Sligo	Ireland	1847/04/23	1847/06/10
Hetherington, Mary	34	Dykes	Sligo	Ireland	1847/04/23	1847/06/10
Hewitt, Ann		Tay	Liverpool	England	1847/05/22	1847/06/23
Hickey, Eliza	4	Bee	Cork	Ireland	1847/04/17	1847/06/12
Hickey, Eliza	4	Bee	Cork	Ireland	1847/04/17	1847/06/12
Hickey, Johanna	2	Bee	Cork	Ireland	1847/04/17	1847/06/12
Hickey, Johanna	5	Bee	Cork	Ireland	1847/04/17	1847/06/12

List of people who died on ships at sea or in quarantine at Grosse Île, in 1847

Name	Age	Vessel	Port	Country	Embarkation	Qc Arrival
Hickey, Michael	1	Medusa	Cork	Ireland	1847/06/03	1847/07/16
Hickey, Owen	40	Wakefield	Cork	Ireland	1847/05/28	1847/07/12
Higgins, Alice	7	Goliah	Liverpool	England	1847/05/21	1847/07/18
Higgins, Ann		Yorkshire	Liverpool	England	1847/06/09	1847/08/10
Higgins, Bryan	62	Tamarac	Liverpool	England	1847/05/26	1847/07/11
Higgins, Daniel	2	Covenanter	Cork	Ireland	1847/06/17	1847/08/09
Higgins, Daniel	21	Sir Henry Pottinger	Cork	Ireland	1847/05/29	1847/08/07
Higgins, Elijah	4	Goliah	Liverpool	England	1847/05/21	1847/07/18
Higgins, John		Emigrant	Liverpool	England	1847/08/11	1847/10/03
Higgins, Margaret	12	Saguenay	Cork	Ireland	1847/06/05	1847/08/22
Higgins, Margaret	35	Emigrant	Liverpool	England	1847/08/11	1847/10/03
Higgins, Mary	22	Jessie	Limerick	Ireland	1847/04/18	1847/06/26
Higgins, Mary Jane		Goliah	Liverpool	England	1847/05/21	1847/07/18
Higgins, Nancy	35	Triton	Liverpool	England	1847/05/14	1847/07/24
Higgins, Owen		Numa	Sligo	Ireland	1847/06/02	1847/07/27
Higgins, Patrick	14	Jessie	Limerick	Ireland	1847/04/18	1847/06/26
Higgins, Peter	40	Ann	Liverpool	England	1847/05/16	1847/06/30
Higgins, Robert	2	Yorkshire	Liverpool	England	1847/06/09	1847/08/10
Higgins, Thomas	4	Yorkshire	Liverpool	England	1847/06/09	1847/08/10
Hill, Catherine	60	John and Robert	Liverpool	England	1847/06/09	1847/08/06
Hill, Mrs.	60	John Munn	Liverpool	England	1847/06/16	1847/08/13
Hill, William	5	John Munn	Liverpool	England	1847/06/16	1847/08/13
Hilliard, Ann		Ajax	Liverpool	England	1847/04/16	1847/06/23
Hilliard, Eliza	3	Washington	Liverpool	England	1847/07/09	1847/08/26
Hilliard, Patrick	3	Washington	Liverpool	England	1847/07/09	1847/08/26
Hilliard, Robert	3	Marchioness of Abercorn	Londonderry	Ireland	1847/06/15	1847/08/05
Hinchy, Elizabeth	14	Progress	New Ross	Ireland	1847/05/05	1847/07/14
Hinchy, Judith	70	Colonist	New Ross	Ireland	1847/07/13	1847/08/29
Hoban, Ann	44	Larch	Sligo	Ireland	1847/07/11	1847/08/20
Hoban, William	17	Larch	Sligo	Ireland	1847/07/11	1847/08/20
Hodgins, Joseph	60	Odessa	Dublin	Ireland	1847/06/09	1847/08/09
Hodnett, Mary	26	Vesta	Limerick	Ireland	1847/06/21	1847/08/09
Hoey, Susan	15	Saguenay	Cork	Ireland	1847/06/05	1847/08/22
Hoey, William	46	Jessie	Limerick	Ireland	1847/04/18	1847/06/26
Hogan, Edmund	42	Asia	Cork	Ireland	1847/06/02	1847/07/27
Hogan, James		Alexander Stewart	Limerick	Ireland	1847/06/04	1847/07/28
Hogan, Nancy	40	Jessie	Limerick	Ireland	1847/04/18	1847/06/26
Hogan, Patrick	66	Albion	Limerick	Ireland	1847/04/19	1847/06/18
Hogan, Patrick		Greenock	Liverpool	England	1847/06/19	1847/07/29
Hogan, Thomas	24	Larch	Sligo	Ireland	1847/07/11	1847/08/20
Hogan, William	60	Lady Campbell	Dublin	Ireland	1847/06/03	1847/08/05
Holden, Bridget	25	Naomi	Liverpool	England	1847/06/15	1847/08/10
Holland, Ellen		Agnes	Cork	Ireland	1847/04/10	1847/06/10
Holland, Joseph	21	Lady Flora Hastings	Cork	Ireland	1847/05/11	1847/06/26
Holland, Margaret		Agnes	Cork	Ireland	1847/04/10	1847/06/10
Hollinger, Thomas	30	Lord Seaton	Belfast	Ireland	1847/04/12	1847/06/10
Holloway, Mary	60	Gilmour	Cork	Ireland	1847/04/24	1847/06/18
Holloway, Michael	18	Lady Flora Hastings	Cork	Ireland	1847/05/11	1847/06/26
Holly, Catherine	30	Scotland	Cork	Ireland	1847/04/13	1847/06/08
Holly, Catherine	2	Scotland	Cork	Ireland	1847/04/13	1847/06/08
Holly, James	2	Scotland	Cork	Ireland	1847/04/13	1847/06/08
Holly, James	2	Scotland	Cork	Ireland	1847/04/13	1847/06/08
Holly, Michael	29	Scotland	Cork	Ireland	1847/04/13	1847/06/08
Holly, Michael	2	Scotland	Cork	Ireland	1847/04/13	1847/06/08
Holmes, Catherine	28	Virginius	Liverpool	England	1847/05/28	1847/08/12
Holmes, Daniel	13	Sisters	Liverpool	England	1847/04/22	1847/06/20
Holmes, Daniel	50	Sisters	Liverpool	England	1847/04/22	1847/06/20
Holmes, Daniel	9	Sisters	Liverpool	England	1847/04/22	1847/06/20
Holmes, Edward	25	Virginius	Liverpool	England	1847/05/28	1847/08/12
Holmes, James	18	Bridgetown	Liverpool	England	1847/07/03	1847/08/29
Holmes, John	24	Sisters	Liverpool	England	1847/04/22	1847/06/20
Holmes, Mary	4	Virginius	Liverpool	England	1847/05/28	1847/08/12
Holmes, Michael	2	Virginius	Liverpool	England	1847/05/28	1847/08/12
Holmes, Mrs.	24	Rosalinda	Belfast	Ireland	1847/06/22	1847/08/07
Holmes, Patrick	20	Sisters	Liverpool	England	1847/04/22	1847/06/20
Holmes, William	25	John Munn	Liverpool	England	1847/06/16	1847/08/13
Homan, Mary		Corea	Liverpool	England	1847/07/02	1847/08/14
Honan, James	30	Covenanter	Cork	Ireland	1847/06/17	1847/08/09
Honan, John	35	Larch	Sligo	Ireland	1847/07/11	1847/08/20
Honan, Mary	6	Covenanter	Cork	Ireland	1847/06/17	1847/08/09
Hone, Bridget	75	Charles Walton	Killala	Ireland	1847/06/24	1847/08/05
Hone, Daniel	40	Bee	Cork	Ireland	1847/04/17	1847/06/12
Hone, J.	45	Bee	Cork	Ireland	1847/04/17	1847/06/12
Hone, Jemmy	1	Bee	Cork	Ireland	1847/04/17	1847/06/12
Hone, John	50	George	Liverpool	England	1847/04/13	1847/06/12
Hood, Elizabeth	44	Columbia	Sligo	Ireland	1847/05/01	1847/06/10
Hoolahan, Abraham	3	Ninian	Limerick	Ireland	1847/04/13	1847/06/12
Hooley, Ann	24	Thistle	Liverpool	England	1847/06/01	1847/07/18
Hooligan, Mary		Thistle	Liverpool	England	1847/06/01	1847/07/18
Hopkins, Bridget	40	Virginius	Liverpool	England	1847/05/28	1847/08/12
Hopkins, Bridget		Sisters	Liverpool	England	1847/04/22	1847/06/20
Hopkins, Catherine	3	Sisters	Liverpool	England	1847/04/22	1847/06/20
Hopkins, Edward	25	Virginius	Liverpool	England	1847/05/28	1847/08/12
Hopkins, Ellen	19	Triton	Liverpool	England	1847/05/14	1847/07/24
Hopkins, Frank	35	Rose	Liverpool	England	1847/04/19	1847/07/01
Hopkins, John	1	Rose	Liverpool	England	1847/04/19	1847/07/01
Hopkins, John	3	Rose	Liverpool	England	1847/04/19	1847/07/01
Hopkins, Margaret	24	Sisters	Liverpool	England	1847/04/22	1847/06/20
Hopkins, Margaret	1	Rose	Liverpool	England	1847/04/19	1847/07/01
Hopkins, Mary	6	Sisters	Liverpool	England	1847/04/22	1847/06/20
Hopkins, Michael	17	Sisters	Liverpool	England	1847/04/22	1847/06/20
Hopkins, Michael	50	Virginius	Liverpool	England	1847/05/28	1847/08/12
Hopkins, Nelly	37	Rose	Liverpool	England	1847/04/19	1847/07/01
Hopkins, Patrick	11	Sisters	Liverpool	England	1847/04/22	1847/06/20
Hopkins, Patrick	12	Rose	Liverpool	England	1847/04/19	1847/07/01
Hopkins, Patrick	42	Virginius	Liverpool	England	1847/05/28	1847/08/12
Horn, John	1	Free Trader	Liverpool	England	1847/06/22	1847/08/14
Horn, Michael		Free Trader	Liverpool	England	1847/06/22	1847/08/14
Horn, Michael	5	Free Trader	Liverpool	England	1847/06/22	1847/08/14
Horrigan, Ellen	2	Avon	Cork	Ireland	1847/05/19	1847/07/26
Horrigan, Ellen	25	Avon	Cork	Ireland	1847/05/19	1847/07/26
Horrigan, J.		Sir Henry Pottinger	Cork	Ireland	1847/05/29	1847/08/07
Hosty, Patrick	32	Sobraon	Liverpool	England	1847/05/08	1847/06/29
Howard, Mary	17	Broom	Liverpool	England	1847/06/13	1847/08/06
Howe, Elizabeth		Sobraon	Liverpool	England	1847/05/08	1847/06/29
Howe, Thomas	1	Sobraon	Liverpool	England	1847/05/08	1847/06/29
Howell, Edmund	4	Mail	Cork	Ireland	1847/04/25	1847/06/19
Howell, Robert	30	Mail	Cork	Ireland	1847/04/25	1847/06/19
Howley, Catherine	36	Marchioness of Breadalbane	Sligo	Ireland	1847/06/11	1847/08/12
Hoy, Cecily	22	Virginius	Liverpool	England	1847/05/28	1847/08/12
Hoy, Mary	16	Virginius	Liverpool	England	1847/05/28	1847/08/12
Hoy, Patrick	1	Sisters	Liverpool	England	1847/04/22	1847/06/20
Hoy, Peter	25	Virginius	Liverpool	England	1847/05/28	1847/08/12
Hubert, John	24	James Moran	Liverpool	England	1847/05/22	1847/07/11
Hucher, John C.	1	General Hewitt	Bremen	Germany	1847/07/22	1847/09/12
Hughes, Anthony	22	Bridgetown	Liverpool	England	1847/07/03	1847/08/29
Hughes, Bridget	3	Sarah	Liverpool	England	1847/05/29	1847/07/19
Hughes, Bridget	50	Bridgetown	Liverpool	England	1847/07/03	1847/08/29
Hughes, Catherine	11	John Bolton	Liverpool	England	1847/04/13	1847/06/10
Hughes, John	45	George	Liverpool	England	1847/04/13	1847/06/12
Hughes, Martin	40	Minerva	Galway	Ireland	1847/06/17	1847/08/14
Hughes, Mary	18	Bridgetown	Liverpool	England	1847/07/03	1847/08/29
Hughes, Mary	7	Champion	Liverpool	England	1847/07/13	1847/08/28
Hughes, Matthew	28	Marinus	Dublin	Ireland	1847/06/05	1847/08/13
Hughes, Patrick	7	George	Liverpool	England	1847/04/13	1847/06/12

List of people who died on ships at sea or in quarantine at Grosse Île, in 1847

Name	Age	Vessel	Port	Country	Embarkation	Qc Arrival
Hughes, Patrick	5	George	Liverpool	England	1847/04/13	1847/06/12
Hughes, Patrick	66	Royal Adelaide	Killala	Ireland	1847/06/09	1847/08/09
Hughes, Patrick	13	Bridgetown	Liverpool	England	1847/07/03	1847/08/29
Hughes, Patrick	11	Bridgetown	Liverpool	England	1847/07/03	1847/08/29
Hughes, Patrick	70	Tay	Sligo	Ireland	1847/05/05	1847/06/09
Hughes, Thomas	8	Bridgetown	Liverpool	England	1847/07/03	1847/08/29
Hurley, Ann	3	Ninian	Limerick	Ireland	1847/04/13	1847/06/12
Hurley, Bridget	30	Ninian	Limerick	Ireland	1847/04/13	1847/06/12
Hurley, Judith	3	Margrette	New Ross	Ireland	1847/05/02	1847/07/08
Hurley, Margaret	1	Ninian	Limerick	Ireland	1847/04/13	1847/06/12
Hurley, Mary	5	Ninian	Limerick	Ireland	1847/04/13	1847/06/12
Hurson, Alexander	2	Tamarac	Liverpool	England	1847/05/26	1847/07/11
Hussey, Thomas	3	Lord Ashburton	Liverpool	England	1847/09/13	1847/11/01
Hylan, Andrew	40	Champion	Liverpool	England	1847/07/13	1847/08/28
Hylan, Margaret	2	Champion	Liverpool	England	1847/07/13	1847/08/28
Hynes, Edward	24	Primrose	Limerick	Ireland	1847/04/07	1847/06/18
Hynes, Michael	1	Lotus	Liverpool	England	1847/04/15	1847/06/24
Hynes, Patrick	35	Lotus	Liverpool	England	1847/04/15	1847/06/24
Hynes, Patrick	2	Lotus	Liverpool	England	1847/04/15	1847/06/24
Ireland, Mary	2	Free Trader	Liverpool	England	1847/06/22	1847/08/14
Irvine, George	2	Yorkshire	Liverpool	England	1847/06/09	1847/08/10
Irvine, James	45	John Bolton	Liverpool	England	1847/04/13	1847/06/10
Irving, Grace	2	Yorkshire	Liverpool	England	1847/06/09	1847/08/10
Ivory, Margaret	3	John Francis	Cork	Ireland	1847/04/10	1847/06/10
Ivory, Patrick	10	John Francis	Cork	Ireland	1847/04/10	1847/06/10
Jack, Julia	25	Sir Henry Pottinger	Cork	Ireland	1847/05/29	1847/08/07
Jackle, Christiana	3	Golden Spring	London	England	1847/05/27	1847/07/13
Jackson, James	19	Goliah	Liverpool	England	1847/05/21	1847/07/18
Jackson, Patrick		Junior	Liverpool	England	1847/05/10	1847/07/03
Jacob, Ellen		Margaret	New Ross	Ireland	1847/05/19	1847/07/02
James, Martin	60	Colonist	New Ross	Ireland	1847/05/19	1847/08/29
Jamieson, James	24	Bridgetown	Liverpool	England	1847/07/03	1847/08/29
Jenkins, Donald	24	Independance	Belfast	Ireland	1847/05/23	1847/07/07
Jennings, Bridget		George	Liverpool	England	1847/04/13	1847/06/12
Jennings, Catherine	2	George	Liverpool	England	1847/04/13	1847/06/12
Jennings, Catherine	4	Tay	Liverpool	England	1847/05/22	1847/06/23
Jennings, Edward	8	George	Liverpool	England	1847/04/13	1847/06/12
Johnson, Owen	20	Rose	Liverpool	England	1847/04/19	1847/07/01
Johnson, William	38	Haubet	Hamburg	Germany	1847/07/02	1847/09/01
Johnston, Alexander	3	Sir Robert Peel	Liverpool	England	1847/07/26	1847/09/19
Johnston, Gunild	7	Haubet	Hamburg	Germany	1847/07/02	1847/09/01
Johnston, John	2	Haubet	Hamburg	Germany	1847/07/02	1847/09/01
Johnston, Juri	10	Haubet	Hamburg	Germany	1847/07/02	1847/09/01
Johnston, M.A.	4	Rosalinda	Belfast	Ireland	1847/06/22	1847/08/07
Johnston, Quile		Haubet	Hamburg	Germany	1847/07/02	1847/09/01
Johnston, Thomas	25	Erin's Queen	Liverpool	England	1847/06/01	1847/07/23
Jolly, Catherine	6	Eliza Caroline	Liverpool	England	1847/05/03	1847/06/14
Jones, Eliza	2	Argo	Liverpool	England	1847/05/04	1847/06/12
Jones, James	2	Sir Henry Pottinger	Belfast	Ireland	1847/07/09	1847/08/29
Jones, John		Sir Henry Pottinger	Belfast	Ireland	1847/07/09	1847/08/29
Jones, John	2	Goliah	Liverpool	England	1847/05/21	1847/07/18
Jones, John	1	Sobraon	Liverpool	England	1847/05/08	1847/06/29
Jones, Mary	31	Argo	Liverpool	England	1847/05/04	1847/06/12
Jones, Nancy		Goliah	Liverpool	England	1847/05/21	1847/07/18
Jordan, Ann	7	Rose	Liverpool	England	1847/04/19	1847/07/01
Jordan, Mrs.	52	Thistle	Liverpool	England	1847/06/01	1847/07/18
Joy, Garrett	25	Sir Henry Pottinger	Cork	Ireland	1847/05/29	1847/08/07
Joyce, Patrick	30	Sobraon	Liverpool	England	1847/05/08	1847/06/29
Joynt, Mary	1	Lady Milton	Liverpool	England	1847/05/05	1847/06/26
Judge, Margaret	3	Marchioness of Breadalbane	Sligo	Ireland	1847/06/11	1847/08/12
Judge, Margaret	3	Marchioness of Breadalbane	Sligo	Ireland	1847/06/11	1847/08/12
Judge, Patrick	4	John Bolton	Liverpool	England	1847/04/13	1847/06/10
Judge, Thomas	62	Asia	Cork	Ireland	1847/06/02	1847/07/27
Judge, Thomas		Sisters	Liverpool	Ireland	1847/04/22	1847/06/20
Keady, Ellen	13	Margrette	New Ross	Ireland	1847/05/02	1847/07/08
Keady, Mary		Margrette	New Ross	Ireland	1847/05/02	1847/07/08
Keady, Thomas	28	Agnes	Cork	Ireland	1847/04/10	1847/06/10
Keady, Winford	70	Douce Davie	Sligo	Ireland	1847/08/11	1847/09/30
Kean, Ann	1	New York Packet	Liverpool	England	1847/04/24	1847/06/29
Kean, Hugh	35	Ganges	Liverpool	England	1847/06/16	1847/08/21
Kean, Thomas	4	Wolfville	Sligo	Ireland	1847/04/25	1847/06/10
Kearney, Alexander	1	Odessa	Dublin	Ireland	1847/06/09	1847/08/09
Kearney, Allison	2	Odessa	Dublin	Ireland	1847/06/09	1847/08/09
Kearney, Bridget	72	Odessa	Dublin	Ireland	1847/06/09	1847/08/09
Kearney, Francis	16	Sir Henry Pottinger	Cork	Ireland	1847/05/29	1847/08/07
Kearney, Honora	20	Yorkshire	Liverpool	England	1847/06/09	1847/08/10
Kearney, James	8	John Munn	Liverpool	England	1847/06/16	1847/08/13
Kearney, John	40	John Munn	Liverpool	England	1847/06/16	1847/08/13
Kearney, John	9	John Munn	Liverpool	England	1847/06/16	1847/08/13
Kearney, John	50	Sir Henry Pottinger	Cork	Ireland	1847/05/29	1847/08/07
Kearney, Mary	37	Virginius	Liverpool	England	1847/05/28	1847/08/12
Kearney, Mary	22	Odessa	Dublin	Ireland	1847/06/09	1847/08/09
Kearney, Michael	2	Yorkshire	Liverpool	England	1847/06/09	1847/08/10
Kearney, Patrick	54	Dominica	Cork	Ireland	1847/05/01	1847/06/14
Kearney, Patrick	50	Sarah	Liverpool	England	1847/05/29	1847/07/19
Kearney, William	6	John Munn	Liverpool	England	1847/06/16	1847/08/13
Kearns, Catherine	3	Admiral	Waterford	Ireland	1847/06/01	1847/07/07
Kearns, Catherine	30	Larch	Sligo	Ireland	1847/07/11	1847/08/20
Kearns, Mary	65	Larch	Sligo	Ireland	1847/07/11	1847/08/20
Kearns, Matilda	36	Ganges	Liverpool	England	1847/06/16	1847/08/21
Kearns, Mrs.	45	Larch	Sligo	Ireland	1847/07/11	1847/08/20
Kearns, Patrick	1	Sisters	Liverpool	England	1847/04/22	1847/06/20
Kearns, Thomas	2	Larch	Sligo	Ireland	1847/07/11	1847/08/20
Keating, Mary	20	Herald	Dublin	Ireland	1847/05/20	1847/06/26
Keating, Mary	75	Herald	Dublin	Ireland	1847/05/20	1847/06/26
Keating, Patrick	1	Ganges	Liverpool	England	1847/06/16	1847/08/21
Keaveny, Ann	3	Ajax	Liverpool	England	1847/04/16	1847/06/23
Keefe, Ann	2	Lady Flora Hastings	Cork	Ireland	1847/05/11	1847/06/26
Keefe, Bridget	70	Progress	New Ross	Ireland	1847/05/05	1847/07/14
Keefe, Bridget	6	Lady Flora Hastings	Cork	Ireland	1847/05/11	1847/06/26
Keefe, Cornelius	48	Lady Flora Hastings	Cork	Ireland	1847/05/11	1847/06/26
Keefe, Cornelius	1	Lady Flora Hastings	Cork	Ireland	1847/05/11	1847/06/26
Keefe, Cornelius		Goliah	Liverpool	England	1847/05/21	1847/07/18
Keefe, Johanna	30	Avon	Cork	Ireland	1847/05/19	1847/07/26
Keefe, John	4	Lady Flora Hastings	Cork	Ireland	1847/05/11	1847/06/26
Keefe, Margaret	23	Scotland	Cork	Ireland	1847/04/13	1847/06/08
Keefe, Margaret	28	Avon	Cork	Ireland	1847/05/19	1847/07/26
Keefe, Mary	3	Avon	Cork	Ireland	1847/05/19	1847/07/26
Keefe, Mary	1	Avon	Cork	Ireland	1847/05/19	1847/07/26
Keefe, Mrs.	40	Scotland	Cork	Ireland	1847/04/13	1847/06/08
Keefe, Owen	1	Avon	Cork	Ireland	1847/05/19	1847/07/26
Keefe, Owen		Avon	Cork	Ireland	1847/05/19	1847/07/26
Keenan, Ellenor	3	Allan Kerr	Sligo	Ireland	1847/06/23	1847/08/04
Keenan, James	3	Sarah	Liverpool	England	1847/05/29	1847/07/19
Keenan, Margaret	35	Sarah	Liverpool	England	1847/05/29	1847/07/19
Keenan, Mary	35	Rose	Liverpool	England	1847/04/19	1847/07/01
Keenan, Peter	40	Sarah	Liverpool	England	1847/05/29	1847/07/19
Keily, Mary	78	Herald	Dublin	Ireland	1847/05/20	1847/06/26
Keith, John		Goliah	Liverpool	England	1847/05/21	1847/07/18
Kelleher, Catherine	12	Saguenay	Cork	Ireland	1847/06/05	1847/08/22

LIST OF PEOPLE WHO DIED ON SHIPS AT SEA OR IN QUARANTINE AT GROSSE ÎLE, IN 1847

Name	Age	Vessel	Port	Country	Embarkation	Qc Arrival
Kelleher, Ellen	30	Sir Henry Pottinger	Cork	Ireland	1847/05/29	1847/08/07
Kelleher, J.		Sir Henry Pottinger	Cork	Ireland	1847/05/29	1847/08/07
Kelleher, J.		Sir Henry Pottinger	Cork	Ireland	1847/05/29	1847/08/07
Kelleher, Jerry	27	Sir Henry Pottinger	Cork	Ireland	1847/05/29	1847/08/07
Kelleher, John	50	Sir Henry Pottinger	Cork	Ireland	1847/05/29	1847/08/07
Kelleher, John	16	Saguenay	Cork	Ireland	1847/06/05	1847/08/22
Kelleher, Margaret	20	Sir Henry Pottinger	Cork	Ireland	1847/05/29	1847/08/07
Kelleher, Mary	4	Sir Henry Pottinger	Cork	Ireland	1847/05/29	1847/08/07
Kelleher, Mary	10	Thompson	Sligo	Ireland	1847/05/05	1847/06/14
Kelleher, Patrick	1	Sisters	Liverpool	England	1847/04/22	1847/06/20
Kelleher, Patrick	21	Goliah	Liverpool	England	1847/05/21	1847/07/18
Kelly, Ann		Naomi	Liverpool	England	1847/06/15	1847/08/10
Kelly, Ann M.	13	George	Liverpool	England	1847/04/13	1847/06/12
Kelly, Bridget	50	Avon	Cork	Ireland	1847/05/19	1847/07/26
Kelly, Bryan	40	Virginius	Liverpool	England	1847/05/28	1847/08/12
Kelly, Catherine	18	Wolfville	Sligo	Ireland	1847/04/25	1847/06/10
Kelly, Catherine	50	Virginius	Liverpool	England	1847/05/28	1847/08/12
Kelly, Catherine		Elliotts	Dublin	Ireland	1847/05/14	1847/06/30
Kelly, Catherine	37	Naomi	Liverpool	England	1847/06/15	1847/08/10
Kelly, Catherine	36	Naomi	Liverpool	England	1847/06/15	1847/08/10
Kelly, Daniel	2	Henrietta Mary	Cork	Ireland	1847/08/18	1847/09/29
Kelly, Denis	10	John Munn	Liverpool	England	1847/06/16	1847/08/13
Kelly, Edward	2	Rose	Liverpool	England	1847/04/19	1847/07/01
Kelly, Ellen	50	Lord Ashburton	Liverpool	England	1847/09/13	1847/11/01
Kelly, Henry		Virginius	Liverpool	England	1847/05/28	1847/08/12
Kelly, James	1	Margrette	New Ross	Ireland	1847/05/02	1847/07/08
Kelly, James	41	Ajax	Liverpool	England	1847/04/16	1847/06/23
Kelly, John	2	Triton	Liverpool	England	1847/05/14	1847/07/24
Kelly, John	2	Ganges	Liverpool	England	1847/06/16	1847/08/21
Kelly, Judith	23	Ajax	Liverpool	England	1847/04/16	1847/06/23
Kelly, Judith	24	Ajax	Liverpool	England	1847/04/16	1847/06/23
Kelly, Margaret	62	Diamond	Bremerhaven	Germany	1847/06/08	1847/07/31
Kelly, Margaret		Greenock	Liverpool	England	1847/06/19	1847/07/29
Kelly, Martin	2	Washington	Liverpool	England	1847/07/09	1847/08/26
Kelly, Mary	32	Christiana	Londonderry	Ireland	1847/04/08	1847/06/10
Kelly, Mary	5	Virginius	Liverpool	England	1847/05/28	1847/08/12
Kelly, Mary	30	Henrietta Mary	Cork	Ireland	1847/08/18	1847/09/29
Kelly, Mary	24	Ajax	Liverpool	England	1847/04/16	1847/06/23
Kelly, Mary	3	Elliotts	Dublin	Ireland	1847/05/14	1847/06/30
Kelly, Mary	2	Alert	Waterford	Ireland	1847/06/05	1847/07/15
Kelly, Mary		Corea	Liverpool	England	1847/07/02	1847/08/14
Kelly, Matthew	2	Sesostris	Londonderry	Ireland	1847/05/14	1847/06/24
Kelly, Matthew		Herald	Dublin	Ireland	1847/05/20	1847/06/26
Kelly, Matthew	4	Wolfville	Sligo	Ireland	1847/04/25	1847/06/10
Kelly, Michael	7	Dykes	Sligo	Ireland	1847/04/23	1847/06/10
Kelly, Nora	24	Gilmour	Cork	Ireland	1847/04/24	1847/06/18
Kelly, Patrick	25	John Bell	New Ross	Ireland	1847/05/10	1847/06/29
Kelly, Patrick	24	Virginius	Liverpool	England	1847/05/28	1847/08/12
Kelly, Peter	3	Margrette	New Ross	Ireland	1847/05/02	1847/07/08
Kelly, Peter	14	Rose	Liverpool	England	1847/04/19	1847/07/01
Kelly, Thomas	2	Wolfville	Sligo	Ireland	1847/04/25	1847/06/10
Kelly, Thomas	2	Rose	Liverpool	England	1847/04/19	1847/07/01
Kelly, Thomas	5	Triton	Liverpool	England	1847/05/14	1847/07/24
Kelly, Thomas		Triton	Liverpool	England	1847/05/14	1847/07/24
Kelly, Timothy	3	John Munn	Liverpool	England	1847/06/16	1847/08/13
Kelly, William	1	Scotland	Cork	Ireland	1847/04/13	1847/06/08
Kelly, William	34	Scotland	Cork	Ireland	1847/04/13	1847/06/08
Kelly, Winford	45	Virginius	Liverpool	England	1847/05/28	1847/08/12
Kelsey, Catherine		City of Derry	London	England	1847/05/23	1847/07/04
Kenelly, Margaret	2	Agnes	Cork	Ireland	1847/04/10	1847/06/10
Kenelly, Mary	1	Agnes	Cork	Ireland	1847/04/10	1847/06/10
Kenna, Johanna		Louisa	Limerick	Ireland	1847/05/08	1847/06/25
Kenna, Johanna		Jessie	Limerick	Ireland	1847/04/18	1847/06/26
Kenna, Michael	25	Bee	Cork	Ireland	1847/04/17	1847/06/12
Kenneally, Bridget	5	Aberdeen	Liverpool	England	1847/05/01	1847/06/13
Kenneally, Helen	30	Agnes	Cork	Ireland	1847/04/10	1847/06/10
Kenneally, Margaret	4	Alexander Stewart	Limerick	Ireland	1847/06/04	1847/07/28
Kennedy, Bridget	5	Araminta	Liverpool	England	1847/05/01	1847/06/20
Kennedy, Bridget	1	Mary	Sligo	Ireland	1847/05/24	1847/07/27
Kennedy, Catherine	9	Tay	Liverpool	England	1847/05/22	1847/06/23
Kennedy, Daniel	25	Gilmour	Cork	Ireland	1847/04/24	1847/06/18
Kennedy, Darby	50	Bridgetown	Liverpool	England	1847/07/03	1847/08/29
Kennedy, Dora	2	John Munn	Liverpool	England	1847/06/16	1847/08/13
Kennedy, Honora		Royal Adelaide	Killala	Ireland	1847/06/09	1847/08/09
Kennedy, Johanna	2	Ninian	Limerick	Ireland	1847/04/13	1847/06/12
Kennedy, John		Sisters	Liverpool	England	1847/04/22	1847/06/20
Kennedy, Julia	45	Bridgetown	Liverpool	England	1847/07/03	1847/08/29
Kennedy, Margaret	3	Lord Seaton	Belfast	Ireland	1847/04/12	1847/06/10
Kennedy, Mary	5	Wolfville	Sligo	Ireland	1847/04/25	1847/06/10
Kennedy, Mary	26	Sir Henry Pottinger	Cork	Ireland	1847/05/29	1847/08/07
Kennedy, Mary	18	Saguenay	Cork	Ireland	1847/06/05	1847/08/22
Kennedy, Mrs.	56	Manchester	Liverpool	England	1847/06/05	1847/07/17
Kennedy, Patrick	1	Sir Robert Peel	Liverpool	England	1847/07/26	1847/09/19
Kennedy, Robert	2	Rosalinda	Belfast	Ireland	1847/06/22	1847/08/07
Kennedy, Robert	2	Rosalinda	Belfast	Ireland	1847/06/22	1847/08/07
Kennedy, Thomas		Ninian	Limerick	Ireland	1847/04/13	1847/06/12
Kennedy, Thomas	19	Sir Henry Pottinger	Cork	Ireland	1847/05/29	1847/08/07
Kennedy, Thomas	5	Columbia	Sligo	Ireland	1847/05/01	1847/06/10
Kenny, Catherine	2	Wolfville	Sligo	Ireland	1847/04/25	1847/06/10
Kenny, Edmond	43	Scotland	Cork	Ireland	1847/04/13	1847/06/08
Kenny, Francis	2	Agamemnon	Liverpool	England	1847/06/24	1847/07/31
Kenny, Margaret	50	George	Liverpool	England	1847/04/13	1847/06/12
Kenny, Michael	55	George	Liverpool	England	1847/04/13	1847/06/12
Kenny, Michael	1	Aberdeen	Liverpool	England	1847/05/01	1847/06/13
Kenny, Michael	1	Araminta	Liverpool	England	1847/05/01	1847/06/20
Kenny, Thomas	10	Argo	Liverpool	England	1847/05/04	1847/06/12
Keogh, Patrick	30	Saguenay	Cork	Ireland	1847/06/05	1847/08/22
Keogh, William		Margaret	New Ross	Ireland	1847/05/19	1847/07/02
Keoghan, Michael		Achsah	Limerick	Ireland	1847/05/11	1847/06/23
Keon, Ann	4	Wolfville	Sligo	Ireland	1847/04/25	1847/06/10
Keon, Miles	40	Rose	Liverpool	England	1847/04/19	1847/07/01
Keribel, Johann		Diamond	Bremerhaven	Germany	1847/06/08	1847/07/31
Kerin, John	50	Mary	Sligo	Ireland	1847/05/24	1847/07/27
Kernan, Catherine	20	Ayrshire	Newry	Ireland	1847/07/04	1847/08/19
Kernan, Margaret	23	Sir Henry Pottinger	Cork	Ireland	1847/05/29	1847/08/07
Kernan, Mary		Ayrshire	Newry	Ireland	1847/07/04	1847/08/19
Kernan, Mary	28	Sir Henry Pottinger	Cork	Ireland	1847/05/29	1847/08/07
Kerovan, Joseph	2	Herald	Dublin	Ireland	1847/05/20	1847/06/26
Kerr, Eliza	17	Larch	Sligo	Ireland	1847/07/11	1847/08/20
Kerr, Helen	3	Larch	Sligo	Ireland	1847/07/11	1847/08/20
Kerr, Henry	3	Marchioness of Abercorn	Londonderry	Ireland	1847/06/15	1847/08/05
Kerr, James	24	Bridgetown	Liverpool	England	1847/07/03	1847/08/29
Kerr, John		Maria and Elizabeth	Liverpool	England	1847/05/06	1847/06/24
Kerr, Margaret	47	Sisters	Liverpool	England	1847/04/22	1847/06/20
Kerr, Robert	3	Sisters	Liverpool	England	1847/04/22	1847/06/20
Kerr, Samuel	50	Sisters	Liverpool	England	1847/04/22	1847/06/20
Kerr, Sarah	7	Larch	Sligo	Ireland	1847/07/11	1847/08/20
Kerr, William	56	Larch	Sligo	Ireland	1847/07/11	1847/08/20
Kerry, Patrick	38	Argo	Liverpool	England	1847/05/04	1847/06/12
Keyes, Eliza A.	2	Rosalinda	Belfast	Ireland	1847/06/22	1847/08/07

LIST OF PEOPLE WHO DIED ON SHIPS AT SEA OR IN QUARANTINE AT GROSSE ÎLE, IN 1847

Name	Age	Vessel	Port	Country	Embarkation	Qc Arrival
Keyes, James	18	Saguenay	Cork	Ireland	1847/06/05	1847/08/22
Keyes, Joseph	5	Manchester	Liverpool	England	1847/06/05	1847/07/17
Keyes, Margaret	30	Scotland	Cork	Ireland	1847/04/13	1847/06/08
Keyes, Patrick	50	Manchester	Liverpool	England	1847/06/05	1847/07/17
Keyes, Samuel	7	Yorkshire	Liverpool	England	1847/06/09	1847/08/10
Keyes, Thomas	3	Princess Royal	Liverpool	England	1847/05/10	1847/06/16
Kidd, Alexander		Junior	Liverpool	England	1847/05/10	1847/07/03
Kilbane, Michael	2	Agamemnon	Liverpool	England	1847/06/24	1847/07/31
Kilbane, Michael	10	George	Liverpool	England	1847/04/13	1847/06/12
Kilgallon, John	2	Dykes	Sligo	Ireland	1847/04/23	1847/06/10
Kilgallon, Thomas	34	Dykes	Sligo	Ireland	1847/04/23	1847/06/10
Kilkelly, Matthew	40	Wolfville	Sligo	Ireland	1847/04/25	1847/06/10
Kilkenny, Thomas		Marchioness of Bute	Belfast	Ireland	1847/06/10	1847/07/31
Killeen, Bridget	9	Lotus	Liverpool	England	1847/04/15	1847/06/24
Kilmartin, Bridget	6	John Francis	Cork	Ireland	1847/04/10	1847/06/10
Kilpatrick, Thomas	1	Sobraon	Liverpool	England	1847/05/08	1847/06/29
Kimble, John		Greenock	Liverpool	England	1847/06/19	1847/07/29
Kinahan, Sarah	20	Wellington	Liverpool	England	1847/07/29	1847/09/20
Kinane, Isabella	2	Euclid	Glasgow	Scotland	1847/06/01	1847/07/29
Kinane, Richard	45	Abbotsford	Dublin	Ireland	1847/04/23	1847/06/21
King, Ellen	18	Sir Henry Pottinger	Cork	Ireland	1847/05/29	1847/08/07
King, James	3	Eliza Caroline	Liverpool	England	1847/05/03	1847/06/14
King, Michael	55	Margaret	New Ross	Ireland	1847/05/19	1847/07/02
Kingle, Anthony	6	Juliet	London	England	1847/07/03	1847/08/28
Kingston, Ann	1	Wellington	Liverpool	England	1847/07/29	1847/09/20
Kingston, Ernest	36	Jessie	Cork	Ireland	1847/06/03	1847/07/24
Kingston, James	6	Lady Flora Hastings	Cork	Ireland	1847/05/11	1847/06/26
Kingston, James	3	Lady Flora Hastings	Cork	Ireland	1847/05/11	1847/06/26
Kingston, John	23	Wellington	Liverpool	England	1847/07/29	1847/09/20
Kingston, Mary	9	Jessie	Cork	Ireland	1847/06/03	1847/07/24
Kingston, Richard	43	Jessie	Cork	Ireland	1847/06/03	1847/07/24
Kingston, Richard	43	Jessie	Cork	Ireland	1847/06/03	1847/07/24
Kingston, Richard		Jessie	Cork	Ireland	1847/06/03	1847/07/24
Kingston, Samuel	7	Jessie	Cork	Ireland	1847/06/03	1847/07/24
Kinighan, Thomas	2	Rose	Liverpool	England	1847/04/19	1847/07/01
Kiniry, Margaret		Margrette	New Ross	Ireland	1847/05/02	1847/07/08
Kinnear, Ann	2	Aberdeen	Liverpool	England	1847/05/01	1847/06/13
Kinnear, Matthew	4	Free Trader	Liverpool	England	1847/06/22	1847/08/14
Kinnear, Richard	2	Free Trader	Liverpool	England	1847/06/22	1847/08/14
Kinnon, Ann	18	Araminta	Liverpool	England	1847/05/01	1847/06/20
Kinsella, Mary		John Bell	New Ross	Ireland	1847/05/10	1847/06/29
Kirby, Eliza	16	Gilmour	Cork	Ireland	1847/04/24	1847/06/18
Kirby, J.		Sir Henry Pottinger	Cork	Ireland	1847/05/29	1847/08/07
Kirby, James	30	Sir Henry Pottinger	Cork	Ireland	1847/05/29	1847/08/07
Kirby, John		Sir Henry Pottinger	Cork	Ireland	1847/05/29	1847/08/07
Kirby, John		Pursuit	Liverpool	England	1847/05/04	1847/06/23
Kirby, John	60	Scotland	Cork	Ireland	1847/04/13	1847/06/08
Kirby, Mary	11	Gilmour	Cork	Ireland	1847/04/24	1847/06/18
Kirrane, John	3	Bridgetown	Liverpool	England	1847/07/03	1847/08/29
Kirsley, Jacob	1	Juliet	London	England	1847/07/03	1847/08/28
Kirwin, John	16	Saguenay	Cork	Ireland	1847/06/05	1847/08/22
Kirwin, Mary	16	Colonist	New Ross	Ireland	1847/07/13	1847/08/29
Kirwin, Michael	60	Saguenay	Cork	Ireland	1847/06/05	1847/08/22
Knight, James	1	Goliah	Liverpool	England	1847/05/21	1847/07/18
Knox, James	4	Greenock	Liverpool	England	1847/06/19	1847/07/29
Knox, Maria		Greenock	Liverpool	England	1847/06/19	1847/07/29
Krugen, Caroline		Leontine	Bremen	Germany	1847/05/28	1847/07/28
Kutehinmuster, Frederick	1	Haubet	Hamburg	Germany	1847/07/02	1847/09/01
Kyle, Eliza	8	Christiana	Londonderry	Ireland	1847/04/08	1847/06/10

Name	Age	Vessel	Port	Country	Embarkation	Qc Arrival
Kyle, Joseph	1	Christiana	Londonderry	Ireland	1847/04/08	1847/06/10
Kyle, Robert	13	Christiana	Londonderry	Ireland	1847/04/08	1847/06/10
Kyne, Christiana	8	Christiana	Londonderry	Ireland	1847/04/08	1847/06/10
Lacey, Margaret	30	Sisters	Liverpool	England	1847/04/22	1847/06/20
Laffey, William		Agnes	Cork	Ireland	1847/04/10	1847/06/10
Lahiff, Catherine	10	Saguenay	Cork	Ireland	1847/06/05	1847/08/22
Lahiff, Michael	8	Saguenay	Cork	Ireland	1847/06/05	1847/08/22
Lahiff, Norry	15	Saguenay	Cork	Ireland	1847/06/05	1847/08/22
Lally, Edward	50	Virginius	Liverpool	England	1847/05/28	1847/08/12
Lally, James	40	Bridgetown	Liverpool	England	1847/07/03	1847/08/29
Lally, Mary	23	Virginius	Liverpool	England	1847/05/28	1847/08/12
Lally, Nancy	13	Virginius	Liverpool	England	1847/05/28	1847/08/12
Lambert, Thomas	24	Lady Flora Hastings	Cork	Ireland	1847/05/11	1847/06/26
Lane, James	22	Sir Henry Pottinger	Cork	Ireland	1847/05/29	1847/08/07
Lane, Thomas	25	Caithness-shire	Belfast	Ireland	1847/04/10	1847/06/12
Lang, Martin	2	Golden Spring	London	England	1847/05/27	1847/07/13
Langton, Elizabeth	6	Scotland	Cork	Ireland	1847/04/13	1847/06/08
Langton, Maurice	3	Scotland	Cork	Ireland	1847/04/13	1847/06/08
Lanigan, Bridget	40	Camillia	Sligo	Ireland	1847/05/19	1847/07/07
Lanigan, Bridget	40	Energy	Limerick	Ireland	1847/05/28	1847/07/05
Lanigan, Jessie		Sobraon	Liverpool	England	1847/05/08	1847/06/29
Lanigan, P.	7	Triton	Liverpool	England	1847/05/14	1847/07/24
Lanigan, Patrick	60	Ganges	Liverpool	England	1847/06/16	1847/08/21
Lanigan, Peter	30	Triton	Liverpool	England	1847/05/14	1847/07/24
Lanigan, Peter	3	Triton	Liverpool	England	1847/05/14	1847/07/24
Lanigan, Thomas	19	Agamemnon	Liverpool	England	1847/06/24	1847/07/31
Lannigan, Silbry	5	Triton	Liverpool	England	1847/05/14	1847/07/24
Larkin, Bridget	18	Avon	Cork	Ireland	1847/05/19	1847/07/26
Larkin, Catherine	60	Herald	Dublin	Ireland	1847/05/20	1847/06/26
Larkin, James	60	Avon	Cork	Ireland	1847/05/19	1847/07/26
Larkin, John		Jane Black	Limerick	Ireland	1847/08/10	1847/09/17
Larkin, Mary	60	Avon	Cork	Ireland	1847/05/19	1847/07/26
Larkin, Michael	20	Herald	Dublin	Ireland	1847/05/20	1847/06/26
Larkin, Thomas	35	Larch	Sligo	Ireland	1847/07/11	1847/08/20
Lashbrook, J.	3	Bridgetown	Liverpool	England	1847/07/03	1847/08/29
Laughlin, Edward	6	Agnes	Cork	Ireland	1847/04/10	1847/06/10
Laughlin, James	26	Gilmour	Cork	Ireland	1847/04/24	1847/06/18
Laughlin, Judith	2	John Bolton	Liverpool	England	1847/04/13	1847/06/10
Laughlin, M.	14	Agnes	Cork	Ireland	1847/04/10	1847/06/10
Laughlin, William	13	John Bolton	Liverpool	England	1847/04/13	1847/06/10
Lavelle, Patrick	6	Larch	Sligo	Ireland	1847/07/11	1847/08/20
Lavelle, Sarah	76	Royal Adelaide	Killala	Ireland	1847/06/09	1847/08/09
Lavin, Henry		Aberdeen	Liverpool	England	1847/05/01	1847/06/13
Lavin, Mary	40	John Bolton	Liverpool	England	1847/04/13	1847/06/10
Lavin, Mary	6	John Bolton	Liverpool	England	1847/04/13	1847/06/10
Lawler, Andrew	70	Herald	Dublin	Ireland	1847/05/20	1847/06/26
Lawlor, Bridget	25	Lady Campbell	Dublin	Ireland	1847/06/03	1847/08/05
Lawlor, Mrs.	52	Lady Campbell	Dublin	Ireland	1847/06/03	1847/08/05
Lawlor, N.	50	Lady Campbell	Dublin	Ireland	1847/06/03	1847/08/05
Lawrence, John	30	Columbia	Sligo	Ireland	1847/05/01	1847/06/10
Lawson, Andrew		Rose	Liverpool	England	1847/04/19	1847/07/01
Lawson, Henry	3	Sobraon	Liverpool	England	1847/05/08	1847/06/29
Lawton, Elizabeth	3	Scotland	Cork	Ireland	1847/04/13	1847/06/08
Lawton, Sarah	2	Odessa	Dublin	Ireland	1847/06/09	1847/08/09
Lean, M.	38	Bee	Cork	Ireland	1847/04/17	1847/06/12
Leary, Catherine	13	Scotland	Cork	Ireland	1847/04/13	1847/06/08
Leary, Catherine	2	Scotland	Cork	Ireland	1847/04/13	1847/06/08
Leary, Dennis	28	Thistle	Liverpool	England	1847/06/01	1847/07/18
Leary, Ellen		Eliza Caroline	Liverpool	England	1847/05/03	1847/06/14
Leary, Ellen	50	Asia	Cork	Ireland	1847/06/02	1847/07/27
Leary, James	25	Asia	Cork	Ireland	1847/06/02	1847/07/27
Leary, Margaret	72	Asia	Cork	Ireland	1847/06/02	1847/07/27
Leary, Mary	1	Bee	Cork	Ireland	1847/04/17	1847/06/12
Leary, P.	25	Emily	Cork	Ireland	1847/05/12	1847/07/06

List of people who died on ships at sea or in quarantine at Grosse Île, in 1847

Name	Age	Vessel	Port	Country	Embarkation	Qc Arrival
Leary, Thomas		Eliza Caroline	Liverpool	England	1847/05/03	1847/06/14
Leddy, Mary		Emigrant	Liverpool	England	1847/08/11	1847/10/03
Leddy, Robert	45	Emigrant	Liverpool	England	1847/08/11	1847/10/03
Lee, Mary	5	Julius Caesar	Liverpool	England	1847/07/13	1847/09/05
Lehan, Ellen		Avon	Cork	Ireland	1847/05/19	1847/07/26
Lehan, Johanna	30	Avon	Cork	Ireland	1847/05/19	1847/07/26
Lehan, Michael	26	Jessie	Cork	Ireland	1847/06/03	1847/07/24
Lenaghan, James	24	Sir Henry Pottinger	Cork	Ireland	1847/05/29	1847/08/07
Lenechan, Ellen	30	Wakefield	Cork	Ireland	1847/05/28	1847/07/12
Lenihan, Denis	24	Urania	Cork	Ireland	1847/04/09	1847/06/10
Lennane, Andrew	50	Rose	Liverpool	England	1847/04/19	1847/07/01
Lennane, Michael	38	Bee	Cork	Ireland	1847/04/17	1847/06/12
Lennane, Nancy	25	Bee	Cork	Ireland	1847/04/17	1847/06/12
Lennane, Patrick	1	Virgilia	Liverpool	England	1847/07/22	1847/09/20
Lennon, Ann	3	Erin's Queen	Liverpool	England	1847/06/01	1847/07/23
Lennon, Bryan	40	Virginius	Liverpool	England	1847/05/28	1847/08/12
Lennon, Darby	5	Virginius	Liverpool	England	1847/05/28	1847/08/12
Lennon, George	19	Wakefield	Cork	Ireland	1847/05/28	1847/07/12
Lennon, Judith	35	Ann	Liverpool	England	1847/05/16	1847/06/30
Lennon, Leonard	60	Triton	Liverpool	England	1847/05/14	1847/07/24
Lennon, Mary	20	Virginius	Liverpool	England	1847/05/28	1847/08/12
Lennon, Mary	65	John Jardine	Liverpool	England	1847/06/04	1847/07/16
Lennon, Michael	50	John Jardine	Liverpool	England	1847/06/04	1847/07/16
Lennon, Michael	30	Erin's Queen	Liverpool	England	1847/06/01	1847/07/23
Lennon, Patrick	75	Rose	Liverpool	England	1847/04/19	1847/07/01
Lennon, Susan	50	Erin's Queen	Liverpool	England	1847/06/01	1847/07/23
Lennon, William	81	Wakefield	Cork	Ireland	1847/05/28	1847/07/12
Leonard, Andrew	4	Greenock	Liverpool	England	1847/06/19	1847/07/29
Leonard, Francis	24	Triton	Liverpool	England	1847/05/14	1847/07/24
Leonard, John	9	Herald	Dublin	Ireland	1847/05/20	1847/06/26
Leonard, Margaret	1	Herald	Dublin	Ireland	1847/05/20	1847/06/26
Leonard, Owen		Lady Gordon	Belfast	Ireland	1847/04/14	1847/06/20
Leonard, Patrick	32	Virginius	Liverpool	England	1847/05/28	1847/08/12
Leslie, James	45	Christiana	Londonderry	Ireland	1847/04/08	1847/06/10
Leslie, Margaret	8	Lord Ashburton	Liverpool	England	1847/09/13	1847/11/01
Leslie, Margaret	3	Lord Ashburton	Liverpool	England	1847/09/13	1847/11/01
Leslie, Thomas	12	Lord Ashburton	Liverpool	England	1847/09/13	1847/11/01
Levall, G.	4	City of Derry	London	England	1847/05/23	1847/07/04
Ley, Godfred		General Hewitt	Bremen	Germany	1847/07/22	1847/09/12
Linden, Thomas		Ann	Liverpool	England	1847/05/16	1847/06/30
Lindsay, Nancy	4	Christiana	Londonderry	Ireland	1847/04/08	1847/06/10
Linehan, Johanna	26	Sir Henry Pottinger	Cork	Ireland	1847/05/29	1847/08/07
Little, Mary	3	Goliah	Liverpool	England	1847/05/21	1847/07/18
Little, William	5	Goliah	Liverpool	England	1847/05/21	1847/07/18
Lockhart, Dolly	5	Goliah	Liverpool	England	1847/05/21	1847/07/18
Lockhart, James	11	Larch	Sligo	Ireland	1847/07/11	1847/08/20
Lockhart, John	5	Larch	Sligo	Ireland	1847/07/11	1847/08/20
Lockhart, Mary	40	Larch	Sligo	Ireland	1847/07/11	1847/08/20
Lockhart, William	9	Larch	Sligo	Ireland	1847/07/11	1847/08/20
Lockhart, William	45	Larch	Sligo	Ireland	1847/07/11	1847/08/20
Loftus, Catherine	5	Sisters	Liverpool	England	1847/04/22	1847/06/20
Loftus, James	33	Triton	Liverpool	England	1847/05/14	1847/07/24
Loftus, James		Royal Adelaide	Killala	Ireland	1847/06/09	1847/08/09
Loftus, Mary	50	Wolfville	Sligo	Ireland	1847/04/25	1847/06/10
Loftus, Mary	2	Sisters	Liverpool	England	1847/04/22	1847/06/20
Loftus, Mary	2	Triton	Liverpool	England	1847/05/14	1847/07/24
Loftus, Patrick	28	Ann	Liverpool	England	1847/05/16	1847/06/30
Loftus, Thomas	3	Triton	Liverpool	England	1847/05/14	1847/07/24
Logan, Maria	1	Nelson's Village	Belfast	Ireland	1847/05/10	1847/06/26
Logan, Patrick	10	Broom	Liverpool	England	1847/06/13	1847/08/06
Lombard, Ellen	20	Lord Sandon	Cork	Ireland	1847/05/11	1847/06/26
Long, Catherine	10	Jessie	Cork	Ireland	1847/06/03	1847/07/24
Long, James	16	Ellen	Sligo	Ireland	1847/05/27	1847/07/10
Long, John	3	Jessie	Cork	Ireland	1847/06/03	1847/07/24
Long, Mary		Lord Sandon	Cork	Ireland	1847/05/11	1847/06/26
Lord, Christopher	7	Pursuit	Liverpool	England	1847/05/04	1847/06/23
Loughran, Michael	80	Herald	Dublin	Ireland	1847/05/20	1847/06/26
Lovett, Charles		Pursuit	Liverpool	England	1847/05/04	1847/06/23
Lovett, Jonah	35	Pursuit	Liverpool	England	1847/05/04	1847/06/23
Lovett, Mary	10	Pursuit	Liverpool	England	1847/05/04	1847/06/23
Lowe, Ann	65	John Jardine	Liverpool	England	1847/06/04	1847/07/16
Lowe, Lawrence	28	Larch	Sligo	Ireland	1847/07/11	1847/08/20
Lowe, Mary	29	Larch	Sligo	Ireland	1847/07/11	1847/08/20
Lowry, Ellen	26	John Francis	Cork	Ireland	1847/04/10	1847/06/10
Lowry, Judith	19	Agnes	Cork	Ireland	1847/04/10	1847/06/10
Lowry, Nancy	65	Larch	Sligo	Ireland	1847/07/11	1847/08/20
Lowry, Owen	22	Mail	Cork	Ireland	1847/04/25	1847/06/19
Lowry, Patrick	80	Royal Adelaide	Killala	Ireland	1847/06/09	1847/08/09
Lucey, Bartholomew	25	Henrietta Mary	Cork	Ireland	1847/08/18	1847/09/29
Lunny, Daniel	2	Julius Caesar	Liverpool	England	1847/07/13	1847/09/05
Lunny, Mary	16	John Bolton	Liverpool	England	1847/04/13	1847/06/10
Lunny, Patrick	3	John Bolton	Liverpool	England	1847/04/13	1847/06/10
Lynan, Elizabeth	50	Naparina	Dublin	Ireland	1847/06/17	1847/08/23
Lynch, Bridget	25	Avon	Cork	Ireland	1847/05/19	1847/07/26
Lynch, Catherine	5	Free Trader	Liverpool	England	1847/06/22	1847/08/14
Lynch, Edward	14	Jane Avery	Dublin	Ireland	1847/05/09	1847/06/25
Lynch, Ellen	20	Avon	Cork	Ireland	1847/05/19	1847/07/26
Lynch, Francis	15	Larch	Sligo	Ireland	1847/07/11	1847/08/20
Lynch, John	15	Larch	Sligo	Ireland	1847/07/11	1847/08/20
Lynch, Mary		Jane Avery	Dublin	Ireland	1847/05/09	1847/06/25
Lynn, Susan	56	Lord Seaton	Belfast	Ireland	1847/04/12	1847/06/10
Lyons, Ann	20	Virginius	Liverpool	England	1847/05/28	1847/08/12
Lyons, Bridget		Lady Flora Hastings	Cork	Ireland	1847/05/11	1847/06/26
Lyons, Ellen	18	Virginius	Liverpool	England	1847/05/28	1847/08/12
Lyons, J.	1	Bridgetown	Liverpool	England	1847/07/03	1847/08/29
Lyons, James	45	Virginius	Liverpool	England	1847/05/28	1847/08/12
Lyons, James	22	Virginius	Liverpool	England	1847/05/28	1847/08/12
Lyons, Jane	56	Sesostris	Londonderry	Ireland	1847/05/14	1847/06/24
Lyons, Jane	36	Virginius	Liverpool	England	1847/05/28	1847/08/12
Lyons, Jane		Herald	Dublin	Ireland	1847/05/20	1847/06/26
Lyons, John	32	Virginius	Liverpool	England	1847/05/28	1847/08/12
Lyons, John	7	Lady Flora Hastings	Cork	Ireland	1847/05/11	1847/06/26
Lyons, Julia	3	Bridgetown	Liverpool	England	1847/07/03	1847/08/29
Lyons, Luke	35	Virginius	Liverpool	England	1847/05/28	1847/08/12
Lyons, Martin	36	Naomi	Liverpool	England	1847/06/15	1847/08/10
Lyons, Mary	17	Virginius	Liverpool	England	1847/05/28	1847/08/12
Lyons, Mary	40	Virginius	Liverpool	England	1847/05/28	1847/08/12
Lyons, Michael	1	Naomi	Liverpool	England	1847/06/15	1847/08/10
Lyons, Patrick	45	Lady Flora Hastings	Cork	Ireland	1847/05/11	1847/06/26
Lyons, Patrick	35	Virginius	Liverpool	England	1847/05/28	1847/08/12
Lyons, Peter	9	Virginius	Liverpool	England	1847/05/28	1847/08/12
Lyons, Sally		Margaret	New Ross	Ireland	1847/05/19	1847/07/02
Lyons, William	48	Pandora	New Ross	Ireland	1847/06/11	1847/08/04
MacElhoyle, Robert	23	Argo	Liverpool	England	1847/05/04	1847/06/12
MacFarlane, Catherine	3	Rose	Liverpool	England	1847/04/19	1847/07/01
Madden, Catherine		Tom	Dublin	Ireland	1847/05/26	1847/07/12
Madden, Edward		Virginius	Liverpool	England	1847/05/28	1847/08/12
Madden, James		Triton	Liverpool	England	1847/05/14	1847/07/24
Madden, Julia	2	Naomi	Liverpool	England	1847/06/15	1847/08/10
Madden, Martin	3	John Bolton	Liverpool	England	1847/04/13	1847/06/10
Madden, Mary	25	Virginius	Liverpool	England	1847/05/28	1847/08/12
Madden, Michael		George	Liverpool	England	1847/04/13	1847/06/12
Madden, Michael	16	Virginius	Liverpool	England	1847/05/28	1847/08/12
Madden, Patrick	3	Triton	Liverpool	England	1847/05/14	1847/07/24
Madden, Patrick	50	Triton	Liverpool	England	1847/05/14	1847/07/24
Madden, William	6	Triton	Liverpool	England	1847/05/14	1847/07/24

LIST OF PEOPLE WHO DIED ON SHIPS AT SEA OR IN QUARANTINE AT GROSSE ÎLE, IN 1847

Name	Age	Vessel	Port	Country	Embarkation	Qc Arrival
Madden, William	26	Triton	Liverpool	England	1847/05/14	1847/07/24
Magnan, Mary	35	Bridgetown	Liverpool	England	1847/07/03	1847/08/29
Magnan, Michael	13	Pursuit	Liverpool	England	1847/05/04	1847/06/23
Magnan, William	35	Bridgetown	Liverpool	England	1847/07/03	1847/08/29
Maguire, Mary	8	John Munn	Liverpool	England	1847/06/16	1847/08/13
Maher, Eliza	15	Odessa	Dublin	Ireland	1847/06/09	1847/08/09
Maher, Henry	15	Agent	New Ross	Ireland	1847/05/20	1847/07/02
Maher, Honora	50	Ann Kenny	Waterford	Ireland	1847/06/27	1847/08/05
Maher, James	1	Energy	Limerick	Ireland	1847/05/28	1847/07/05
Maher, John	2	New York Packet	Liverpool	England	1847/04/24	1847/06/29
Maher, John	50	Agent	New Ross	Ireland	1847/05/20	1847/07/02
Maher, John	39	Independance	Belfast	Ireland	1847/05/23	1847/07/07
Maher, John		Agent	New Ross	Ireland	1847/05/20	1847/07/02
Maher, Julia	22	Scotland	Cork	Ireland	1847/04/13	1847/06/08
Maher, Julia	26	Scotland	Cork	Ireland	1847/04/13	1847/06/08
Maher, Margaret	3	Margrette	New Ross	Ireland	1847/05/02	1847/07/04
Maher, Mary	2	Aberfoyle	Waterford	Ireland	1847/05/27	1847/07/04
Maher, Mary	1	Venilia	Limerick	Ireland	1847/05/28	1847/07/11
Maher, Patrick	3	Energy	Limerick	Ireland	1847/05/28	1847/07/05
Maher, Sarah	54	Odessa	Dublin	Ireland	1847/06/09	1847/08/09
Maher, Thomas	5	Lord Ashburton	Liverpool	England	1847/09/13	1847/11/01
Maher, William	2.50	Lord Ashburton	Liverpool	England	1847/09/13	1847/11/01
Mahon, Catherine		Lotus	Liverpool	England	1847/04/15	1847/06/24
Mahon, Mary	55	Naomi	Liverpool	England	1847/06/15	1847/08/10
Mahon, Mrs.	28	Sobraon	Liverpool	England	1847/05/08	1847/06/29
Mahon, Patrick	22	Energy	Limerick	Ireland	1847/05/28	1847/07/05
Mahon, Peter	6	Sobraon	Liverpool	England	1847/05/08	1847/06/29
Mahon, Thomas		Pursuit	Liverpool	England	1847/05/04	1847/06/23
Mahon, Thomas	3	Lotus	Liverpool	England	1847/04/15	1847/06/24
Mahoney, Catherine	28	Wakefield	Cork	Ireland	1847/05/28	1847/07/12
Mahoney, Daniel	23	Sir Henry Pottinger	Cork	Ireland	1847/05/29	1847/08/07
Mahoney, David	25	Scotland	Cork	Ireland	1847/04/13	1847/06/08
Mahoney, David	25	Scotland	Cork	Ireland	1847/04/13	1847/06/08
Mahoney, Ellen	2	Covenanter	Cork	Ireland	1847/06/17	1847/08/09
Mahoney, Jane	2	Urania	Cork	Ireland	1847/04/09	1847/06/10
Mahoney, Johanna	20	Primrose	Limerick	Ireland	1847/04/07	1847/06/18
Mahoney, John	21	Bridgetown	Liverpool	England	1847/07/03	1847/08/29
Mahoney, John	45	Sir Henry Pottinger	Cork	Ireland	1847/05/29	1847/08/07
Mahoney, Margaret	9	Urania	Cork	Ireland	1847/04/09	1847/06/10
Mahoney, Margaret	2	Emily	Cork	Ireland	1847/05/12	1847/07/06
Mahoney, Margaret	30	Emily	Cork	Ireland	1847/05/12	1847/07/06
Mahoney, Mary	4	Sisters	Liverpool	England	1847/04/22	1847/06/20
Mahoney, Mary	26	Thistle	Liverpool	England	1847/06/01	1847/07/18
Mahoney, Mary	4	Covenanter	Cork	Ireland	1847/06/17	1847/08/09
Mahoney, Michael	31	Urania	Cork	Ireland	1847/04/09	1847/06/10
Mahoney, Michael	50	Pursuit	Liverpool	England	1847/05/04	1847/06/23
Mahoney, Patrick	60	John Francis	Cork	Ireland	1847/04/10	1847/06/10
Mahoney, Patrick	23	Avon	Cork	Ireland	1847/05/19	1847/07/26
Mahoney, Patrick		Horatio	Limerick	Ireland	1847/07/18	1847/09/03
Malley, Bridget	75	Larch	Sligo	Ireland	1847/07/11	1847/08/20
Malley, Catherine	30	Ann	Liverpool	England	1847/05/16	1847/06/30
Malley, Ellen		Tay	Liverpool	England	1847/05/22	1847/06/23
Malley, Hubert	1	Larch	Sligo	Ireland	1847/07/11	1847/08/20
Malley, James	45	Larch	Sligo	Ireland	1847/07/11	1847/08/20
Malley, John	30	Ann	Liverpool	England	1847/05/16	1847/06/30
Malley, Mary	3	Tay	Liverpool	England	1847/05/22	1847/06/23
Malley, Patrick	70	Larch	Sligo	Ireland	1847/07/11	1847/08/20
Malley, Thomas	7	Rose	Liverpool	England	1847/04/19	1847/07/01
Malley, Thomas		Ann	Liverpool	England	1847/05/16	1847/06/30
Malone, James	5	Free Trader	Liverpool	England	1847/06/22	1847/08/14
Malone, John	1	Ninian	Limerick	Ireland	1847/04/13	1847/06/12
Malone, Martin	42	Argo	Liverpool	England	1847/05/04	1847/06/12
Malone, Mary	3	Free Trader	Liverpool	England	1847/06/22	1847/08/14
Malone, Matthew	4	Free Trader	Liverpool	England	1847/06/22	1847/08/14
Malone, Michael	56	Eagle	Dublin	Ireland	1847/05/12	1847/06/25
Malone, William	7	Free Trader	Liverpool	England	1847/06/22	1847/08/14
Malone, William	35	Free Trader	Liverpool	England	1847/06/22	1847/08/14
Maloney, Bridget	4	Wolfville	Sligo	Ireland	1847/04/25	1847/06/10
Maloney, Burnet	25	Charles Richard	Sligo	Ireland	1847/05/27	1847/07/16
Maloney, David	47	Ganges	Liverpool	England	1847/06/16	1847/08/21
Maloney, Honora	4	Camillia	Sligo	Ireland	1847/05/19	1847/07/07
Maloney, James	1	Argo	Liverpool	England	1847/05/04	1847/06/12
Maloney, Nancy		Goliah	Liverpool	England	1847/05/21	1847/07/18
Maloney, Nancy	26	Wolfville	Sligo	Ireland	1847/04/25	1847/06/10
Maloney, Nancy	50	Virginius	Liverpool	England	1847/05/28	1847/08/12
Maloney, Patrick	18	Virginius	Liverpool	England	1847/05/28	1847/08/12
Maloney, Thomas	2	Argo	Liverpool	England	1847/05/04	1847/06/12
Mangan, Sally	48	James Moran	Liverpool	England	1847/05/22	1847/07/11
Manley, Ann	60	Ganges	Liverpool	England	1847/06/16	1847/08/21
Manley, John	26	Sir Henry Pottinger	Cork	Ireland	1847/05/29	1847/08/07
Manley, Kate	40	Sir Henry Pottinger	Cork	Ireland	1847/05/29	1847/08/07
Manley, Michael	39	Sir Henry Pottinger	Cork	Ireland	1847/05/29	1847/08/07
Manley, Patrick	22	Sir Henry Pottinger	Cork	Ireland	1847/05/29	1847/08/07
Mannihan, Eliza		Sesostris	Londonderry	Ireland	1847/05/14	1847/06/24
Mannihan, Eliza		Herald	Dublin	Ireland	1847/05/20	1847/06/26
Manning, Catherine	22	Avon	Cork	Ireland	1847/05/19	1847/07/26
Manning, Edward	1	Henrietta Mary	Cork	Ireland	1847/08/18	1847/09/29
Manning, Mary		John Bell	New Ross	Ireland	1847/05/10	1847/06/29
Mannion, John	56	Mary Brack	Limerick	Ireland	1847/05/03	1847/06/12
Manor, William	35	Bridgetown	Liverpool	England	1847/07/03	1847/08/29
Mara, Elizabeth	70	Progress	New Ross	Ireland	1847/05/05	1847/07/14
Mara, James	63	Progress	New Ross	Ireland	1847/05/05	1847/07/14
Mara, Patrick		Sir Robert Peel	Liverpool	England	1847/07/26	1847/09/19
Mareas, Anna	4	Canton	Bremen	Germany	1847/06/20	1847/08/07
Markey, Andrew	5	Lotus	Liverpool	England	1847/04/15	1847/06/24
Markham, A.		Ganges	Liverpool	England	1847/06/16	1847/08/21
Markham, James	5	Ganges	Liverpool	England	1847/06/16	1847/08/21
Marley, James		Goliah	Liverpool	England	1847/05/21	1847/07/18
Marley, Martin		Ann	Liverpool	England	1847/05/16	1847/06/30
Marshall, John	70	Rose	Liverpool	England	1847/04/19	1847/07/01
Martin, Dennis	50	Eliza Caroline	Liverpool	England	1847/05/03	1847/06/14
Martin, Eleanor		Goliah	Liverpool	England	1847/05/21	1847/07/18
Martin, Johanna		General Hewitt	Bremen	Germany	1847/07/22	1847/09/29
Martin, Mary	7	Bridgetown	Liverpool	England	1847/07/03	1847/08/29
Martin, Michael	30	Bridgetown	Liverpool	England	1847/07/03	1847/08/29
Martin, Patrick	47	Ganges	Liverpool	England	1847/06/16	1847/08/21
Martin, Thomas	12	Wellington	Liverpool	England	1847/07/29	1847/09/20
Mason, B.	25	Bee	Cork	Ireland	1847/04/17	1847/06/12
Mason, J.	3	Bee	Cork	Ireland	1847/04/17	1847/06/12
Massey, Ann		Ninian	Limerick	Ireland	1847/04/13	1847/06/12
Massey, William	2	Ninian	Limerick	Ireland	1847/04/13	1847/06/12
Masterson, Frank	68	Tamarac	Liverpool	England	1847/05/26	1847/07/11
Masterson, James		Corea	Liverpool	England	1847/07/02	1847/08/14
Matheson, Donald		Eliza	Glasgow	Scotland	1847/07/17	1847/09/17
Matthewson, Alexander	3	Eliza	Glasgow	Scotland	1847/07/17	1847/09/17
Maxwell, Mary Jane	1	Eliza Caroline	Liverpool	England	1847/05/03	1847/06/14
May, Martin	2	Lord Ashburton	Liverpool	England	1847/09/13	1847/11/01
Mays, Bridget	16	Ajax	Liverpool	England	1847/04/16	1847/06/23
McAdam, Joseph		Sobraon	Liverpool	England	1847/05/08	1847/06/29
McAleer, Bridget	22	Albion	Cork	Ireland	1847/08/13	1847/09/29
McAleer, Ellen	15	Rose	Liverpool	England	1847/04/19	1847/07/01
McAleese, Mary	4	Tamarac	Liverpool	England	1847/05/26	1847/07/11
McAllen, Sarah	4	Lord Glenelg	Limerick	Ireland	1847/05/06	1847/06/19
McAllen, Thomas	2	Goliah	Liverpool	England	1847/05/21	1847/07/18

85

List of people who died on ships at sea or in quarantine at Grosse Île, in 1847

Name	Age	Vessel	Port	Country	Embarkation	Qc Arrival
McAllister, Samuel	1	Constitution	Belfast	Ireland	1847/04/21	1847/06/08
McAnally, Mary	1	Sobraon	Liverpool	England	1847/05/08	1847/06/29
McAnally, Mary	3	Rose	Liverpool	England	1847/04/19	1847/07/01
McAndrew, James		Larch	Sligo	Ireland	1847/07/11	1847/08/20
McAndrew, John	34	Columbia	Sligo	Ireland	1847/05/01	1847/06/10
McAndrew, John	2	Numa	Sligo	Ireland	1847/06/02	1847/07/27
McAneny, Mary		Wellington	Liverpool	England	1847/07/29	1847/09/20
McAnulty, Bridget	31	Wolfville	Sligo	Ireland	1847/04/25	1847/06/10
McAnulty, Daniel	64	Sesostris	Londonderry	Ireland	1847/05/14	1847/06/24
McAnulty, Eleanor	40	Wolfville	Sligo	Ireland	1847/04/25	1847/06/10
McAnulty, John	35	Wolfville	Sligo	Ireland	1847/04/25	1847/06/10
McAnulty, Margaret	17	Wolfville	Sligo	Ireland	1847/04/25	1847/06/10
McAnulty, Mary	10	Wolfville	Sligo	Ireland	1847/04/25	1847/06/10
McArdle, Francis	10	Lotus	Liverpool	England	1847/04/15	1847/06/24
McArdle, Jane	42	Jessie	Limerick	Ireland	1847/04/18	1847/06/26
McArdle, John	11	Lord Ashburton	Liverpool	England	1847/09/13	1847/11/01
McArdle, Nancy	8	Lord Ashburton	Liverpool	England	1847/09/13	1847/11/01
McArdle, Rose	18	Lotus	Liverpool	England	1847/04/15	1847/06/24
McArdle, Rose	18	Lotus	Liverpool	England	1847/04/19	1847/06/24
McArthur, Christie	50	Rose	Liverpool	England	1847/04/19	1847/07/01
McArthur, Margaret	11	Canada	Glasgow	Scotland	1847/07/14	1847/09/04
McAuley, Catherine		Covenanter	Cork	Ireland	1847/06/17	1847/08/09
McAuley, James	60	Rose	Liverpool	England	1847/04/19	1847/07/01
McAuley, Mary	55	Coromandel	Dublin	Ireland	1847/05/13	1847/07/02
McAuley, Mary	6	Covenanter	Cork	Ireland	1847/06/17	1847/08/09
McAuley, Morris	60	Coromandel	Dublin	Ireland	1847/05/13	1847/07/02
McAuley, Thomas	35	Coromandel	Dublin	Ireland	1847/05/13	1847/07/02
McAuliffe, Bartholomew	1	Covenanter	Cork	Ireland	1847/06/17	1847/08/09
McAuliffe, Mary	8	Triton	Liverpool	England	1847/05/14	1847/07/24
McCabe, Bridget	40	Sarah	Liverpool	England	1847/05/29	1847/07/19
McCabe, Francis	9	Julius Caesar	Liverpool	England	1847/07/13	1847/09/05
McCabe, Mary	11	John Bolton	Liverpool	England	1847/04/13	1847/06/10
McCabe, Michael	10	Blenheim	Cork	Ireland	1847/06/16	1847/07/29
McCabe, Thomas	10	John Bolton	Liverpool	England	1847/04/13	1847/06/10
McCaffery, Michael	60	Sisters	Liverpool	England	1847/04/22	1847/06/20
McCaffery, Thomas	50	Rose	Liverpool	England	1847/04/19	1847/07/01
McCahan, Eliza	69	Lotus	Liverpool	England	1847/04/15	1847/06/24
McCain, Maria		Goliah	Liverpool	England	1847/05/21	1847/07/18
McCain, Patrick		George	Liverpool	England	1847/04/13	1847/06/12
McCall, Ann	1	Erin's Queen	Liverpool	England	1847/06/01	1847/07/23
McCall, Honora	30	Erin's Queen	Liverpool	England	1847/06/01	1847/07/23
McCall, James	13	John Bolton	Liverpool	England	1847/04/13	1847/06/10
McCall, Mary	40	Lotus	Liverpool	England	1847/04/15	1847/06/24
McCallum, Andrew	40	Rose	Liverpool	England	1847/04/19	1847/07/01
McCallum, Angus	1	Louisa	Limerick	Ireland	1847/05/08	1847/06/25
McCallum, James	40	Rose	Liverpool	England	1847/04/19	1847/07/01
McCandless, Catherine	2	Sisters	Liverpool	England	1847/04/22	1847/06/20
McCandless, Mary	26	Sisters	Liverpool	England	1847/04/22	1847/06/20
McCandless, Thomas	3	Sisters	Liverpool	England	1847/04/22	1847/06/20
McCann, John	60	Sobraon	Liverpool	England	1847/05/08	1847/06/29
McCarrick, Martin		Greenock	Liverpool	England	1847/06/19	1847/07/29
McCarroll, Margaret		Corea	Liverpool	England	1847/07/02	1847/08/14
McCarron, John	35	Sisters	Liverpool	England	1847/04/22	1847/06/20
McCarron, Terrence	16	Rose	Liverpool	England	1847/04/19	1847/07/01
McCarry, Bridget	14	Argo	Liverpool	England	1847/05/04	1847/06/12
McCarter, Mary	38	Lord Ashburton	Liverpool	England	1847/09/13	1847/11/01
McCarthy, Daniel	90	Gilmour	Cork	Ireland	1847/04/24	1847/06/18
McCarthy, Dennis	21	Triton	Liverpool	England	1847/05/14	1847/07/24
McCarthy, Johanna	35	Julius Caesar	Liverpool	England	1847/07/13	1847/09/05
McCarthy, John	24	Avon	Cork	Ireland	1847/05/19	1847/07/26
McCarthy, Mary	13	Lady Flora Hastings	Cork	Ireland	1847/05/11	1847/06/26
McCarthy, Mary Jane	3	Lord Ashburton	Liverpool	England	1847/09/13	1847/11/01
McCarthy, Owen	6	Triton	Liverpool	England	1847/05/14	1847/07/24
McCarthy, Patrick	36	Bee	Cork	Ireland	1847/04/17	1847/06/12
McCarthy, Patrick	36	Bee	Cork	Ireland	1847/04/17	1847/06/12
McCarthy, Patrick	0.5	Lord Ashburton	Liverpool	England	1847/09/13	1847/11/01
McCarthy, Thomas	44	Pursuit	Liverpool	England	1847/05/04	1847/06/23
McCarty, Ann	6	Canada	Glasgow	Scotland	1847/07/14	1847/09/04
McCarty, Bridget	3	Wakefield	Cork	Ireland	1847/05/28	1847/07/12
McCarty, Daniel	10	Covenanter	Cork	Ireland	1847/06/17	1847/08/09
McCarty, Denis		Triton	Liverpool	England	1847/05/14	1847/07/24
McCarty, Edward	4	Triton	Liverpool	England	1847/05/14	1847/07/24
McCarty, James	26	Lord Ashburton	Liverpool	England	1847/09/13	1847/11/01
McCarty, John	20	Saguenay	Cork	Ireland	1847/06/05	1847/08/22
McCarty, John	45	Lord Ashburton	Liverpool	England	1847/09/13	1847/11/01
McCarty, Judith	26	Mail	Cork	Ireland	1847/04/25	1847/06/19
McCarty, Julia	34	Triton	Liverpool	England	1847/05/14	1847/07/24
McCarty, Mary	25	Pursuit	Liverpool	England	1847/05/04	1847/06/23
McCarty, Mary	4	Emigrant	Liverpool	England	1847/08/11	1847/10/03
McCarty, Michael	36	Sir Henry Pottinger	Cork	Ireland	1847/05/29	1847/08/07
McCarty, Michael	21	Royal Adelaide	Killala	Ireland	1847/06/09	1847/08/09
McCarty, Michael	12	Bridgetown	Liverpool	England	1847/07/03	1847/08/29
McCarty, Neill	4	Canada	Glasgow	Scotland	1847/07/14	1847/09/04
McCarty, Thomas	15	Pursuit	Liverpool	England	1847/05/04	1847/06/23
McCarty, Timothy	38	Covenanter	Cork	Ireland	1847/06/17	1847/08/09
McClaskey, Mary	2	Tamarac	Liverpool	England	1847/05/26	1847/07/11
McCleary, John	4	Independance	Belfast	Ireland	1847/05/23	1847/07/07
McClellan, Thomas	4	Tamarac	Liverpool	England	1847/05/26	1847/07/11
McClenaghan, Nancy	50	New Zealand	Newry	Ireland	1847/05/20	1847/07/03
McClosky, Mrs.	60	Manchester	Liverpool	England	1847/06/05	1847/07/17
McClughan, Duncan	58	Broom	Liverpool	England	1847/06/13	1847/08/06
McClughan, Jessie	1	Broom	Liverpool	England	1847/06/13	1847/08/06
McClure, Donald		Euclid	Glasgow	Scotland	1847/06/01	1847/07/29
McClure, Edward	2	Sobraon	Liverpool	England	1847/05/08	1847/06/29
McClure, Robert		Sobraon	Liverpool	England	1847/05/08	1847/06/29
McClusky, Henry	14	Wellington	Liverpool	England	1847/07/29	1847/09/20
McComb, Robert	36	Ganges	Liverpool	England	1847/06/16	1847/08/21
McConaghy, Francis	1	Christiana	Londonderry	Ireland	1847/04/08	1847/06/10
McConnell, James	20	Erin's Queen	Liverpool	England	1847/06/01	1847/07/23
McConnell, John		Lady Gordon	Belfast	Ireland	1847/04/14	1847/06/20
McConnell, John James	1	Christiana	Londonderry	Ireland	1847/04/08	1847/06/10
McCool, Sally		George	Liverpool	England	1847/04/13	1847/06/12
McCool, Sally	9	George	Liverpool	England	1847/04/13	1847/06/12
McCormick, Ann	7	Pursuit	Liverpool	England	1847/05/04	1847/06/23
McCormick, Ann	29	Erin's Queen	Liverpool	England	1847/06/01	1847/07/23
McCormick, J.	6	John Munn	Liverpool	England	1847/06/16	1847/08/13
McCormick, James	26	Larch	Sligo	Ireland	1847/07/11	1847/08/20
McCormick, John	3	John Munn	Liverpool	England	1847/06/16	1847/08/13
McCormick, Mary		Naomi	Liverpool	England	1847/06/15	1847/08/10
McCormick, Mary	30	Abbeylands	Liverpool	England	1847/06/15	1847/07/31
McCormick, Owen	66	Naomi	Liverpool	England	1847/06/15	1847/08/10
McCormick, Thomas	40	John Munn	Liverpool	England	1847/06/16	1847/08/13
McCormick, Thomas	6	John Munn	Liverpool	England	1847/06/16	1847/08/13
McCormick, Winford		Naomi	Liverpool	England	1847/06/15	1847/08/10
McCracken, William	1	Sisters	Liverpool	England	1847/04/22	1847/06/20
McCrea, Mary		Lord Ashburton	Liverpool	England	1847/09/13	1847/11/01
McCrea, Michael	40	Pursuit	Liverpool	England	1847/05/04	1847/06/23
McCrea, Thomas	4	Eliza Caroline	Liverpool	England	1847/05/03	1847/06/14
McCrea, William	4	Leander	Londonderry	Ireland	1847/06/13	1847/07/31
McCristol, Catherine	50	Marchioness of Bute	Belfast	Ireland	1847/06/10	1847/07/31
McCristol, John	60	Marchioness of Bute	Belfast	Ireland	1847/06/10	1847/07/31
McCulloch, Catherine	4	Christiana	Londonderry	Ireland	1847/04/08	1847/06/10
McCutcheon, Eliza	2	Araminta	Liverpool	England	1847/05/01	1847/06/20
McCutcheon, Eliza	2	Aberdeen	Liverpool	England	1847/05/01	1847/06/13
McDermott, Ann	10	Naomi	Liverpool	England	1847/06/15	1847/08/10
McDermott, Ellen	1	Sir Robert Peel	Liverpool	England	1847/07/26	1847/09/19

List of people who died on ships at sea or in quarantine at Grosse Île, in 1847

Name	Age	Vessel	Port	Country	Embarkation	Qc Arrival
McDermott, Hannah	2	Naomi	Liverpool	England	1847/06/15	1847/08/10
McDermott, James	26	Larch	Sligo	Ireland	1847/07/11	1847/08/20
McDermott, John	1	Tamarac	Liverpool	England	1847/05/26	1847/07/11
McDermott, Mary	37	Naomi	Liverpool	England	1847/06/15	1847/08/10
McDermott, Patrick	21	Lotus	Liverpool	England	1847/04/15	1847/06/24
McDermott, Peter	35	Larch	Sligo	Ireland	1847/07/11	1847/08/20
McDermott, Thomas	43	Naomi	Liverpool	England	1847/06/15	1847/08/10
McDonagh, Ann	22	Bridgetown	Liverpool	England	1847/07/03	1847/08/29
McDonagh, Bridget	65	Rose	Liverpool	England	1847/04/19	1847/07/01
McDonagh, Michael	60	Rose	Liverpool	England	1847/04/19	1847/07/01
McDonald, Alexander		Eliza	Glasgow	Scotland	1847/07/17	1847/09/17
McDonald, Arthur		Lady Gordon	Belfast	Ireland	1847/04/14	1847/06/20
McDonald, Donald	3	Sir Robert Peel	Liverpool	England	1847/07/26	1847/09/19
McDonald, Dougald	49	Ann Rankin	Glasgow	Scotland	1847/06/27	1847/08/09
McDonald, George	25	Ellen Simpson	Limerick	Ireland	1847/06/11	1847/08/14
McDonald, James		Lady Gordon	Belfast	Ireland	1847/04/14	1847/06/20
McDonald, James	40	Free Trader	Liverpool	England	1847/06/22	1847/08/14
McDonald, Jane		Lady Gordon	Belfast	Ireland	1847/04/14	1847/06/20
McDonald, John	51	Ann Rankin	Glasgow	Scotland	1847/06/27	1847/08/09
McDonald, John	1	Sir Robert Peel	Liverpool	England	1847/07/26	1847/09/19
McDonald, Judith	30	Sarah	Liverpool	England	1847/05/29	1847/07/19
McDonald, Margaret		Corea	Liverpool	England	1847/07/02	1847/08/14
McDonald, Margaret	5	Sir Robert Peel	Liverpool	England	1847/07/26	1847/09/19
McDonald, Mary	3	Ajax	Liverpool	England	1847/04/16	1847/06/23
McDonald, Michael	40	Ganges	Liverpool	England	1847/06/16	1847/08/21
McDonald, Mrs.	40	Ajax	Liverpool	England	1847/04/16	1847/06/23
McDonald, Nancy	18	Ajax	Liverpool	England	1847/04/16	1847/06/23
McDonald, Neil		Eliza	Glasgow	Scotland	1847/07/17	1847/09/17
McDonald, Patrick	12	Ajax	Liverpool	England	1847/04/16	1847/06/23
McDonald, Peter	40	John Bolton	Liverpool	England	1847/04/13	1847/06/10
McDonald, Ronald	30	Oregon	Killala	Ireland	1847/06/09	1847/08/02
McDonald, Ronald	49	Bridgetown	Liverpool	England	1847/07/03	1847/08/29
McDonnell, Ann	3	Sarah	Liverpool	England	1847/05/29	1847/07/19
McDonnell, Edward	22	Sarah	Liverpool	England	1847/05/29	1847/07/19
McDonnell, Eliza	2	Ganges	Liverpool	England	1847/06/16	1847/08/21
McDonnell, Eliza		Corea	Liverpool	England	1847/07/02	1847/08/14
McDonnell, Honora	7	Ganges	Liverpool	England	1847/06/16	1847/08/21
McDonnell, James	2	Ajax	Liverpool	England	1847/04/16	1847/06/23
McDonnell, James	2	Ajax	Liverpool	England	1847/04/16	1847/06/23
McDonnell, James	60	Oregon	Killala	Ireland	1847/06/09	1847/08/02
McDonnell, Margaret	19	Virginius	Liverpool	England	1847/05/28	1847/08/12
McDonnell, Mary	3	Sarah	Liverpool	England	1847/05/29	1847/07/19
McDonnell, Mary		Progress	New Ross	Ireland	1847/05/05	1847/07/14
McDonnell, Mary	8	Ajax	Liverpool	England	1847/04/16	1847/06/23
McDonnell, Mrs.	60	Ajax	Liverpool	England	1847/04/16	1847/06/23
McDonnell, Owen	3	Erin's Queen	Liverpool	England	1847/06/01	1847/07/23
McDonnell, Patrick		Erin's Queen	Liverpool	England	1847/06/01	1847/07/23
McDonnell, Winford	30	Ganges	Liverpool	England	1847/06/16	1847/08/21
McDougal, Jerry	40	Broom	Liverpool	England	1847/06/13	1847/08/06
McElrone, Nancy	60	Lord Seaton	Belfast	Ireland	1847/04/12	1847/06/10
McEwen, Barney		Sobraon	Liverpool	England	1847/05/08	1847/06/29
McFadden, John	50	Eliza	Glasgow	Scotland	1847/07/17	1847/09/17
McFadden, Mary	60	Marchioness of Bute	Belfast	Ireland	1847/06/10	1847/07/31
McFadden, Mary	60	Eliza	Glasgow	Scotland	1847/07/17	1847/09/17
McFadden, Nancy	8	Eliza	Glasgow	Scotland	1847/07/17	1847/09/17
McFarlane, Andrew	45	Rose	Liverpool	England	1847/04/19	1847/07/01
McFarlane, James	2	New York Packet	Liverpool	England	1847/04/24	1847/06/29
McFarlane, James	45	Broom	Liverpool	England	1847/06/13	1847/08/06
McFarlane, James	2	Broom	Liverpool	England	1847/06/13	1847/08/06
McFarlane, Jane	67	Broom	Liverpool	England	1847/06/13	1847/08/06
McFerran, Daniel	50	Lotus	Liverpool	England	1847/04/15	1847/06/24
McGann, Mary	2	George	Liverpool	England	1847/04/13	1847/06/12
McGann, Patrick	3	George	Liverpool	England	1847/04/13	1847/06/12
McGarry, William	45	Marchioness of Bute	Belfast	Ireland	1847/06/10	1847/07/31
McGaughey, Owen	2	Abbeylands	Liverpool	England	1847/06/15	1847/07/31
McGauran, Francis	30	Marinus	Dublin	Ireland	1847/06/05	1847/08/13
McGavin, Bridget	6	Sisters	Liverpool	England	1847/04/22	1847/06/20
McGee, Ann	3	Lord Ashburton	Liverpool	England	1847/09/13	1847/11/01
McGee, Ann	32	Lord Ashburton	Liverpool	England	1847/09/13	1847/11/01
McGee, Bridget	25	Lady Milton	Liverpool	England	1847/05/05	1847/06/26
McGee, Bridget	25	Lady Milton	Liverpool	England	1847/05/05	1847/06/26
McGee, Catherine	2	Araminta	Liverpool	England	1847/05/01	1847/06/20
McGee, Mary	5	Sisters	Liverpool	England	1847/04/22	1847/06/20
McGee, Mary		Lady Milton	Liverpool	England	1847/05/05	1847/06/26
McGee, Mary		Lady Milton	Liverpool	England	1847/05/05	1847/06/26
McGee, Patrick	13	Araminta	Liverpool	England	1847/05/01	1847/06/20
McGee, Sarah	1	Lord Ashburton	Liverpool	England	1847/09/13	1847/11/01
McGee, Thomas	20	Araminta	Liverpool	England	1847/05/01	1847/06/20
McGee, William	5	Lord Ashburton	Liverpool	England	1847/09/13	1847/11/01
McGennis, Bridget	1	John Munn	Liverpool	England	1847/06/16	1847/08/13
McGennis, Helen		John Munn	Liverpool	England	1847/06/16	1847/08/13
McGennis, James		John Munn	Liverpool	England	1847/06/16	1847/08/13
McGennis, Margaret		John Munn	Liverpool	England	1847/06/16	1847/08/13
McGennis, Mary	70	John Munn	Liverpool	England	1847/06/16	1847/08/13
McGerity, Mary	12	Julius Caesar	Liverpool	England	1847/07/13	1847/09/05
McGettigan, Britley	45	Pursuit	Liverpool	England	1847/05/04	1847/06/23
McGibbon, Elizabeth	8	Sobraon	Liverpool	England	1847/05/08	1847/06/29
McGill, Barney	20	Columbia	Sligo	Ireland	1847/05/01	1847/06/10
McGlinchey, Anthony	2	Christiana	Londonderry	Ireland	1847/04/08	1847/06/10
McGlinchey, James	25	Caithness-shire	Belfast	Ireland	1847/04/10	1847/06/12
McGlinchey, Mary	3	Caithness-shire	Belfast	Ireland	1847/04/10	1847/06/12
McGlynn, Michael		Naomi	Liverpool	England	1847/06/15	1847/08/10
McGlynn, Owen	2	Lotus	Liverpool	England	1847/04/15	1847/06/24
McGlynn, Peter	35	Naomi	Liverpool	England	1847/06/15	1847/08/10
McGlynn, Peter		Naomi	Liverpool	England	1847/06/15	1847/08/10
McGoldrick, Catherine	1	Larch	Sligo	Ireland	1847/07/11	1847/08/20
McGoldrick, John	2	Allan Kerr	Sligo	Ireland	1847/06/23	1847/08/04
McGough, David		Wellington	Liverpool	England	1847/07/29	1847/09/20
McGowan, Bridget	6	Yorkshire	Liverpool	England	1847/06/09	1847/08/10
McGowan, Daniel	36	Larch	Sligo	Ireland	1847/07/11	1847/08/20
McGowan, Elleanor	10	John Bolton	Liverpool	England	1847/04/13	1847/06/10
McGowan, Nancy	35	Yorkshire	Liverpool	England	1847/06/09	1847/08/10
McGowan, Nancy		Yorkshire	Liverpool	England	1847/06/09	1847/08/10
McGowan, Thomas	3	Yorkshire	Liverpool	England	1847/06/09	1847/08/10
McGrady, Sarah	1	Tay	Liverpool	England	1847/05/22	1847/06/23
McGrath, Andrew		Manchester	Liverpool	England	1847/06/05	1847/07/17
McGrath, Catherine	2	Aberdeen	Liverpool	England	1847/05/01	1847/06/13
McGrath, Catherine	2	Larch	Sligo	Ireland	1847/07/11	1847/08/20
McGrath, Hannah	50	John Bolton	Liverpool	England	1847/04/13	1847/06/10
McGrath, J.		Larch	Sligo	Ireland	1847/07/11	1847/08/20
McGrath, John	20	Aberdeen	Liverpool	England	1847/05/01	1847/06/13
McGrath, John	7	Jessie	Cork	Ireland	1847/06/03	1847/07/24
McGrath, John	39	Avon	Cork	Ireland	1847/05/19	1847/07/26
McGrath, John	35	Ellen Simpson	Limerick	Ireland	1847/06/11	1847/08/14
McGrath, Michael	35	Pursuit	Liverpool	England	1847/05/04	1847/06/23
McGrath, Michael	25	Saguenay	Cork	Ireland	1847/06/05	1847/08/22
McGrath, Patrick	3	Aberdeen	Liverpool	England	1847/05/01	1847/06/13
McGrath, Patrick	3	Pursuit	Liverpool	England	1847/05/04	1847/06/23
McGrath, Patrick	27	Sir Henry Pottinger	Cork	Ireland	1847/05/29	1847/08/07
McGrath, Peter		Lady Gordon	Belfast	Ireland	1847/04/14	1847/06/20
McGrath, Thomas	35	Larch	Sligo	Ireland	1847/07/11	1847/08/20
McGrath, Thomas	35	Jessie	Cork	Ireland	1847/06/03	1847/07/24
McGreal, John	5	Eliza Caroline	Liverpool	England	1847/05/03	1847/06/14
McGreal, Thomas	45	Eliza Caroline	Liverpool	England	1847/05/03	1847/06/14
McGreevey, John	12	Lord Ashburton	Liverpool	England	1847/09/13	1847/11/01
McGuane, Grace		Broom	Liverpool	England	1847/06/13	1847/08/06
McGuinn, Ann	11	John Bolton	Liverpool	England	1847/04/13	1847/06/10

LIST OF PEOPLE WHO DIED ON SHIPS AT SEA OR IN QUARANTINE AT GROSSE ÎLE, IN 1847

Name	Age	Vessel	Port	Country	Embarkation	Qc Arrival
McGuinness, Ann	30	Eliza	Glasgow	Scotland	1847/07/17	1847/09/17
McGuinness, Ann	4	Canada	Glasgow	Scotland	1847/07/14	1847/09/04
McGuinness, Bryan	20	Ann	Liverpool	England	1847/05/16	1847/06/30
McGuinness, Catherine		Eliza	Glasgow	Scotland	1847/07/17	1847/09/17
McGuinness, Catherine		Sir Robert Peel	Liverpool	England	1847/07/26	1847/09/19
McGuinness, Hector	12	Sir Robert Peel	Liverpool	England	1847/07/26	1847/09/19
McGuinness, James	35	Larch	Sligo	Ireland	1847/07/11	1847/08/20
McGuinness, James		Ann	Liverpool	England	1847/05/16	1847/06/30
McGuinness, John	1	Canada	Glasgow	Scotland	1847/07/14	1847/09/04
McGuinness, Margaret	2	Canada	Glasgow	Scotland	1847/07/14	1847/09/04
McGuinness, Neill	1	Emigrant	Liverpool	England	1847/08/11	1847/10/03
McGuire, Barney		Naomi	Liverpool	England	1847/06/15	1847/08/10
McGuire, Bridget	16	Virginius	Liverpool	England	1847/05/28	1847/08/12
McGuire, Catherine	3	Christiana	Londonderry	Ireland	1847/04/08	1847/06/10
McGuire, Catherine	18	Virginius	Liverpool	England	1847/05/28	1847/08/12
McGuire, Charles	8	Bridgetown	Liverpool	England	1847/07/03	1847/08/29
McGuire, Charles	40	Virginius	Liverpool	England	1847/05/28	1847/08/12
McGuire, Elizabeth	16	Virginius	Liverpool	England	1847/05/28	1847/08/12
McGuire, James	46	Virginius	Liverpool	England	1847/05/28	1847/08/12
McGuire, James	2	Allan Kerr	Sligo	Ireland	1847/06/23	1847/08/04
McGuire, John	30	James Moran	Liverpool	England	1847/05/22	1847/07/11
McGuire, Joseph	9	Virginius	Liverpool	England	1847/05/28	1847/08/12
McGuire, Maria	20	Virginius	Liverpool	England	1847/05/28	1847/08/12
McGuire, Mary		Frankfield	Liverpool	England	1847/06/29	1847/08/09
McGuire, Mary	3	Naomi	Liverpool	England	1847/06/15	1847/08/10
McHale, Bridget	1	Aberdeen	Liverpool	England	1847/05/01	1847/06/13
McHale, Bridget	1	Araminta	Liverpool	England	1847/05/01	1847/06/20
McHale, Edward		George	Liverpool	England	1847/04/13	1847/06/12
McHale, Elizabeth	2	Sisters	Liverpool	England	1847/04/22	1847/06/20
McHale, Patrick		Sisters	Liverpool	England	1847/04/22	1847/06/20
McHale, Patrick	4	Agamemnon	Liverpool	England	1847/06/24	1847/07/31
McHale, Sally	4	Agamemnon	Liverpool	England	1847/06/24	1847/07/31
McHenry, Ellen	1	Energy	Limerick	Ireland	1847/05/28	1847/07/05
McHenry, Mary	24	Lady Flora Hastings	Cork	Ireland	1847/05/11	1847/06/26
McHenry, Patrick	4	Sarah	Liverpool	England	1847/05/29	1847/07/19
McHugh, Mary	35	Sesostris	Londonderry	Ireland	1847/05/14	1847/06/24
McHugh, Mary		Herald	Dublin	Ireland	1847/05/20	1847/06/26
McHugh, Thomas	60	Westmoreland	Sligo	Ireland	1847/06/12	1847/08/10
McInerney, Mary	2	Argo	Liverpool	England	1847/05/04	1847/06/12
McInerney, Thomas	64	Anna Maria	Limerick	Ireland	1847/07/03	1847/08/11
McIntyre, Alexander	3	Eliza	Glasgow	Scotland	1847/07/17	1847/09/17
McIntyre, Margaret	1	Christiana	Londonderry	Ireland	1847/04/08	1847/06/10
McIver, James	4	Lord Seaton	Belfast	Ireland	1847/04/12	1847/06/10
McIver, John	2	Argo	Liverpool	England	1847/05/04	1847/06/12
McKay, F.	3	Sir Robert Peel	Liverpool	England	1847/07/26	1847/09/19
McKay, Farquhar	2	Eliza	Glasgow	Scotland	1847/07/17	1847/09/17
McKay, Jane	5	Sir Robert Peel	Liverpool	England	1847/07/26	1847/09/19
McKay, Jeremiah	30	John Bolton	Liverpool	England	1847/04/13	1847/06/10
McKay, John	34	Eliza	Glasgow	Scotland	1847/07/17	1847/09/17
McKay, Kenith	15	Eliza	Glasgow	Scotland	1847/07/17	1847/09/17
McKay, Mary	7	George	Liverpool	England	1847/04/13	1847/06/12
McKay, Michael	1	Free Trader	Liverpool	England	1847/06/22	1847/08/14
McKay, Murdock	27	Sir Robert Peel	Liverpool	England	1847/07/26	1847/09/19
McKay, Patrick	6	Free Trader	Liverpool	England	1847/06/22	1847/08/14
McKay, Robert	52	Caithness-shire	Belfast	Ireland	1847/04/10	1847/06/12
McKay, William	40	Free Trader	Liverpool	England	1847/06/22	1847/08/14
McKee, Ann	22	Lord Ashburton	Liverpool	England	1847/09/13	1847/11/01
McKee, James	27	Marchioness of Bute	Belfast	Ireland	1847/06/10	1847/07/31
McKellor, Rowland	60	Mail	Cork	Ireland	1847/04/25	1847/06/19
McKendry, Patrick	8	Marchioness of Bute	Belfast	Ireland	1847/06/10	1847/07/31
McKenna, Catherine	1	Sisters	Liverpool	England	1847/04/22	1847/06/20
McKenna, Ellen	11	John Bolton	Liverpool	England	1847/04/13	1847/06/10
McKenna, Mary	2	Sarah	Liverpool	England	1847/05/29	1847/07/19
McKenzie, Alexander	3	Eliza	Glasgow	Scotland	1847/07/17	1847/09/17
McKenzie, Christopher	2	Sir Robert Peel	Liverpool	England	1847/07/26	1847/09/19
McKenzie, Donald	30	Eliza	Glasgow	Scotland	1847/07/17	1847/09/17
McKeon, John	30	Wolfville	Sligo	Ireland	1847/04/25	1847/06/10
McKeon, Patrick	26	Wolfville	Sligo	Ireland	1847/04/25	1847/06/10
McKinley, Margaret	32	Julius Caesar	Liverpool	England	1847/07/13	1847/09/05
McKinney, Mary	24	Wellington	Liverpool	England	1847/07/29	1847/09/20
McKinnon, Alexander		Eliza	Glasgow	Scotland	1847/07/17	1847/09/17
McKinnon, Catherine	30	Canada	Glasgow	Scotland	1847/07/14	1847/09/04
McKinnon, Donald		Eliza	Glasgow	Scotland	1847/07/17	1847/09/17
McKinnon, Donald	12	Eliza	Glasgow	Scotland	1847/07/17	1847/09/17
McKinnon, Dougald	57	Eliza	Glasgow	Scotland	1847/07/17	1847/09/17
McKinnon, Malcolm	1	Eliza	Glasgow	Scotland	1847/07/17	1847/09/17
McKinnon, Mary	50	Eliza	Glasgow	Scotland	1847/07/17	1847/09/17
McKinnon, Neil	32	Eliza	Glasgow	Scotland	1847/07/17	1847/09/17
McKinnon, Robert	3	Christiana	Londonderry	Ireland	1847/04/08	1847/06/10
McKinnon, William	3	Eliza	Glasgow	Scotland	1847/07/17	1847/09/17
McKitrick, John	4	Washington	Liverpool	England	1847/07/09	1847/08/26
McKitterick, Thomas	3	Washington	Liverpool	England	1847/07/09	1847/08/26
McLaughlin, Ann	3	Ann Rankin	Glasgow	Scotland	1847/06/27	1847/08/09
McLaughlin, Bernard		Lady Milton	Liverpool	England	1847/05/05	1847/06/26
McLaughlin, John	1	Christiana	Londonderry	Ireland	1847/04/08	1847/06/10
McLaughlin, Mary	2	Dykes	Sligo	Ireland	1847/04/23	1847/06/10
McLaughlin, Mary		Lady Milton	Liverpool	England	1847/05/05	1847/06/26
McLaughlin, Philip	30	Ellen	Sligo	Ireland	1847/05/27	1847/07/10
McLean, Donald	20	Eliza	Glasgow	Scotland	1847/07/17	1847/09/17
McLean, Ellen	4	Christiana	Londonderry	Ireland	1847/04/08	1847/06/10
McLean, Jannet	4	Argo	Liverpool	England	1847/05/04	1847/06/12
McLean, John	60	Eliza	Glasgow	Scotland	1847/07/17	1847/09/17
McLean, Margaret	38	Marchioness of Bute	Belfast	Ireland	1847/06/10	1847/07/31
McLean, Mary	2	Christiana	Londonderry	Ireland	1847/04/08	1847/06/10
McLean, Mary	4	Christiana	Londonderry	Ireland	1847/04/08	1847/06/10
McLean, Patrick	2	Triton	Liverpool	England	1847/05/14	1847/07/24
McLennon, Eliza	1	Nelson's Village	Belfast	Ireland	1847/05/10	1847/06/26
McLeod, Mr.	13	Larch	Sligo	Ireland	1847/07/11	1847/08/20
McMahon, Ann	7	Free Trader	Liverpool	England	1847/06/22	1847/08/14
McMahon, Eliza	9	Mary Brack	Limerick	Ireland	1847/05/03	1847/06/12
McMahon, Jane	13	John Munn	Liverpool	England	1847/06/16	1847/08/13
McMahon, Mary Jane	1	Sir Robert Peel	Liverpool	England	1847/07/26	1847/09/19
McMahon, Michael		Manchester	Liverpool	England	1847/06/05	1847/07/17
McMahon, Mrs.	59	Manchester	Liverpool	England	1847/06/05	1847/07/17
McMahon, Patrick	1	Jessie	Cork	Ireland	1847/06/03	1847/07/24
McMahon, Thomas	40	John Munn	Liverpool	England	1847/06/16	1847/08/13
McManamy, Catherine	16	Rose	Liverpool	England	1847/04/19	1847/07/01
McManamy, Michael	1	Rose	Liverpool	England	1847/04/19	1847/07/01
McManus, Ann		Princess Royal	Liverpool	England	1847/05/05	1847/06/16
McManus, Bridget	4	Princess Royal	Liverpool	England	1847/05/05	1847/06/16
McManus, James	2	Princess Royal	Liverpool	England	1847/05/05	1847/06/16
McManus, John		Rose	Liverpool	England	1847/04/19	1847/07/01
McManus, Patrick		Princess Royal	Liverpool	England	1847/05/05	1847/06/16
McManus, Richard		Princess Royal	Liverpool	England	1847/05/05	1847/06/16
McMaster, Jane	2	Julius Caesar	Liverpool	England	1847/07/13	1847/09/05
McMeekin, Catherine	14	Champion	Liverpool	England	1847/07/13	1847/08/28
McMeekin, Mary Ann	3	Champion	Liverpool	England	1847/07/13	1847/08/28
McMillan, Ann		John Munn	Liverpool	England	1847/06/16	1847/08/13
McMillan, Samuel	1	Rosalinda	Belfast	Ireland	1847/06/22	1847/08/07
McMinn, John		George	Liverpool	England	1847/04/13	1847/06/12
McMullen, Hugh	23	Bridgetown	Liverpool	England	1847/07/03	1847/08/29
McNab, Barney	38	Rose	Liverpool	England	1847/04/19	1847/07/01
McNamara, Anthony	1	Washington	Liverpool	England	1847/07/09	1847/08/26
McNamara, Mary	3	Rose	Liverpool	England	1847/04/19	1847/07/01
McNeilan, Mary	7	Margrette	New Ross	Ireland	1847/05/02	1847/07/08

List of people who died on ships at sea or in quarantine at Grosse Île, in 1847

Name	Age	Vessel	Port	Country	Embarkation	Qc Arrival
McNeill, Francis		Lotus	Liverpool	England	1847/04/15	1847/06/24
McNeill, John	40	Virginius	Liverpool	England	1847/05/28	1847/08/12
McNeill, John	36	Virginius	Liverpool	England	1847/05/28	1847/08/12
McNeill, M.	40	John Munn	Liverpool	England	1847/06/16	1847/08/13
McNeill, Margaret	6	Virginius	Liverpool	England	1847/05/28	1847/08/12
McNeill, Maria	2	Virginius	Liverpool	England	1847/05/28	1847/08/12
McNeill, Mary	55	Royal Adelaide	Killala	Ireland	1847/06/09	1847/08/09
McNeill, Patrick	38	Virginius	Liverpool	England	1847/05/28	1847/08/12
McNeill, Patrick		Virginius	Liverpool	England	1847/05/28	1847/08/12
McNeill, Sally	5	Virginius	Liverpool	England	1847/05/28	1847/08/12
McNeill, Sally		Virginius	Liverpool	England	1847/05/28	1847/08/12
McNickle, Daniel	50	Unicorn	Londonderry	Ireland	1847/05/23	1847/07/09
McNickle, Patrick	40	Broom	Liverpool	England	1847/06/13	1847/08/06
McNider, Mary	20	James Moran	Liverpool	England	1847/05/22	1847/07/11
McNiece, Mrs.	42	John Munn	Liverpool	England	1847/06/16	1847/08/13
McNulty, Daniel		Herald	Dublin	Ireland	1847/05/20	1847/06/26
McNulty, Mary	12	Free Trader	Liverpool	England	1847/06/01	1847/08/14
McPherson, Agnes	1	Lord Seaton	Belfast	Ireland	1847/04/12	1847/06/10
McPherson, Hector	1	Lord Seaton	Belfast	Ireland	1847/04/12	1847/06/10
McPherson, Roderick		Eliza	Glasgow	Scotland	1847/07/17	1847/09/17
McQuinn, Helen	24	George	Liverpool	England	1847/04/13	1847/06/12
McSweeney, Edward		Rose	Liverpool	England	1847/04/19	1847/07/01
McTavish, Mary	50	Ann Rankin	Glasgow	Scotland	1847/06/27	1847/08/09
McTeague, Mary		Erin's Queen	Liverpool	England	1847/06/01	1847/07/23
McTeague, Michael	27	Erin's Queen	Liverpool	England	1847/06/01	1847/07/23
McTernan, Mary	2	Charles Richard	Sligo	Ireland	1847/05/27	1847/07/16
McTiffin, Anny	1	General Hewitt	Bremen	Germany	1847/07/22	1847/09/12
McVeigh, Ann	4	John Munn	Liverpool	England	1847/06/16	1847/08/13
McVeigh, Bridget	18	John Munn	Liverpool	England	1847/06/16	1847/08/13
McVeigh, Isaac		Lotus	Liverpool	England	1847/04/15	1847/06/24
McVeigh, James	50	Emily	Cork	Ireland	1847/05/12	1847/07/06
McVeigh, Jane	5	John Munn	Liverpool	England	1847/06/16	1847/08/13
McVeigh, Mary	8	John Munn	Liverpool	England	1847/06/16	1847/08/13
Mea, Bridget	3	Bee	Cork	Ireland	1847/04/17	1847/06/12
Meade, Bridget	3	Bee	Cork	Ireland	1847/04/17	1847/06/12
Meany, Jane	65	Lord Glenelg	Limerick	Ireland	1847/05/06	1847/06/19
Meara, Martin	2	Wellington	Liverpool	England	1847/07/29	1847/09/20
Meara, Mary	20	Ellen Simpson	Limerick	Ireland	1847/06/11	1847/08/14
Meara, Owen	15	Ajax	Liverpool	England	1847/04/16	1847/06/23
Meara, Patrick	56	Jessie	Limerick	Ireland	1847/04/18	1847/06/26
Mears, James	3	Bridgetown	Liverpool	England	1847/07/03	1847/08/29
Meehan, Dennis	2	Scotland	Cork	Ireland	1847/04/13	1847/06/08
Meehan, Dennis	24	Scotland	Cork	Ireland	1847/04/13	1847/06/08
Meehan, Edward		Larch	Sligo	Ireland	1847/07/11	1847/08/20
Meehan, Elizabeth	5	Larch	Sligo	Ireland	1847/07/11	1847/08/20
Meehan, John	35	Larch	Sligo	Ireland	1847/07/11	1847/08/20
Meehan, John	40	Covenanter	Cork	Ireland	1847/06/17	1847/08/09
Meehan, Luke	5	Larch	Sligo	Ireland	1847/07/11	1847/08/20
Meehan, Mary	3	Larch	Sligo	Ireland	1847/07/11	1847/08/20
Meehan, Patrick		Westmoreland	Sligo	Ireland	1847/06/12	1847/08/10
Meehan, Patrick		Larch	Sligo	Ireland	1847/07/11	1847/08/20
Meehan, Thomas	2	Allan Kerr	Sligo	Ireland	1847/06/23	1847/08/04
Meenan, Ann	1	John Munn	Liverpool	England	1847/06/16	1847/08/13
Meenan, Judith		Champion	Liverpool	England	1847/07/13	1847/08/28
Melville, Ann	3	Lady Milton	Liverpool	England	1847/05/05	1847/06/26
Melville, Bridget	7	George	Liverpool	England	1847/04/13	1847/06/12
Memel, Kermgund	2	Elza Anne	Hamburg	Germany	1847/06/17	1847/08/11
Mense, Edward		Nelson's Village	Belfast	Ireland	1847/05/10	1847/06/26
Merrick, Anthony	2	Sisters	Liverpool	England	1847/04/22	1847/06/20
Merrick, Bridget	4	Sisters	Liverpool	England	1847/04/22	1847/06/20
Merrick, John	30	Sisters	Liverpool	England	1847/04/22	1847/06/20
Merrick, Margaret	1	Lord Ashburton	Liverpool	England	1847/09/13	1847/11/01
Merrick, Mary	18	Triton	Liverpool	England	1847/05/14	1847/07/24
Merrick, Mary	37	Julius Caesar	Liverpool	England	1847/07/13	1847/09/05
Mesner, Margaret	1	General Hewitt	Bremen	Germany	1847/07/22	1847/09/12
Millan, Daniel		Lady Flora Hastings	Cork	Ireland	1847/05/11	1847/06/26
Miller, Ann	1	Argo	Liverpool	England	1847/05/04	1847/06/12
Miller, Hugh	23	Ann	Donegal	Ireland	1847/05/29	1847/07/26
Miller, John	22	Triton	Liverpool	England	1847/05/14	1847/07/24
Miller, Michael	30	Lotus	Liverpool	England	1847/04/15	1847/06/24
Miller, Robert	30	Bridgetown	Liverpool	England	1847/07/03	1847/08/29
Miller, Sarah	5	Argo	Liverpool	England	1847/05/04	1847/06/12
Millett, John	40	Ann	Liverpool	England	1847/05/16	1847/06/30
Milligan, Michael	60	Wolfville	Sligo	Ireland	1847/04/25	1847/06/10
Mills, George	8	Ajax	Liverpool	England	1847/04/16	1847/06/23
Mills, John	30	Mail	Cork	Ireland	1847/04/25	1847/06/19
Mills, John		Ajax	Liverpool	England	1847/04/16	1847/06/23
Mills, Margaret	2	Ajax	Liverpool	England	1847/04/16	1847/06/23
Mills, Samuel	53	Unicorn	Londonderry	Ireland	1847/05/23	1847/07/09
Minihane, Cornelius	60	John Francis	Cork	Ireland	1847/04/10	1847/06/10
Minihane, James	25	Agnes	Cork	Ireland	1847/04/10	1847/06/10
Minnock, Peter	1	Triton	Liverpool	England	1847/05/14	1847/07/24
Mitchell, Alexander	30	Greenock	Liverpool	England	1847/06/19	1847/07/29
Mitchell, John		Aberdeen	Liverpool	England	1847/05/01	1847/06/13
Mitchell, Joseph		Araminta	Liverpool	England	1847/05/01	1847/06/20
Mitchell, Mary	85	Emigrant	Liverpool	England	1847/08/11	1847/10/03
Molloy, Bridget	35	Virginius	Liverpool	England	1847/05/28	1847/08/12
Molloy, Catherine	30	Wolfville	Sligo	Ireland	1847/04/25	1847/06/10
Molloy, Margaret	2	Wolfville	Sligo	Ireland	1847/04/25	1847/06/10
Molloy, Michael	48	Virginius	Liverpool	England	1847/05/28	1847/08/12
Molloy, Nancy	58	Standard	New Ross	Ireland	1847/04/22	1847/06/19
Molloy, William	58	Sobraon	Liverpool	England	1847/05/08	1847/06/29
Monaghan, Catherine	31	Progress	New Ross	Ireland	1847/05/05	1847/07/14
Monaghan, Cornelius	6	Agnes	Cork	Ireland	1847/04/10	1847/06/10
Monaghan, Daniel	36	Agnes	Cork	Ireland	1847/04/10	1847/06/10
Monaghan, Ellen	10	Agnes	Cork	Ireland	1847/04/10	1847/06/10
Monaghan, John	2	Abbotsford	Dublin	Ireland	1847/04/23	1847/06/21
Monaghan, Margaret	30	Agnes	Cork	Ireland	1847/04/10	1847/06/10
Monaghan, Patrick	1	Progress	New Ross	Ireland	1847/05/05	1847/07/14
Monaghan, Thomas	11	Virginius	Liverpool	England	1847/05/28	1847/08/12
Monday, Bridget	2	John Bolton	Liverpool	England	1847/04/13	1847/06/12
Monnelly, Catherine	60	Oregon	Killala	Ireland	1847/06/09	1847/08/02
Montgomery, Jane	1	Free Trader	Liverpool	England	1847/06/22	1847/08/14
Montgomery, Mary	1	Free Trader	Liverpool	England	1847/06/22	1847/08/14
Moody, Mary	1	Argo	Liverpool	England	1847/05/04	1847/06/12
Mooney, Ann	8	John Jardine	Liverpool	England	1847/06/04	1847/07/16
Mooney, Bridget	12	Corea	Liverpool	England	1847/07/02	1847/08/14
Mooney, Edward	29	Scotland	Cork	Ireland	1847/04/13	1847/06/08
Mooney, Mary		Mail	Cork	Ireland	1847/04/25	1847/06/19
Mooney, Mary	2	Horatio	Limerick	Ireland	1847/07/18	1847/09/03
Mooney, Mary		Corea	Liverpool	England	1847/07/02	1847/08/14
Mooney, Nancy	60	Wolfville	Sligo	Ireland	1847/04/25	1847/06/10
Mooney, Noreen	7	Avon	Cork	Ireland	1847/05/19	1847/07/26
Mooney, Patrick	80	Avon	Cork	Ireland	1847/05/19	1847/07/26
Mooney, Sarah		Sisters	Liverpool	England	1847/04/22	1847/06/20
Mooney, Thomas	20	Jessie	Cork	Ireland	1847/06/03	1847/07/24
Moore, Andrew		Lotus	Liverpool	England	1847/04/15	1847/06/24
Moore, Ann	16	Triton	Liverpool	England	1847/05/14	1847/07/24
Moore, Anthony	50	Triton	Liverpool	England	1847/05/14	1847/07/24
Moore, Arthur	3	Triton	Liverpool	England	1847/05/14	1847/07/24
Moore, Elizabeth	34	Lotus	Liverpool	England	1847/04/15	1847/06/24
Moore, Ellen	4	Coromandel	Dublin	Ireland	1847/05/13	1847/07/02
Moore, Ellen	25	Virginius	Liverpool	England	1847/05/28	1847/08/12
Moore, James	1	Collingwood	Londonderry	Ireland	1847/05/27	1847/07/13
Moore, Mary	60	Sisters	Liverpool	England	1847/04/22	1847/06/20
Moore, Mary	2	Lotus	Liverpool	England	1847/04/15	1847/06/24
Moore, Mary Jane	38	Marchioness of Bute	Belfast	Ireland	1847/06/10	1847/07/31

LIST OF PEOPLE WHO DIED ON SHIPS AT SEA OR IN QUARANTINE AT GROSSE ÎLE, IN 1847

Name	Age	Vessel	Port	Country	Embarkation	Qc Arrival
Moore, Patrick	54	Virginius	Liverpool	England	1847/05/28	1847/08/12
Moore, Patrick	59	Avon	Cork	Ireland	1847/05/19	1847/07/26
Moore, Sarah		Marchioness of Bute	Belfast	Ireland	1847/06/10	1847/07/31
Moore, Thomas	20	Ellen	Sligo	Ireland	1847/05/27	1847/07/10
Moran, Ann	18	Thistle	Liverpool	England	1847/06/01	1847/07/18
Moran, Bridget	35	Emigrant	Liverpool	England	1847/08/11	1847/10/03
Moran, Bridget	3	Argo	Liverpool	England	1847/05/04	1847/06/12
Moran, Edmund	60	Emigrant	Liverpool	England	1847/08/11	1847/10/03
Moran, Edward		Emigrant	Liverpool	England	1847/08/11	1847/10/03
Moran, Ellen	60	Ganges	Liverpool	England	1847/06/16	1847/08/21
Moran, J.		Marinus	Dublin	Ireland	1847/06/05	1847/08/13
Moran, John	30	Washington	Liverpool	England	1847/07/09	1847/08/26
Moran, Mary	1	Argo	Liverpool	England	1847/05/04	1847/06/12
Moran, Winifred	20	James Moran	Liverpool	England	1847/05/22	1847/07/11
Morey, Patrick		Pursuit	Liverpool	England	1847/05/04	1847/06/23
Morgan, Daniel		Sir Henry Pottinger	Cork	Ireland	1847/05/29	1847/08/07
Morgan, Daniel	35	Sir Henry Pottinger	Cork	Ireland	1847/05/29	1847/08/07
Morgan, James		Naomi	Liverpool	England	1847/06/15	1847/08/10
Morgan, John	50	Larch	Sligo	Ireland	1847/07/11	1847/08/20
Morgan, Margaret	22	Scotland	Cork	Ireland	1847/04/13	1847/06/08
Morgan, Margaret	24	Scotland	Cork	Ireland	1847/04/13	1847/06/08
Morgan, Patrick	70	Naomi	Liverpool	England	1847/06/15	1847/08/10
Moriarty, Charles	50	John Bolton	Liverpool	England	1847/04/13	1847/06/10
Moriarty, Ellen	55	Wakefield	Cork	Ireland	1847/05/28	1847/07/12
Moriarty, James	20	Sir Henry Pottinger	Cork	Ireland	1847/05/29	1847/08/07
Moriarty, James	29	Sir Henry Pottinger	Cork	Ireland	1847/05/29	1847/08/07
Moriarty, Julia	29	Sir Henry Pottinger	Cork	Ireland	1847/05/29	1847/08/07
Moriarty, Mary	19	Sir Henry Pottinger	Cork	Ireland	1847/05/29	1847/08/07
Moriarty, Mary	17	Sir Henry Pottinger	Cork	Ireland	1847/05/29	1847/08/07
Moriarty, Mary	20	Sir Henry Pottinger	Cork	Ireland	1847/05/29	1847/08/07
Moriarty, Mora	3	Free Trader	Liverpool	England	1847/06/22	1847/08/14
Morissey, Ellen	1	Alert	Waterford	Ireland	1847/06/05	1847/07/15
Morissey, William	21	Venilia	Limerick	Ireland	1847/05/28	1847/07/11
Moroney, Timothy	35	Avon	Cork	Ireland	1847/05/19	1847/07/26
Morris, Ann		Junior	Liverpool	England	1847/05/10	1847/07/03
Morris, Catherine	16	Avon	Cork	Ireland	1847/05/19	1847/07/26
Morris, Jane	2	Araminta	Liverpool	England	1847/05/01	1847/06/20
Morris, Jane	2	Aberdeen	Liverpool	England	1847/05/01	1847/06/13
Morris, John	13	Jane Avery	Dublin	Ireland	1847/05/09	1847/06/25
Morris, Patrick	5	Goliah	Liverpool	England	1847/05/21	1847/07/18
Morris, Peter		City of Derry	London	England	1847/05/23	1847/07/04
Morris, Peter	2	John and Robert	Liverpool	England	1847/06/09	1847/08/06
Morris, William	1	Aberdeen	Liverpool	England	1847/05/01	1847/06/13
Morris, William	12	Araminta	Liverpool	England	1847/05/01	1847/06/20
Morrison, Catherine	1	Aberfoyle	Waterford	Ireland	1847/05/27	1847/07/04
Morrison, J.		Sobraon	Liverpool	England	1847/05/08	1847/06/29
Morrow, Alexander	2	Tamarac	Liverpool	England	1847/05/26	1847/07/11
Morrow, Jane		George	Liverpool	England	1847/04/13	1847/06/12
Morrow, Jane	50	George	Liverpool	England	1847/04/13	1847/06/12
Morrow, John	50	George	Liverpool	England	1847/04/13	1847/06/12
Morrow, Mary		George	Liverpool	England	1847/04/13	1847/06/12
Morton, Ann	16	Columbia	Sligo	Ireland	1847/05/01	1847/06/10
Morton, George	9	John Bolton	Liverpool	England	1847/04/13	1847/06/10
Mountain, Dennis	9	Bee	Cork	Ireland	1847/04/17	1847/06/12
Mountain, Dennis	1	Bee	Cork	Ireland	1847/04/17	1847/06/12
Mulally, Daniel	3	Virginius	Liverpool	England	1847/05/28	1847/08/12
Mulhall, Honora		Oregon	Killala	Ireland	1847/06/09	1847/08/02
Mulhall, James	36	Pandora	New Ross	Ireland	1847/06/11	1847/08/04
Mulhern, Anthony	6	George	Liverpool	England	1847/04/13	1847/06/12
Mulhern, Mary	21	George	Liverpool	England	1847/04/13	1847/06/12
Mulholland, Henry	65	Nelson's Village	Belfast	Ireland	1847/05/10	1847/06/26
Mulholland, James	9	Numa	Sligo	Ireland	1847/06/02	1847/07/27
Mulholland, Patrick	15	Agnes and Ann	Newry	Ireland	1847/05/15	1847/07/02
Mulholland, William	55	Numa	Sligo	Ireland	1847/06/02	1847/07/27
Mullaney, C.	60	Numa	Sligo	Ireland	1847/06/02	1847/07/27
Mullany, Martin		Westmoreland	Sligo	Ireland	1847/06/12	1847/08/10
Mullen, Ann	24	Virginius	Liverpool	England	1847/05/28	1847/08/12
Mullen, Bridget	27	Triton	Liverpool	England	1847/05/14	1847/07/24
Mullen, Catherine	50	Naomi	Liverpool	England	1847/06/15	1847/08/10
Mullen, Catherine	2	John Munn	Liverpool	England	1847/06/16	1847/08/13
Mullen, Eliza	1	Sir Robert Peel	Liverpool	England	1847/07/26	1847/09/19
Mullen, John	20	Virginius	Liverpool	England	1847/05/28	1847/08/12
Mullen, John	60	Virginius	Liverpool	England	1847/05/28	1847/08/12
Mullen, Mary	43	Agamemnon	Liverpool	England	1847/06/24	1847/07/31
Mullen, Michael	13	Julius Caesar	Liverpool	England	1847/07/13	1847/09/05
Mullen, Michael	16	Virginius	Liverpool	England	1847/05/28	1847/08/12
Mullen, Patrick	50	Virginius	Liverpool	England	1847/05/28	1847/08/12
Mullen, Richard	1	Ninian	Limerick	Ireland	1847/04/13	1847/06/12
Mulligan, Bernard		Greenock	Liverpool	England	1847/06/19	1847/07/29
Mulligan, Mary	28	Lady Milton	Liverpool	England	1847/05/05	1847/06/26
Mulligan, Mary	30	Broom	Liverpool	England	1847/06/13	1847/08/06
Mulligan, Michael	45	Lady Milton	Liverpool	England	1847/05/05	1847/06/26
Mulligan, Michael		Lady Milton	Liverpool	England	1847/05/05	1847/06/26
Mullins, Ellen	6	Avon	Cork	Ireland	1847/05/19	1847/07/26
Mullins, John		Avon	Cork	Ireland	1847/05/19	1847/07/26
Mullins, Julia	1	Avon	Cork	Ireland	1847/05/19	1847/07/26
Mullins, Mary	50	Saguenay	Cork	Ireland	1847/06/05	1847/08/22
Mullins, Mary	29	Avon	Cork	Ireland	1847/05/19	1847/07/26
Mullowny, Anthony	22	Larch	Sligo	Ireland	1847/07/11	1847/08/20
Mulrooney, Mary	30	Urania	Cork	Ireland	1847/04/09	1847/06/10
Mulroy, Catherine	30	Ann	Liverpool	England	1847/05/16	1847/06/30
Mulroy, James	30	Princess Royal	Liverpool	England	1847/05/05	1847/06/16
Mulroy, John	3	Wellington	Liverpool	England	1847/07/29	1847/09/20
Mulroy, Mary	6	Wellington	Liverpool	England	1847/07/29	1847/09/20
Mulroy, Mary	8	Ann	Liverpool	England	1847/05/16	1847/06/30
Mulroy, Michael	1	Bridgetown	Liverpool	England	1847/07/03	1847/08/29
Mulvey, Patrick	2	Bridgetown	Liverpool	England	1847/07/03	1847/08/29
Murphy, Ann	1	Progress	New Ross	Ireland	1847/05/05	1847/07/14
Murphy, Ann		Junior	Liverpool	England	1847/05/10	1847/07/03
Murphy, Ann		Pandora	New Ross	Ireland	1847/06/11	1847/08/04
Murphy, Bridget	25	Aberdeen	Liverpool	England	1847/05/01	1847/06/13
Murphy, Bridget	25	Araminta	Liverpool	England	1847/05/01	1847/06/20
Murphy, Bridget	16	Sarah	Liverpool	England	1847/05/29	1847/07/19
Murphy, Bryan	20	Ann	Liverpool	England	1847/05/16	1847/06/30
Murphy, Bryan	27	Margaret	New Ross	Ireland	1847/05/19	1847/07/02
Murphy, Catherine	2	Progress	New Ross	Ireland	1847/05/05	1847/07/14
Murphy, Catherine	61	Avon	Cork	Ireland	1847/05/19	1847/07/26
Murphy, Charles	13	Lord Ashburton	Liverpool	England	1847/09/13	1847/11/01
Murphy, Darby	3	Sarah	Liverpool	England	1847/05/29	1847/07/19
Murphy, Dennis	9	John Bolton	Liverpool	England	1847/04/13	1847/06/10
Murphy, Eliza	15	Covenanter	Cork	Ireland	1847/06/17	1847/08/09
Murphy, Ellen		Avon	Cork	Ireland	1847/05/19	1847/07/26
Murphy, Harriet		Lillias	Dublin	Ireland	1847/07/01	1847/08/16
Murphy, James	13	Bee	Cork	Ireland	1847/04/17	1847/06/12
Murphy, James	13	Bee	Cork	Ireland	1847/04/17	1847/06/12
Murphy, James	50	Ann	Liverpool	England	1847/05/16	1847/06/30
Murphy, James		Ann	Liverpool	England	1847/05/16	1847/06/30
Murphy, Jerry	16	Lady Flora Hastings	Cork	Ireland	1847/05/11	1847/06/26
Murphy, Johanna	49	Mail	Cork	Ireland	1847/04/25	1847/06/19
Murphy, Johanna	5	John Bolton	Liverpool	England	1847/04/13	1847/06/10
Murphy, John	6	Gilmour	Cork	Ireland	1847/04/24	1847/06/18
Murphy, John		Junior	Liverpool	England	1847/05/10	1847/07/03
Murphy, John	41	Naomi	Liverpool	England	1847/06/15	1847/08/10
Murphy, John	60	John Bell	New Ross	Ireland	1847/05/10	1847/06/29

LIST OF PEOPLE WHO DIED ON SHIPS AT SEA OR IN QUARANTINE AT GROSSE ÎLE, IN 1847

Name	Age	Vessel	Port	Country	Embarkation	Qc Arrival
Murphy, John	2	Bridgetown	Liverpool	England	1847/07/03	1847/08/29
Murphy, Julia		Greenock	Liverpool	England	1847/06/19	1847/07/29
Murphy, Margaret	9	Naomi	Liverpool	England	1847/06/15	1847/08/10
Murphy, Mary		Agnes	Cork	Ireland	1847/04/10	1847/06/10
Murphy, Mary	45	Mail	Cork	Ireland	1847/04/25	1847/06/19
Murphy, Mary	40	Scotland	Cork	Ireland	1847/04/13	1847/06/08
Murphy, Mary	4	Wakefield	Cork	Ireland	1847/05/28	1847/07/12
Murphy, Mary	50	Naomi	Liverpool	England	1847/06/15	1847/08/10
Murphy, Mary	6	John Bolton	Liverpool	England	1847/04/13	1847/06/10
Murphy, Matthew	50	New Zealand	Newry	Ireland	1847/05/20	1847/07/03
Murphy, Michael	30	Avon	Cork	Ireland	1847/05/19	1847/07/26
Murphy, Michael		Naomi	Liverpool	England	1847/06/15	1847/08/10
Murphy, Michael	55	Oregon	Killala	Ireland	1847/06/09	1847/08/02
Murphy, Michael	14	Lord Ashburton	Liverpool	England	1847/09/13	1847/11/01
Murphy, Michael	26	Jessie	Cork	Ireland	1847/06/03	1847/07/24
Murphy, Michael	35	Saguenay	Cork	Ireland	1847/06/05	1847/08/22
Murphy, Mrs.	35	Eliza Caroline	Liverpool	England	1847/05/03	1847/06/14
Murphy, Owen	55	Princess Royal	Liverpool	England	1847/05/05	1847/06/16
Murphy, P.		Junior	Liverpool	England	1847/05/10	1847/07/03
Murphy, Patrick	16	John Bolton	Liverpool	England	1847/04/13	1847/06/10
Murphy, Patrick	3	Avon	Cork	Ireland	1847/05/19	1847/07/26
Murphy, Patrick	50	Naomi	Liverpool	England	1847/06/15	1847/08/10
Murphy, Patrick	3	Emigrant	Liverpool	England	1847/08/11	1847/10/03
Murphy, Patrick		Naomi	Liverpool	England	1847/06/15	1847/08/10
Murphy, Peter		Eliza Caroline	Liverpool	England	1847/05/03	1847/06/14
Murphy, Sarah	4	Covenanter	Cork	Ireland	1847/06/17	1847/08/09
Murphy, Thomas	2	Odessa	Dublin	Ireland	1847/06/09	1847/08/09
Murphy, Thomas	20	Naomi	Liverpool	England	1847/06/15	1847/08/10
Murphy, William		Agent	New Ross	Ireland	1847/05/20	1847/07/02
Murray, Ann	50	Naomi	Liverpool	England	1847/06/15	1847/08/10
Murray, Bridget	17	Virginius	Liverpool	England	1847/05/28	1847/08/12
Murray, Christiana	42	Broom	Liverpool	England	1847/06/13	1847/08/06
Murray, Christopher	25	Ajax	Liverpool	England	1847/04/16	1847/06/23
Murray, Christopher	29	Ajax	Liverpool	England	1847/04/16	1847/06/23
Murray, Garret	26	Julius Caesar	Liverpool	England	1847/07/13	1847/09/05
Murray, Helen	2	Free Trader	Liverpool	England	1847/06/22	1847/08/14
Murray, Hugh		Naomi	Liverpool	England	1847/06/15	1847/08/10
Murray, James	3	John Bolton	Liverpool	England	1847/04/13	1847/06/10
Murray, James	1	Pursuit	Liverpool	England	1847/05/04	1847/06/23
Murray, John	45	Broom	Liverpool	England	1847/06/13	1847/08/06
Murray, John	3	Naomi	Liverpool	England	1847/06/15	1847/08/10
Murray, Luke	70	Naomi	Liverpool	England	1847/06/15	1847/08/10
Murray, Margaret	3	Lord Ashburton	Liverpool	England	1847/09/13	1847/11/01
Murray, Mary		Naomi	Liverpool	England	1847/06/15	1847/08/10
Murray, Mary	9	Virginius	Liverpool	England	1847/05/28	1847/08/12
Murray, Mary	40	Virginius	Liverpool	England	1847/05/28	1847/08/12
Murray, Michael	2	Virginius	Liverpool	England	1847/05/28	1847/08/12
Murray, Patrick	15	Virginius	Liverpool	England	1847/05/28	1847/08/12
Murray, Sarah	4	Pursuit	Liverpool	England	1847/05/04	1847/06/23
Murray, Theodore	50	Virginius	Liverpool	England	1847/05/28	1847/08/12
Murray, Thomas	60	James Moran	Liverpool	England	1847/05/22	1847/07/11
Murray, William	27	John Munn	Liverpool	England	1847/06/16	1847/08/13
Murtagh, Patrick	27	Scotland	Cork	Ireland	1847/04/13	1847/06/08
Myers, Catherine	3	Nerio	Limerick	Ireland	1847/08/05	1847/09/28
Nagle, Ellen	21	Bee	Cork	Ireland	1847/04/17	1847/06/12
Nagle, Ellen	21	Bee	Cork	Ireland	1847/04/17	1847/06/12
Nagle, Margaret	2	Dominica	Cork	Ireland	1847/05/01	1847/06/14
Nally, John M.	55	Eliza Caroline	Liverpool	England	1847/05/03	1847/06/14
Nangle, Timothy	26	Lord Ashburton	Liverpool	England	1847/09/13	1847/11/01
Nash, Mary	35	Scotland	Cork	Ireland	1847/04/13	1847/06/08
Naughton, Ann	2	Triton	Liverpool	England	1847/05/14	1847/07/24
Naughton, Mary	6	Triton	Liverpool	England	1847/05/14	1847/07/24
Navin, Martin		Larch	Sligo	Ireland	1847/07/11	1847/08/20
Naylor, Patrick	18	Rose	Liverpool	England	1847/04/19	1847/07/01
Neal, Andrew		Progress	New Ross	Ireland	1847/05/05	1847/07/14
Neal, Cornelius	7	Covenanter	Cork	Ireland	1847/06/17	1847/08/09
Neal, Daniel	20	Avon	Cork	Ireland	1847/05/19	1847/07/26
Neal, George	1	Lord Seaton	Belfast	Ireland	1847/04/12	1847/06/10
Neal, John	20	Champion	Liverpool	England	1847/07/13	1847/08/28
Neale, Margaret	50	Avon	Cork	Ireland	1847/05/19	1847/07/26
Neale, Mary	69	Progress	New Ross	Ireland	1847/05/05	1847/07/14
Neale, Owen	62	Progress	New Ross	Ireland	1847/05/05	1847/07/14
Needham, Patrick	35	Bee	Cork	Ireland	1847/04/17	1847/06/12
Neenan, Bridget	3	Bee	Cork	Ireland	1847/04/17	1847/06/12
Neenan, Dennis	2	Agnes	Cork	Ireland	1847/04/10	1847/06/10
Neilan, Elizabeth	65	Ninian	Limerick	Ireland	1847/04/13	1847/06/12
Neilan, Johanna		Ninian	Limerick	Ireland	1847/04/13	1847/06/12
Neilan, Mary	5	Ninian	Limerick	Ireland	1847/04/13	1847/06/12
Neilan, Mary	5	Lord Glenelg	Limerick	Ireland	1847/05/06	1847/06/19
Neilan, Owen	27	Triton	Liverpool	England	1847/05/14	1847/07/24
Neilan, Patrick	70	Ninian	Limerick	Ireland	1847/04/13	1847/06/12
Neilan, Patrick	3	Ninian	Limerick	Ireland	1847/04/13	1847/06/12
Neilan, Patrick		Charles Walton	Killala	Ireland	1847/06/24	1847/08/05
Neill, Andrew	25	Agnes	Cork	Ireland	1847/04/10	1847/06/10
Neill, John	50	Avon	Cork	Ireland	1847/05/19	1847/07/26
Neill, John	71	Albion	Cork	Ireland	1847/08/13	1847/09/29
Neill, Judith	18	Albion	Cork	Ireland	1847/08/13	1847/09/29
Neill, Mary	50	Standard	New Ross	Ireland	1847/04/22	1847/06/19
Nestor, Bridget	60	Lady Milton	Liverpool	England	1847/05/05	1847/06/26
Neville, Catherine	4	Minerva	Galway	Ireland	1847/06/17	1847/08/14
Neville, Martin	35	Minerva	Galway	Ireland	1847/06/17	1847/08/14
Neville, Michael	6	Minerva	Galway	Ireland	1847/06/17	1847/08/14
Newman, Michael	26	Primrose	Limerick	Ireland	1847/04/07	1847/06/18
Nicholas, Michael		Horatio	Limerick	Ireland	1847/07/18	1847/09/03
Nicholson, Richard	40	Manchester	Liverpool	England	1847/06/05	1847/07/17
Nocton, Honora	42	John Jardine	Liverpool	England	1847/06/04	1847/07/16
Nocton, Patrick	56	John Jardine	Liverpool	England	1847/06/04	1847/07/16
Nogiel, Christopher	41	Henrietta Sophia	Hamburg	Germany	1847/05/12	1847/07/21
Nolan, James	20	Blenheim	Cork	Ireland	1847/06/16	1847/07/29
Nolan, John		Greenock	Liverpool	England	1847/06/19	1847/07/29
Nolan, Judith	1	Progress	New Ross	Ireland	1847/05/05	1847/07/14
Nolan, Margaret	1	Tay	Sligo	Ireland	1847/05/05	1847/06/09
Nolan, Mary	15	Albion	Limerick	Ireland	1847/04/19	1847/06/18
Nolan, Mary	10	John Bolton	Liverpool	England	1847/04/13	1847/06/10
Nolan, Mary	86	Margaret	New Ross	Ireland	1847/05/19	1847/07/02
Nolan, Peter	50	Princess Royal	Liverpool	England	1847/05/05	1847/06/16
Nolan, Thomas	21	Greenock	Liverpool	England	1847/06/19	1847/07/29
Noonan, Dennis	20	Avon	Cork	Ireland	1847/05/19	1847/07/26
Noonan, John	40	Avon	Cork	Ireland	1847/05/19	1847/07/26
Noone, Bridget	3	Virginius	Liverpool	England	1847/05/28	1847/08/12
Noone, Bridget	30	Larch	Sligo	Ireland	1847/07/11	1847/08/20
Noone, David	13	Sarah	Liverpool	England	1847/05/29	1847/07/19
Noone, Michael	60	Mary	Sligo	Ireland	1847/05/24	1847/07/27
Norris, Alice	24	Avon	Cork	Ireland	1847/05/19	1847/07/26
Norris, John	3	Jessie	Cork	Ireland	1847/06/03	1847/07/24
Norris, Mrs.	32	Jessie	Cork	Ireland	1847/06/03	1847/07/24
Nugent, Bridget		Virginius	Liverpool	England	1847/05/28	1847/08/12
Nugent, Catherine		Atalanta	Dublin	Ireland	1847/07/30	1847/09/12
Nugent, Margaret		Corea	Liverpool	England	1847/07/02	1847/08/14
Nugent, Mary	8	Virginius	Liverpool	England	1847/05/28	1847/08/12
Nugent, Mary	1	Lady Flora Hastings	Cork	Ireland	1847/05/11	1847/06/26
Nugent, N.	35	Emigrant	Liverpool	England	1847/08/11	1847/10/03
Nugent, Sarah	35	Virginius	Liverpool	England	1847/05/28	1847/08/12
Nyhan, Sarah	1.5	Lord Ashburton	Liverpool	England	1847/09/13	1847/11/01
O'Boyle, C.	24	Triton	Liverpool	England	1847/05/14	1847/07/24
O'Boyle, John	1	Triton	Liverpool	England	1847/05/14	1847/07/24
O'Boyle, Mary		Lady Milton	Liverpool	England	1847/05/05	1847/06/26
O'Boyle, Nancy	3	Triton	Liverpool	England	1847/05/14	1847/07/24
O'Boyle, Patrick	4	Triton	Liverpool	England	1847/05/14	1847/07/24

List of people who died on ships at sea or in quarantine at Grosse Île, in 1847

Name	Age	Vessel	Port	Country	Embarkation	Qc Arrival
O'Boyle, Peter	3	Triton	Liverpool	England	1847/05/14	1847/07/24
O'Boyle, Peter	36	Triton	Liverpool	England	1847/05/14	1847/07/24
O'Brien, Andrew	2	Eliza Caroline	Liverpool	England	1847/05/03	1847/06/14
O'Brien, Austin	27	Ninian	Limerick	Ireland	1847/04/13	1847/06/12
O'Brien, Catherine	3	Tamarac	Liverpool	England	1847/05/26	1847/07/11
O'Brien, Charles	32	Mary Brack	Limerick	Ireland	1847/05/03	1847/06/12
O'Brien, Daniel	52	Mail	Cork	Ireland	1847/04/25	1847/06/19
O'Brien, Daniel		Mail	Cork	Ireland	1847/04/25	1847/06/19
O'Brien, Denis	5	Blenheim	Cork	Ireland	1847/06/16	1847/07/29
O'Brien, John	73	Horatio	Limerick	Ireland	1847/07/18	1847/09/03
O'Brien, Mary	60	Mail	Cork	Ireland	1847/04/25	1847/06/19
O'Brien, Mary	25	Mail	Cork	Ireland	1847/04/25	1847/06/19
O'Brien, Mary	12	Bridgetown	Liverpool	England	1847/07/03	1847/08/29
O'Brien, Mary	60	Horatio	Limerick	Ireland	1847/07/18	1847/09/03
O'Brien, Michael	36	Margaret	New Ross	Ireland	1847/05/19	1847/07/02
O'Brien, Michael	16	Blenheim	Cork	Ireland	1847/06/16	1847/07/29
O'Brien, Patrick	55	Blenheim	Cork	Ireland	1847/06/16	1847/07/29
O'Brien, Sarah	42	Ellen Simpson	Limerick	Ireland	1847/06/11	1847/08/14
O'Brien, Thomas	2	Tamarac	Liverpool	England	1847/05/26	1847/07/11
O'Connell, Anthony	3	John Bolton	Liverpool	England	1847/04/13	1847/06/10
O'Connell, Mary	60	John Bolton	Liverpool	England	1847/04/13	1847/06/10
O'Connell, Mary	4	John Bolton	Liverpool	England	1847/04/13	1847/06/10
O'Connell, Michael	11	John Bolton	Liverpool	England	1847/04/13	1847/06/10
O'Donnell, Cornelius	3	Lady Milton	Liverpool	England	1847/05/05	1847/06/26
O'Donnell, Edward	13	Larch	Sligo	Ireland	1847/07/11	1847/08/20
O'Donnell, Michael	35	Saguenay	Cork	Ireland	1847/06/05	1847/08/22
O'Dowd, Mary	4	Larch	Sligo	Ireland	1847/07/11	1847/08/20
O'Dowd, Patrick	2	Larch	Sligo	Ireland	1847/07/11	1847/08/20
O'Gahan, Bridget		Covenanter	Cork	Ireland	1847/06/17	1847/08/09
O'Halloran, Judith		Horatio	Limerick	Ireland	1847/07/18	1847/09/03
O'Hanlon, Mary	11	Caithness-shire	Belfast	Ireland	1847/04/10	1847/06/12
O'Hara, Catherine	7	Charlotte Harrison	Greenock	Scotland	1847/05/14	1847/06/18
O'Hara, Catherine	17	Naomi	Liverpool	England	1847/06/15	1847/08/10
O'Hara, Ellen	40	Naomi	Liverpool	England	1847/06/15	1847/08/10
O'Hara, John	44	Naomi	Liverpool	England	1847/06/15	1847/08/10
O'Hara, John	8	Naomi	Liverpool	England	1847/06/15	1847/08/10
O'Hara, Luke	17	Virginius	Liverpool	England	1847/05/28	1847/08/12
O'Hara, Michael	1	Marchioness of Breadalbane	Sligo	Ireland	1847/06/11	1847/08/12
O'Hara, Michael	50	Marchioness of Breadalbane	Sligo	Ireland	1847/06/11	1847/08/12
O'Hara, Michael	22	Virginius	Liverpool	England	1847/05/28	1847/08/12
O'Hara, Michael	40	Virginius	Liverpool	England	1847/05/28	1847/08/12
O'Hara, Michael	16	Naomi	Liverpool	England	1847/06/15	1847/08/10
O'Hara, Michael	50	Virginius	Liverpool	England	1847/05/28	1847/08/12
O'Hara, Peter	17	Naomi	Liverpool	England	1847/06/15	1847/08/10
O'Heron, Margaret	62	Araminta	Liverpool	England	1847/05/01	1847/06/20
O'Kane, Stephen	1	Argo	Liverpool	England	1847/05/04	1847/06/12
O'Keefe, Denis	20	Sir Henry Pottinger	Cork	Ireland	1847/05/29	1847/08/07
O'Keefe, J.		Sir Henry Pottinger	Cork	Ireland	1847/05/29	1847/08/07
O'Laughlin, Patrick	20	Champion	Liverpool	England	1847/07/13	1847/08/28
O'Neill, Ann	40	Christiana	Londonderry	Ireland	1847/04/08	1847/06/10
O'Neill, Ann	1	Lord Ashburton	Liverpool	England	1847/09/13	1847/11/01
O'Neill, Bridget		Margaret	New Ross	Ireland	1847/05/19	1847/07/02
O'Neill, Jennifer	2	Urania	Cork	Ireland	1847/04/09	1847/06/10
O'Neill, Jeremiah	25	Julius Caesar	Liverpool	England	1847/07/13	1847/09/05
O'Neill, Mary	2	Christiana	Londonderry	Ireland	1847/04/08	1847/06/10
O'Neill, Nancy	3	John Bolton	Liverpool	England	1847/04/13	1847/06/10
O'Neill, William	3	Triton	Liverpool	England	1847/05/14	1847/07/24
O'Niell, Brien	30	Larch	Sligo	Ireland	1847/07/11	1847/08/20
O'Rourke, Farrell	65	Larch	Sligo	Ireland	1847/07/11	1847/08/20
Oakley, Mary		Sobraon	Liverpool	England	1847/05/08	1847/06/29
Oliver, John	42	Manchester	Liverpool	England	1847/06/05	1847/07/17
Olson, Alexander		Haubet	Hamburg	Germany	1847/07/02	1847/09/01
Olson, Garry	1	Haubet	Hamburg	Germany	1847/07/02	1847/09/01
Olson, Gunild	5	Haubet	Hamburg	Germany	1847/07/02	1847/09/01
Olson, Hirard	1	Haubet	Hamburg	Germany	1847/07/02	1847/09/01
Orr, John	2	Yorkshire	Liverpool	England	1847/06/09	1847/08/10
Osborne, Catherine		Jessie	Limerick	Ireland	1847/04/18	1847/06/26
Osborne, Edward		Charlotte	Plymouth	England	1847/06/02	1847/07/13
Owens, Beck	15	Naomi	Liverpool	England	1847/06/15	1847/08/10
Owens, Bridget	4	Ganges	Liverpool	England	1847/06/16	1847/08/21
Owens, John	1	Eliza Caroline	Liverpool	England	1847/05/03	1847/06/14
Padden, Joseph	8	John Bolton	Liverpool	England	1847/04/13	1847/06/10
Padden, Patrick		Sisters	Liverpool	England	1847/04/22	1847/06/20
Paisley, Joseph	26	John Francis	Cork	Ireland	1847/04/10	1847/06/10
Palmer, John		Lotus	Liverpool	England	1847/05/15	1847/06/24
Panier, Emily		Henrietta Sophia	Hamburg	Germany	1847/05/12	1847/07/21
Parker, Edward	25	Sisters	Liverpool	England	1847/04/22	1847/06/20
Parkinson, Eliza	75	Coromandel	Dublin	Ireland	1847/05/13	1847/07/02
Parr, Johanna	1	Juliet	London	England	1847/07/03	1847/08/28
Partlan, J.	2	Mary	Sligo	Ireland	1847/05/24	1847/07/27
Partlan, Martin	3	Larch	Sligo	Ireland	1847/07/11	1847/08/20
Partridge, John	6	Sobraon	Liverpool	England	1847/05/08	1847/06/29
Patrick, Matthew	32	Margaret	New Ross	Ireland	1847/05/19	1847/07/02
Patten, Martin	35	Larch	Sligo	Ireland	1847/07/11	1847/08/20
Patterson, Ann M.	6	John Bolton	Liverpool	England	1847/04/13	1847/06/10
Patterson, Margaret	2	Marchioness of Bute	Belfast	Ireland	1847/06/10	1847/07/31
Patterson, Thomas	3	Lord Seaton	Belfast	Ireland	1847/04/12	1847/06/10
Patton, Agnes		Sobraon	Liverpool	England	1847/05/08	1847/06/29
Patton, Mary	7	Pursuit	Liverpool	England	1847/05/04	1847/06/23
Patton, Mary		Lady Gordon	Belfast	Ireland	1847/04/14	1847/06/20
Patton, Thomas	1	Pursuit	Liverpool	England	1847/05/04	1847/06/23
Patton, William John	3	Sobraon	Liverpool	England	1847/05/08	1847/06/29
Payne, Margaret	2	Sobraon	Liverpool	England	1847/05/08	1847/06/29
Peel, John	14	Pursuit	Liverpool	England	1847/05/04	1847/06/23
Peel, William	6	Pursuit	Liverpool	England	1847/05/04	1847/06/23
Perrott, Catherine	26	Jessie	Cork	Ireland	1847/06/03	1847/07/24
Perrott, David		Jessie	Cork	Ireland	1847/06/03	1847/07/24
Perry, Catherine	2	Agnes and Ann	Newry	Ireland	1847/05/15	1847/07/02
Phelan, Catherine	39	Progress	New Ross	Ireland	1847/05/05	1847/07/14
Phelan, Henry	40	Erin's Queen	Liverpool	England	1847/06/01	1847/07/23
Phelan, James	25	Ajax	Liverpool	England	1847/04/16	1847/06/23
Phelan, James	30	Ajax	Liverpool	England	1847/04/16	1847/06/23
Phelan, Mrs.	40	Ajax	Liverpool	England	1847/04/16	1847/06/23
Philips, Mary	1	Emigrant	Liverpool	England	1847/08/11	1847/10/03
Philips, Richard	9	John Bolton	Liverpool	England	1847/04/13	1847/06/10
Pickering, Gibson		Goliah	Liverpool	England	1847/05/21	1847/07/18
Pidgeon, Patrick	26	Wolfville	Sligo	Ireland	1847/04/25	1847/06/10
Pierce, Eliza	67	Jessie	Limerick	Ireland	1847/04/18	1847/06/26
Pierce, Eliza	1	Jessie	Limerick	Ireland	1847/04/18	1847/06/26
Pierce, Hugh	65	Larch	Sligo	Ireland	1847/07/11	1847/08/20
Pigott, Catherine	26	John Francis	Cork	Ireland	1847/04/10	1847/06/10
Pigott, Maurice	27	Wakefield	Cork	Ireland	1847/05/28	1847/07/12
Pilling, Friedrich	1	Henrietta Sophia	Hamburg	Germany	1847/05/12	1847/07/21
Piper, Henry	60	Jessie	Limerick	Ireland	1847/04/18	1847/06/26
Plunkett, Andrew		Naparina	Dublin	Ireland	1847/06/17	1847/08/23
Plunkett, Patrick	30	Emigrant	Liverpool	England	1847/08/11	1847/10/03
Porter, Robert	1	Tay	Sligo	Ireland	1847/05/05	1847/06/09
Powell, Bridget	27	Virginius	Liverpool	England	1847/05/28	1847/08/12
Powell, James	30	Virginius	Liverpool	England	1847/05/28	1847/08/12
Powell, Patrick		Virginius	Liverpool	England	1847/05/28	1847/08/12
Power, John	4	Bee	Cork	Ireland	1847/04/17	1847/06/12
Prendergast, James	2	Avon	Cork	Ireland	1847/05/19	1847/07/26
Preston, Mary	58	Naomi	Liverpool	England	1847/06/15	1847/08/10
Preston, Patrick	3	Naomi	Liverpool	England	1847/06/15	1847/08/10
Preston, Richard	20	Naomi	Liverpool	England	1847/06/15	1847/08/10
Priest, James	13	Wellington	Liverpool	England	1847/07/29	1847/09/20
Proude, Mary	33	Jessie	Limerick	Ireland	1847/04/18	1847/06/26

LIST OF PEOPLE WHO DIED ON SHIPS AT SEA OR IN QUARANTINE AT GROSSE ÎLE, IN 1847

Name	Age	Vessel	Port	Country	Embarkation	Qc Arrival
Purcell, Mary	4	Abbotsford	Dublin	Ireland	1847/04/23	1847/06/21
Purvis, Roseanna	1	Aberdeen	Liverpool	England	1847/05/01	1847/06/13
Queally, John		Lady Campbell	Dublin	Ireland	1847/06/03	1847/08/05
Quigley, Hugh	4	Lotus	Liverpool	England	1847/04/15	1847/06/24
Quigley, Mary	39	James Moran	Liverpool	England	1847/05/22	1847/07/11
Quigley, Thomas	2	John Munn	Liverpool	England	1847/06/16	1847/08/13
Quinane, Thomas		Thompson	Sligo	Ireland	1847/05/05	1847/06/14
Quincy, James	30	Covenanter	Cork	Ireland	1847/06/17	1847/08/09
Quinlan, Bridget		Lotus	Liverpool	England	1847/04/15	1847/06/24
Quinlan, Denis		Gilmour	Cork	Ireland	1847/04/24	1847/06/18
Quinlan, Timothy		Lotus	Liverpool	England	1847/04/15	1847/06/24
Quinn, Ann	60	Naomi	Liverpool	England	1847/06/15	1847/08/10
Quinn, Bridget	3	Julius Caesar	Liverpool	England	1847/07/13	1847/09/05
Quinn, Bridget	36	Naomi	Liverpool	England	1847/06/15	1847/08/10
Quinn, Catherine	45	Oregon	Killala	Ireland	1847/06/09	1847/08/02
Quinn, Ellen	28	Lady Campbell	Dublin	Ireland	1847/06/03	1847/08/05
Quinn, James		Naomi	Liverpool	England	1847/06/15	1847/08/10
Quinn, James	6	New Zealand	Newry	Ireland	1847/05/20	1847/07/03
Quinn, Joseph		Naomi	Liverpool	England	1847/06/15	1847/08/10
Quinn, Michael	40	John Munn	Liverpool	England	1847/06/16	1847/08/13
Quinn, Michael	6	Naomi	Liverpool	England	1847/06/15	1847/08/10
Quinn, Patrick	35	Julius Caesar	Liverpool	England	1847/07/13	1847/09/05
Quinn, Sarah		Sisters	Liverpool	England	1847/04/22	1847/06/20
Quinn, Thadeus		Tom	Dublin	Ireland	1847/05/26	1847/07/12
Quinn, Thomas	11	Sisters	Liverpool	England	1847/04/22	1847/06/20
Quinn, Thomas	27	Tay	Liverpool	England	1847/05/22	1847/06/23
Quinney, Ellen	3	Triton	Liverpool	England	1847/05/14	1847/07/24
Quirke, Mary		Lord Sandon	Cork	Ireland	1847/05/11	1847/06/26
Quirke, Mary	7	Triton	Liverpool	England	1847/05/14	1847/07/24
Quirke, Michael		Triton	Liverpool	England	1847/05/14	1847/07/24
Quirke, Timothy	6	Triton	Liverpool	England	1847/05/14	1847/07/24
Rafferty, Mary	19	Sarah	Liverpool	England	1847/05/29	1847/07/19
Rafferty, Patrick	30	John Munn	Liverpool	England	1847/06/16	1847/08/13
Ralph, James	35	Larch	Sligo	Ireland	1847/07/11	1847/08/20
Ralph, Margaret	40	Larch	Sligo	Ireland	1847/07/11	1847/08/20
Ralph, Margaret	38	Larch	Sligo	Ireland	1847/07/11	1847/08/20
Ratcliffe, Agnes	9	Lord Seaton	Belfast	Ireland	1847/04/12	1847/06/10
Reardon, Ellen	16	Jessie	Cork	Ireland	1847/06/03	1847/07/24
Reardon, Judith	7	Ninian	Limerick	Ireland	1847/04/13	1847/06/12
Reardon, Mrs.	22	Saguenay	Cork	Ireland	1847/06/05	1847/08/22
Reddin, Eugene	19	Washington	Liverpool	England	1847/07/09	1847/08/26
Reddington, Helen		Princess Royal	Liverpool	England	1847/05/05	1847/06/16
Reddington, Michael	40	Sisters	Liverpool	England	1847/04/22	1847/06/20
Reddy, Anthony	10	John Bolton	Liverpool	England	1847/04/13	1847/06/10
Reddy, Hugh	2	Greenock	Liverpool	England	1847/06/19	1847/07/29
Reddy, John	2	Fose	Liverpool	England	1847/04/19	1847/07/01
Reddy, William	48	Goliah	Liverpool	England	1847/05/21	1847/07/18
Redmond, Edward		Greenock	Liverpool	England	1847/06/19	1847/07/29
Regan, Ann	9	Agamemnon	Liverpool	England	1847/06/24	1847/07/31
Regan, Ann	16	Bridgetown	Liverpool	England	1847/07/03	1847/08/29
Regan, Bridget	7	Pursuit	Liverpool	England	1847/05/04	1847/06/23
Regan, Bryan	50	Bridgetown	Liverpool	England	1847/07/03	1847/08/29
Regan, Charles	10	Pursuit	Liverpool	England	1847/05/04	1847/06/23
Regan, F.		Larch	Sligo	Ireland	1847/07/11	1847/08/20
Regan, Honora	2	Larch	Sligo	Ireland	1847/07/11	1847/08/20
Regan, James	35	Bee	Cork	Ireland	1847/04/17	1847/06/12
Regan, Jerry	30	Bridgetown	Liverpool	England	1847/07/03	1847/08/29
Regan, Lawrence	25	Bridgetown	Liverpool	England	1847/07/03	1847/08/29
Regan, Mary	26	Larch	Sligo	Ireland	1847/07/11	1847/08/20
Regan, Michael	45	Bridgetown	Liverpool	England	1847/07/03	1847/08/29
Regan, Patrick	6	Lady Flora Hastings	Cork	Ireland	1847/05/11	1847/06/26
Regan, Sally	2	Agamemnon	Liverpool	England	1847/06/24	1847/07/31
Regan, Thomas	3	Bridgetown	Liverpool	England	1847/07/03	1847/08/29
Regan, Timothy	2	Frankfield	Liverpool	England	1847/06/29	1847/08/09
Reid, Eliza		Lady Gordon	Belfast	Ireland	1847/04/14	1847/06/20
Reid, John	3	Agnes	Cork	Ireland	1847/04/10	1847/06/10
Reid, Margaret	52	Marchioness of Bute	Belfast	Ireland	1847/06/10	1847/07/31
Reid, Mary Jane	2	Eliza Caroline	Liverpool	England	1847/05/03	1847/06/14
Reid, Robert	2	Marchioness of Bute	Belfast	Ireland	1847/06/10	1847/07/31
Reid, Robert	70	Yorkshire	Liverpool	England	1847/06/09	1847/08/10
Reid, William	55	Countess of Arran	Donegal	Ireland	1847/06/30	1847/08/10
Reilly, Ann	4	Odessa	Dublin	Ireland	1847/06/09	1847/08/09
Reilly, Ann	35	Rose	Liverpool	England	1847/04/19	1847/07/01
Reilly, Anthony		George	Liverpool	England	1847/04/13	1847/06/12
Reilly, Bridget		Maria and Elizabeth	Liverpool	England	1847/05/06	1847/06/24
Reilly, Daniel	5	John Bolton	Liverpool	England	1847/04/13	1847/06/10
Reilly, Ellen	3	John Bolton	Liverpool	England	1847/04/13	1847/06/10
Reilly, John	9	Columbia	Sligo	Ireland	1847/05/01	1847/06/10
Reilly, John	30	Abbotsford	Dublin	Ireland	1847/04/23	1847/06/21
Reilly, John	4	John Bolton	Liverpool	England	1847/04/13	1847/06/10
Reilly, John	27	Ajax	Liverpool	England	1847/04/16	1847/06/23
Reilly, John		Bridgetown	Liverpool	England	1847/07/03	1847/08/29
Reilly, John	5	John Bolton	Liverpool	England	1847/04/13	1847/06/10
Reilly, John	25	Sir Henry Pottinger	Cork	Ireland	1847/05/29	1847/08/07
Reilly, Margaret	60	Bee	Cork	Ireland	1847/04/17	1847/06/12
Reilly, Margaret	46	Bridgetown	Liverpool	England	1847/07/03	1847/08/29
Reilly, Margaret	60	Bee	Cork	Ireland	1847/04/17	1847/06/12
Reilly, Maria	22	Bridgetown	Liverpool	England	1847/07/03	1847/08/29
Reilly, Mary	2	Triton	Liverpool	England	1847/05/14	1847/07/24
Reilly, Mary	2	Aberdeen	Liverpool	England	1847/05/01	1847/06/13
Reilly, Mary	1	Triton	Liverpool	England	1847/05/14	1847/07/24
Reilly, Michael	17	John Bolton	Liverpool	England	1847/04/13	1847/06/10
Reilly, Michael	1	Triton	Liverpool	England	1847/05/14	1847/07/24
Reilly, Patrick	4	Odessa	Dublin	Ireland	1847/06/09	1847/08/09
Reilly, Patrick	7	Ajax	Liverpool	England	1847/04/16	1847/06/23
Reilly, Rose		Junior	Liverpool	England	1847/05/10	1847/07/03
Reilly, Sarah	16	John Bolton	Liverpool	England	1847/04/13	1847/06/10
Reilly, Thomas	15	John Bolton	Liverpool	England	1847/04/13	1847/06/10
Reilly, Thomas	1	Atalanta	Dublin	Ireland	1847/07/30	1847/09/12
Reilly, William		Broom	Liverpool	England	1847/06/13	1847/08/06
Renchel, Wolfgang	1	Henrietta Sophia	Hamburg	Germany	1847/05/12	1847/07/21
Reunet, Susan	4	City of Derry	London	England	1847/05/23	1847/07/04
Reynolds, James	23	Atalanta	Dublin	Ireland	1847/07/30	1847/09/12
Reynolds, John	1	Champion	Liverpool	England	1847/07/13	1847/08/28
Reynolds, John		John Munn	Liverpool	England	1847/06/16	1847/08/13
Reynolds, John	50	Lillias	Dublin	Ireland	1847/07/01	1847/08/16
Reynolds, Mary		Naomi	Liverpool	England	1847/06/15	1847/08/10
Reynolds, Mary	55	Naomi	Liverpool	England	1847/06/15	1847/08/10
Reynolds, Mary Ann	1	Emigrant	Liverpool	England	1847/08/11	1847/10/03
Reynolds, Patrick	32	Bridgetown	Liverpool	England	1847/07/03	1847/08/29
Rice, Ann	55	Caithness-shire	Belfast	Ireland	1847/04/10	1847/06/12
Rice, James	20	Free Trader	Liverpool	England	1847/06/22	1847/08/14
Rice, William	44	Wave	Dublin	Ireland	1847/04/30	1847/06/09
Richard, Ann	3	Nelson's Village	Belfast	Ireland	1847/05/10	1847/06/26
Richard, Maria	2	Nelson's Village	Belfast	Ireland	1847/05/10	1847/06/26
Richard, Mary Ann		Lotus	Liverpool	England	1847/04/15	1847/06/24
Richardson, Joseph		Sobraon	Liverpool	England	1847/05/08	1847/06/29
Riddell, Edward	3	Sobraon	Liverpool	England	1847/05/08	1847/06/29
Riordan, John		Saguenay	Cork	Ireland	1847/06/05	1847/08/22
Ritchie, Isabella	3	Christiana	Londonderry	Ireland	1847/04/08	1847/06/10
Roach, J.	60	Pacha	Cork	Ireland	1847/05/05	1847/06/14
Roach, Mary	60	Avon	Cork	Ireland	1847/05/19	1847/07/26
Roach, Michael	30	Avon	Cork	Ireland	1847/05/19	1847/07/26
Robb, Alexander	7	Tamarac	Liverpool	England	1847/05/26	1847/07/11
Robb, Catherine	3	Lady Flora Hastings	Cork	Ireland	1847/05/11	1847/06/26
Robb, Eliza	12	Rose	Liverpool	England	1847/04/19	1847/07/01

LIST OF PEOPLE WHO DIED ON SHIPS AT SEA OR IN QUARANTINE AT GROSSE ÎLE, IN 1847

Name	Age	Vessel	Port	Country	Embarkation	Qc Arrival
Robb, Eliza	9	Tamarac	Liverpool	England	1847/05/26	1847/07/11
Robb, James	6	Goliah	Liverpool	England	1847/05/21	1847/07/18
Roberts, John	26	Scotland	Cork	Ireland	1847/04/13	1847/06/08
Roberts, Mary		Lord Sandon	Cork	Ireland	1847/05/11	1847/06/26
Roberts, Mary	30	Lord Sandon	Cork	Ireland	1847/05/11	1847/06/26
Roberts, Michael	29	Scotland	Cork	Ireland	1847/04/13	1847/06/08
Roberts, Nicholas	34	Scotland	Cork	Ireland	1847/04/13	1847/06/08
Robinson, Andrew	76	Nelson's Village	Belfast	Ireland	1847/05/10	1847/06/26
Robinson, James	2	Yorkshire	Liverpool	England	1847/06/09	1847/08/10
Robinson, John		Yorkshire	Liverpool	England	1847/06/09	1847/08/10
Robinson, Nancy	60	Emigrant	Liverpool	England	1847/08/11	1847/10/03
Robinson, Peter	30	John Munn	Liverpool	England	1847/06/16	1847/08/13
Roche, Ann	12	Bridgetown	Liverpool	England	1847/07/03	1847/08/29
Roche, Bridget		Tay	Liverpool	England	1847/05/22	1847/06/23
Roche, Bridget	40	Mary	Sligo	Ireland	1847/05/24	1847/07/27
Roche, Mary	31	Bridgetown	Liverpool	England	1847/07/03	1847/08/29
Roche, Patrick	3	Champion	Liverpool	England	1847/07/13	1847/08/28
Rocheford, Lawrence	60	Avon	Cork	Ireland	1847/05/19	1847/07/26
Rock, Richard	19	Yorkshire	Liverpool	England	1847/06/09	1847/08/10
Rodgers, John	40	Covenanter	Cork	Ireland	1847/06/17	1847/08/09
Rodgers, William	45	Jessie	Limerick	Ireland	1847/04/18	1847/06/26
Rogan, Catherine	25	Agamemnon	Liverpool	England	1847/06/24	1847/07/31
Rogan, James	30	Agnes	Cork	Ireland	1847/04/10	1847/06/10
Rogan, James	35	Bee	Cork	Ireland	1847/04/17	1847/06/12
Rogan, Jennifer	3	Bee	Cork	Ireland	1847/04/17	1847/06/12
Rogan, John	35	Bee	Cork	Ireland	1847/04/17	1847/06/12
Rohan, Bridget	4	John Munn	Liverpool	England	1847/06/16	1847/08/13
Rohan, James	40	Lotus	Liverpool	England	1847/04/15	1847/06/24
Rohan, Mary		John Munn	Liverpool	England	1847/06/16	1847/08/13
Rolan, Catherine		Venilia	Limerick	Ireland	1847/05/28	1847/07/11
Rooney, Bernard	1	Rosalinda	Belfast	Ireland	1847/06/22	1847/08/07
Rooney, Bridget	80	Rosalinda	Belfast	Ireland	1847/06/22	1847/08/07
Rooney, John	3	Lord Ashburton	Liverpool	England	1847/09/13	1847/11/01
Rooney, Patrick	5	Agamemnon	Liverpool	England	1847/06/24	1847/07/31
Ross, Catherine		Lotus	Liverpool	England	1847/04/15	1847/06/24
Ross, Henry	10	Saguenay	Cork	Ireland	1847/06/05	1847/08/22
Ross, James		George	Liverpool	England	1847/04/13	1847/06/12
Ross, Margaret	9	George	Liverpool	England	1847/04/13	1847/06/12
Ross, Mary	6	Lotus	Liverpool	England	1847/04/15	1847/06/24
Ross, Matthew	50	Lillias	Dublin	Ireland	1847/07/01	1847/08/16
Ross, Michael	1	Lotus	Liverpool	England	1847/04/15	1847/06/24
Ross, Thomas		George	Liverpool	England	1847/04/13	1847/06/12
Ross, Thomas	3	George	Liverpool	England	1847/04/13	1847/06/12
Ross, William	35	Saguenay	Cork	Ireland	1847/06/05	1847/08/22
Ross, William	5	George	Liverpool	England	1847/04/13	1847/06/12
Rourke, Bridget	1	Charles Richard	Sligo	Ireland	1847/05/27	1847/07/16
Rourke, Daniel		Westmoreland	Sligo	Ireland	1847/06/12	1847/08/10
Rourke, Patrick	1	Sir Henry Pottinger	Cork	Ireland	1847/05/29	1847/08/07
Rovimberg, Friedrich	28	City of Derry	London	England	1847/05/23	1847/07/04
Rowan, Michael	30	James Moran	Liverpool	England	1847/05/22	1847/07/11
Rowan, Thomas	19	Emigrant	Liverpool	England	1847/08/11	1847/10/03
Rowe, Thomas	3	Jessie	Limerick	Ireland	1847/04/18	1847/06/26
Rowe, Thomas		Marchioness of Abercorn	Londonderry	Ireland	1847/06/15	1847/08/05
Ruddle, David	66	Yorkshire	Liverpool	England	1847/06/09	1847/08/10
Ruddock, Catherine	4	Saguenay	Cork	Ireland	1847/06/05	1847/08/22
Ruddy, Edward	17	Greenock	Liverpool	England	1847/06/19	1847/07/29
Rulseek, Catherine		City of Derry	London	England	1847/05/23	1847/07/04
Rush, B.		Naomi	Liverpool	England	1847/06/15	1847/08/10
Rush, James	35	Naomi	Liverpool	England	1847/06/15	1847/08/10
Rush, James	36	Naomi	Liverpool	England	1847/06/15	1847/08/10
Rush, John	45	Naomi	Liverpool	England	1847/06/15	1847/08/10
Rush, Mary	25	Naomi	Liverpool	England	1847/06/15	1847/08/10
Rush, Mary	47	Naomi	Liverpool	England	1847/06/15	1847/08/10
Rush, Thomas	37	Naomi	Liverpool	England	1847/06/15	1847/08/10
Ruth, John	7	Albion	Limerick	Ireland	1847/04/19	1847/06/18
Ruth, John	44	Albion	Limerick	Ireland	1847/04/19	1847/06/18
Ruth, Margaret	1	Albion	Limerick	Ireland	1847/04/19	1847/06/18
Rutledge, William	20	Larch	Sligo	Ireland	1847/07/11	1847/08/20
Rutledge, William	3	Larch	Sligo	Ireland	1847/07/11	1847/08/20
Rutledge, Winifred	30	Larch	Sligo	Ireland	1847/07/11	1847/08/20
Rutsek, Mary	38	City of Derry	London	England	1847/05/23	1847/07/04
Ruttle, John	14	Pursuit	Liverpool	England	1847/05/04	1847/06/23
Ryan, Allen	18	Lady Flora Hastings	Cork	Ireland	1847/05/11	1847/06/26
Ryan, Anthony		Julius Caesar	Liverpool	England	1847/07/13	1847/09/05
Ryan, Bridget	6	John Munn	Liverpool	England	1847/06/16	1847/08/13
Ryan, Edward	6	Emigrant	Liverpool	England	1847/08/11	1847/10/03
Ryan, James		Ninian	Limerick	Ireland	1847/04/13	1847/06/12
Ryan, James		Sir Henry Pottinger	Cork	Ireland	1847/05/29	1847/08/07
Ryan, Jemmy	3	Bee	Cork	Ireland	1847/04/17	1847/06/12
Ryan, Johanna	1	Avon	Cork	Ireland	1847/05/19	1847/07/26
Ryan, John	1	Bee	Cork	Ireland	1847/04/17	1847/06/12
Ryan, John	30	Scotland	Cork	Ireland	1847/04/13	1847/06/08
Ryan, John	15	Lady Milton	Liverpool	England	1847/05/05	1847/06/26
Ryan, John	2	John Munn	Liverpool	England	1847/06/16	1847/08/13
Ryan, John		John Munn	Liverpool	England	1847/06/16	1847/08/13
Ryan, Judith	7	Eagle	Dublin	Ireland	1847/05/12	1847/06/25
Ryan, Kerry	20	Lady Flora Hastings	Cork	Ireland	1847/05/11	1847/06/26
Ryan, Lawrence	48	Emily	Cork	Ireland	1847/05/12	1847/07/06
Ryan, Margaret	7	Alexander Stewart	Limerick	Ireland	1847/06/04	1847/07/28
Ryan, Margaret	2	Wakefield	Cork	Ireland	1847/05/28	1847/07/12
Ryan, Mary	30	Bee	Cork	Ireland	1847/04/17	1847/06/12
Ryan, Mary	1	John Bell	New Ross	Ireland	1847/05/10	1847/06/29
Ryan, Mary	30	Saguenay	Cork	Ireland	1847/06/05	1847/08/22
Ryan, Mary	2	Abbeylands	Liverpool	England	1847/06/15	1847/07/31
Ryan, Michael	3	Ninian	Limerick	Ireland	1847/04/13	1847/06/12
Ryan, Michael	4	John Bolton	Liverpool	England	1847/04/13	1847/06/10
Ryan, Mrs.	40	Coromandel	Dublin	Ireland	1847/05/13	1847/07/02
Ryan, Nancy	30	Bee	Cork	Ireland	1847/04/17	1847/06/12
Ryan, Nell	5	John Munn	Liverpool	England	1847/06/16	1847/08/13
Ryan, Patrick	8	Coromandel	Dublin	Ireland	1847/05/13	1847/07/02
Ryan, Richard	5	New York Packet	Liverpool	England	1847/04/24	1847/06/29
Ryan, Theresa	1	Wolfville	Sligo	Ireland	1847/04/25	1847/06/10
Ryan, Thomas	6	Abbeylands	Liverpool	England	1847/06/15	1847/07/31
Ryan, Timothy	25	Broom	Liverpool	England	1847/07/13	1847/08/06
Ryder, Allan		Goliah	Liverpool	England	1847/05/21	1847/07/18
Ryder, Margaret	1	Sir Robert Peel	Liverpool	England	1847/07/26	1847/09/19
Ryder, Peter	3	Sir Robert Peel	Liverpool	England	1847/07/26	1847/09/19
Sanders, John		Naomi	Liverpool	England	1847/06/15	1847/08/10
Sanders, Robert	2	Allan Kerr	Sligo	Ireland	1847/06/23	1847/08/04
Sanderson, Lander		Haubet	Hamburg	Germany	1847/07/02	1847/09/01
Sanderson, Margaret		Haubet	Hamburg	Germany	1847/07/02	1847/09/01
Santry, Patrick	10	Douce Davie	Sligo	Ireland	1847/08/11	1847/09/30
Saunders, Catherine	4	Avon	Cork	Ireland	1847/05/19	1847/07/26
Saunders, Margaret	28	Avon	Cork	Ireland	1847/05/19	1847/07/26
Saunders, Mary		Avon	Cork	Ireland	1847/05/19	1847/07/26
Saurin, Honora		Araminta	Liverpool	England	1847/05/01	1847/06/20
Saurin, John	1	Emigrant	Liverpool	England	1847/08/11	1847/10/03
Savin, Thomas		Larch	Sligo	Ireland	1847/07/11	1847/08/20
Scally, Bridget	23	Virginius	Liverpool	England	1847/05/28	1847/08/12
Scally, Bridget	55	Virginius	Liverpool	England	1847/05/28	1847/08/12
Scally, Elizabeth	8	Covenanter	Cork	Ireland	1847/06/17	1847/08/09
Scally, Jane	9	Covenanter	Cork	Ireland	1847/06/17	1847/08/09
Scally, Patrick	28	Virginius	Liverpool	England	1847/05/28	1847/08/12
Scally, Robert	70	Covenanter	Cork	Ireland	1847/06/17	1847/08/09

LIST OF PEOPLE WHO DIED ON SHIPS AT SEA OR IN QUARANTINE AT GROSSE ÎLE, IN 1847

Name	Age	Vessel	Port	Country	Embarkation	Qc Arrival
Scally, Sally	11	Covenanter	Cork	Ireland	1847/06/17	1847/08/09
Scally, Thomas	60	Covenanter	Cork	Ireland	1847/06/17	1847/08/09
Scally, Thomas	4	Covenanter	Cork	Ireland	1847/06/17	1847/08/09
Scanlan, Ann	12	Larch	Sligo	Ireland	1847/07/11	1847/08/20
Scanlan, John		Ann Kenny	Waterford	Ireland	1847/06/27	1847/08/05
Scanlan, Patrick	35	Dykes	Sligo	Ireland	1847/04/23	1847/06/10
Scanlan, Thomas	18	Larch	Sligo	Ireland	1847/07/11	1847/08/20
Scannell, Caroline	32	Agamemnon	Liverpool	England	1847/06/24	1847/07/31
Scannell, Francis	1	Agamemnon	Liverpool	England	1847/06/24	1847/07/31
Scheuter, Philomena	2	Henrietta Sophia	Hamburg	Germany	1847/05/12	1847/07/21
Schmidt, Catherine	5	Leontine	Bremen	Germany	1847/05/28	1847/07/28
Schmidt, Elizabeth	36	Leontine	Bremen	Germany	1847/05/28	1847/07/28
Scott, Francis	1	Ajax	Liverpool	England	1847/04/16	1847/06/23
Scott, Francis	2	Ajax	Liverpool	England	1847/04/16	1847/06/23
Scott, John	2	Douce Davie	Sligo	Ireland	1847/08/11	1847/09/30
Scott, Mrs.	46	Ajax	Liverpool	England	1847/04/16	1847/06/23
Scott, Mrs.	44	Ajax	Liverpool	England	1847/04/16	1847/06/23
Scott, Thomas	50	Ajax	Liverpool	England	1847/04/16	1847/06/23
Scott, Thomas		Ajax	Liverpool	England	1847/04/16	1847/06/23
Scott, Thomas		Ajax	Liverpool	England	1847/04/16	1847/06/23
Scott, William	50	Eliza Caroline	Liverpool	England	1847/05/03	1847/06/14
Scully, Catherine	55	Sisters	Liverpool	England	1847/04/22	1847/06/20
Scully, John	3	Agamemnon	Liverpool	England	1847/06/24	1847/07/31
Scully, Maria	1	Agamemnon	Liverpool	England	1847/06/24	1847/07/31
Seed, Thomas	24	Urania	Cork	Ireland	1847/04/09	1847/06/10
Sexton, Michael	24	Bee	Cork	Ireland	1847/04/17	1847/06/12
Sexton, Patrick	25	Bee	Cork	Ireland	1847/04/17	1847/06/12
Sexton, Patrick	25	Bee	Cork	Ireland	1847/04/17	1847/06/12
Seymour, Margaret	29	Corea	Liverpool	England	1847/07/02	1847/08/14
Seymour, Maria		Eagle	Dublin	Ireland	1847/05/12	1847/06/25
Shanahan, J.		Sir Henry Pottinger	Cork	Ireland	1847/05/29	1847/08/07
Shanahan, John	30	Avon	Cork	Ireland	1847/05/19	1847/07/26
Shanahan, John		Sir Henry Pottinger	Cork	Ireland	1847/05/29	1847/08/07
Shanley, James		Virginius	Liverpool	England	1847/05/28	1847/08/12
Shanley, Michael	17	Marchioness of Breadalbane	Sligo	Ireland	1847/06/11	1847/08/12
Shanlon, John	75	Larch	Sligo	Ireland	1847/07/11	1847/08/20
Shannon, Bridget	5	Sisters	Liverpool	England	1847/04/22	1847/06/20
Shannon, Daniel	6	Washington	Liverpool	England	1847/07/09	1847/08/26
Shannon, Edward	6	Independance	Belfast	Ireland	1847/05/23	1847/07/07
Shannon, Jane	9	Thetis	Limerick	Ireland	1847/05/10	1847/06/20
Shannon, Michael	54	Larch	Sligo	Ireland	1847/07/11	1847/08/20
Shannon, Sarah	1	Washington	Liverpool	England	1847/07/09	1847/08/26
Sharkey, Catherine	20	Virginius	Liverpool	England	1847/05/28	1847/08/12
Sharkey, John	16	Virginius	Liverpool	England	1847/05/28	1847/08/12
Sharkey, Margaret		Greenock	Liverpool	England	1847/06/19	1847/07/29
Shaw, John	4	Ann	Liverpool	England	1847/05/16	1847/06/30
Shaw, Joseph		Rosalinda	Belfast	Ireland	1847/06/22	1847/08/07
Shea, Ellen	3	Mail	Cork	Ireland	1847/04/25	1847/06/19
Shea, Honora	56	Mary Brack	Limerick	Ireland	1847/05/03	1847/06/12
Shea, Jane	30	Agnes	Cork	Ireland	1847/04/10	1847/06/10
Shea, Johanna	50	Avon	Cork	Ireland	1847/05/19	1847/07/26
Shea, John	20	Avon	Cork	Ireland	1847/05/19	1847/07/26
Shea, John	5	Avon	Cork	Ireland	1847/05/19	1847/07/26
Shea, John		Corea	Liverpool	England	1847/07/02	1847/08/14
Shea, John	29	Sir Henry Pottinger	Cork	Ireland	1847/05/29	1847/08/07
Shea, John	24	Urania	Cork	Ireland	1847/04/09	1847/06/10
Shea, Margaret		Avon	Cork	Ireland	1847/05/19	1847/07/26
Shea, Mary	3	Avon	Cork	Ireland	1847/05/19	1847/07/26
Shea, Mary	13	Bridgetown	Liverpool	England	1847/07/03	1847/08/29
Shea, Michael	17	Lord Ashburton	Liverpool	England	1847/09/13	1847/11/01
Shea, Patrick	1	Lady Flora Hastings	Cork	Ireland	1847/05/11	1847/06/26
Shea, Stephen	25	Saguenay	Cork	Ireland	1847/06/05	1847/08/22
Shearer, Stephen		Free Briton	Cork	Ireland	1847/05/25	1847/07/10
Sheehan, Catherine	5	Avon	Cork	Ireland	1847/05/19	1847/07/26
Sheehan, Catherine	22	Asia	Cork	Ireland	1847/06/02	1847/07/27
Sheehan, Ellen	12	Avon	Cork	Ireland	1847/05/19	1847/07/26
Sheehan, Honora		Asia	Cork	Ireland	1847/06/02	1847/07/27
Sheehan, James	28	Gilmour	Cork	Ireland	1847/04/24	1847/06/18
Sheehan, Margaret	9	Avon	Cork	Ireland	1847/05/19	1847/07/26
Sheehan, Mary	5	Avon	Cork	Ireland	1847/05/19	1847/07/26
Sheehan, Mary	20	Lady Flora Hastings	Cork	Ireland	1847/05/11	1847/06/26
Sheehan, Mary	18	Saguenay	Cork	Ireland	1847/06/05	1847/08/22
Sheehan, Morris	35	Asia	Cork	Ireland	1847/06/02	1847/07/27
Sheehey, Bridget	4	Champion	Liverpool	England	1847/07/13	1847/08/28
Sheehey, Mary	24	Champion	Liverpool	England	1847/07/13	1847/08/28
Sheehey, Thomas	30	Champion	Liverpool	England	1847/07/13	1847/08/28
Sheeran, Bryan	45	Emigrant	Liverpool	England	1847/08/11	1847/10/03
Sheridan, Ann	38	Eliza Caroline	Liverpool	England	1847/05/03	1847/06/14
Sheridan, Bridget		Naomi	Liverpool	England	1847/06/15	1847/08/10
Sheridan, Bridget	3	Colonist	New Ross	Ireland	1847/07/13	1847/08/29
Sheridan, James	60	Naomi	Liverpool	England	1847/06/15	1847/08/10
Sheridan, John	22	Naomi	Liverpool	England	1847/06/15	1847/08/10
Sheridan, Matthew	11	Sarah	Liverpool	England	1847/05/29	1847/07/19
Sheridan, Michael	3	Erin's Queen	Liverpool	England	1847/06/01	1847/07/23
Sherlock, Ann	4	Wolfville	Sligo	Ireland	1847/04/25	1847/06/10
Sherlock, Maria	2	Wolfville	Sligo	Ireland	1847/04/25	1847/06/10
Sherman, Ann		Lotus	Liverpool	England	1847/04/15	1847/06/24
Sherman, James	10	Lotus	Liverpool	England	1847/04/15	1847/06/24
Sherone, Martin	28	Lady Milton	Liverpool	England	1847/05/05	1847/06/26
Sherrard, Mary	5	Rose	Liverpool	England	1847/04/19	1847/07/01
Sherrard, Oliver	25	Emigrant	Liverpool	England	1847/08/11	1847/10/03
Sherrard, Warthy		Emigrant	Liverpool	England	1847/08/11	1847/10/03
Sherry, Isabella	7	Argo	Liverpool	England	1847/05/04	1847/06/12
Sherry, James	1	Argo	Liverpool	England	1847/05/04	1847/06/12
Sherry, James	1	Argo	Liverpool	England	1847/05/04	1847/06/12
Sherry, John	1	Agnes	Cork	Ireland	1847/04/10	1847/06/10
Sherry, Mary	9	Argo	Liverpool	England	1847/05/04	1847/06/12
Sherry, Richard	12	Agnes	Cork	Ireland	1847/04/10	1847/06/10
Shiel, Ann	60	Wellington	Liverpool	England	1847/07/29	1847/09/20
Shiel, Jane	40	Bridgetown	Liverpool	England	1847/07/03	1847/08/29
Shiel, Mary	21	Lady Flora Hastings	Cork	Ireland	1847/05/11	1847/06/26
Shiel, Sydney	1	Leander	Londonderry	Ireland	1847/06/13	1847/07/31
Shields, Sarah		Ganges	Liverpool	England	1847/06/16	1847/08/21
Shortt, Mary	20	Goliah	Liverpool	England	1847/05/21	1847/07/18
Silke, Johanna	18	Dominica	Cork	Ireland	1847/05/01	1847/06/14
Simms, William S.	3	Agamemnon	Liverpool	England	1847/06/24	1847/07/31
Simpson, Margaret	4	Tamarac	Liverpool	England	1847/05/26	1847/07/11
Simpson, Mary	68	Larch	Sligo	Ireland	1847/07/11	1847/08/20
Simpson, William	2	Tamarac	Liverpool	England	1847/05/26	1847/07/11
Sinclair, Andrew	17	Scotland	Cork	Ireland	1847/04/13	1847/06/08
Skerrett, Walter	2	Emigrant	Liverpool	England	1847/08/11	1847/10/03
Slater, John	16	Emigrant	Liverpool	England	1847/08/11	1847/10/03
Sleith, Johanna	30	Juliet	London	England	1847/07/03	1847/08/28
Sloan, Margaret	3	Goliah	Liverpool	England	1847/05/21	1847/07/18
Sloan, Randolph	1	Juliet	London	England	1847/07/03	1847/08/28
Sloan, Robert	30	Goliah	Liverpool	England	1847/05/21	1847/07/18
Small, Bridget	1	Venilia	Limerick	Ireland	1847/05/28	1847/07/11
Smart, Celina	3	John Bolton	Liverpool	England	1847/04/13	1847/06/10
Smith, Ann		Lord Ashburton	Liverpool	England	1847/09/13	1847/11/01
Smith, Bridget	2	Virginius	Liverpool	England	1847/05/28	1847/08/12
Smith, Charles	23	Triton	Liverpool	England	1847/05/14	1847/07/24
Smith, David	8	Wellington	Liverpool	England	1847/07/29	1847/09/20
Smith, Edward	12	Ajax	Liverpool	England	1847/04/16	1847/06/23
Smith, Elizabeth	18	Lotus	Liverpool	England	1847/04/15	1847/06/24

List of people who died on ships at sea or in quarantine at Grosse Île, in 1847

Name	Age	Vessel	Port	Country	Embarkation	Qc Arrival
Smith, Elizabeth	1	Juliet	London	England	1847/07/03	1847/08/28
Smith, James	4	John Bolton	Liverpool	England	1847/04/13	1847/06/10
Smith, Jerry		Junior	Liverpool	England	1847/05/10	1847/07/03
Smith, Mary		George	Liverpool	England	1847/04/13	1847/06/12
Smith, Mary	55	Emigrant	Liverpool	England	1847/08/11	1847/10/03
Smith, Matthew	26	Margaret	New Ross	Ireland	1847/05/19	1847/07/02
Smith, William		Trade	Waterford	Ireland	1847/04/17	1847/06/26
Smyth, Andrew	70	Herald	Dublin	Ireland	1847/05/20	1847/06/26
Smyth, Patrick	52	Virginius	Liverpool	England	1847/05/28	1847/08/12
Smyth, Thomas	34	Yorkshire	Liverpool	England	1847/06/09	1847/08/10
Spears, Margaret		Goliah	Liverpool	England	1847/05/21	1847/07/18
Spellman, Bridget	13	John Bolton	Liverpool	England	1847/04/13	1847/06/10
Spence, John		Margrette	New Ross	Ireland	1847/05/02	1847/07/08
Spillane, Eliza	5	Agnes	Cork	Ireland	1847/04/10	1847/06/10
Stack, John	1	Triton	Liverpool	England	1847/05/14	1847/07/24
Stack, Mary	4	Triton	Liverpool	England	1847/05/14	1847/07/24
Stack, Thomas	2	Tay	Sligo	Ireland	1847/05/05	1847/06/09
Stack, William	7	Triton	Liverpool	England	1847/05/14	1847/07/24
Stanton, Alexander		New Zealand	Newry	Ireland	1847/05/20	1847/07/03
Stanton, John	50	George	Liverpool	England	1847/04/13	1847/06/12
Stanton, Michael	24	Bee	Cork	Ireland	1847/04/17	1847/06/12
Stanton, Michael	23	Triton	Liverpool	England	1847/05/14	1847/07/24
Starr, Thomas	70	Jessie	Limerick	Ireland	1847/06/25	1847/08/09
Steel, Hugh	18	Leander	Londonderry	Ireland	1847/06/13	1847/07/31
Steel, James	4	Sir Henry Pottinger	Belfast	Ireland	1847/07/09	1847/08/29
Steel, John	20	Aberdeen	Liverpool	England	1847/05/01	1847/06/13
Steel, John	48	Aberdeen	Liverpool	England	1847/05/01	1847/06/13
Steel, John	3	Araminta	Liverpool	England	1847/05/01	1847/06/20
Steel, John	48	Araminta	Liverpool	England	1847/05/01	1847/06/20
Steel, Margaret	42	Araminta	Liverpool	England	1847/05/01	1847/06/20
Steel, Margaret Jane	1	Marchioness of Abercorn	Londonderry	Ireland	1847/06/15	1847/08/05
Steel, Martha	8	Araminta	Liverpool	England	1847/05/01	1847/06/20
Steel, Martha	8	Aberdeen	Liverpool	England	1847/05/01	1847/06/13
Steel, Mary	42	Aberdeen	Liverpool	England	1847/05/01	1847/06/13
Steel, Robert		Aberdeen	Liverpool	England	1847/05/01	1847/06/13
Steel, Robert		Araminta	Liverpool	England	1847/05/01	1847/06/20
Steenson, James		Sesostris	Londonderry	Ireland	1847/05/14	1847/06/24
Stenson, James		Herald	Dublin	Ireland	1847/05/20	1847/06/26
Stone, James	23	Sir Henry Pottinger	Cork	Ireland	1847/05/29	1847/08/07
Stone, James	30	Sir Henry Pottinger	Cork	Ireland	1847/05/29	1847/08/07
Stoop, Sarah	2	Tamarac	Liverpool	England	1847/05/26	1847/07/11
Storey, William	1	Aberdeen	Liverpool	England	1847/05/01	1847/06/13
Storey, William		Araminta	Liverpool	England	1847/05/01	1847/06/20
Strahan, George	34	Larch	Sligo	Ireland	1847/07/11	1847/08/20
Straren, Wilhelm		General Hewitt	Bremen	Germany	1847/07/22	1847/09/12
Strecht, Herman	2	Henrietta Sophia	Hamburg	Germany	1847/05/12	1847/07/21
Stringer, C.	5	Lord Seaton	Belfast	Ireland	1847/04/12	1847/06/10
Stringer, Prudence	1	Lord Seaton	Belfast	Ireland	1847/04/12	1847/06/10
Stritch, Johanna	2	Canton	Bremen	Germany	1847/06/20	1847/08/07
Stritch, John	1	Lotus	Liverpool	England	1847/04/15	1847/06/24
Stritch, Maria	6	Canton	Bremen	Germany	1847/06/20	1847/08/07
Stritch, Mary		Lotus	Liverpool	England	1847/04/15	1847/06/24
Stuart, David	1	Marchioness of Abercorn	Londonderry	Ireland	1847/06/15	1847/08/05
Stuart, Eliza	3	Goliah	Liverpool	England	1847/05/21	1847/07/18
Stuart, John	4	Marchioness of Abercorn	Londonderry	Ireland	1847/06/15	1847/08/05
Stuart, Margaret Jane	6	Marchioness of Abercorn	Londonberry	Ireland	1847/06/15	1847/08/05
Stuart, Mary Ann	1	Julius Caesar	Liverpool	England	1847/07/13	1847/09/05
Stuart, Patrick		Tay	Liverpool	England	1847/05/22	1847/06/23
Stuart, Sarah		Emigrant	Liverpool	England	1847/08/11	1847/10/03
Stuart, William	3	Marchioness of Abercorn	Londonderry	Ireland	1847/06/15	1847/08/05
Sullivan, Ann	40	Avon	Cork	Ireland	1847/05/19	1847/07/26
Sullivan, Bridget	17	Agnes	Cork	Ireland	1847/04/10	1847/06/10
Sullivan, Bridget	4	Eliza Caroline	Liverpool	England	1847/05/03	1847/06/14
Sullivan, Bridget	17	Agnes	Cork	Ireland	1847/04/10	1847/06/10
Sullivan, Catherine	2	Pacha	Cork	Ireland	1847/05/05	1847/06/14
Sullivan, Catherine	50	Scotland	Cork	Ireland	1847/04/13	1847/06/08
Sullivan, Catherine	25	Sir Henry Pottinger	Cork	Ireland	1847/05/29	1847/08/07
Sullivan, Catherine	60	Naparina	Dublin	Ireland	1847/06/17	1847/08/23
Sullivan, Catherine	3	Bee	Cork	Ireland	1847/04/17	1847/06/12
Sullivan, Catherine	3	Bee	Cork	Ireland	1847/04/17	1847/06/12
Sullivan, Catherine		Lord Sandon	Cork	Ireland	1847/05/11	1847/06/26
Sullivan, Catherine	2	Avon	Cork	Ireland	1847/05/19	1847/07/26
Sullivan, Cornelius	15	Covenanter	Cork	Ireland	1847/06/17	1847/08/09
Sullivan, Daniel	2	Charles Richard	Sligo	Ireland	1847/05/27	1847/07/16
Sullivan, Daniel	2	Greenock	Liverpool	England	1847/06/19	1847/07/29
Sullivan, Daniel	30	Washington	Liverpool	England	1847/07/09	1847/08/26
Sullivan, Daniel	2	Julius Caesar	Liverpool	England	1847/07/13	1847/09/05
Sullivan, Daniel	23	Sir Robert Peel	Liverpool	England	1847/07/26	1847/09/19
Sullivan, Darby	14	Lady Flora Hastings	Cork	Ireland	1847/05/11	1847/06/26
Sullivan, Denis	24	Bridgetown	Liverpool	England	1847/07/03	1847/08/29
Sullivan, Dennis	26	Avon	Cork	Ireland	1847/05/19	1847/07/26
Sullivan, Ellen	5	Avon	Cork	Ireland	1847/05/19	1847/07/26
Sullivan, Ellen	2	Sir Robert Peel	Liverpool	England	1847/07/26	1847/09/19
Sullivan, Ellen	13	Saguenay	Cork	Ireland	1847/06/05	1847/08/22
Sullivan, Humphrey	32	Agnes	Cork	Ireland	1847/04/10	1847/06/10
Sullivan, James	23	Scotland	Cork	Ireland	1847/04/13	1847/06/08
Sullivan, James	16	Lady Flora Hastings	Cork	Ireland	1847/05/11	1847/06/26
Sullivan, James	6	Scotland	Cork	Ireland	1847/04/13	1847/06/08
Sullivan, James	1	Scotland	Cork	Ireland	1847/04/13	1847/06/08
Sullivan, James	24	Urania	Cork	Ireland	1847/04/09	1847/06/10
Sullivan, Jemmy	7	Pacha	Cork	Ireland	1847/05/05	1847/06/14
Sullivan, Jennifer	3	John Francis	Cork	Ireland	1847/04/10	1847/06/10
Sullivan, Jerry	4	Pacha	Cork	Ireland	1847/05/05	1847/06/14
Sullivan, Johanna	5	Avon	Cork	Ireland	1847/05/19	1847/07/26
Sullivan, John		Agnes	Cork	Ireland	1847/04/10	1847/06/10
Sullivan, John	28	Mail	Cork	Ireland	1847/04/25	1847/06/19
Sullivan, John	1	Sir Henry Pottinger	Cork	Ireland	1847/05/29	1847/08/07
Sullivan, John	9	Saguenay	Cork	Ireland	1847/06/05	1847/08/22
Sullivan, John		Jessie	Cork	Ireland	1847/06/03	1847/07/24
Sullivan, John	20	Jessie	Cork	Ireland	1847/06/03	1847/07/24
Sullivan, Judith	22	Agnes	Cork	Ireland	1847/04/10	1847/06/10
Sullivan, Judith	1	Agnes	Cork	Ireland	1847/04/10	1847/06/10
Sullivan, Mary	30	Agnes	Cork	Ireland	1847/04/10	1847/06/10
Sullivan, Mary	20	Avon	Cork	Ireland	1847/05/19	1847/07/26
Sullivan, Mary	24	Sir Henry Pottinger	Cork	Ireland	1847/05/29	1847/08/07
Sullivan, Mary	16	Saguenay	Cork	Ireland	1847/06/05	1847/08/22
Sullivan, Mary	4	Covenanter	Cork	Ireland	1847/06/17	1847/08/09
Sullivan, Mary	6	George	Liverpool	England	1847/04/13	1847/06/12
Sullivan, Mary		Avon	Cork	Ireland	1847/05/19	1847/07/26
Sullivan, Michael	9	Avon	Cork	Ireland	1847/05/19	1847/07/26
Sullivan, Patrick	1	Lady Flora Hastings	Cork	Ireland	1847/05/11	1847/06/26
Sullivan, Patrick	28	Wakefield	Cork	Ireland	1847/05/28	1847/07/12
Sullivan, Patrick	35	Wakefield	Cork	Ireland	1847/05/28	1847/07/12
Sullivan, Patrick		Avon	Cork	Ireland	1847/05/19	1847/07/26
Sullivan, Patrick	2	Lord Ashburton	Liverpool	England	1847/09/13	1847/11/01
Sullivan, Patrick		Lotus	Liverpool	England	1847/04/15	1847/06/24
Sullivan, Sarah		Pursuit	Liverpool	England	1847/05/04	1847/06/23
Sullivan, Simon	28	Mail	Cork	Ireland	1847/04/25	1847/06/19
Sullivan, Timothy	1	Julius Caesar	Liverpool	England	1847/07/13	1847/09/05
Sullivan, Timothy	4	Lord Sandon	Cork	Ireland	1847/05/11	1847/06/26

List of people who died on ships at sea or in quarantine at Grosse Île, in 1847

Name	Age	Vessel	Port	Country	Embarkation	Qc Arrival
Sullivan, William		Avon	Cork	Ireland	1847/05/19	1847/07/26
Sutton, Peter	25	Columbia	Sligo	Ireland	1847/05/01	1847/06/10
Swally, Daniel		Lady Milton	Liverpool	England	1847/05/05	1847/06/26
Swanton, Barry	3	Covenanter	Cork	Ireland	1847/06/17	1847/08/09
Sweeney, Brian	29	Mail	Cork	Ireland	1847/04/25	1847/06/19
Sweeney, Cornelius	20	Avon	Cork	Ireland	1847/05/19	1847/07/26
Sweeney, David	4	Washington	Liverpool	England	1847/07/09	1847/08/26
Sweeney, Johanna		Mail	Cork	Ireland	1847/04/25	1847/06/19
Sweeney, John	3	Tay	Sligo	Ireland	1847/05/05	1847/06/09
Sweeney, John	8	Lotus	Liverpool	England	1847/04/15	1847/06/24
Sweeney, Margaret	3	Margrette	New Ross	Ireland	1847/05/02	1847/07/08
Sweeney, Mary	25	Douce Davie	Sligo		1847/08/11	1847/09/30
Sweeney, Owen	25	Saguenay	Cork	Ireland	1847/06/05	1847/08/22
Sweeney, Terrence	40	Avon	Cork	Ireland	1847/05/19	1847/07/26
Swift, Jane	2	Wolfville	Sligo	Ireland	1847/04/25	1847/06/10
Switzer, Michael		Primrose	Limerick	Ireland	1847/04/07	1847/06/18
Synge, Patrick	6	El en	Sligo	Ireland	1847/05/27	1847/07/10
Taaffe, Ellen	8	Saguenay	Cork	Ireland	1847/06/05	1847/08/22
Taaffe, Mary	8	Saguenay	Cork	Ireland	1847/06/05	1847/08/22
Talbot, Mary	2	Saguenay	Cork	Ireland	1847/06/05	1847/08/22
Tally, Denis	9	Wellington	Liverpool	England	1847/07/29	1847/09/20
Tansey, Dennis	26	Dykes	Sligo	Ireland	1847/04/23	1847/06/10
Tansey, James	2	Dykes	Sligo	Ireland	1847/04/23	1847/06/10
Tarrant, Edward	45	James Moran	Liverpool	England	1847/05/22	1847/07/11
Tate, James		Julius Caesar	Liverpool	England	1847/07/13	1847/09/05
Tate, Margaret	40	Larch	Sligo	Ireland	1847/07/11	1847/08/20
Taylor, Catherine	6	Larch	Sligo	Ireland	1847/07/11	1847/08/20
Taylor, Edward	53	Larch	Sligo	Ireland	1847/07/11	1847/08/20
Taylor, Jane	35	Westmoreland	Sligo	Ireland	1847/06/12	1847/08/10
Taylor, John		Larch	Sligo	Ireland	1847/07/11	1847/08/20
Taylor, John	40	Larch	Sligo	Ireland	1847/07/11	1847/08/20
Taylor, John		Westmoreland	Sligo	Ireland	1847/06/12	1847/08/10
Taylor, Mary	42	Larch	Sligo	Ireland	1847/07/11	1847/08/20
Taylor, Robert	3	Westmoreland	Sligo	Ireland	1847/06/12	1847/08/10
Teague, Anthony		Royal Adelaide	Killala	Ireland	1847/06/09	1847/08/09
Teague, Bridget	4	John Bolton	Liverpool	England	1847/04/13	1847/06/10
Teague, James	43	Larch	Sligo	Ireland	1847/07/11	1847/08/20
Teague, Mary	12	John Bolton	Liverpool	England	1847/04/13	1847/06/10
Teague, Rodger	2	Washington	Liverpool	England	1847/07/09	1847/08/26
Teague, Sarah		Washington	Liverpool	England	1847/07/09	1847/08/26
Teahan, Bridget	23	Lady Flora Hastings	Cork	Ireland	1847/05/11	1847/06/26
Teahan, Henry		Mary	Sligo	Ireland	1847/05/24	1847/07/27
Temple, Jerry	1	Josepha	Belfast	Ireland	1847/05/09	1847/06/18
Thompson, Ann	1	Charles Richard	Sligo	Ireland	1847/05/27	1847/07/16
Thompson, Eliza	46	Marchioness of Bute	Belfast	Ireland	1847/06/10	1847/07/31
Thompson, James		Goliah	Liverpool	England	1847/05/21	1847/07/18
Thompson, James		Goliah	Liverpool	England	1847/05/21	1847/07/18
Thompson, James	84	Larch	Sligo	Ireland	1847/07/11	1847/08/20
Thompson, James	7	Tamarac	Liverpool	England	1847/05/26	1847/07/11
Thompson, Maria	4	Lady Milton	Liverpool	England	1847/05/05	1847/06/26
Thompson, Theresa	2	Yorkshire	Liverpool	England	1847/06/09	1847/08/10
Thompson, Thomas	50	Marchioness of Bute	Belfast	Ireland	1847/06/10	1847/07/31
Thompson, William	1	Sir Henry Pottinger	Cork	Ireland	1847/05/29	1847/08/07
Thornton, Elizabeth	17	James Moran	Liverpool	England	1847/05/22	1847/07/11
Thornton, Theresa		Yorkshire	Liverpool	England	1847/06/09	1847/08/10
Thynne, Eliza	2	Lord Sandon	Cork	Ireland	1847/05/11	1847/06/26
Tierney, Ann	50	Corea	Liverpool	England	1847/07/02	1847/08/14
Tierney, Bridget	7	Rose	Liverpool	England	1847/04/19	1847/07/01
Tierney, Bridget	4	Agamemnon	Liverpool	England	1847/06/24	1847/07/31
Tierney, Catherine	25	Rose	Liverpool	England	1847/04/19	1847/07/01
Tierney, James	9	Jessie	Limerick	Ireland	1847/04/18	1847/06/26
Tierney, James	4	Rose	Liverpool	England	1847/04/19	1847/07/01
Tierney, John	45	James Moran	Liverpool	England	1847/05/22	1847/07/11
Tierney, Mary		Goliah	Liverpool	England	1847/05/21	1847/07/18
Tierney, Michael	4	Rose	Liverpool	England	1847/04/19	1847/07/01
Tierney, Nancy	45	Jessie	Limerick	Ireland	1847/04/18	1847/06/26
Timlin, Honora	8	Eliza Caroline	Liverpool	England	1847/05/03	1847/06/14
Timlin, Mary	2	Eliza Caroline	Liverpool	England	1847/05/03	1847/06/14
Timmons, Andrew	60	Tay	Sligo	Ireland	1847/05/05	1847/06/09
Timmons, John	11	Columbia	Sligo	Ireland	1847/05/01	1847/06/10
Timmons, John	45	Eliza Caroline	Liverpool	England	1847/05/03	1847/06/14
Timmons, Philip	6	Columbia	Sligo	Ireland	1847/05/01	1847/06/10
Timony, Bartholomew	22	Gilmour	Cork	Ireland	1847/04/24	1847/06/18
Timony, Patrick	6	Wolfville	Sligo	Ireland	1847/04/25	1847/06/10
Toal, Mary	20	Scotland	Cork	Ireland	1847/04/13	1847/06/08
Tobin, Bridget	50	Saguenay	Cork	Ireland	1847/06/05	1847/08/22
Tobin, Elizabeth	25	Agnes	Cork	Ireland	1847/04/10	1847/06/10
Tobin, James	18	Jessie	Cork	Ireland	1847/06/03	1847/07/24
Tobin, John	28	Jessie	Cork	Ireland	1847/06/03	1847/07/24
Tobin, John	30	Sobraon	Liverpool	England	1847/05/08	1847/06/29
Tobin, Judith	22	Jessie	Cork	Ireland	1847/06/03	1847/07/24
Tobin, Michael	2	Jane Black	Limerick	Ireland	1847/08/10	1847/09/17
Tobin, Nancy	2	Agnes	Cork	Ireland	1847/04/10	1847/06/10
Tolan, Mary	2	Sisters	Liverpool	England	1847/04/22	1847/06/20
Tomelty, Ellen	8	Saguenay	Cork	Ireland	1847/06/05	1847/08/22
Toner, William	5	Goliah	Liverpool	England	1847/05/21	1847/07/18
Toole, Catherine	2	Sisters	Liverpool	England	1847/04/22	1847/06/20
Toole, James	1	Argo	Liverpool	England	1847/05/04	1847/06/12
Toole, Michael	1	Ninian	Limerick	Ireland	1847/04/13	1847/06/12
Toole, Simpson	30	Ajax	Liverpool	England	1847/04/16	1847/06/23
Toomey, Ellen	3	Avon	Cork	Ireland	1847/05/19	1847/07/26
Toomey, Mary	30	Avon	Cork	Ireland	1847/05/19	1847/07/26
Tracey, Catherine	20	Sir Henry Pottinger	Cork	Ireland	1847/05/29	1847/08/07
Tracey, John	12	Jessie	Limerick	Ireland	1847/06/25	1847/08/09
Tracey, John	11	Agamemnon	Liverpool	England	1847/06/24	1847/07/31
Tracey, Margaret	28	Lord Ashburton	Liverpool	England	1847/09/13	1847/11/01
Trainor, Armstrong		Frankfield	Liverpool	England	1847/06/29	1847/08/09
Trainor, Mary	24	Yorkshire	Liverpool	England	1847/06/09	1847/08/10
Travers, Patrick		Sisters	Liverpool	England	1847/04/22	1847/06/20
Traynor, Peter	40	Lillias	Dublin	Ireland	1847/07/01	1847/08/16
Trotter, Henry	7	Bridgetown	Liverpool	England	1847/07/03	1847/08/29
Trotter, Mary	2	Ajax	Liverpool	England	1847/04/16	1847/06/23
Trotter, Mary	40	Bridgetown	Liverpool	England	1847/07/03	1847/08/29
Trotter, Melinda		Ajax	Liverpool	England	1847/04/16	1847/06/23
Trotter, Morris	2	Tamarac	Liverpool	England	1847/05/26	1847/07/11
Trotter, Walter	40	Bridgetown	Liverpool	England	1847/07/03	1847/08/29
Tuchs, Margarete	57	Henrietta Sophia	Hamburg	Germany	1847/05/12	1847/07/21
Tucker, Ann		Larch	Sligo	Ireland	1847/07/11	1847/08/20
Tucker, Patrick	35	Larch	Sligo	Ireland	1847/07/11	1847/08/20
Tully, John		Naomi	Liverpool	England	1847/06/15	1847/08/10
Tunny, Michael	40	Avon	Cork	Ireland	1847/05/19	1847/07/26
Turnbull, Daniel	3	Yorkshire	Liverpool	England	1847/06/09	1847/08/10
Turnbull, John		Yorkshire	Liverpool	England	1847/06/09	1847/08/10
Turnbull, Robert	2	Yorkshire	Liverpool	England	1847/06/09	1847/08/10
Turner, Elizabeth	50	Naomi	Liverpool	England	1847/06/15	1847/08/10
Turner, James	16	Naomi	Liverpool	England	1847/06/15	1847/08/10
Turner, John	6	Naomi	Liverpool	England	1847/06/15	1847/08/10
Turner, Mary	52	Naomi	Liverpool	England	1847/06/15	1847/08/10
Turner, Mary	57	Collingwood	Londonderry	Ireland	1847/05/27	1847/07/13
Turner, Thomas	60	Collingwood	Londonderry	Ireland	1847/05/27	1847/07/13
Twohig, John	1	Ninian	Limerick	Ireland	1847/04/13	1847/06/12
Tyrrell, John	33	Sir Henry Pottinger	Cork	Ireland	1847/05/29	1847/08/07
Tyrrell, Patrick	1	Odessa	Dublin	Ireland	1847/06/09	1847/08/09
Unknown		Agnes	Cork	Ireland	1847/04/10	1847/06/10
Unknown		Agnes	Cork	Ireland	1847/04/10	1847/06/10

LIST OF PEOPLE WHO DIED ON SHIPS AT SEA OR IN QUARANTINE AT GROSSE ÎLE, IN 1847

Name	Age	Vessel	Port	Country	Embarkation	Qc Arrival
Unknown		Agnes	Cork	Ireland	1847/04/10	1847/06/10
Unknown		Agnes	Cork	Ireland	1847/04/10	1847/06/10
Unknown		Agnes	Cork	Ireland	1847/04/10	1847/06/10
Unknown		Agnes	Cork	Ireland	1847/04/10	1847/06/10
Unknown		Agnes	Cork	Ireland	1847/04/10	1847/06/10
Unknown		Saguenay	Cork	Ireland	1847/06/05	1847/08/22
Unknown		Saguenay	Cork	Ireland	1847/06/05	1847/08/22
Unknown		Saguenay	Cork	Ireland	1847/06/05	1847/08/22
Unknown		Saguenay	Cork	Ireland	1847/06/05	1847/08/22
Unknown		Saguenay	Cork	Ireland	1847/06/05	1847/08/22
Unknown		Saguenay	Cork	Ireland	1847/06/05	1847/08/22
Unknown		Saguenay	Cork	Ireland	1847/06/05	1847/08/22
Unknown		Saguenay	Cork	Ireland	1847/06/05	1847/08/22
Unknown		Saguenay	Cork	Ireland	1847/06/05	1847/08/22
Unknown		Saguenay	Cork	Ireland	1847/06/05	1847/08/22
Unknown		Saguenay	Cork	Ireland	1847/06/05	1847/08/22
Unknown		Saguenay	Cork	Ireland	1847/06/05	1847/08/22
Unknown		Saguenay	Cork	Ireland	1847/06/05	1847/08/22
Unknown		Saguenay	Cork	Ireland	1847/06/05	1847/08/22
Unknown		Saguenay	Cork	Ireland	1847/06/05	1847/08/22
Unknown		Saguenay	Cork	Ireland	1847/06/05	1847/08/22
Unknown		Saguenay	Cork	Ireland	1847/06/05	1847/08/22
Unknown		Saguenay	Cork	Ireland	1847/06/05	1847/08/22
Unknown		Saguenay	Cork	Ireland	1847/06/05	1847/08/22
Unknown		Saguenay	Cork	Ireland	1847/06/05	1847/08/22
Unknown		Saguenay	Cork	Ireland	1847/06/05	1847/08/22
Unknown		Saguenay	Cork	Ireland	1847/06/05	1847/08/22
Unknown		Saguenay	Cork	Ireland	1847/06/05	1847/08/22
Unknown		Saguenay	Cork	Ireland	1847/06/05	1847/08/22
Unknown		Saguenay	Cork	Ireland	1847/06/05	1847/08/22
Unknown		Saguenay	Cork	Ireland	1847/06/05	1847/08/22
Unknown		Saguenay	Cork	Ireland	1847/06/05	1847/08/22
Unknown		Saguenay	Cork	Ireland	1847/06/05	1847/08/22
Unknown		Saguenay	Cork	Ireland	1847/06/05	1847/08/22
Unknown		Saguenay	Cork	Ireland	1847/06/05	1847/08/22
Unknown		Henrietta Mary	Cork	Ireland	1847/08/18	1847/09/29
Unknown		Lord Ashburton	Liverpool	England	1847/09/13	1847/11/01
Unknown		Lord Ashburton	Liverpool	England	1847/09/13	1847/11/01
Unknown		Lord Ashburton	Liverpool	England	1847/09/13	1847/11/01
Unknown		Agnes	Cork	Ireland	1847/04/10	1847/06/10
Unknown		Agnes	Cork	Ireland	1847/04/10	1847/06/10
Vandine, Ellen		Mary	Sligo	Ireland	1847/05/24	1847/07/27
Vandine, Patrick	35	Bee	Cork	Ireland	1847/04/17	1847/06/12
Vaughan, Martin	60	Anna Maria	Limerick	Ireland	1847/07/03	1847/08/11
Verdon, Thomas	28	Bee	Cork	Ireland	1847/04/17	1847/06/12
Verling, Bridget	24	Bee	Cork	Ireland	1847/04/17	1847/06/12
Waddell, David	2	Yorkshire	Liverpool	England	1847/06/09	1847/08/10
Waddell, James	40	Ayrshire	Newry	Ireland	1847/07/04	1847/08/19
Wade, Ann	3	Blenheim	Cork	Ireland	1847/06/16	1847/07/29
Wade, Bridget	6	Blenheim	Cork	Ireland	1847/06/16	1847/07/29
Waldron, Alearnia	5	George	Liverpool	England	1847/04/13	1847/06/12
Waldron, Ann		George	Liverpool	England	1847/04/13	1847/06/12
Waleys, Charles	25	Dominica	Cork	Ireland	1847/05/01	1847/06/14
Walker, Jane	3	Lord Seaton	Belfast	Ireland	1847/04/12	1847/06/10
Walker, Janet	1	Sobraon	Liverpool	England	1847/05/08	1847/06/29
Walker, Mary Ann	1	Lord Seaton	Belfast	Ireland	1847/04/12	1847/06/10
Walker, Thomas	34	Sobraon	Liverpool	England	1847/05/08	1847/06/29
Wall, John	24	Rose	Liverpool	England	1847/04/19	1847/07/01
Wall, Mary	60	Odessa	Dublin	Ireland	1847/06/09	1847/08/09
Wall, Mary	2	Odessa	Dublin	Ireland	1847/06/09	1847/08/09
Wall, Thomas	45	Bee	Cork	Ireland	1847/04/17	1847/06/12
Wall, Thomas	45	Bee	Cork	Ireland	1847/04/17	1847/06/12
Wallace, Ellen	1	Covenanter	Cork	Ireland	1847/06/17	1847/08/09
Wallace, James	2	Progress	New Ross	Ireland	1847/05/05	1847/07/14
Wallace, Thomas	18	Covenanter	Cork	Ireland	1847/06/17	1847/08/09
Waller, Patrick	28	James Moran	Liverpool	England	1847/05/22	1847/07/11
Walsh, Ann	2	Lord Ashburton	Liverpool	England	1847/09/13	1847/11/01
Walsh, Bridget	22	Scotland	Cork	Ireland	1847/04/13	1847/06/08
Walsh, Daniel	10	Saguenay	Cork	Ireland	1847/06/05	1847/08/22
Walsh, Edward	8	Triton	Liverpool	England	1847/05/14	1847/07/24
Walsh, Ellen		Naparina	Dublin	Ireland	1847/06/17	1847/08/23
Walsh, Henry	58	Rosalinda	Belfast	Ireland	1847/06/22	1847/08/07
Walsh, J.		Lady Campbell	Dublin	Ireland	1847/06/03	1847/08/05
Walsh, James	28	Saguenay	Cork	Ireland	1847/06/05	1847/08/22
Walsh, James	40	Blenheim	Cork	Ireland	1847/06/16	1847/07/29
Walsh, John	40	Naparina	Dublin	Ireland	1847/06/17	1847/08/23
Walsh, John	32	Saguenay	Cork	Ireland	1847/06/05	1847/08/22
Walsh, Judith	3	Emigrant	Liverpool	England	1847/08/11	1847/10/03
Walsh, Mary	5	Gilmour	Cork	Ireland	1847/04/24	1847/06/18
Walsh, Mary	24	Ajax	Liverpool	England	1847/04/16	1847/06/23
Walsh, Mary	3	Asia	Cork	Ireland	1847/06/02	1847/07/27
Walsh, Mary	12	Gilmour	Cork	Ireland	1847/04/24	1847/06/18
Walsh, Mary	10	Triton	Liverpool	England	1847/05/14	1847/07/24
Walsh, Maurice	45	Saguenay	Cork	Ireland	1847/06/05	1847/08/22
Walsh, Michael	6	Ninian	Limerick	Ireland	1847/04/13	1847/06/12
Walsh, Michael	23	Saguenay	Cork	Ireland	1847/06/05	1847/08/22
Walsh, Michael	4	Lady Campbell	Dublin	Ireland	1847/06/03	1847/08/05
Walsh, William	21	Triton	Liverpool	England	1847/05/14	1847/07/24
Ward, Ann	40	Virginius	Liverpool	England	1847/05/28	1847/08/12
Ward, Ann	21	Bridgetown	Liverpool	England	1847/07/03	1847/08/29
Ward, James	10	Virginius	Liverpool	England	1847/05/28	1847/08/12
Ward, John	21	Virginius	Liverpool	England	1847/05/28	1847/08/12
Ward, John	2	Aberdeen	Liverpool	England	1847/05/01	1847/06/13
Ward, Mary	50	Rose	Liverpool	England	1847/04/19	1847/07/01
Ward, Mary	3	Sarah	Liverpool	England	1847/05/29	1847/07/19
Ward, Patrick	4	Sarah	Liverpool	England	1847/05/29	1847/07/19
Ward, Sarah	7	Lord Seaton	Belfast	Ireland	1847/04/12	1847/06/10
Ward, Timothy		Goliah	Liverpool	England	1847/05/21	1847/07/18
Warnock, Barbara		Golden Spring	London	England	1847/05/27	1847/07/13
Warren, John	30	Scotland	Cork	Ireland	1847/04/13	1847/06/08
Warren, John	6	Scotland	Cork	Ireland	1847/04/13	1847/06/08
Waters, Helen	18	Larch	Sligo	Ireland	1847/07/11	1847/08/20
Waters, Jane	60	Numa	Sligo	Ireland	1847/06/02	1847/07/27
Waters, Mary	3.5	Richard Watson	Sligo	Ireland	1847/09/13	1847/11/08
Waters, Mary Ann	14	Yorkshire	Liverpool	England	1847/06/09	1847/08/10
Waters, Patrick	10	Richard Watson	Sligo	Ireland	1847/09/13	1847/11/08
Watson, Bridget	35	Unicorn	Londonderry	Ireland	1847/05/23	1847/07/09
Watson, Ellen	10	Yorkshire	Liverpool	England	1847/06/09	1847/08/10
Watson, William	3	Ann Rankin	Glasgow	Scotland	1847/06/27	1847/08/09
Watt, Alexander	32	Bridgetown	Liverpool	England	1847/07/03	1847/08/29
Watt, Margaret	3	Bridgetown	Liverpool	England	1847/07/03	1847/08/29
Webb, Ann	18	Bridgetown	Liverpool	England	1847/07/03	1847/08/29
Webb, George		Saguenay	Cork	Ireland	1847/06/05	1847/08/22
Webb, Henry	5	Saguenay	Cork	Ireland	1847/06/05	1847/08/22
Webb, James	9	Bridgetown	Liverpool	England	1847/07/03	1847/08/29
Webb, Mary	6	Saguenay	Cork	Ireland	1847/06/05	1847/08/22
Webb, Mary	6	Saguenay	Cork	Ireland	1847/06/05	1847/08/22
Webber, Bartholomew		Frankfield	Liverpool	England	1847/06/29	1847/08/09
Welch, Ann	2	Sarah	Liverpool	England	1847/05/29	1847/07/19
Welch, Catherine	13	Marchioness of Breadalbane	Sligo	Ireland	1847/06/11	1847/08/12
Welch, Elizabeth	14	Progress	New Ross	Ireland	1847/05/05	1847/07/14
Welch, James	3	Ninian	Limerick	Ireland	1847/04/13	1847/06/12

LIST OF PEOPLE WHO DIED ON SHIPS AT SEA OR IN QUARANTINE AT GROSSE ÎLE, IN 1847

Name	Age	Vessel	Port	Country	Embarkation	Qc Arrival
Welch, Johanna	2	Avon	Cork	Ireland	1847/05/19	1847/07/26
Welch, John	40	Princess Royal	Liverpool	England	1847/05/05	1847/06/16
Welch, Mary	35	Ninian	Limerick	Ireland	1847/04/13	1847/06/12
Welch, Mary	3	Sarah	Liverpool	England	1847/05/29	1847/07/19
Welch, Mary	4	Agamemnon	Liverpool	England	1847/06/24	1847/07/31
Welch, Mary	40	Tay	Sligo	Ireland	1847/05/05	1847/06/09
Welch, Maurice	23	Saguenay	Cork	Ireland	1847/06/05	1847/08/22
Welch, Patrick	20	Tay	Sligo	Ireland	1847/05/05	1847/06/09
Welch, Patrick	35	Princess Royal	Liverpool	England	1847/05/05	1847/06/16
Welch, Patrick	1	Aberfoyle	Waterford	Ireland	1847/05/27	1847/07/04
Welch, Thomas		Wellington	Liverpool	England	1847/07/29	1847/09/20
Welch, William	9	Trade	Waterford	Ireland	1847/04/17	1847/06/26
Weldon, James	1	Venilia	Limerick	Ireland	1847/05/28	1847/07/11
Wells, Jacob	69	Sisters	Liverpool	England	1847/04/22	1847/06/20
Whelan, James	70	Admiral	Waterford	Ireland	1847/06/01	1847/07/07
Whelan, James	63	Champion	Liverpool	England	1847/07/13	1847/08/28
Whelan, Jane	44	Wave	Dublin	Ireland	1847/04/30	1847/06/09
Whelan, Jane	2	Margrette	New Ross	Ireland	1847/05/02	1847/07/08
Whelan, Jane	50	Rosalinda	Belfast	Ireland	1847/06/22	1847/08/07
Whelan, Maria		Ninian	Limerick	Ireland	1847/04/13	1847/06/12
Whelan, Mary		George	Liverpool	England	1847/04/13	1847/06/12
Whelan, Mary		Progress	New Ross	Ireland	1847/05/05	1847/07/14
Whelan, Mary	32	Naparina	Dublin	Ireland	1847/06/17	1847/08/23
Whelan, Mary		Corea	Liverpool	England	1847/07/02	1847/08/14
Whelan, Mary	4	Margrette	New Ross	Ireland	1847/05/02	1847/07/08
Whelan, Michael	4	Margrette	New Ross	Ireland	1847/05/02	1847/07/08
Whelan, William	2	Frankfield	Liverpool	England	1847/06/29	1847/08/09
White, Ann	42	Leander	Londonderry	Ireland	1847/06/13	1847/07/31
White, Catherine	1	Agnes	Cork	Ireland	1847/04/10	1847/06/10
White, Catherine	13	Champion	Liverpool	England	1847/07/13	1847/08/28
White, Daniel		Lady Flora Hastings	Cork	Ireland	1847/05/11	1847/06/26
White, Edmund	9	Saguenay	Cork	Ireland	1847/06/05	1847/08/22
White, James	2	Lady Flora Hastings	Cork	Ireland	1847/05/11	1847/06/26
White, Jane	7	Pursuit	Liverpool	England	1847/05/04	1847/06/23
White, John	18	Lady Flora Hastings	Cork	Ireland	1847/05/11	1847/06/26
White, Julia	25	Pursuit	Liverpool	England	1847/05/04	1847/06/23
White, Mary	58	Eliza Caroline	Liverpool	England	1847/05/03	1847/06/14
White, Mary	70	Harald	Dublin	Ireland	1847/05/20	1847/06/26
White, Thomas	7	Saguenay	Cork	Ireland	1847/06/05	1847/08/22
White, William	4	Pursuit	Liverpool	England	1847/05/04	1847/06/23
Whitehead, John	30	Triton	Liverpool	England	1847/05/14	1847/07/24
Whiteside, John	7	Wolfville	Sligo	Ireland	1847/04/25	1847/06/10
Whiteside, Maria	4	Wolfville	Sligo	Ireland	1847/04/25	1847/06/10
Whiteside, Nathaniel	4	Wolfville	Sligo	Ireland	1847/04/25	1847/06/10
Whitney, Joseph	65	Emigrant	Liverpool	England	1847/08/11	1847/10/03
Whitton, Catherine	75	Argo	Liverpool	England	1847/05/04	1847/06/12
Whitton, Peter	13	Emily	Cork	Ireland	1847/05/12	1847/07/06
Wiener, Christiana	1	General Hewitt	Bremen	Germany	1847/07/22	1847/09/12
Wilcox, Agnes	1	Broom	Liverpool	England	1847/06/13	1847/08/06
Wilcox, Thomas	29	Covenanter	Cork	Ireland	1847/06/17	1847/08/09
Williams, David	25	Free Trader	Liverpool	England	1847/06/22	1847/08/14
Williams, James	30	Free Trader	Liverpool	England	1847/06/22	1847/08/14
Williams, William	1	Washington	Liverpool	England	1847/07/09	1847/08/26
Williamson, George	34	Larch	Sligo	Ireland	1847/07/11	1847/08/20
Willis, Martha	10	Jessie	Limerick	Ireland	1847/04/18	1847/06/26
Willis, William	27	John Bolton	Liverpool	England	1847/04/13	1847/06/10
Wilmot, Mary	2	Lady Flora Hastings	Cork	Ireland	1847/05/11	1847/06/26
Wilson, Edward	21	Sarah Maria	Sligo	Ireland	1847/05/07	1847/06/28
Wilson, Joseph	55	John and Robert	Liverpool	England	1847/06/09	1847/08/06
Wilson, Joseph	26	Yorkshire	Liverpool	England	1847/06/09	1847/08/10
Wilson, Margaret		Herald	Dublin	Ireland	1847/05/20	1847/06/26
Wilson, Margaret		Sesostris	Londonderry	Ireland	1847/05/14	1847/06/24
Wilson, Margaret	60	Sarah Maria	Sligo	Ireland	1847/05/07	1847/06/28
Wilson, Seth	1	Argo	Liverpool	England	1847/05/04	1847/06/12
Wilton, Joseph		General Hewitt	Bremen	Germany	1847/07/22	1847/09/12
Wistnis, Ernestina	1	General Hewitt	Bremen	Germany	1847/07/22	1847/09/12
Wittell, Johann	1	General Hewitt	Bremen	Germany	1847/07/22	1847/09/12
Woods, Ann	3	Caithness-shire	Belfast	Ireland	1847/04/10	1847/06/12
Woods, Ann	3	Sarah	Liverpool	England	1847/05/29	1847/07/19
Woods, James		Lord Ashburton	Liverpool	England	1847/09/13	1847/11/01
Woods, John	2	Ann	Liverpool	England	1847/05/16	1847/06/30
Woods, Margaret		Lord Ashburton	Liverpool	England	1847/09/13	1847/11/01
Woods, Margaret	3	Sobraon	Liverpool	England	1847/05/08	1847/06/29
Woods, Mrs.	53	Agnes and Ann	Newry	Ireland	1847/05/15	1847/07/02
Woods, Nelly		Agnes and Ann	Newry	Ireland	1847/05/15	1847/07/02
Wright, Ann	12	John Bolton	Liverpool	England	1847/04/13	1847/06/10
Wright, Charles	1	Lord Seaton	Belfast	Ireland	1847/04/12	1847/06/10
Wright, Margaret	1	Sisters	Liverpool	England	1847/04/22	1847/06/20
Wright, William		Sisters	Liverpool	England	1847/04/22	1847/06/20
Wylie, Ann	1	New York Packet	Liverpool	England	1847/04/24	1847/06/29
Wynne, Denis	22	Bridgetown	Liverpool	England	1847/07/03	1847/08/29
Wynne, Elizabeth A.	2	Agnes and Ann	Newry	Ireland	1847/05/15	1847/07/02
Wynne, J.	2	Araminta	Liverpool	England	1847/05/01	1847/06/20
Wynne, Margaret	1	Erin's Queen	Liverpool	England	1847/06/01	1847/07/23

Appendix 1

LIST OF MARRIED WOMEN WHO DIED AND WERE BURIED ON GROSSE ÎLE, IN 1847

Maiden name	Age	Vessel	Port	Country	Reference
Arlwekle, Martha	40	Rankin	Liverpool	England	Craig, Martha
Armstrong, Margaret	82	Lotus	Liverpool	England	McCullough, Margaret
Banniford, Anne	35	Free Trader	Liverpool	England	William, Anne
Barry, Margaret	32	Avon	Cork	Ireland	Reilly, Margaret
Blair, Eliza					Galbot, Eliza
Blair, Mary	36				Conlan, Mary
Cook, Margaret	42	Araminta	Liverpool	England	Steele, Margaret
Henry, Alicia		Broom	Liverpool	England	Sweade, Alicia
Holmes, Anny		Rosalinda	Belfast	Ireland	Henry, Anny
Maxwell, Ann		Eliza Caroline	Liverpool	England	Barron, Ann
Maxwell, Jane	30	Eliza Caroline	Liverpool	England	Barnes, Jane
McGuiness, Christiana					McDonald, Christiana
Moore, Jane	26	Agnes	Cork	Ireland	Skews, Jane
Munro, Mary	50	Caithness-shire	Belfast	Ireland	Mack, Mary
Pharson, Ann	30				Brown, Ann
Rain, Mary	46	Odessa	Dublin	Ireland	Ireland, Mary
Reid, Elizabeth					Irvine, Elizabeth
Swallow, Elizabeth	34	John Munn	Liverpool	Ireland	McMullen, Elizabeth
Tolarton, Mary	54	Lord Seaton	Belfast	Ireland	Morrow, Mary
Williams, Catherine		Saguenay	Cork	Ireland	Galbot, Catherine

Appendix 2

LIST OF SHIPS THAT ARRIVED AT GROSSE ÎLE AND QUÉBEC CITY, IN 1847

Vessel	Country of origin	Port of origin	Departure date	Arrival at Québec	Number of pass.	Deaths at sea	Deaths vessel qua.	Deaths hosp. qua.	Deaths total
Abbeylands	England	Liverpool	1847/06/15	1847/07/31	398	4	0	1	5
Abbotsford	Ireland	Dublin	1847/04/23	1847/06/21	382	9	7	5	21
Aberdeen	England	Liverpool	1847/05/01	1847/06/13	411	9	21	31	61
Aberfoyle	Ireland	Waterford	1847/05/27	1847/07/04	328	7	0	0	7
Achilles	England	Liverpool	1847/04/15	1847/06/08	413	42	0	9	51
Achsah	Ireland	Limerick	1847/05/11	1847/06/23	174	2	0	0	2
Admiral	Ireland	Waterford	1847/06/01	1847/07/07	480	6	0	0	6
Agamemnon	England	Liverpool	1847/06/24	1847/07/31	646	23	19	3	45
Agent	Ireland	New Ross	1847/05/20	1847/07/02	387	8	1	4	13
Agnes	Germany	Bremen	1847/05/15	1847/07/04	334	8	0	0	8
Agnes	Ireland	Cork	1847/04/10	1847/06/10	430	39	35	96	170
Agnes King	Ireland	Limerick	1847/05/15	1847/06/26	176	6	0	3	9
Agnes and Ann	Ireland	Newry	1847/05/15	1847/07/02	297	7	0	0	7
Ajax	England	Liverpool	1847/04/16	1847/06/23	259	36	33	18	87
Albion	Scotland	Glasgow		1847/06/05	18	0	0	0	0
Albion	Scotland	Glasgow	1847/08/09	1847/09/09	64	0	0	0	0
Albion	Ireland	Limerick	1847/04/19	1847/06/18	189	17	2	0	19
Albion	Ireland	Cork	1847/08/13	1847/09/29	184	5	0	1	6
Albion	Ireland	Galway	1847/05/03	1847/05/29	211	3	2	1	6
Alert	Ireland	Waterford	1847/06/05	1847/07/15	234	4	1	1	6
Alexander Stewart	Ireland	Limerick	1847/06/04	1847/07/28	103	3	3	2	8
Allan Kerr	Ireland	Sligo	1847/06/23	1847/08/04	416	9	5	1	15
Amy	Germany	Bremen	1847/06/25	1847/08/11	292	1	0	0	1
Ann	England	Liverpool		1847/05/15	3	0	0	0	0
Ann	England	Liverpool	1847/05/16	1847/06/30	348	31	1	18	50
Ann	Ireland	Limerick	1847/04/13	1847/06/02	119	4	0	0	4
Ann	Ireland	Donegal	1847/05/29	1847/07/26	109	1	0	0	1
Ann	Ireland	Limerick	1847/08/11	1847/09/25	116	0	0	0	0
Ann Kenny	Ireland	Waterford	1847/06/27	1847/08/05	360	4	0	6	10
Ann Rankin	Scotland	Glasgow	1847/06/27	1847/08/09	336	2	5	1	8
Anna Maria	Ireland	Limerick	1847/07/03	1847/08/11	119	2	0	0	2
Annette Gilbert	England	Chepstow		1847/07/19	1	0	0	0	0
Annie	Ireland	Belfast	1847/04/29	1847/05/28	429	1	0	0	1
Anteris	Canada	Arichat	1847/10/14		46	0			
Apollo	Canada	Halifax	1847/06/01		0	0		1	1
Aquamarine	England	Liverpool	1847/04/22	1847/05/26	27	0	0	0	0
Araminta	England	Liverpool	1847/05/01	1847/06/20	416	13	16	21	50
Argent	Ireland	Limerick	1847/05/02	1847/06/02	127	0	0	1	1
Argo	England	Liverpool	1847/05/04	1847/06/12	593	11	32	28	71
Argo	Ireland	Sligo	1847/06/11	1847/07/31	127	3	0	0	3
Argyle	England	Newport	1847/08/05	1847/09/19	364	5	0	7	12
Ariel	Ireland	Kilrush	1847/08/09	1847/09/25	119	0	0	0	0
Asia	Ireland	Cork	1847/06/02	1847/07/27	409	11	5	20	36
Astrea	England	Weymouth		1847/06/14	4	0	0	0	0
Atalanta	Ireland	Dublin	1847/07/30	1847/09/12	226	4	1	0	5
Augusta Melina	Germany	Bremen	1847/06/07	1847/08/01	150	1	1	0	2
Auguste	Germany	Bremen	1847/06/15	1847/08/11	170	0	0	0	0
Avon	Ireland	Cork	1847/05/19	1847/07/26	552	137	26	84	247
Ayrshire	Ireland	Newry	1847/07/04	1847/08/19	434	3	0	8	11
Bee	Ireland	Cork	1847/04/17	1847/06/12	373	77	29	59	165
Belleisle	Scotland	Glasgow	1847/03/27	1847/05/27	35	1	0	0	1
Belleisle	Scotland	Glasgow	1847/08/12	1847/09/12	28	0	0	0	0
Bellona	Scotland	Glasgow		1847/05/22	10	0	0	0	0
Birman	England	London	1847/04/29	1847/06/16	193	0	0	0	0
Blenheim	Ireland	Cork	1847/06/16	1847/07/29	384	10	2	4	16

APPENDIX 2

Vessel	Country of origin	Port of origin	Departure date	Arrival at Québec	Number of pass.	Deaths at sea	Deaths vessel qua.	Deaths hosp. qua.	Deaths total
Blonde	England	Liverpool	1847/05/01	1847/06/08	424	5	6	8	19
Bolton	Ireland	Dublin	1847/05/26	1847/07/07	208	2	1	1	4
Bridgetown	England	Liverpool	1847/07/03	1847/08/29	480	74	24	63	161
Britain								1	1
Britannia	Scotland	Greenock	1847/07/12	1847/08/15	388	7	0	3	10
British Queen	Ireland	Limerick	1847/04/28	1847/06/08	190	1	0	0	1
Broom	England	Liverpool	1847/06/13	1847/08/06	515	16	9	39	64
Brothers	Ireland	Dublin	1847/07/05	1847/08/15	321	4	0	11	15
Brougham								2	2
Bryan Abbs	Ireland	Limerick	1847/04/14	1847/06/02	194	5	0	1	6
Bryan Abbs	Ireland	Limerick	1847/08/13	1847/10/13	179	5	0	0	5
Caithness-shire	Ireland	Belfast	1847/04/10	1847/06/12	250	10	4	16	30
Caledonia	Scotland	Glasgow		1847/05/19	15	0	0	0	0
Caledonia	Scotland	Glasgow	1847/07/29	1847/09/01	45	0	0	1	1
Cambria	Scotland	Glasgow		1847/05/09	19	0	0	0	0
Cambria	Scotland	Glasgow	1847/07/22	1847/09/03	67	1	0	0	1
Camillia	Ireland	Sligo	1847/05/19	1847/07/07	138	4	0	0	4
Canada	Scotland	Glasgow		1847/05/13	3	0	0	0	0
Canada	Scotland	Glasgow	1847/07/14	1847/09/04	136	9	0	0	9
Canton	Germany	Bremen	1847/06/20	1847/08/07	240	6	0	0	6
Cape Breton	Ireland	Dublin	1847/05/06	1847/06/19	176	0	2	6	8
Catherine	Canada	Sydney	1847/06/10	1847/06/19	47	0		1	1
Celeste	Ireland	Limerick	1847/04/13	1847/05/23	199	1	0	0	1
Ceylon	USA	New York	1847/06/16		0	1		1	2
Champion	England	Liverpool	1847/07/13	1847/08/28	422	29	0	65	94
Charles	Ireland	Limerick	1847/05/27	1847/07/02	125	1	0	0	1
Charles	Ireland	Youghal	1847/08/06	1847/09/17	65	0	0	0	0
Charles Richard	Ireland	Sligo	1847/05/27	1847/07/16	178	9	0	8	17
Charles Walton	Ireland	Killala	1847/06/24	1847/08/05	272	5	9	2	16
Charlotte	England	Plymouth	1847/06/02	1847/07/13	336	2	0	0	2
Charlotte Harrison	Scotland	Greenock	1847/05/14	1847/06/18	305	2	0	0	2
Cherokee	Scotland	Glasgow		1847/05/25	14	0	0	0	0
Cherokee	Scotland	Glasgow		1847/09/24	5	0	0	0	0
Chieftain	England	Liverpool		1847/08/23	6	0	0	0	0
Chieftain	Ireland	Belfast	1847/04/12	1847/05/27	267	1	1	0	2
Chieftain	Ireland	Belfast	1847/08/10	1847/09/25	98	1	0	0	1
Christiana	Ireland	Londonderry	1847/04/08	1847/06/10	480	10	18	12	40
Cistus								3	3
City of Derry	England	London	1847/05/23	1847/07/04	295	8	0	0	8
Clansman	Scotland	Greenock	1847/05/27	1847/07/05	218	0	0	1	1
Clarendon	England	Liverpool	1847/04/02	1847/06/08	287	18	0	36	54
Clio	England	Padstow	1847/08/28	1847/10/15	227	0	0	0	0
Clio	England	Padstow	1847/04/10	1847/05/29	328	2	0	0	2
Coeur-de-Lion	England	Liverpool		1847/05/09	3	0	0	0	0
Collingwood	Ireland	Londonderry	1847/05/27	1847/07/13	202	4	0	0	4
Colloony	Scotland	Glasgow		1847/05/21	6	0	0	0	0
Colonist	Ireland	New Ross	1847/07/13	1847/08/29	453	12	0	13	25
Columbia	Ireland	Sligo	1847/05/01	1847/06/10	250	15	7	12	34
Concord	Ireland	Dublin	1847/04/30	1847/05/27	183	3	0	0	3
Congress	Ireland	Sligo	1847/04/24	1847/06/10	219	38	10	6	54
Constance	England	Bristol		1847/05/29	15	0	0	0	0
Constance	England	Bristol		1847/10/08	9	0	0	0	0
Constitution	Ireland	Belfast	1847/04/21	1847/06/08	394	6	0	14	20
Constitution	Ireland	Sligo	1847/04/16	1847/06/01	166	16	2	0	18
Corea	England	Liverpool	1847/07/02	1847/08/14	512	17	0	8	25
Coromandel	Ireland	Dublin	1847/05/13	1847/07/02	446	10	2	15	27
Corsair	England	Bristol	1847/06/27	1847/08/09	45	0	0	0	0
Countess of Arran	Ireland	Donegal	1847/06/30	1847/08/10	207	2	0	0	2
Courier								3	3
Covenanter	Ireland	Cork	1847/06/17	1847/08/09	400	43	16	71	130
Cumberland	Germany	Bremerhaven	1847/06/08	1847/07/30	365	1	0	0	1
Curraghmore	Ireland	Waterford	1847/06/20	1847/08/03	214	1	0	0	1
Cygnet	Ireland	Londonderry	1847/06/07	1847/08/01	210	0	0	0	0
Daniel Ranken								1	1

List of ships that arrived at Grosse Île and Québec City, in 1847

Vessel	Country of origin	Port of origin	Departure date	Arrival at Québec	Number of pass.	Deaths at sea	Deaths vessel qua.	Deaths hosp. qua.	Deaths total
Delia	England	Poole		1847/05/19	4	0	0	0	0
Delta	Germany	Bremen	1847/05/24	1847/07/29	143	2	0	0	2
Despatch	Ireland	Waterford	1847/04/23	1847/06/18	255	5	0	1	6
Dew Drop	Ireland	Westport	1847/04/22	1847/06/05	33	0	0	0	0
Diamond	Germany	Bremerhaven	1847/06/08	1847/07/31	166	5	0	0	5
Dominica	Ireland	Cork	1847/05/01	1847/06/14	254	0	5	6	11
Douce Davie	Ireland	Sligo	1847/08/11	1847/09/30	307	6	0	2	8
Douglas	England	London	1847/04/05	1847/05/25	47	0	0	0	0
Douglas	England	London	1847/08/25	1847/10/06	21	0	0	0	0
Douglas	England	Hull		1847/11/04	10	0	0	0	0
Drabs	Holland	Amsterdam	1847/07/26		0	0	0	0	0
Duchess of Beaufort	Spain	Benicarlo		1847/07/14	3	0	0	0	0
Dunbrody	Ireland	New Ross		1847/09/05	12	0	0	0	0
Dunbrody	Ireland	New Ross	1847/04/12	1847/05/25	312	5	0	3	8
Dundonald	Wales	Milford	1847/07/02	1847/09/03	32	0	0	0	0
Durham	England	Liverpool	1847/05/18	1847/07/04	269	7	0	1	8
Dykes	Ireland	Sligo	1847/04/23	1847/06/10	170	16	3	6	25
Eagle	England	Padstow	1847/04/16	1847/05/25	129	0	0	0	0
Eagle	Ireland	Dublin	1847/05/12	1847/06/25	211	6	0	1	7
Earl Powis	Scotland	Dundee	1847/04/04	1847/05/23	52	0	0	0	0
Earl Powis	Scotland	Dundee	1847/08/19	1847/10/10	20	0	0	0	0
Ebenezer	Jersey	Saint-Hélier	1847/05/26	1847/07/03	19	0	0	0	0
Edward Kenny	Ireland	Belfast	1847/06/12	1847/08/02	245	0	0	0	0
Egbert	Germany	Bremen	1847/05/22	1847/08/03	164	0	0	0	0
Eleonora & Henrietta	Germany	Bremen	1847/05/19	1847/07/04	125	3	0	0	3
Eliza	Scotland	Glasgow	1847/07/17	1847/09/17	269	29	0	16	45
Eliza Ann	Ireland	Limerick	1847/06/30	1847/08/01	112	0	0	0	0
Eliza Caroline	England	Liverpool	1847/05/03	1847/06/14	540	16	33	30	79
Eliza Morrison	Ireland	Belfast	1847/05/23	1847/07/04	471	7	0	10	17
Eliza and Sara					276	22	0	0	22
Elizabeth	England	Liverpool		1847/06/19	2	0	0	0	0
Elizabeth	England	Liverpool	1847/05/21	1847/06/29	434	19	7	10	36
Elizabeth	England	Liverpool	1847/04/24	1847/06/20	347	12	10	4	26
Elizabeth	Ireland	Limerick	1847/05/29	1847/07/04	112	0	0	0	0
Ellen	England	Plymouth	1847/07/18	1847/08/29	164	0	0	0	0
Ellen	Ireland	Sligo	1847/05/27	1847/07/10	248	6	0	2	8
Ellen Forristal	Ireland	Limerick	1847/05/29	1847/07/02	130	1	0	0	1
Ellen Simpson	Ireland	Limerick	1847/06/11	1847/08/14	192	4	0	2	6
Ellen Thompson	Ireland	Londonderry	1847/04/16	1847/05/25	371	4	0	1	5
Elliotts	Ireland	Dublin	1847/05/14	1847/06/30	197	12	0	3	15
Elza Anne	Germany	Hamburg	1847/06/17	1847/08/11	143	1	0	0	1
Emarance	Canada	Richibucto	1847/06/29	1847/07/16	15	0			
Emerald	Ireland	Newry	1847/08/07	1847/09/17	85	1	0	0	1
Emigrant	England	Liverpool	1847/08/11	1847/10/03	529	46	2	40	88
Emily	Ireland	Cork	1847/05/12	1847/07/06	157	9	0	6	15
Emma	Ireland	Limerick	1847/07/04	1847/08/24	118	2	0	0	2
Emperor	England	Plymouth		1847/09/25	5	0	0	0	0
Empress	England	Sunderland		1847/08/14	3	0	0	0	0
Energy	Ireland	Limerick	1847/05/28	1847/07/05	209	6	0	0	6
England	England	Stockton		1847/06/23	3	0	0	0	0
Erin	Ireland	New Ross	1847/04/13	1847/06/07	120	2	1	0	3
Erin's Queen	England	Liverpool	1847/06/01	1847/07/23	518	45	20	71	136
Estafette	Germany	Bremen	1847/04/23	1847/05/27	127	0	0	0	0
Euclid	Scotland	Glasgow	1847/06/01	1847/07/29	330	3	4	9	16
Fame	Ireland	Limerick	1847/05/04	1847/05/26	208	1	0	0	1
Favourite	Germany	Bremen	1847/06/08	1847/08/02	201	1	0	0	1
Favourite	Scotland	Glasgow	1847/04/05	1847/05/27	81	1	2	0	3
Favourite	Scotland	Greenock		1847/10/03	19	0	0	0	0
Febulon	Canada	Prince Edward Island	1847/07/08		52	0			
Fenella	England	London	1847/06/09	1847/08/06	19	2	0	0	2
Fergus	England	Hull	1847/04/10	1847/05/23	131	0	0	0	0
Florence	England	Plymouth		1847/09/24	11	0	0	0	0
Florence	Wales	Cardiff		1847/09/25	1	0	0	0	0

APPENDIX 2

Vessel	Country of origin	Port of origin	Departure date	Arrival at Québec	Number of pass.	Deaths at sea	Deaths vessel qua.	Deaths hosp. qua.	Deaths total
Forester								1	1
Frankfield	England	Liverpool	1847/06/29	1847/08/09	529	8	2	3	13
Free Briton	Ireland	Cork	1847/05/27	1847/07/10	185	6	0	3	9
Free Trader	England	Liverpool	1847/06/22	1847/08/14	481	40	13	85	138
Friendship	Ireland	Dublin	1847/05/23	1847/07/24	202	1	0	0	1
Ganges	England	Liverpool	1847/06/16	1847/08/21	393	45	9	44	98
Ganges	Ireland	Cork	1847/04/12	1847/05/26	412	4	0	1	5
General Hewitt	Germany	Bremen	1847/07/22	1847/09/12	516	12	0	0	12
Gentoo	England	Plymouth	1847/08/18	1847/09/25	52	0	0	0	0
George	England	Liverpool	1847/04/13	1847/06/12	397	40	35	75	150
George	Ireland	Dublin	1847/05/30	1847/08/03	104	7	0	4	11
George Ramsay	Ireland	New Ross	1847/07/23	1847/09/14	26	0	0	0	0
Georgiana	Ireland	Dublin	1847/05/16	1847/06/29	184	2	0	0	2
Gilmour	Ireland	Cork	1847/04/24	1847/06/18	368	19	9	44	72
Glenswilly	Scotland	Glasgow	1847/04/10	1847/05/21	43	0	0	0	0
Globe	Germany	Bremen	1847/05/24	1847/08/01	159	0	0	0	0
Golden Spring	England	London	1847/05/27	1847/07/13	149	3	0	0	3
Goliah	England	Liverpool	1847/05/21	1847/07/18	603	41	20	28	89
Grace	Ireland	Westport	1847/06/18	1847/08/06	41	1	0	0	1
Graham	England	Southampton	1847/05/15	1847/07/04	250	0	0	0	0
Great Britain	England	London		1847/09/12	13	0	0	0	0
Greenoch	England	Liverpool	1847/06/19	1847/07/29	816	12	26	42	80
Han Rumney	England	Hull	1847/04/10	1847/06/10	178	1	0	0	1
Harry Lorrequer								1	1
Haubet	Germany	Hamburg	1847/07/02	1847/09/01	199	13	0	0	13
Helen	Germany	Bremen	1847/05/03	1847/06/23	138	0	0	0	0
Helen	Ireland	Belfast	1847/06/02	1847/08/05	212	0	0	0	0
Henrietta Mary	Ireland	Cork	1847/08/18	1847/09/29	267	12	0	7	19
Henrietta Sophia	Germany	Hamburg	1847/05/12	1847/07/21	186	8	0	1	9
Henry	Scotland	Montrose	1847/03/31	1847/06/11	25	0			
Henry	Ireland	Donegal	1847/04/13	1847/06/07	170	10	0	6	16
Henry Volante	Ireland	Ballyshannon	1847/06/16	1847/08/10	66	0	0	0	0
Herald	Ireland	Dublin	1847/05/20	1847/06/26	569	26	1	3	30
Hercules								2	2
Heroine	Scotland	Aberdeen	1847/05/29	1847/07/28	81	0	0	0	0
Heromanga	Scotland	Glasgow	1847/08/08	1847/09/12	56	0	0	0	0
Hibernia								1	1
Highland Mary	Ireland	Cork	1847/07/20	1847/09/09	100	4	1	2	7
Hope	England	Maryport	1847/05/02	1847/06/07	24	0	0	0	0
Horatio	Ireland	Limerick	1847/07/18	1847/09/03	277	10	0	1	11
Huron	Ireland	Belfast	1847/05/26	1847/07/11	329	9	5	6	20
Independance	Canada	Miramichi	1847/08/07	1847/08/25	23	0			
Independance	Ireland	Belfast	1847/05/23	1847/07/07	432	5	2	12	19
Industry	Ireland	Sligo	1847/07/07	1847/08/30	178	7	0	2	9
Industry	Ireland	Dublin	1847/04/19	1847/05/28	301	3	0	3	6
Isabella	England	Whitehaven		1847/05/25	2	0	0	0	0
Isabella	Ireland	Killala	1847/07/17	1847/09/17	236	8	0	4	12
Jamaica	Scotland	Greenock	1847/06/11	1847/07/30	212	0	0	2	2
James Moran	England	Liverpool	1847/05/22	1847/07/11	353	9	4	43	56
Jane	Ireland	Limerick	1847/04/03	1847/05/23	201	1	0	0	1
Jane Avery	Ireland	Dublin	1847/05/09	1847/06/25	183	10	0	14	24
Jane Black	Ireland	Limerick	1847/08/10	1847/09/17	395	3	2	0	5
Jane Black	Ireland	Limerick	1847/04/02	1847/05/23	426	13	0	6	19
Jane Blane	Ireland	Sligo	1847/05/16	1847/06/26	225	6	0	1	7
Jane and Ann	England	Stockton		1847/06/07	4	0	0	0	0
Jessie	Ireland	Cork	1847/06/03	1847/07/24	441	36	7	40	83
Jessie	Ireland	Limerick	1847/04/18	1847/06/26	489	26	10	22	58
Jessie	Ireland	Sligo	1847/04/24	1847/05/25	243	6	0	4	10
Jessie	Ireland	Limerick	1847/06/25	1847/08/09	108	2	0	0	2
Johana								1	1
John Bell	Ireland	New Ross	1847/05/10	1847/06/29	254	7	0	0	7
John Bolton	England	Liverpool	1847/04/13	1847/06/10	578	74	35	34	143
John Bull	England	London		1847/09/12	23	0	0	0	0
John Campbell	Germany	Bremen	1847/06/14	1847/07/21	371	0	0	0	0

List of ships that arrived at Grosse Île and Québec City, in 1847

Vessel	Country of origin	Port of origin	Departure date	Arrival at Québec	Number of pass.	Deaths at sea	Deaths vessel qua.	Deaths hosp. qua.	Deaths total
John Christophe	Germany	Bremen	1847/06/09	1847/08/05	173	0	0	0	0
John Francis	Ireland	Cork	1847/04/10	1847/06/10	260	16	7	46	69
John Hawkes	Ireland	Limerick	1847/08/24	1847/10/12	114	5	0	0	5
John Jardine	England	Liverpool	1847/06/04	1847/07/16	389	12	0	6	18
John Munn	England	Liverpool	1847/06/16	1847/08/13	452	59	11	118	188
John Smith	Germany	Bremen	1847/05/14	1847/07/04	404	8	0	0	8
John and Robert	England	Liverpool	1847/06/09	1847/08/06	346	7	7	20	34
Josepha	Ireland	Belfast	1847/05/09	1847/06/18	301	2	0	0	2
Juliet	England	London	1847/07/03	1847/08/28	271	16	0	0	16
Julius Caesar	England	Liverpool	1847/07/13	1847/09/05	471	35	0	20	55
Junior	England	Liverpool	1847/05/10	1847/07/03	356	13	0	21	34
Juverna	Ireland	Waterford	1847/05/20	1847/06/25	182	1	0	0	1
Kate Robinson	Ireland	Youghal	1847/05/29	1847/07/04	25	0	0	0	0
Kennedy	Scotland	Glasgow	1847/07/14		135	12	0	0	12
Kilblain	England	London	1847/06/06	1847/07/31	258	0	0	0	0
Lady Bagot	Ireland	Dublin						1	1
Lady Campbell	Ireland	Dublin	1847/06/03	1847/08/05	242	13	2	26	41
Lady Flora Hastings	Ireland	Cork	1847/05/11	1847/06/26	454	48	15	19	82
Lady Gordon	Ireland	Belfast	1847/04/14	1847/06/20	204	10	4	5	19
Lady Milton	England	Liverpool	1847/05/05	1847/06/26	445	21	20	16	57
Lady Seaton	England	London	1847/03/31	1847/05/24	21	0	0	0	0
Larch	Ireland	Sligo	1847/07/11	1847/08/20	440	113	24	62	199
Lawrence Forristal	Ireland	Waterford	1847/05/20	1847/06/25	143	3	0	0	3
Leander	Ireland	Londonderry	1847/06/13	1847/07/31	427	4	0	2	6
Leo	England	Liverpool		1847/07/29	20	0	0	0	0
Leontine	Germany	Bremen	1847/05/28	1847/07/28	326	6	2	0	8
Leveret	Ireland	Limerick	1847/04/15	1847/06/07	125	0	0	0	0
Liberia	Germany	Hamburg	1847/06/01	1847/08/02	153	0	0	0	0
Lillias	Ireland	Dublin	1847/07/01	1847/08/16	214	6	0	6	12
Linden	Ireland	Limerick	1847/05/19	1847/07/02	179	1	0	1	2
Lively	Ireland	Cork	1847/05/26	1847/07/14	189	31	0	14	45
Lloyds	England	London	1847/06/01	1847/07/14	215	2	0	0	2
Lord Ashburton	England	Liverpool	1847/09/13	1847/11/01	491	107	0	0	107
Lord Glenelg	Ireland	Limerick	1847/05/06	1847/06/19	264	7	0	1	8
Lord Metcalfe	Scotland	Aberdeen	1847/08/19	1847/10/10	51	0	0	0	0
Lord Panmure	Scotland	Glasgow	1847/05/27	1847/07/04	175	0	0	0	0
Lord Ramsay	England	Bideford		1847/05/29	10	0	0	0	0
Lord Sandon	Ireland	Cork	1847/05/11	1847/06/26	246	17	2	8	27
Lord Seaton	Ireland	Belfast	1847/04/12	1847/06/10	301	20	9	22	51
Lotus	England	Liverpool	1847/04/15	1847/06/24	546	51	22	27	100
Louisa	Ireland	Limerick	1847/05/08	1847/06/25	213	4	0	0	4
Magnet	Germany	Bremen	1847/05/01	1847/06/10	202	1	0	0	1
Mahaica	England	Liverpool		1847/05/18	1	0	0	0	0
Maid of the Mill	Scotland	Glasgow		1847/06/22	8	0	0	0	0
Mail	Ireland	Cork	1847/04/25	1847/06/19	289	12	17	7	36
Manchester	England	Liverpool	1847/06/05	1847/07/17	512	11	0	17	28
Marchioness of Abercorn	Ireland	Londonderry	1847/06/15	1847/08/05	416	10	0	7	17
Marchioness of Ailsa	Scotland	Glasgow		1847/08/09	1	0	0	0	0
Marchioness of Breadalbane	Ireland	Sligo	1847/06/11	1847/08/12	187	10	9	8	27
Marchioness of Bute	Ireland	Belfast	1847/06/10	1847/07/31	497	15	6	5	26
Marchioness of Queensbury	Scotland	Glasgow		1847/05/23	14	0	0	0	0
Margaret	Ireland	New Ross	1847/05/19	1847/07/02	531	10	5	11	26
Margrette	Ireland	New Ross	1847/05/02	1847/07/08	399	21	5	0	26
Maria	Ireland	Limerick	1847/06/19	1847/08/03	132	0	0	0	0
Maria Julia	Canada	Gaspé		1847/07/08	21				
Maria Somes	Ireland	Cork	1847/07/13	1847/09/10	329	17	0	33	50
Maria and Elizabeth	England	Liverpool	1847/05/06	1847/06/24	81	2	2	0	4
Marinus	Ireland	Dublin	1847/06/05	1847/08/13	202	6	2	38	46
Marquis of Bute	Wales	Cardiff		1847/06/05	8	0	0	0	0
Marquis of Normandy	Ireland	Dublin	1847/07/09	1847/09/03	11	0	0	0	0
Martengale	Germany	Hamburg	1847/06/25	1847/08/01	168	0	0	0	0

APPENDIX 2

Vessel	Country of origin	Port of origin	Departure date	Arrival at Québec	Number of pass.	Deaths at sea	Deaths vessel qua.	Deaths hosp. qua.	Deaths total
Martha	Germany	Bremen	1847/07/08	1847/08/30	229	0	0	0	0
Mary	England	Liverpool	1847/05/04	1847/06/08	38	1	0	0	1
Mary	Scotland	Glasgow	1847/05/06	1847/06/10	32	3	0	0	3
Mary	Scotland	Glasgow		1847/10/08	20	0	0	0	0
Mary	Ireland	Sligo	1847/05/24	1847/07/27	154	9	2	1	12
Mary Brack	Ireland	Limerick	1847/05/03	1847/06/12	184	7	1	1	9
Mary and Harriett	Ireland	Limerick	1847/04/18	1847/06/22	178	9	0	0	9
Matador	Germany	Bremen	1847/05/07	1847/06/16	164	1	0	0	1
Mecca	Ireland	Dublin	1847/07/08	1847/08/26	74	1	0	0	1
Medusa	Ireland	Cork	1847/06/03	1847/07/16	205	2	0	0	2
Mersey	England	Torquay		1847/05/22	5	0	0	0	0
Mersey	England	Torquay		1847/09/12	8	0	0	0	0
Messenger	England	Liverpool	1847/08/24	1847/10/14	227	12	0	1	13
Minerva	Ireland	Waterford	1847/07/13	1847/08/29	126	0	0	0	0
Minerva	Ireland	Galway	1847/06/17	1847/08/14	138	4	5	13	22
Miscou	Canada	Miramichi	1847/08/19	1847/09/06	19	0			
Mountaineer	England	Hull	1847/05/05	1847/06/18	31	0	0	0	0
Naomi	England	Liverpool	1847/06/15	1847/08/10	334	78	31	87	196
Naparina	Ireland	Dublin	1847/06/17	1847/08/23	229	24	0	17	41
Nelson's Village	Ireland	Belfast	1847/05/10	1847/06/26	264	16	1	1	18
Nerio	Ireland	Limerick	1847/08/05	1847/09/28	134	3	0	3	6
Nerio	Ireland	Limerick	1847/04/14	1847/06/03	132	3	0	1	4
Nestor	England	Maryport		1847/05/27	7	0	0	0	0
New York Packet	England	Liverpool	1847/04/24	1847/06/29	470	9	0	1	10
New Zealand	Ireland	Newry	1847/05/20	1847/07/03	477	6	1	0	7
Niger	Canada	Sydney	1847/06/04	1847/06/18	104	1			
Ninian	Ireland	Limerick	1847/08/30	1847/10/15	109	1	0	0	1
Ninian	Ireland	Limerick	1847/04/13	1847/06/12	261	20	10	1	31
Norna	England	Sunderland		1847/06/05	4	0	0	0	0
Numa	Ireland	Sligo	1847/06/02	1847/07/27	257	10	0	27	37
Ocean Queen	England	Bristol	1847/04/01	1847/05/18	83	0	0	1	1
Ocean Queen	Ireland	Cork	1847/06/29	1847/08/03	498	2	3	1	6
Odessa	Ireland	Dublin	1847/06/09	1847/08/09	242	22	4	49	75
Ophelia and Mary	Germany	Hamburg	1847/05/20	1847/08/01	183	3	0	0	3
Oregon	Ireland	Killala	1847/06/09	1847/08/02	231	8	1	2	11
Orlando	Ireland	Newry	1847/04/29	1847/06/08	209	4	0	4	8
Ottawa	England	London	1847/07/18	1847/09/08	45	0	0	0	0
Ottawa	England	Bridgwater	1847/04/13	1847/05/27	55	0	0	0	0
Pacha	Ireland	Cork	1847/05/05	1847/06/14	218	11	0	4	15
Pacific	Ireland	Waterford	1847/05/04	1847/06/18	197	1	0	0	1
Pallas	Germany	Bremen	1847/05/19	1847/07/17	153	2	0	0	2
Panama	Scotland	Loch Saxford	1847/06/21	1847/07/29	279	0	0	0	0
Pandora	Ireland	New Ross	1847/06/11	1847/08/04	401	12	3	9	24
Panope	Ireland	Dublin	1847/05/05	1847/06/29	112	1	0	1	2
Paragon	England	Falmouth	1847/04/14	1847/06/10	105	0	0	0	0
Pearl	England	London		1847/05/15	11	0	0	0	0
Pearl	England	London		1847/09/19	12	0	0	0	0
Perseverance	Germany	Hamburg	1847/05/18	1847/07/14	165	4	0	0	4
Perseverance	Ireland	Dublin	1847/04/13	1847/05/23	311	9	0	10	19
Peruvian	Scotland	Glasgow	1847/05/28	1847/06/26	43	0	0	0	0
Peruvian	Scotland	Glasgow		1847/10/09	1	0	0	0	0
Phoenix	England	Liverpool	1847/04/13	1847/06/05	286	4	0	3	7
Pomona	Germany	Bremen	1847/06/10	1847/08/10	227	0	0	0	0
Primrose	Ireland	Limerick	1847/04/07	1847/06/18	337	12	1	2	15
Prince George								1	1
Princess	Germany	Bremen	1847/05/23	1847/07/16	320	1	0	0	1
Princess Royal	England	Liverpool	1847/05/05	1847/06/16	599	14	10	6	30
Progress	Ireland	New Ross	1847/05/05	1847/07/14	555	27	5	31	63
Provincialist	Ireland	Londonderry	1847/07/19	1847/09/04	205	0	0	0	0
Pursuit	England	Liverpool	1847/05/04	1847/06/23	472	37	7	30	74
Quebec	Scotland	Glasgow		1847/07/01	10	0	0	0	0
Rainbow	England	Southampton		1847/05/19	2	0	0	0	0
Rankin	England	Liverpool	1847/05/05	1847/06/14	579	5	13	33	51
Redwing								1	1

List of ships that arrived at Grosse Île and Québec City, in 1847

Vessel	Country of origin	Port of origin	Departure date	Arrival at Québec	Number of pass.	Deaths at sea	Deaths vessel qua.	Deaths hosp. qua.	Deaths total
Rega	Ireland	Cork	1847/06/20	1847/07/26	132	3	0	0	3
Resolution	England	Penzance	1847/04/15	1847/06/12	66	0	0	0	0
Richard Watson	Ireland	Sligo	1847/09/13	1847/11/08	170	4	0	0	4
Robert Newton	Ireland	Limerick	1847/07/18	1847/08/29	206	1	0	0	1
Robert and Isabella	Germany	Hamburg	1847/04/17	1847/05/28	170	2	1	0	3
Rockshire	England	Liverpool	1847/06/13	1847/08/03	48	0	0	0	0
Rodeng	Ireland	Cork	1847/05/20	1847/07/07	94	2	0	0	2
Rosalinda	Ireland	Belfast	1847/06/22	1847/08/07	508	17	0	2	19
Rose	England	Liverpool	1847/04/19	1847/07/01	384	52	47	40	139
Roseanna	Ireland	Cork	1847/06/01	1847/07/18	272	3	0	7	10
Roslin Castle	England	Falmouth	1847/04/10	1847/05/26	214	0	0	0	0
Ross-shire	Ireland	Limerick	1847/05/05	1847/06/22	212	0	0	0	0
Royal Adelaide	Ireland	Waterford	1847/05/29	1847/07/14	198	0	0	0	0
Royal Adelaide	Ireland	Killala	1847/06/09	1847/08/09	367	7	4	10	21
Royal Albert	England	London	1847/05/14	1847/07/08	178	0	0	0	0
Royalist	England	Liverpool	1847/04/23	1847/06/07	437	26	0	10	36
Royalist	Ireland	Limerick	1847/07/13	1847/08/29	168	1	0	0	1
Saguenay	Ireland	Cork	1847/06/05	1847/08/22	476	104	16	47	167
Saint-Roch	Canada	Gaspé	1847/06/20		20	0			
Samson								1	1
Sarah	England	Liverpool		1847/05/18	2	0	0	0	0
Sarah	England	Liverpool	1847/05/29	1847/07/19	255	31	0	39	70
Sarah (Ramin)								1	1
Sarah Maria	Ireland	Sligo	1847/05/07	1847/06/28	116	6	0	8	14
Sarah Milledge	Ireland	Galway	1847/08/15	1847/10/09	270	5	0	3	8
Sceptre	Germany	Hamburg	1847/05/04	1847/06/19	134	2	0	1	3
Scotland	Ireland	Cork	1847/04/13	1847/06/08	564	60	34	72	166
Secret	Canada	Charlottetown	1847/06/17		26	0			
Segastus								1	1
Sesostris	Ireland	Londonderry	1847/05/14	1847/06/24	428	8	4	5	17
Sir Colin Campbell	Ireland	Belfast	1847/04/28	1847/05/27	383	2	1	0	3
Sir Henry Pottinger	Ireland	Belfast	1847/07/09	1847/08/29	253	5	0	30	35
Sir Henry Pottinger	Ireland	Cork	1847/05/29	1847/08/07	400	101	7	22	130
Sir John Campbell	Ireland	Belfast	1847/08/25	1847/10/07	385	2	0	0	2
Sir Robert Peel	England	Liverpool	1847/07/26	1847/09/19	480	31	2	16	49
Sisters	England	Liverpool	1847/04/22	1847/06/20	507	58	44	17	119
Sobraon	England	Liverpool	1847/05/08	1847/06/29	607	31	16	20	67
Solway	Ireland	New Ross	1847/05/27	1847/06/30	364	3	0	1	4
Sophia	Germany	Bremen	1847/05/06	1847/07/05	105	0	0	0	0
Sophia	Ireland	Waterford	1847/08/08	1847/09/25	23	0	0	0	0
Sophia Moffatt	England	London		1847/05/14	4	0	0	0	0
Souvenir	Ireland	Limerick	1847/05/01	1847/05/28	124	1	0	0	1
Sovereign								2	2
Spermaceti	England	Plymouth	1847/04/13	1847/05/25	251	1	0	0	1
Spermaceti	England	Plymouth	1847/07/30	1847/09/12	206	0	0	0	0
Springhill	Ireland	Sligo	1847/05/01	1847/06/10	227	9	0	0	9
St. George								4	4
St. Lawrence	Scotland	Aberdeen	1847/08/28	1847/10/13	28	0	0	0	0
St. Lawrence	Scotland	Aberdeen	1847/04/15	1847/06/10	212	0	0	0	0
Standard	Ireland	New Ross	1847/04/22	1847/06/19	369	6	4	2	12
Superior	Ireland	Londonderry	1847/07/18	1847/09/17	366	18	8	45	71
Swallow	Ireland	Limerick	1847/05/15	1847/06/25	147	1	0	0	1
Syria	England	Liverpool	1847/03/28	1847/05/20	245	9	0	40	49
Tadoussac	Canada	New Foundland	1847/06/10	1847/07/02	5				
Tamarac	England	Liverpool	1847/05/26	1847/07/11	497	20	13	9	42
Tamerlane	Wales	Aberystwyth	1847/06/01	1847/07/29	243	1	0	0	1
Tay	England	Liverpool	1847/05/02	1847/06/23	371	9	4	0	13
Tay	Ireland	Sligo	1847/05/05	1847/06/09	303	11	0	1	12
Thetis	Ireland	Limerick	1847/05/10	1847/06/20	161	3	0	0	3
Thistle	England	Liverpool	1847/06/01	1847/07/18	382	4	3	6	13
Thistle	Ireland	Waterford	1847/04/16	1847/06/10	176	0	0	0	0
Thomas Hanford	Ireland	Limerick	1847/05/11	1847/06/18	155	1	0	0	1
Thompson	Ireland	Sligo	1847/05/05	1847/06/14	159	7	5	0	12
Tom	Ireland	Dublin	1847/05/26	1847/07/12	115	4	0	0	4

APPENDIX 2

Vessel	Country of origin	Port of origin	Departure date	Arrival at Québec	Number of pass.	Deaths at sea	Deaths vessel qua.	Deaths hosp. qua.	Deaths total
Tottenham	Ireland	Youghal	1847/04/05	1847/05/26	228	2	0	1	3
Tottenham	Ireland	New Ross		1847/09/12	5	0	0	0	0
Trade	Ireland	Waterford	1847/04/17	1847/06/26	134	5	0	2	7
Transit	Ireland	Sligo	1847/05/01	1847/06/03	158	6	0	0	6
Trinity	Ireland	Limerick	1847/06/19	1847/08/11	89	0	0	0	0
Triton	England	Liverpool	1847/05/14	1847/07/24	493	93	10	83	186
Triumph	Ireland	Donegal	1847/05/28	1847/07/04	115	0	0	0	0
Tropic	England	London	1847/07/02	1847/08/09	86	0	0	0	0
Try Again	Ireland	Cork	1847/04/10	1847/06/07	182	10	0	6	16
Unicorn	Ireland	Londonderry	1847/05/23	1847/07/09	178	4	0	8	12
Union	Ireland	Limerick	1847/06/05	1847/08/02	54	1	0	15	16
Urania	Ireland	Cork	1847/04/09	1847/06/10	200	11	5	20	36
Venilia	Ireland	Limerick	1847/05/28	1847/07/11	391	13	0	1	14
Vesta	Ireland	Limerick	1847/06/21	1847/08/09	118	1	1	0	2
Victoria	England	St.Ives		1847/05/23	22	0	0	0	0
Victoria	England	St.Ives	1847/08/10	1847/09/25	44	0	0	0	0
Victoria	Canada	Miramichi	1847/07/31	1847/08/09	31	0			
Victory	England	Bristol		1847/06/05	5	0	0	0	0
Virgilia	England	Liverpool	1847/07/22	1847/09/20	208	12	0	5	17
Virginius	England	Liverpool	1847/05/28	1847/08/12	476	159	19	90	268
Wakefield	Ireland	Cork	1847/05/28	1847/07/12	398	26	9	37	72
Wallace	England	Liverpool	1847/04/22	1847/05/25	417	4	0	1	5
Wanderer								1	1
Wandsworth	Ireland	Dublin	1847/04/07	1847/05/25	527	51	0	54	105
Washington	England	Liverpool	1847/07/09	1847/08/26	308	22	3	22	47
Watchful	Germany	Hamburg	1847/06/02	1847/08/11	145	0	0	0	0
Wave	Ireland	Dublin	1847/04/30	1847/06/09	396	5	0	0	5
Wellington	England	Liverpool	1847/07/29	1847/09/20	439	27	0	17	44
Wellington	England	Bideford		1847/06/14	9	0	0	0	0
Westmoreland	Ireland	Sligo	1847/06/12	1847/08/10	207	5	4	6	15
Wilhelmina	Ireland	Belfast	1847/05/08	1847/06/20	276	4	0	0	4
William Pirie	Ireland	Belfast	1847/05/01	1847/06/20	414	7	3	4	14
Wm S. Hamilton	Ireland	New Ross	1847/05/20	1847/07/07	207	4	2	18	24
Wolfville	Ireland	Sligo	1847/04/25	1847/06/10	311	37	16	32	85
Wonder	Ireland	Sligo	1847/06/03	1847/07/15	178	2	0	1	3
Woodbine	Ireland	Londonderry	1847/05/27	1847/07/02	243	0	0	1	1
Wyke Regis	England	Poole		1847/06/26	6	0	0	0	0
X. L.	Ireland	Galway	1847/06/10	1847/08/01	130	2	0	2	4
Yeoman								2	2
Yorkshire	England	Liverpool	1847/06/09	1847/08/10	416	47	10	27	84
Yorkshire	Ireland	Donegal	1847/05/01	1847/06/10	235	2	0	0	2
Yorkshire Lass	Ireland	Killala	1847/05/24	1847/07/06	282	5	0	40	45
Zealous	England	London	1847/06/17	1847/08/09	124	1	0	3	4

SOURCES Archives nationales du Québec à Québec, Greffe Saxton Campbell.

Archives nationales du Québec à Québec, Anglican Travelling Missionaries District of Quebec, 1826 to 1848.

Archives du diocèse de Sainte-Anne-de-la-Pocatière, Registre d'état civil, Saint-Luc-de-la-Grosse-Île, 1834-1932.

Irish University Press, British Parliamentary Papers, Colonies, Correspondance 1847-1848 and 1848.

Le Canadien, 1847.

Mitchell, Brian, *Irish Passenger Lists 1847-1871,* Genealogical Publishing Co., Baltimore, 1992, 333 pages.

National Archives of Canada, RG 4, C, 1, Provincial Secretary's Office, vol. 203, 208 and 209.

Public Record Office, C.O. 42, vol. 542 and 551.

The Quebec Morning Chronicle, 1847.

BACK COVER Report of Vessel Boarded at the Quarantine Station Grosse Isle: from the 14th May 1847 to 22nd May 1847. (NAC, RG 4, C, 1, vol. 203, no 1.)

Ann Martin's burying act. (Extract of the Registre catholique d'état civil de Saint-Luc-de-la-Grosse-Île, Archives du diocèse de Sainte-Anne-de-la-Pocatière, folio 36, 20th May 1847.)

Printed on recycled
and alkaline paper.